CHOICE OVER CHANCE

CHOICE OVER CHANCE

ECONOMIC AND ENERGY OPTIONS
FOR THE FUTURE

William F. Thompson
Jerome J. Karaganis
Kenneth D. Wilson

PRAEGER SPECIAL STUDIES • PRAEGER SCIENTIFIC

Library of Congress Cataloging in Publication Data

Thompson, William F.
  Choice over chance.
  Bibliography: p. 259
  Includes index.
    1. United States—Economic policy—
1971-   . 2. Energy policy—United States.
3. Environmental policy—United States.
I. Karaganis, Jerome J. II. Wilson, Kenneth D.
III. Title.
HC106.7.T48   333.79′0973   81-15851
ISBN 0-03-059554-1   AACR2
ISBN 0-03-059556-8 (pbk.)

Published in 1981 by Praeger Publishers
CBS Educational and Professional Publishing
A Division of CBS, Inc.
521 Fifth Avenue, New York, New York 10175 U.S.A.

© 1981 by Edison Electric Institute

123456789   056   987654321

Printed in the United States of America

FOREWORD

by Kenneth Boulding

This volume is designed to improve our understanding of the future, and to clarify both the choices we must consider and the contingencies we cannot control but for which we must plan. The premise underlying this careful research and analysis is that, beyond a certain degree, uncertainty is irreducible. Logic then leads to three inescapable realities: one, uncertainty plays an important role in determining the future; two, in spite of uncertainty, choices can and must be made; and three, under these circumstances, long-term decisions made today must be flexible in order to accommodate a wide range of possible tomorrows.

Uncertainty remains a given in any dynamic system—its source an incomplete knowledge of the system's dynamics. Incomplete knowledge may stem from human ignorance, which can be emended, or from irreducible randomness in the system itself. Although the source of uncertainty is always the same—incomplete knowledge that skews our ability to make accurate predictions—the manner in which uncertainty manifests itself can vary widely from system to system. We can only predict and avoid uncertainty when nothing is happening. As soon as anything begins to happen, uncertainty rises. Equilibrium systems offer the best examples of situations in which predictability increases as uncertainty decreases. Take a physical system that presents very little uncertainty and for which predictability is very accurate. For example, the celestial mechanics of the solar system is an equilibrium system in space-time, the dynamics of which are very accurately understood. There well may have been a time in the early history of the solar system when the uncertainties would have been quite large, if anybody had been around to observe them. Now, however, the solar system has very stable parameters. By careful observation we can find out what these are and then we can use them to predict the future positions of the planets, at least relative to the sun, with great accuracy.

Ecosystems that reach something like an equilibrium are also fairly predictable. We disturb an old pond, for instance, by taking a certain proportion of the fish out of it. In a year or two the species will be back to their original numbers and proportions. Even in social systems, loose equilibrium systems of this kind are not uncommon. At a given level of technology and knowledge, the relative price and output structure of different commodities has a kind of ecological stability. Disturb it, as we did for the liquor industry under Prohibition and, of course, it will change. Once the disturbance is removed, however, the system tends to fall back into something like its old position.

Where there are cybernetic systems with servomechanisms, like a thermostat, that involve an apparatus whereby disturbances from some equilibrium position will set in motion changes that will correct it, again, uncertainty is diminished and prediction becomes more accurate. One can certainly predict the temperature inside a room with a thermostat much more successfully than one can predict the temperature outside. Even certain growth processes have this cybernetic quality. If the growth of an organism from a fertilized egg is checked by starvation or disease, then when the check is removed the organism often comes back to its equilibrium development path. Japan today, at least in terms of its gross national product per capita, seems to be very much where it would have been if its prewar processes had not been interrupted by the enormous catastrophe of World War II.

The general principle here is that if a process involves the working out and the realization of some previously established potential, whether this is the fertilized egg of an organism or the growth of an organization or a whole society from the potential of its origins, there seems to be something like an equilibrium path—what the biologist Waddington called a "creodic" path. There is then quite a strong tendency for divergencies to be corrected and the path to be fulfilled, though, of course, a fatal interruption is always possible. The difficulty here, of course, is understanding what constitutes the potential. We have a pretty fair idea as to what constitutes the creodic path of the fertilized human egg, simply because we have observed it so many times. But we do not really understand exactly how it happens, and we cannot deduce it from our knowledge, limited as it is, of the fertilized egg itself. In social systems, it is even more difficult to recognize potential, except after the fact, because social variables are much more difficult to identify and understand than physical or biological variables.

Another very important type of situation from which uncertainty arises is what I have called "watershed systems," where very slight and perhaps random causes can produce very large differences in results. A raindrop on the Continental Divide may go to the Atlantic or to the Pacific, depending on a chance puff of wind. There are many systems like this in meteorological dynamics: a storm may develop, and only if it goes past a certain point will it become a hurricane or create a 100-year flood; a volcano may start to get active, as Mount Baker did a few years ago, and then fall back into quiescence, or it may go beyond a certain level and explode, like Mount St. Helens.

"Watersheds" are not uncommon in social systems. Thus, in the Cuban crisis during the Kennedy administration, we clearly were moving up a hill toward a watershed, the other side of which was a mile-high precipice of nuclear war. Fortunately, the momentum of the movement did not carry us that far and we fell back again into detente and a more normal international position. Sometimes a firm moves toward bankruptcy and then is saved, perhaps by a change of policy or administration. When a recession becomes a great depression, or inflation turns into hyperinflation, we have examples of systems that go over some kind of irretrievable watershed. The U.S. economy exhibited fairly stable growth in the 1920s and again from 1950 to 1970 or so. In the first case it collapsed into the Great Depression, almost like Crater Lake. In the second case, it has gone off into severe inflation, the future of which is extremely hard to predict.

In addition to the uncertainty inherent in our perceptions of equilibrium and watershed systems, one decision maker's actions can foster uncertainty by changing the environment in which others attempt to plan for the future. This phenomenon has been explored very intensively in game theory, in conflict theory, and in the "policy sciences." Conflict situations are particularly common sources of uncertainty; otherwise sport would not be so large an occasion for gambling. Predicting the outcome of a football game is not much easier than predicting the outcome of the spin of a roulette wheel, though it may have slightly more nonrandom elements in the system. The most general conflict situation is one in which change in the state of the world makes one party better off and one party worse off, each in their own estimation. When the new state of the world is the result of the choices of both parties in an interactive mode (A does something, that makes B do something, that makes A do something, and so on), the uncertainty becomes even larger. The international system is a particularly good example of this mode. Arms races and the very uncertain outcomes in war of either victory or defeat make the concept of the rational pursuit of a known national interest almost preposterous.

When we come to the profit-making business firm, of which the regulated public utility is a very peculiar case, perhaps the most significant dynamic system, and one of the most uncertain, is the market environment, that is, the relative price structure of all the things that the firm buys and sells. Conventional economic theory gives high marks to competitive markets and low marks to monopoly. From the point of view of the general interest, it is certainly true that monopoly, as we can see in the Organization of Petroleum Exporting Countries (OPEC), is capable of creating substantial transfers toward the monopolists from all who purchase and use the monopolists' product, which is hard to justify in any theory of social justice. Nevertheless, the competitive markets also are engaged constantly in redistributing net worth among those who market as the relative price structure changes, and whatever we may think about the gambling aspects of market speculations, there is no doubt that they increase the uncertainties of those who have to make decisions that involve purchase and sale.

There is little doubt, for instance, that the price supports that have been a prime feature of U.S. agricultural policy for almost 50 years may not have been very successful from the point of view of distributional justice, for they certainly subsidized the rich rather than the poor. Nevertheless, the very diminution in price uncertainty that they produce for the individual farmer undoubtedly had a lot to do with the extraordinary increase in agricultural productivity over this same period.

The fear of loss rather than the hope of gain may be a much more important motivation in limiting both the amount of investment and the willingness to make risky investments. If public policy or even private organizations like insurance companies limit this loss, the willingness to invest and to take risks may be augmented substantially. We see somewhat the same phenomenon in the public utilities, which also in effect have "price supports," and also have been willing to take investment risks, for instance in hydropower and even more in nuclear energy. The utilities, significantly, have exhibited a marked increase in productivity over the years.

The hypothesis that a declining rate of increase in productivity in U.S. society in the last decade results from increasing uncertainties, particularly as a result of legislation and changes in the legal structure, is hard to test, but it is at least worth taking seriously. The role of the environmental movement in this problem is particularly interesting. There is no doubt that the environmental movement and environmental legislation arose out of a quite legitimate feeling that certain public goods and public "bads," especially in terms of air and water pollution, and in terms of the destruction of certain natural habitats, were not being taken into account in the overall decision-making process. GNP may be a poor indicator of public goods, though it includes them as a component at cost. The measurement and estimation problem here is very severe, but we certainly should make some allowance for them in estimating overall productivity. Insofar as declining productivity, as reflected in GNP statistics, is a result of an unmeasured shift from private goods into public goods, it may not be as bad as it looks.

The possibility, however, that these public goods are being obtained at too high a cost is very real and deserves serious investigation. High costs are particularly likely to develop where the attempt to solve environmental problems involves extensive litigation and an "adversary process," which can easily have a very high, but hidden, social cost in terms of increasing uncertainty and encouraging delays. The adversary mode of Anglo-American law has many virtues, but there are many situations in which it is very costly and in which a mode of resolving conflict that involves more dialogue and reconciliation could achieve the same end at much lower cost. We see this in the rise of arbitration and conciliation as a paralegal profession. The social cost of increasing uncertainty is apt to be invisible and, hence, underestimated. This book does an important service in calling attention to that fact.

Knowledge of the dynamics of any social system enables us to project, with varying degrees of accuracy, potential futures and, as such, remains the principal antidote to the ill-effects of uncertainty. We gain such knowledge by examining the histories of systems, seeking to discover stable relationships. The perception of trends (stable patterns of change) combined with the perception of episodes (discrete series of events that follow the realization of some previously established potential) allows us to reduce uncertainty. Trends can be quite complex, as when, for instance, the baseball player projects the trajectory of a ball and catches it; certainly, without his realizing it, his nervous system is solving differential equations, perhaps up to the third degree. Episodes are also quite common. For example, we have extraordinary confidence that a kitten, if it grows up at all, will grow up into a cat and not into a hippopotamus. In social systems, however, it is usually harder to recognize an episode, even when it is beginning. Social kittens often look distressingly like baby hippopotamuses and it is hard to tell one episode from another. Furthermore, the difficulty of identifying and distinguishing between episodic events decreases the accuracy of our predictions about trends. The impact of a hippopotamus upon an ecosystem greatly differs from the impact of a kitten. At least, however, constructing hypothetical episodes that would alter trends by changing the causal relationships at work within them forewarns us of the degree of uncertainty that chance may create in the future.

Our inherent inability to predict chance occurrences compounds our sense of uncertainty in our environment. Moreover, any attempt to separate modeling results of the future into choice and chance components inevitably will be somewhat arbitrary and, in this respect, the results of this book undoubtedly will be open to criticism. There is nothing unreasonable in this, however, for the very attempt to distinguish choice from chance involves both choice elements and chance elements and will not be exempt from the uncertainty of the world that it attempts to describe. This book, however, is a very important pioneering work and should have an impact on many reports to come. It no doubt will be possible to refine the technique. We may be able, for instance, to identify chance elements of varying degrees of probability, therefore involving varying degrees of choice.

Sometimes by choice we can diminish chance, which is almost universally beneficial, and it may be possible to identify more exactly particular social structures and decisions, legal frameworks, and so on, that reduce chance and illuminate choice. The present volume, however, is a great improvement on those studies of the future that simply attempt to give a most probable outcome, without indicating the necessity of preparing also for the improbable, and even on those studies that give a range of alternatives without indicating what choice factors may affect them.

With all its difficulties, the distinction that the book makes between choice and chance as determinants of the future is a very important one. It is perhaps as important psychologically as it is technically. On the one side it saves us from the apathy of despair, which arises out of the feeling that everything is due to chance and out of our control. The malaise of the 1960s, particularly as it affected what was really a fairly small percentage (though a very visible one) of young people, arose out of a sense of impotence and the absence of choices. The Vietnam War and the military draft in part may be responsible for this, for any form of involuntary servitude produces a sense of impotence, the sense that all things are due to chance and none to choice. It could well be that the abolition of the draft created the much more cheerful atmosphere of the 1970s among young people, especially on college campuses, and its reinstatement is likely to have profound psychological costs, whatever the military arguments.

On the other side, the emphasis that chance is an important element of the future preserves us from the delusions of grandeur that arise from thinking that we can choose everything and control the future to our own sweet will. This, too, is very dangerous and produces illusions of certainty and perhaps accounts for some of the catastrophic decisions that were made by President Johnson. There is a kind of mystique, by no means absent from the political or business communities, associated with the "great leader" who brushes aside all doubts and uncertainties, mistakes his own intuitions for the voice of God, rejects all criticism, distorts his own information system to the point where he lives in an increasingly unreal world, and makes decisions about futures that become increasingly imaginary and unrealistic. This phenomenon, again, is a sure recipe for catastrophe. We have seen it many times in human history—Napoleon, Hitler, and I think we can now add Khomeini. The only defense against these dangerous delusions is a wide general cultural awareness of the tremendous importance of chance and the decent humility that this awareness produces. Cultures that emphasize that everything has to be "just right" and make no allowances for good and bad luck are in danger of grave pathologies that can easily carry them from bad to worse, and there are many examples of this in human history.

The difficulty of distinguishing choice from chance is illustrated by the uncertainties involved in the rewriting of history, which is a pleasant occupation with highly uncertain results. What would have happened if the Persians had won at Marathon, if Caesar had lost to Pompey, if Jesus had been killed in infancy by Herod, if Mohammed had died young, if the Ming emperors had not called off their great voyages, if Hitler had been killed in World War I? One could multiply the list indefinitely. In some cases, indeed, the answer might well be that things would not have been different. As somebody once said, "How could Columbus miss it?" When Western Europeans became capable of sailing 3,000 miles in a straight line, it was hard for them not to discover America, though it is a bit of a puzzle why the Chinese did not beat the Europeans to it.

The human race indeed seems to hover between the fatalistic determinism that argues that all things are foreordained by Jehovah, Allah, or dialectical materialism, and a much rarer, cynical nihilism, which sees the human race lost in the sea of randomness, alternately buffeted about and smiled upon by inscrutable fates. Even where the deterministic view prevails—and one suspects that a very large percentage of human beings have held this view simply because of our overwhelming fear of randomness—the knowledge of this deterministic system is rarely believed to be granted, and then only to oracles, from Delphi to the modern economists, who speak in ambiguities that are very hard to test.

In the constant search for the reduction of uncertainty, we look first for the necessities, for the things that cannot be otherwise, the great permanent structures and identities that constitute the real hard core of human knowledge. We start with mathematics. The mathematician has an extraordinary capacity for elaborating the obvious, and even the consequences of things that are not immediately obvious. This is why mathematics is such a powerful, though occasionally treacherous, tool in expanding our knowledge of the real world.

Beyond mathematics there are what might be called the "empirical necessities," things like the law of conservation, which says that if we have a fixed quantity of anything, all we can do is push it around, so that a plus somewhere must mean a minus somewhere else. This law applies to a great diversity of things, from energy and materials even to balances of payments, when there is a fixed quantity of money. The conservation principle, however, is a special case of a more general one, which I frivolously have called the "bathtub theorem": a change in the stock of anything is equal to additions minus the subtractions. If subtractions are more than additions (this is true of all exhaustible resources), the stock will diminish. This fact is one of the underlying identities of our present energy and materials crisis.

Beyond this, there are what might be called the "empirical stabilities," which are not necessities in the sense that they may have been arrived at by processes that involve a good deal of chance, but are stable at least in our time span. The patterns of the solar system and the general physical geography of the earth are good examples.

We always have to be careful, however, with merely empirical regularities. They are not necessities, and their parameters may change, as Mount St. Helens illustrates dramatically.

Social systems exhibit much larger parametric change than most physical and biological systems and therefore are inherently much less predictable. Nevertheless, the search for the knowledge both of its necessities and its empirical regularities is essential for wise choices to be made. An example from the last 50 years would be the contrasting experience of Australia and New Zealand on the one hand and Argentina and Uruguay on the other. In terms of their physical environments and their positions in the world economic system, they are very similar. Yet in the last 50 years they have diverged strikingly. Their per capita incomes were very similar 50 or 60 years ago. Today Australia and New Zealand are two or three times as rich as Argentina and Uruguay. Australia and New Zealand have remained free democratic societies; Argentina and Uruguay have gone downhill into tragic dictatorships and depressions. Chance cannot be blamed for this. It is a result of choice, that is, of decisions made under different images of the world. It is hard to believe that the images that governed the decisions in Australia and New Zealand were not much more realistic than those that governed the decisions in Argentina and Uruguay. Just how unrealistic views of the world develop is a process that may have some elements of chance in it, but that these learning processes by which we develop our images of the world can be improved is something that hardly can be doubted and is "a consummation devoutly to be wished."

From an understanding of the importance of the choice and chance factors in the decision-making process we logically derive some insight into how to plan for the future. The general rule is that in the presence of uncertainty, decisions should seek to be flexible and assets adaptable and liquid. All decisions, even bad ones, involve planning, as all decisions involve a choice among alternative images of the future. Under uncertainty, however, it is essential that information be received constantly that is realistic and reflects changes in the real world and that plans should be revised at frequent intervals in light of this information.

We cannot, of course, achieve complete flexibility. There are things to which we have to commit ourselves, and we must be prepared to suffer the consequences if we have bad luck and things turn out wrong. Nevertheless, it is very important to have contingency planning, even for quite extreme positions of the system. The Three Mile Island incident is an excellent example of the need for thinking about extreme and improbable positions of any system in advance of when they take place, and doing at least some preliminary preparation for them. All driver training should include some discussion of what to do in a skid on ice when the old rules suddenly fail. Here, the careful study of the episodes of the past may be very important, so that we will recognize them and be ready for them when they threaten in the future.

It is a critical and quite difficult question as to how much "contingency investment" there ought to be. There is a certain danger that if we have too much of this it might bring on the feared contingency, just as a civil defense program might increase the probability of nuclear war. There are limits, also, as to the extent to which we can remain uncommitted and to the amount of resources that we can afford to put into contingency planning. Somewhere between cocksureness and indecisiveness we have to find a middle way of wisdom. It could be that the principle of at least one egg in all the baskets is a good one, and that no contingency should be excluded completely from our consideration, although we certainly should not brood too much over the more remote ones.

Many events, like our own death, are certain to happen but at an uncertain date. We do plan for such things by insurance, making wills, and so on. For the individual person, bound as we are into our nonrecombinable DNA, the crown of a good life may well be the preparations we have made for our departure from it. Societies, of course, are potentially less mortal than individuals—which actually makes the problem of preparing for the unknown future harder. Their social DNA continually is recombined and renewed, as old individuals vacate their roles and new and usually younger individuals take their places. There is an underlying problem here, of what might be called the "moral resource," as to whether this is renewable or exhaustible. It appears that in societies like Argentina and Uruguay, for example, in some curious way that we do not understand, the underlying moral resources seem to have been exhausted about 1930, and the societies have stagnated economically and have gone downhill politically, especially in terms of basic human rights, with a frightening momentum.

This volume, I am sure, was not designed primarily to renew our society's moral resource. Nevertheless, it may have some effect. Its breadth of vision and its moderate and concerned tone should be a challenge to those who consider themselves to be a moral resource, who are concerned about larger issues than their own immediate personal welfare, who care about where our society is going and earnestly want it to move toward the better rather than toward the worse. The morally concerned, however, are always in danger of substituting the intensity of concern for the wisdom of it. This book is addressed not only to those who have to make public policy decisions, but to a much wider audience, and if it will stimulate discussion in universities and churches, and schools and political circles, it will perform a very valuable function. Its greatest strength is that it illustrates the process of learning under changing conditions.

This volume is very different from earlier economic and energy studies. Some seven years of learning in a very rapidly changing world have gone into it, and there will be, one hopes, future revisions, which will represent still more and new learning processes. But it is not a final revelation of truth. Therein, indeed, is its strength. It deserves to be read carefully and taken seriously by all those who are concerned about the future.

PREFACE

This volume presents the results of a major policy study completed in 1981 under the sponsorship of the Edison Electric Institute (EEI), the association of investor-owned electric utilities. Primary impetus for this project came from a committee of utility industry senior executives chaired by Jack K. Horton, chairman of the executive committee, Southern California Edison Company, and formerly chairman of the board and chief executive officer; and including T. L. Austin, Jr., chairman of the board, Texas Utilities Company; Gordon Corey, retired vice-chairman, Commonwealth Edison Company; W. Donham Crawford, chairman of the board, Gulf States Utilities Company; and William McCollam, Jr., president, Edison Electric Institute. In seeking to contribute to the ongoing growth policy dialogue, this book examines carefully the future of economic growth and of energy prospects over the next 50 years. Like *Economic Growth in the Future* (McGraw-Hill, 1976), upon which it is based, this volume builds on a broad social perspective and a detailed analysis of the components of economic growth, considering the implications for energy and electricity in the context of the U.S. economy at large.

In the intervening years between *Economic Growth in the Future* and this endeavor, major social and political changes have occurred, changes that have shaped the approach and design of this book and enlarged the audience to whom it is addressed. The heightened public awareness of economic and energy issues has been coupled with constantly changing government and private-sector policies and policy makers, new programs in energy management and policy, and technological breakthroughs. Consequently, the present volume's readership will be more diversified than that of *Economic Growth in the Future*. This readership embraces government policy makers and their staffs, academics, business planners, and concerned laymen; considering the diversity of this group, the authors chose to present historical, theoretical, and technical materials whenever it was felt they would facilitate the readers' understanding of either the book's methodology or its results.

This volume's organization illustrates how energy-economic studies are conducted. Chapter 1 presents a historical perspective on societal forces that have dominated the past 30 years. This perspective on our past forms the context for this analysis and functions as a qualitative modeling system.

Chapter 2 translates this qualitative model into a quantitative form by telescoping these social forces into an analytical representation of the economy. It incorporates uncertainty, which plays a major role in future economic and energy growth, into the scenario design by distinguishing between variables determined primarily by choice and variables determined largely by chance. Chapter 2 also explains the specific modeling systems used for the short term, midterm, and long term and the relationships between them.

Chapter 3 details the book's major input assumptions, classifying variables under the general categories of demographics, labor force, productivity, investment, government expenditures, fiscal policies, and energy. The chapter emphasizes the input information required for the midterm analysis, but sections of it also provide detail about the short- and long-term assumptions.

Chapter 4 describes and interprets the modeling results of the five basic scenarios as well as the results of the judgmental analysis that complemented the modeling work. It also includes a qualitative description of other futures—ultrahigh and negative growth—that lie outside the range of the modeled scenarios.

Chapter 5 articulates the book's policy recommendations, which serve as prescriptions for sustaining a healthy economy and for securing the energy future of the United States. Although these recommendations are divided into two principal categories — economic vitality and energy security — it is not as individual recommendations, but only as an integrated set of mutually reinforcing choices, that they can lead to a preferred future.

The present volume observes the United States at one of the most decisive points in its history. Domestic and international policies formulated in the early 1980s and implemented during the remainder of the decade will do much to determine whether the nation prospers, stagnates, or declines during the rest of the twentieth century and the first part of the next. Much may be said for the widely held thesis that stagnant growth and chronic inflation will characterize the 1980s—a sad legacy of the confused 1970s. However, an even stronger case can be made for the nation's ability to profit from the lessons of history, improve its policy choices, and initiate a remarkable rejuvenation of spirit and growth during the 1980s—a rejuvenation that can extend into the next century.

Any such rejuvenation requires careful discrimination between choice and chance, admitting the presence of chance effects where they truly dominate, but rejecting the excuses of bad luck frequently advanced when poor choices have been made. This book's design accounts for this distinction. Its different scenarios, which depict the likely outcomes of various combinations of choice and chance factors, present a wide range of possible economic and energy futures. Based on these outcomes, the present volume sets forth a number of policy recommendations for both the economy and energy sectors.*

Economic Growth in the Future-II: An Executive Summary (Washington, D.C.: Edison Electric Institute, 1980) encapsulates this volume's research and findings.

ACKNOWLEDGMENTS

The research for the present volume was conducted between 1978 and 1981. The analysis employed the most advanced econometric and energy models currently available. The study's core models, the Hudson-Jorgenson and Baughman-Joskow models, allowed the authors to focus their policy recommendations on the midterm. Additionally, the Wharton Annual Model, the Evans Economics Model, and the Energy Technology Assessment-Macro Model were used for near- and long-term analyses. With the exception of the Evans Economics Model, these models were made available through ongoing research contracts with the Electric Power Research Institute (EPRI) in Palo Alto, California. EPRI staff members Stephen Peck, E. Victor Neimeyer, and Lewis Rubin joined with the authors to form an Advisory Committee for both the present volume and EPRI's Continuing Projects Concerning Energy-Economy Interactions. Certainly, both projects benefited from the cooperative spirit in which EEI and EPRI approached these distinct but complementary undertakings.

The list of consultants and advisors who contributed to this book reveals one of the foremost concerns that characterized the planning and execution of this project. A diversity of opinions was sought to ensure that this volume represented a balanced perspective. Thus, the assistance of individuals with wide-ranging views on society, on the economy, and on the energy sector were solicited—individuals whose collective contribution would not be to justify the principle of growth, but instead to evaluate objectively the scenario design. The authors apologize in advance for any omissions in their attempt to list those individuals who assisted in the preparation of the book: Peter Auer, Cornell University; Douglas Bauer, Edison Electric Institute; Raymond Beauregard, Northeast Utilities Service Company; Anne Carter, Brandeis University; Herman Daly, Louisiana State University; Vijaya Duggal, Wharton Econometric Forecasting Associates; Michael Evans, Evans Economics, Inc.; Ted Gordon, The Futures Group; David Hoff, Puget Sound Power and Light Company; William Hogan, Harvard University; Connie Holmes, National Coal Association; Edward Hudson, Dale W. Jorgenson Associates; Edward Hyman, University of San Francisco; Dale W. Jorgenson, Harvard University; Lawrence Klein, University of Pennsylvania; Seymour Lipset, Stanford University; Dennis Little, Library of Congress; Thomas McMillan, Texas Power and Light Company; William Nordhaus, Yale University; Peter Passell, The *New York Times;* Jack Schenck, Edison Electric Institute; George Schink,

Wharton Econometric Forecasting Associates; Ben Schlesinger, American Gas Association; Sidney Sonenblum, Energy Consultant; Hoff Stauffer, ICF Inc.; William Stitt, ICF Inc.; Edwin Wiggin, Atomic Industrial Forum; Ian Wilson, General Electric; and Saad Zara, Detroit Edison. The authors express special appreciation to Kenneth Boulding of the University of Colorado for his assistance throughout the project and for writing the book's thought-provoking Foreword.

These acknowledgments would not be complete without crediting the technical and editorial staff for its work throughout the project. Norm Rubenstein served as the project's general editor and Jane Nunnelee as the staff writer. Clara Gordon, the staff researcher, was invaluable in constructing many of the tables and figures and in shepherding drafts of the manuscript. Harry Stickler provided the text's illustrations. Lyn Cannastra produced the book and Charlene Corbin designed it. In addition, writers Mary Wayne, Henry Simmons, and Mark Reynolds assisted the authors in the preparation of the manuscript. The authors also are indebted to Norma Beimbrink and her word processing staff for patiently and carefully typing the manuscript.

This volume represents the combined efforts of all the participants. The broad spectrum of views it presents ensures that some contributors will not agree with certain of its conclusions or recommendations. Any errors must be attributed to the authors.

CONTENTS

TABLES

FIGURES

Chapter 1

HISTORICAL FORCES IN THE ECONOMY

Contemporary economic-energy literature describes a world radically different from the world that forms its history; prior to the Arab oil embargo of 1973, many of the economic and energy factors for which the present volume must account neither existed nor were foreseen. In conducting this research, consideration was given to a variety of economic factors associated with the U.S. recovery from the 1974–75 recession, including the stagnation of private-sector labor productivity, the unprecedented decline of the savings rate, an alarming slowdown in capital investment per employed person, a general shift from investment to consumption, overexpansive federal fiscal and monetary policies, and sudden and dramatic increases in oil prices and inflation.

In addition to purely economic concerns, the present volume's results reflect the effects of the failure of the United States to adopt a coherent energy policy in a timely manner. The most dramatic evidence of this failure is the increase in U.S. reliance on imported petroleum from 38 percent in 1974 to 46 percent in 1979, an increased dependence that has been accompanied by a more than doubling of prices.

To profit from history we must review it carefully, examining the basic philosophies behind both the policies that have proven ineffective over the last 20 years and those that have proven successful. Such a historical review of the recent past's economic and energy surprises and of the policies they have generated indicates the enormous growth of uncertainty in the U.S. social and economic system and in the world at large. One purpose of studies such as the present volume is to reduce uncertainty by acquiring more knowledge about energy-economy interactions.

The eclectic methodology of this work combines two principal techniques: judgmental analysis and energy modeling. Without a social perspective, however, judgmental analysis and energy modeling lack the scope and the proper inductive basis to lend confidence to the process of making policy recommendations. The scenarios set forth in the following chapters reflect assumptions about the way social, economic, and political forces will operate in the future. A perception of the evolution of these forces over the past 30 years was instrumental in deriving these assumptions and in designing the scenarios. The result is a range of possibilities from which the actual future might unfold and, within this range, a preferred alternative that would depend upon flexible policy choices.

Social Sectors and Forces

The United States has experienced an extraordinarily rich history since World War II, a history too often ignored or incompletely understood by policy makers. Policy recommendations that ignore both the dramatic social changes and the influential societal forces of the last three decades are little more than advice out of context. To identify these dominant social forces the authors have defined five major social sectors: people, business, government, international relations, and resources. Figure 1.1 depicts each sector and the dominant force that has characterized its postwar evolution.

Productivity, the dominant force in the business sector, demonstrates how each of the five forces both acts upon and is acted upon by forces associated with the other sectors. Productivity, heavily dependent upon the capital formation process, is one measure of our society's standard of living. Its relationship to factors such as rates of inflation and employment indicates its importance in the people sector, where the degree of productivity we enjoy influences the savings rate, decisions about whether or not to have children, or whether to join the labor force, and so on. In its attempts to insure economic well-being, the government sector responds to productivity fluctuations by adjusting fiscal and monetary policy. Productivity also affects the international relations sector, for how competitive we can be determines the proportions of the goods we import and export. Also, because productivity rates reflect the availability not only of capital and labor, but of materials, productivity both influences the use of our resources and is influenced by resource availability.

A perception of these forces and of the ways that they change in magnitude, direction, and horizon of influence is the basis for the assumptions in Chapter 3. In the people sector, the authors note that the once widely accepted image of the U.S. population as sharing uniform social goals and values has faded. In fact, the awareness of fragmentation within our society has grown progressively as Americans have questioned more openly and frequently the social order that existed just after World War II. The key force identified in the resource sector is availability. The burgeoning concern with our physical environment's ability to renew itself, with our ability to substitute resources, and with the depletion of fuel supplies suggests the various directions this force of availability has taken in the last three decades. In the international relations sector, the focus is on the oscillation toward and away from interdependence, an international strategy with both economic and security implications. The dominant force characterizing the government sector is its concern with the public's general welfare. Over the historical period this book examines, this concern has amounted to growing regulation and various attempts to effect income redistribution through a growth in government expenditures.

While writing the historical perspective, the authors frequently were reminded that reality, unlike a social science diagram, does not reduce to discrete social sectors. To acknowledge this fact, they have depicted Figure 1.1 in a circular form to suggest its interrelationships. Obviously, singling out five principal forces, like dividing society into five sectors, is a simplification; but this book is intended to illustrate that the viability of any policy decision depends upon our awareness that social forces do not

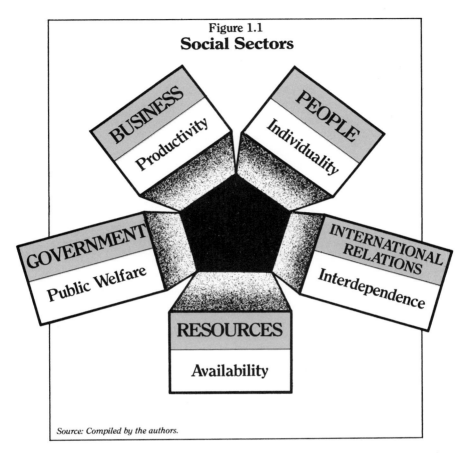

Figure 1.1
Social Sectors

BUSINESS
Productivity

PEOPLE
Individuality

GOVERNMENT
Public Welfare

INTERNATIONAL RELATIONS
Interdependence

RESOURCES
Availability

Source: Compiled by the authors.

act in isolation from one another. Moreover, the five dominant forces discussed are actually organizing metaphors—categories that incorporate a host of related social forces and demonstrate the highly integrative nature of society.

The People Sector

Loss of a Single American Identity

The people sector is composed of some 220 million individuals belonging to one or more disparate social groups defined by factors such as age, race, religion, sex, national heritage, income, profession, political persuasion, and geography. Together these individuals comprise an extraordinarily diverse national population—over half of whom were born after World War II. At that time, the United States enjoyed the reputation of a melting pot, accepting diversity and creating a mixture stronger and better than any of its single ingredients, a mixture that was uniquely American.

However, the past 30 years have witnessed the loss of that apparently homogeneous American identity. Illustrations of this fragmentation abound, although it has no single explanation. A series of extremely vocal civil rights movements, for example, have called attention, not to problems shared by all Americans, but to the specific status of groups such as black Americans, female Americans, Hispanic Americans, or gay Americans. As more education and better sources of information have made us better informed, they also have made us more confused about our place as Americans in a constantly changing world. If the fragmentation of our national personality has no single cause, however, it does have one principal consequence: a social consensus in the United States is harder to achieve now than it was 30 years ago. The melting pot that produced homogeneous Americans in the early postwar years has given way to a salad bar, the ingredients of which are recognizable and distinct.

The Evolution of American Society

Members of the generation born after World War II, on the whole, tend to demonstrate a greater diversity of beliefs and attitudes than their parents. Over time, the U.S. consciousness has shifted in response to business-sector and governmental forces, a changing physical universe, and a new conception of what it means on an international level to be a contemporary U.S. citizen. The shift has been toward greater individualism, an individualism both of ideology and of action. Today's generation emphasizes realizing one's individual potential, safeguarding the physical environment, and sharing in a good life equitably defined. It questions much of what post-World War II society apparently held dear: its conception of the work ethic, of the traditional family, and of a notion of progress defined in purely technological and economic terms.

When U.S. soldiers returned from World War II, the society welcoming them back was equal to their expectations. They had to weather an inevitable postwar recession, as the United States adjusted to a peacetime economy; soon, however, the men and women of the late 1940s and early 1950s acquired the middle class rewards of home ownership, employment, and public education to which they had aspired. Characteristic of that generation of U.S. citizens, they accepted the wartime roles they had played with the psychological ease that comes from conviction, conviction that one's actions are justified and one's principles worth underscoring with one's life.

Less certainty characterized the response of draft-age Americans during the era of the Vietnam War. Reponses to that conflict symbolize the difference between the two generations' senses of their relation to government. The generation returning from World War II concentrated on improving material standards of living and broadening educational opportunities for their children. This emphasis on education in the last 30 years explains not only the expanding professional class, but also shifts in the way that class has come to view traditional American values. Educating their children, however, did not guarantee those paying tuition that the next generation necessarily would embrace their values. In fact, the generation schooled after the Korean War learned to question and challenge those very values. As such, formerly shared consensuses dissolved. Much to the concern of tradition-minded U.S. citizens, many college-aged Americans argued that their country was not defending freedom in Vietnam but propping up a corrupt government; some felt that compared to third world countries, the United States consumed a disproportionate share of world resources. For that reason and others, some concluded that having as many children as their parents had was unconscionable. Increasing numbers decided that living with someone made more sense than contributing to rising divorce statistics.

Shifting Economic and Political Realities

As time passed, the capacity of the job market to absorb this flood of highly educated new workers diminished and, with it, the economic opportunities of all U.S. citizens reflected shifting realities that both generations had to face. By the mid-1970s the employment picture darkened further as a result of slower economic growth. Liberal arts degrees no longer guaranteed employment. Salaries that compared favorably with job-wage ratios of the previous generation no longer could keep pace with the costs of housing, food, and fuel, much less luxuries like movies, eating out, and vacations.

When the nation's economic performance was stronger, its citizens' dissatisfaction with government focused largely on political issues, such as Vietnam or Watergate. During the 1970s, however, that sense of alienation was aggravated by the economic repercussions of government policies. For example, supporting government social programs that raise the standard of living of the disadvantaged and improve the quality of the environment further shrinks each citizen's paycheck, which already is shrinking in real terms. Consequently, individuals who once fought to institutionalize pollution control or transfer payment programs now rank social goals somewhat differently, especially when the costs of these programs must vie with the rising costs of rearing children. Although the average number of children per family has dropped from 3.2 to 1.7 in the last 30 years, the expense of their upbringing and education continues to climb. Moreover, members of the postwar generation might accept more readily the cost of government programs, such as Social Security and Medicare, if they could be assured that these programs would be solvent in the future when they might need them.

Much about life in the United States today differs from life in the 1950s. Not only are we a better educated society now, but the media explosion allows us to act with better information than U.S. citizens had access to a generation ago. Only 9 percent of U.S. families had television sets in 1950; in 1980, households are likely to have more than one set and constant access to daily news, often while it is happening. Critics of the networks' emphasis on the visual claim that it often precludes in-depth reporting; nevertheless, many U.S. citizens who have not served in the armed forces have seen for themselves the effects of war. They have seen men walking on the moon, the Kennedy-Nixon debates, President Kennedy's funeral, the Watergate hearings, Abscam coverage, and many other events that helped shape their beliefs and attitudes.

While the media have educated us in one way, the marketplace has educated us in another. For example, 30 years ago roomy sedans and Sunday driving were a way of life. Today, facing resource depletion, consumers are looking for energy-efficient compact cars. The emergence of OPEC (Organization of Petroleum Exporting Countries) and long gasoline lines have made us necessarily more energy conscious than we ever had to be before. Meanwhile, until recently Detroit continued to manufacture mostly gas guzzlers and only foreign competitors offered small cars with good mileage ratings. The consequence has been the public's decision not to support U.S. business automatically but instead to make purchases on an economic basis.

The cost of gasoline and its scarcity, both in 1973 and 1979, were far more than energy lessons to aware U.S. consumers. They were cause for a growing suspicion both of business and government—business because rising prices triggered the consumer's sense of large oil companies' collusion in the gas shortage, and government because it apparently had learned nothing from the 1973 embargo to prevent a similar occurrence six years later. U.S. citizens expected their government to anticipate and prevent shortages of commodities essential to their style of living. Gasoline shortages, like earlier supply interruptions of coffee and sugar, cast doubt on the government's ability to protect its constituents' welfare.

The Rise of the Special Interest Group

The fragmentation of a seemingly uniform postwar U.S. identity also results in part from the increasing visibility of special interest groups, groups that share rather exclusive common goals or problems. Individuals have joined together because of sexual, cultural, or racial bonds and have produced a modern American character that, more than the national personality of 30 years ago, emphasizes its citizens' individuality.

Take, for example, the way in which women today both perceive themselves and are perceived differently than they were in 1950. No longer resigned to being treated as silent partners, women have fought for increased recognition of their contributions to society and for greater opportunities to contribute. Certain technological innovations have helped make possible this struggle for equality. The development and market penetration of labor-saving products and services have given women more discretionary time. In addition, the Pill, introduced in 1960, presented them with a more effective means for preventing unwanted pregnancies.

Significant advances for women, at least in the aggregate, mark the last few decades: child care centers for working mothers, safe abortions, the right of single women to obtain birth control, the ability to establish credit independently, and so on. However, the work force best reflects how much women's roles have shifted in the past 30 years. Between 1950 and 1978, the number of employed U.S. women rose 125 percent; the jump signals women's growing desire or need for careers of their own or for additional income. Their struggle for acceptance as individuals also partially may explain the virtual doubling of single-person households in this time period. For both men and women, marriage has become more of a conscious choice than a social expectation. Although women have yet to see the Equal Rights Amendment ratified, their struggle to have it incorporated into the U.S. Constitution powerfully symbolizes the evolution of their postwar role.

As a cause, the postwar struggle for equal rights did not originate with women. In fact, as a national concern, its cry first was associated with minority rights, particularly the rights of U.S. blacks and, more recently, those of Hispanic Americans. The opportunities for housing, education, and employment that greeted returning white soldiers in the late 1940s did not always exist for blacks, who came to know the frustration of battlefield equality revoked back home. By the time that black Air Force veteran James Meredith attempted to enter the University of Mississippi in 1961, blacks already had won the *Brown* vs. *Board of Education* Supreme Court victory declaring racial segregation unconstitutional. Overturning the separate but equal doctrine in 1954 neither created equal educational opportunities nor translated into voting, housing, or employment equality. The emergence of Dr. Martin Luther King, Jr. provided alienated blacks with a forceful and charismatic leader. In 1957 the Civil Rights Commission was established and an epoch of history-making events, including demonstrations, sit-ins, the Freedom Rides, and black boycotts of discriminatory businesses, began.

Predictably, the black separatist movement of the mid- and late 1960s evolved, at least in part, as a result of the failure of government, business, and other elements of the people sector to address blacks' economic grievances as consistently and rapidly as they had expected them to. A 1967 census report confirmed that income levels were far lower, the numbers of blacks inhabiting subsistence housing far higher, and the unemployment rates twice as high for blacks as for whites. Clearly, the grounds for dissatisfaction among blacks were far more than purely theoretical—they were as basic as where and how one could sustain a decent standard of living.

Such economic concerns now occupy the nation's rapidly growing Spanish-speaking population. As immigration, both legal and illegal, from Mexico, Cuba, Haiti, and South America increases, the economic and social needs of the Hispanic population in the United States will exert influences on government and business. One example is the current pressure for multilingual education in the U.S. public school system. Furthermore, immigration's impact on the other social sectors is more complex than one might initially expect. How government foreign policy handles the immigration issue is politically significant for our international relations and a factor in our negotiating power with countries who can supply us with resources we are now compelled to import.

Race, sex, and age are not the only identifying characteristics that have given rise to special interest groups in the modern United States. For example, a growing national concern with individual rights has led to building-code legislation that ensures access for the handicapped. In addition, television programs frequently offer "signing" for deaf viewers and some buses have been equipped with lifts for wheelchairs. In another vein, U.S. citizens, aroused over the dangers of carcinogens and pollutants, have worked together to legislate government health and safety controls. Whole agencies, the Occupational Safety and Health Administration (OSHA) and the Environmental Protection Agency (EPA), for example, testify to the institutionalization of such concerns. As Nader's Raiders work to establish a more risk-free society, organizations such as Common Cause seek to make government at all levels more responsive to its constituencies.

Summary

During the last three decades, U.S. citizens increasingly have demonstrated a sense of themselves in which "American" modifies some other social identity (women, black, Indian, and so on). The striking diversity of beliefs and attitudes that characterizes contemporary U.S. society evolved in part as a consequence of the struggle for economic equality. All Americans share a vested interest in some issues, such as those on which the economic growth debate centers. The authors of this book note, however, that as U.S. citizens have formed special interest groups to achieve their economic aims, our national personality has fragmented. It seems to be the case that when a group, like U.S. blacks, must struggle to obtain an acceptable, much less equal, standard of living in relation to its fellow citizens, its members first focus on economic attainments. As their struggle begins to produce material rewards and as standards of living equalize, group members then, and only then, direct their attention to other social issues, issues that seem less significant to individuals without jobs or job prospects.

The Business Sector

A burst of economic growth took place in the United States in the first two decades following World War II. It was accompanied—in fact, propelled—by a pervasive, seemingly automatic, and continuous increase in productivity, the efficiency with which the private sector combines the factors of production (capital, labor, energy, and materials). In fact, over the period from 1948 through 1969, real national income grew at a rate twice as fast as the amount of productive factor inputs. Of course, the deferring of costs, such as the underpricing of rapidly depleting resources, accounted for some of this growth, but productivity increases, the key to our economic future, were the principal source of this economic surge.

In general, the early postwar characteristics of the other four sectors complemented business, reinforcing and stimulating its performance. Underconsumption, both in the 1930s because of low incomes and during the war because of production constraints on consumer goods, led to a burst of demand following the war. This demand, coupled with forced savings during the war, provided a strong and predictable market and the buying power to spur the economy. U.S. families consistently put aside a little of their paychecks every week, saving for a second car, a new house, or their children's educations; therefore, business could borrow money easily for new and more efficient plants and equipment. Low inflation rates—partly the result of restrained government fiscal and monetary policies—also encouraged productive investment. War-ravaged Europe, dependent on U.S. goods and grain, provided the United States with an eager export market. The raw materials of production, especially fossil fuels, were readily available and relatively inexpensive. Business and each of the other sectors reinforced one another, resulting in unparalleled productivity increases during the first half of the postwar era. Consequently, Americans' standard of living as measured by real gross national product (GNP) per capita rose 60 percent in the 20 years after the war.

The strong performance of the business sector, in turn, helped shape the evolution of the other social sectors. It assured the swelling middle class ranks of their own financial security and enabled them to begin focusing on social issues rather than on simply acquiring the physical necessities of life. It permitted the government to begin progressive programs to aid disadvantaged Americans, to improve education, housing, diet, medical care, and the environment. It also allowed the government to devote larger amounts of money, time, and energy to the world's developing nations in an attempt to maintain good international relations and the balance of world power.

As the other sectors evolved, however, their impacts on the business sector naturally changed. Today people save a smaller percentage of their incomes than they have at any time during the past 30 years. Inflation has become a household word. The impact of our production processes on the environment has become glaringly obvious and of increasing concern. Oil prices have skyrocketed while our dependence on imports has grown. Government intervention in the business sector has increased progressively. Meanwhile, the relative productivity of many foreign countries has grown dramatically, costing the United States traditional markets at home and abroad. Even so, prior to the 1970s, whenever productivity growth faltered, the pause was only temporary. However, in 1974 and again in early 1978 productivity growth not only stalled, it actually turned negative, events unprecedented in U.S. postwar economic history.

Investment: A Key to Productivity

Productivity advances are not magical. Over the past 30 years, they have depended primarily upon two kinds of investment. Investment in intangibles—such as research and development, and education and training—improves the quality and efficiency of both workers and production processes. Investment in tangibles—such as structures and equipment, and the development of natural resources—then combines with these improvements to advance productivity.

The performance of the business sector's agricultural component dramatically illustrates the returns on such investments. The rapid mechanization of farming and improvements in methods of growing, harvesting, and processing farm products over the postwar era not only have allowed Americans to eat better than ever before, but also to produce record surpluses for export, and to do both while employing fewer people and less land. The development of higher yielding, more disease-resistant crops and more effective fertilizers and pesticides increased farm output per acre. New and improved mechanical equipment made it less time-consuming to cultivate those acres. Meanwhile, the same phenomenon was occurring in beef, pork, and poultry production. As a consequence, millions of workers who would have been on the farm were enabled to pursue other careers as farming became increasingly capital intensive.

However, in the past 15 years the business sector has faced fundamental social changes that have depressed both the level of investment and the economic efficiency with which that investment is translated into increased productivity. Funds once exclusively targeted for productive investment now must satisfy a variety of new demands imposed by the changing nature of the other four sectors.

Influence of the People Sector

One illustration of these changes is the character of the labor force, which looks different, performs different functions, and approaches its work differently today than it did in the early postwar years. A crucial explanation for the recent productivity decline is the rapid infusion of unskilled and inexperienced people into the labor force from the mid-1960s to 1980. From 1968 to 1979 the civilian work force expanded by 2.5 percent annually, a rate almost twice as fast as that of the 1948– 68 period. As the baby-boom generation has come of age and women of all ages have entered the work force in record numbers, the amount of fixed investment per employee has declined, reversing the U.S. economy's trend toward capital intensity and resulting in a less efficient mix of production factors. Capital investment could not keep pace with the surge in the labor force, and capital stock per worker declined at an average annual rate of 1.9 percent from 1976 to 1979. Furthermore, these new workers naturally are less productive than "old hands," although their future impact on productivity growth will grow progressively more positive as they gain experience to complement their better education and training.

However, this same education along with greater access to the media has increased society's knowledge of the tolls its production processes and products exact on the environment and people's health. The 1953 invention of a light-weight plastic valve mechanism for aerosol cans, for example, sharply lowered production costs and made these cans practical for consumer use. A packaging revolution followed as companies marketed countless consumer products propelled by freon gas from low-cost containers. By the 1970s, nearly a million tons of freon were being released each year worldwide and concern began to focus on the earth's apparently shrinking ozone layer. After learning how to become more productive at their work, people have learned that investments must be made to preserve the world. They have come to see their work and the business sector as only a part—albeit a very important part—of their lives and, consequently, one that must respond to and reflect their changing priorities. New attitudes about leisure time, personal development, concern for the physical environment, and the need for reasonably risk-free working conditions have expanded the focus of investment. This expansion often has been mandated federally.

Influence of the Government Sector

During World War II all government policies were quite naturally and single-mindedly directed to one obvious goal: ending the war victoriously. Immediately after the war, the domestic objective of rebuilding the private economy gained precedence. More recently, as government has juggled a greater number of objectives, its impact on productivity has grown stronger and increasingly negative.

The number of governmental regulations to which business must adhere has grown exponentially over the last 15 years. The cost of complying with them has been compounded by their ever-changing scope and requirements. For example, as a result of federal policy, New Jersey's Deepwater Generating Station was forced to switch fuels four times in 12 years: from dirty coal to cleaner oil in 1969, from scarce oil to abundant coal in 1973, from dirty coal to cleaner oil in 1974, and, finally, back to the more abundant, although dirtier, coal in 1980.

Inevitably, as the number of social goods that the government seeks to attain has multiplied, so too have confusion, conflict, and uncertainty. For example, OSHA advocates exposing workers to the lowest level of hazardous substances technically feasible, while EPA uses more flexible standards, comparing risks with costs. EPA restricts the use of pesticides, while the Department of Agriculture (USDA) promotes their use. The National Highway Traffic Safety Administration (NHTSA) mandates weight-adding safety equipment for cars, yet the Department of Transportation (DOT) pushes for lighter vehicles that conserve gasoline. The government wants to reduce the nation's dependence on imported resources but severely restricts resource exploration and development on public lands.

In addition, projects delayed by regulation face unproductive carrying costs — for example, those associated with interest and inflation. As the costs compound, so do uncertainties associated with changing project completion dates. As Pat Choate documents in *As Time Goes By*, when inflation hovers at 15 to 18 percent, as it did in the early months of 1980, almost $6.6 billion in additional costs are incurred by a 30-day delay in the nation's total investment in structures and producers' durable goods.[1] Nuclear power plant construction offers the classic example of time's negative effect on productivity. It now can take more than 12 years to bring a nuclear power plant on line in the United States, twice as long as it did in the 1960s and twice as long as it does in Japan today. Fixed-fee construction contracts are impossible because of inflation and changing regulatory requirements.

Inflation also has depressed business investment by rendering depreciation allowances insufficient. Under existing laws, plant and equipment depreciation is figured on a "historic cost" basis, although replacement costs are, of course, much higher. Likewise, if original prices are used for tax purposes, the cost of raw materials used in production is underestimated when it is deducted from annual sales figures. Automatically, the share of profits transferred to the government has increased. Even though reported earnings have soared to all-time highs during the 1970s and have grown 430 percent from 1950 to 1979, according to Department of Commerce calculations, real profits, after adjusting for inflation, have grown only 72 percent, peaking in the mid-1960s. Not surprisingly, since then investment as a percentage of GNP has declined steadily.

The persistently high inflation that has plagued the United States for more than a decade has depressed investment by shrinking the pool of real capital resources that the business sector traditionally has been able to tap. As U.S. citizens have found it more and more difficult to maintain their standard of living, they have been saving less and less. Well over half of the U.S. population today has no memory of the Great Depression and, for them, retirement seems years and years away. Consequently, even those who have the money might not rank saving for tomorrow as a top priority.

Moreover, critics of government social welfare programs have argued that transfer payments—food stamps, unemployment compensation, social security benefits—are too easy to get and large enough to decrease Americans' incentive to prepare for and secure their own futures independent of government assistance.

Reduced investment means reduced productivity growth. The relationship between inflation and productivity is double-edged, however. Not only do escalating prices depress productivity, slowed productivity causes inflation to accelerate. As productivity decreases, labor cost and therefore the cost of goods and services rises, creating what is known as the wage-price spiral.

Influence of the Resource Sector

The U.S. economy's impressive performance during the 1950s and 1960s was based on cheap and accessible supplies of oil and gas. Transportation systems, plant sites, production processes, and end products were developed accordingly. The energy outlook was so bright that the estimated long-term return on energy-saving investments often did not justify their immediate expense. Government policies and pronouncements encouraged the perception that clean, cheap, and abundant fuel supplies would be available through the end of the century. Consequently, the demand for, and production of, coal fell as the United States used more oil and gas. However, domestic production of oil and gas peaked in the early 1970s and the United States became increasingly dependent on foreign oil, importing 3.4 million barrels a day in 1970 and 8.4 million in 1979.

In less than a decade, the resource sector evolved from a strong, stable force contributing to the productivity of U.S. business to an equally strong but negative force. Prices soared to unheard-of heights. The oil import bill rose from $2.7 billion in 1970 to $56.5 billion in 1979. The 1973–74 oil embargo and the 1979 Iranian cutoff dramatized our nation's dependence on the goodwill and political stability of foreign countries. Consumer purchases suddenly became the wrong ones. Likewise, energy-intensive industrial production processes and equipment automatically became outmoded and inefficient. Uncertainty about future prices and the availability of gas and oil has made resource-related investment choices more difficult—a difficulty compounded by concerns about the environmental consequences of increasing the nation's reliance on coal-generated and nuclear energy. The recessions of 1974–75 and 1980 relate directly to the price increases and disruption in world crude oil supply, but many other countries, also dependent on OPEC oil, have weathered these same events while continuing to make strong productivity advances.

Influence of the International Sector

The United States emerged from World War II with an enormous absolute productivity lead over all other nations in terms of real gross domestic product per employed person, and it still enjoys an absolute but narrow lead. During the 1970s, however, foreign competition ousted a number of major U.S. firms, such as U.S. Steel, from their positions as the number-one suppliers of their product. U.S. productivity growth lagged, while the most devastated economies—Japan, West Germany, Italy, and

France—achieved productivity growth rates two to three times larger than the United States.

A direct consequence of this superior foreign productivity performance has been a declining U.S. share of world trade. In 1960 U.S. products accounted for more than one-quarter of the manufacturing exports of industrial nations. By 1979 they constituted less than one-fifth of the total. Imported products comprised only 2 percent of domestic manufacturing sales in 1960, but almost 7 percent in 1979. Most of the ground was lost in the 1970s, despite the 40 percent depreciation in the value of the dollar, which made U.S. exports cheaper and foreign imports more expensive.

Part of our widening trade deficit can be attributed to higher investment rates in the postwar economies of Japan and Europe; but our government and business decision makers are also partly responsible. For example, the automobile industry ignored the growing demand for small fuel-efficient cars, and, as a result, imports, which were negligible in 1960, captured over 20 percent of the U.S. market in 1979. Government policies such as the Foreign Corrupt Practices Act, trade embargoes, antitrust laws, and Export-Import Bank restrictions, in addition to the desired effects they achieve, have worked in combination to reduce U.S. trade advantages. Not surprisingly, every major industrialized country in the free world not facing such constraints has increased its productive capacity by a greater percentage than the United States during the 1970s, even though they have been grappling with many of the same problems (oil prices, acute inflation, and so on). Only Britain, which has invested a smaller percentage of its income over the same time period, has experienced less growth.

Influence of Age

To some extent, this poor U.S. performance may result from the overall maturation of our economy, a process that began with the end of World War II. After all the easy productivity gains of speed, scale, and efficiency have been achieved through technological progress, productivity growth becomes increasingly more difficult and less dramatic. Each new increment of growth becomes smaller and more costly than previous increments, not unlike the pursuit of absolute zero in physics laboratories. Furthermore, some of these smaller advances in one segment of the economy or even in one facet of a business are achieved occasionally at the expense of productivity growth in another. The net effect is not always positive.

For example, one consequence of the U.S. maturation is the rapid expansion of service-providing businesses. This expansion was made possible by the strong early productivity advances in both agriculture and industry. As our economy has grown since the war and has become increasingly efficient at producing the goods people need and want—cars, houses, food, furniture—more and more people have been able to obtain them with a relative amount of ease. Consequently, the demand for services —haircuts and permanents, movies and restaurants, auto repair, and health care—has grown. The number of people employed in providing services is growing more rapidly than in commodity-producing industries. In 1948 about 51 percent of all U.S. workers were employed in service industries. By 1969 the percentage had grown to almost 61 and it is currently about 65 percent. Of course, this rapid expansion is an integral part of our rising standard of living. Nonetheless, the dominance of the service component, in turn, has dampened the overall rate of productivity growth. Only so many haircuts can be given in an hour, regardless of the type of barbershop, the barber's education, or the kind of equipment he uses. Historically, services have been labor intensive, and, consequently, their productivity advances have been harder to come by.

However, many exceptions to this rule have occurred. The productivity growth curve cannot flatten totally because technology itself is not static; advancing technology continually expands the horizons for productive improvements, even in the service component of the business sector. For example, investments in research have led to the development of computers with increased capabilities and reduced costs. As a consequence, computers have found their way into almost every aspect of American life: companies use them to turn out product designs, bill-payers use them to balance their checkbooks, students use them to take chemistry exams, and children play games with them. As service-providing businesses—banks, libraries, automotive repair shops, and so on—become increasingly cybernetic, they can be expected to become increasingly productive. The health care industry has become progressively more automated and, therefore, more capital intensive. Dozens of blood chemistry analysis tests now are performed automatically, with one lab technician monitoring a machine rather than several technicians conducting the same tests manually. Grocery stores recently have been investing in computerized check-out and inventory equipment that dramatically improve their efficiency. The microelectronic revolution still offers the business sector many unexploited opportunities—both in commodity-producing industries and service-providing ones. Of course, how soon and to what extent the business sector can capitalize on any new technology depends on the availability of investment capital, which, in turn, depends on the other social sectors.

Summary

The American people—consumers, politicians, business executives, and workers—are becoming aware of the relationships between the choices they have made and their weakened ability to raise the U.S. standard of living. Many of the negative factors contributing to our recent productivity performance can be altered by shifts in public policy. For the most part such shifts need not represent any fundamental repudiation of our social goals of equality and environmental protection. Instead, what is needed is a rethinking of our economic system, its goals and capabilities, and of the way in which business, labor, and government must cooperate to make advances in the quality of life compatible with acceptable degrees of productivity.

The Government Sector

Ensuring the general welfare of the American people has always been our government's primary goal. To this end, since the Great Depression government has involved itself to a greater degree and more directly in the lives of U.S. citizens than ever before. The growth of both regulation and transfer payments, which testifies to this new involvement, has redirected productive investment to health, safety, and equity expenditures. Because of this shift in priorities, U.S. productivity has suffered, an indirect consequence of government's conscious decision to redefine its role as defender of the public's general welfare. Sociologist Amitai Etzioni has labeled the decision between productive or nonproductive investment one that determines the government's "core project," which can emphasize either quality of life or economic development, but not both.[2]

Influence of the New Deal

The transition from the Hoover administration's reluctance to intervene in the lives of its citizens to the Roosevelt administration's forceful and dynamic New Deal marks the first major step in the evolution of modern U.S. government. The New Deal set in motion the idea that the central government should assure its citizens not only equal economic opportunities but also more equal sharing of our economic rewards. Once planted, this seed of government involvement grew during the next half century into a vast forest of federal regulatory and transfer activity with decisive social and economic consequences for the entire nation.

The New Deal justified its innovative income transfer programs and increased regulation by the severity of the economic emergency of the times. It is arguable whether New Deal programs dealt very successfully with the central economic problems of the Great Depression; but they undeniably conveyed an unprecedented concern—a commitment on the part of government to help individuals cope with a host of problems that, in the laissez faire past, were seen as private matters quite beyond the notice and constitutional authority of the federal government. Such programs brought about banking and securities reforms, new labor laws, the minimum wage, the social security program, federal housing and mortgage insurance, farm production and price stabilization, and numerous new agencies to administer and enforce the federal government's new role. If these New Deal interventions seem rather mild today, they nevertheless represented an important breaking of new ground, the formerly sacred turf of the marketplace.

In fact, the New Deal was only the beginning. The Full Employment Act of 1946 is evidence of the Truman administration's desire to continue the social initiatives Roosevelt began. To achieve this goal, Truman raised federal expenditures at a more rapid rate than any other president in peacetime, Roosevelt and Johnson included. Nevertheless, two chief endeavors characterized both his and Eisenhower's administrations: a vast reshaping of U.S. relations with the rest of the world and the creation and maintenance of a peacetime security establishment appropriate to the new U.S. role as leader of the Western world. To the extent that the Eisenhower administration focused on domestic needs, the emphasis was almost invariably on building things, and usually on projects with some application to national security. The Interstate Highway System—known formally as the National System of Interstate and Defense Highways—typifies the philosophy of the Eisenhower administration. The Federal Highway Act of 1956 authorized the construction of the 42,500-mile Interstate

System linking major urban centers. The effects of this highway expansion rippled across the entire business sector. The act indirectly stimulated the productivity of trucking firms, intercity business, motor vehicle producers, and oil companies because traveling distances and times and therefore costs were reduced. Trolley cars became a thing of the past and railroads began abandoning their unprofitable passenger services. Meanwhile, the number of cars in the United States doubled, from 40 million in 1950 to 80 million in 1970, and the number of trucks grew from over 8 million in 1951 to almost 18 million in 1970. As long as gasoline was plentiful and cheap—and from 1950 to 1970 the price per gallon rose less than 10 cents—from 27 to 36 cents—our increased use of and dependence on motor vehicle travel, whether for business or pleasure, made economic sense. All businesses and consumers who depended on the increasingly efficient trucking industry for deliveries of either production materials or finished products shared in the gains. Demand was boosted for all kinds of products and services, from tires to radio advertising. Construction boomed as suburbs, and shopping centers to serve them, dotted the wide expanses of previously unused land made accessible by this highway construction.

After the Eisenhower administration came John F. Kennedy's New Frontier, and the focus on national security shifted to a growing competition between the United States and the Soviet Union and international communism. For example, Eisenhower decided that it would be pointless to engage in a costly space race with the Soviet Union; alternatively, Kennedy was determined that the United States should be second to none in exploring "this new ocean" and committed the United States to land a man on the moon during the 1960s.

However, more important to postwar domestic life in the United States than achievements like the National Highway System or the success of the Apollo missions, or even the bitter experience of the Vietnam War, were the Great Society programs of Lyndon Johnson and the powerful political forces they mobilized. These new programs dominated the U.S. domestic political scene through the administrations of Richard Nixon and Gerald Ford, becoming essentially permanent federal activities.

Income Redistributions

Beginning with President Johnson's campaign against poverty in Appalachia, and followed by his much broader War on Poverty, U.S. citizens were exposed as never before to the plight of their most economically disadvantaged fellow Americans. Because of the scope of the problem, the federal government assumed the responsibility for solving it, a responsibility government met through the rapid creation and expansion of programs providing food stamps, subsidies for home purchase or rental, aid for dependent children, Medicare, Medicaid, and other direct government assistance. Accompanying these direct income redistribution programs was an equally vast expansion of indirect federal support for housing, education and training, regional and community development, health services, and other social goals.

However, once the responsibility for the social and economic welfare of U.S. citizens shifted from the private to the public sector, the authority to make social choices shifted as well. One of the inevitable consequences of transferring these social responsibilities to the government is the growth in the total government claim on national income. During the postwar period, government's share of national income has edged steadily upward. In 1950 the government spent roughly one-quarter of total national income. By 1960 it claimed more than one-third of national income. The initial cause of this increase was the demand of peacetime national security, heavier than in the prewar era, reflecting our new dominant position in the Western world. Defense spending (including foreign aid) accounted for about 10.8 percent of national income in 1960, and transfer payments accounted for less than 6.6 percent. By 1970 total government spending, driven by the domestic demands of the Great Society and the external demands of the Vietnam War, had climbed to almost 40 percent of total national income. It was a watershed year: for the first time, transfer payments to individuals exceeded total expenditures for national security. Total nondefense expenditures amounted to almost 30 percent of national income, raising the nondefense/defense expenditure ratio from the approximately two-to-one split that had prevailed during the earlier two decades to three-to-one.

Since 1970 the total government claim has continued to climb. In 1978 government spent almost 40 percent of national income. The defense share, which had been shrinking over the decade, amounted to only 5.7 percent. Spending for domestic purposes amounted to over 34 percent of national income. Transfer payments alone accounted for 12.5 percent of national income. Clearly, these changing spending priorities indicate that government's role as the guarantor of individual Americans' general welfare has become a U.S. institution.

Regulation

A new burst of federal regulation has accompanied this major reallocation of federal outlays over the last 20 years. The civil rights legislation of the mid-1960s opened a tremendous new vista for judicial and regulatory exploration. School desegregation orders and communitywide busing, affirmative action proceedings, and legal action related to discriminatory practices have become commonplace. This federal protection against discrimination, initially provided for racial minorities, since has been extended to women, the aged, and the physically and mentally handicapped. New laws have been enacted that seek to place all Americans on an equal footing.

Government intervention by no means has been confined to adjusting the rights and obligations of individual Americans with respect to one another. It has spread to areas as diverse as safeguarding the environment, consumer product safety, and safety in the workplace. These safety measures were all born of a handful of common impulses: quality of life takes precedence over economic cost; an individual's life should be made as risk-free as possible; a healthy environment is our first priority; and an individual or class of persons must be compensated fully for any injury, with the damages assessed against the party most able to bear them. One illuminating indicator of how much regulation has grown is simply the annual page count of the *Federal Register*, a daily government publication that presents all of the proposed and final rulings of the federal government. During the last decade, the register almost quadrupled in volume, reaching a total page count of almost 77,500 in 1979. Interestingly, this staggering output came in a peacetime year, and it was almost 4.5 times greater than the peak reached in World War II when the nation's entire economy — finance, commerce, industry, and agriculture — was mobilized for war purposes.

The direct economic burden of this regulation has been documented amply, but the indirect burden has not. Every public and private entity touched by regulation or receiving federal benefits establishes an internal bureaucracy that mirrors the federal bureaucracy to which it must answer. The volume and variety of reporting required by federal regulation has become awesome. The chairman of one large U.S. oil company has observed that each quarter his corporation dispatches several miles of computer tape to the Department of Energy alone.

In part because of the oil price shock and the ensuing severe inflation and recession of the mid-1970s, Congress began to recognize the high costs imposed by regulation. Not the least of these costs was the drag that regulation imposed on our ability to respond rapidly to such shocks. The result was a greater reluctance to intervene than the federal government had demonstrated previously. An initiative to dismember the largest U.S. oil companies foundered, as did repeated attempts to establish an Agency for Consumer Advocacy. Other special-interest legislation also failed, including an effort to make common site picketing for the construction trades legal, a general labor law reform to make it harder for management to resist unionization, and a cargo preference law to require shipments in U.S. flag vessels. Congress also directly overturned certain regulatory efforts, such as an ignition interlock system called for by the Department of Transportation and a Food and Drug Administration (FDA) rule banning saccharine as a sugar substitute.

These scattered setbacks testify to a rising public concern with the growth of government regulation. Evidence exists that the economic concept of diminishing returns characterizes Congress's recent consideration of regulatory legislation. For example, significant improvement in auto safety was achieved in the early 1970s at a relatively modest cost per automobile simply by requiring the addition of seatbelts, padded dashboards and sunvisors, collapsible steering wheels, and secure doorlocks. The National Highway Transportation Safety Agency has argued that another significant improvement can be achieved by mandating the use of automatically inflatable airbags to protect the driver and front-seat passenger. This safety improvement would cost several hundred dollars per vehicle. In deliberating this measure, Congress seems inclined to give manufacturers two options: installing airbags or seatbelts that fasten automatically. Despite NHTSA arguments that many car buyers likely would remove the automatic belts and otherwise subvert them, Congress is attempting to weigh costs and benefits.

Summary

The congressional inclination to reexamine existing rulings also seems likely to extend to nonregulatory areas. Ensuring a minimum wage for all workers and indexing transfer payments exemplify possible areas subject to future government reappraisal. Indeed, the possibility that the current regulations governing welfare eligibility may be keeping some workers out of the productive mainstream of the economy is fueling some citizens' desire to modify our entire welfare system.

No sizable contraction in the present scope of federal regulation reasonably can be anticipated. However, it is obvious that great latitude for regulatory reform remains. Of course, the speed and scope of any such reform is a source of considerable uncertainty. It is equally difficult to estimate the future direction of federal transfer payments to individuals and communities as a share of GNP. As a force, the government's decision to protect, through active involvement, the future general welfare of U.S. citizens will depend primarily on the priorities of the American people. Social programs and regulation have improved significantly the quality of life in the postwar United States. To forget this fact in an effort to streamline an inefficient system would be like throwing out the baby with the bath water. Unfortunately, social and economic goals often conflict and choices must be made, although economic growth and increased productivity by no means preclude qualitative social improvements but, in fact, have been largely responsible for them.

The Resource Sector

Now, more than ever, policy decisions concerning the environment and the proper use and protection of natural resources require difficult choices. As a force, resource availability—the consequence of how we have managed the physical world and its assets—in part has dictated our economic present and will continue to play a decisive role in the future.

Because U.S. citizens have felt the sting of inadequate resource availability in a variety of ways since World War II (for example, higher fuel prices and longer gasoline lines), they tend to think of resource availability as a recent concern. However, even prior to a series of eye-opening books in the 1930s and 1940s, including Fairfield Osborne's *Our Plundered Planet,* Paul Sears' *Deserts on the March,* and William Vogt's *Road to Survival,* [3] Americans began to face the growing problems associated with resource management and environmental protection and preservation. Early on, the federal government involved itself in ways to safeguard the environment, from Teddy Roosevelt's park and forest conservation drive to the creation of the Fish and Wildlife Service. It was not long before a host of private conservation groups formed to promote more parks, to spark an interest in forestry, and to spotlight issues like soil erosion. Banding together around 1950, these groups devised an entirely new tactic for dealing with environmental problems: the mode of litigation.

Specific events over this time span—some related to environmental protection and some to resource management—created broader public support for these special interest groups. For example, in 1948, 22 people died near Pittsburgh because of a combination of industrial pollution and bad weather conditions. Over the next 14 years, growing fears about the health effects of commonly used pesticides led to Rachel Carson's *Silent Spring,* a book that squarely equated dangers to wildlife and men with pesticides, such as DDT.[4] Federal legislation during the 1960s, including the

Wilderness Act of 1964, the Clean Air and Water Act of 1965, the Clear Water Restoration Act of 1966, the Air Quality Act of 1967, and the National Environmental Policy Act of 1969, marked a concerted government effort to resolve environmental concerns.

During this period events related to environmental safety and cleanliness were only one side of the coin; resource availability was the other. In 1948 the government responded to a temporary energy shortage by calling for voluntary reductions in gasoline, fuel oil, and natural gas use. Four years later the President's Materials Policy Commission, declaring that U.S. citizens could reduce consumption and waste of liquid fuels, recommended the creation of a federal energy agency, a call not heeded until 1974. Meanwhile, echoes of Malthus' warnings, by Osborne in 1953, by Paul Ehrlich, who founded Zero Population Growth in 1968, and by the Club of Rome in the early 1970s, periodically reasserted the relation between resource availability and population, although somewhat stridently for some people.

In 1970 two related events symbolized the U.S. population's response to the force of availability—both of a clean environment and of adequate natural resources. April 21 was named Earth Day and a mass demonstration was held to protest pollution of the planet's ecology. Its symbolic value was obviously to present environmentalism as a mainstream concern. In response President Nixon created the Environmental Protection Agency and charged it with setting and enforcing environmental standards.

A New Era

The passage of the National Environmental Policy Act (NEPA) in 1969 and the establishment of an agency to enforce it a year later are landmarks in U.S. resource history. The act established the Council on Environmental Quality (CEQ) within the executive branch, marking a major governmental commitment to the idea of organizing its resource-sector activity. In a sense, NEPA moved the government into direct planning with the business sector by requiring both private institutions and federal agencies to submit environmental impact statements of proposed actions. Each impact statement offered the public a chance to utilize its legal "veto." Objections by environmental groups to the Trans-Alaska pipeline impact statement led to a revised statement, equally unsatisfactory to its critics. Although the Department of the Interior still approved the project, this adversary relationship between government and citizens had major economic consequences. The right to "delay" projects imposed significant real costs on the business sector and, ultimately, on all citizens. After prolonged delays due to court challenges, the Trans-Alaska project was completed in 1977 at a cost in excess of $7 billion. If construction had proceeded according to original estimates, the cost would have been about $1 billion and the line would have produced up to one-half million barrels of oil per day at the time of the Arab oil embargo in 1973. This additional U.S. production might have altered significantly the political equation in the Middle East at the time and might even have prevented the embargo entirely.

Initial environmental impact statements emphasized quality of life over cost. Recently, however, the executive branch has pressured its regulatory agencies into preparing cost/benefit analyses; these analyses balance potentially incremental environmental gains against what may be exponentially rising costs. A world with unlimited resources—physical and economic—might not have to consider either the management of its materials or the economics of their use. In the past decade, however, as U.S. productivity and economic growth have slowed, the costs of environmental protection and clean-up activities have demanded a rethinking. The mood of the 1980s seems to be one of refining the environmental resource decision-making process; critics have called for new methods of quantifying both costs and benefits and thereby making cost/benefit analysis less subjective.

New scientific and economic information and the recent emphasis on cost/benefit analysis have led to a reexamination of those regulations conceived during the 1960s and 1970s. Many of these regulations—for example, those dealing with mercury levels in swordfish, the effects of asbestos, food coloring, or saccharine, and so on—reflect people's awareness of man-made dangers to their own health and to the ecosystem. Only time will tell which dangers were real, but one new dilemma has resulted from the government's involvement in environmental planning and regulation: the mass of agencies and regulations has led to a great bureaucracy now requiring its own management cost/benefit analyses. Within the past decade, some individuals, such as economist Murray Weidenbaum, have argued that our regulations have produced less progress and simply more regulations.

U.S. Energy History

Many observers argue that earlier attention to the costs and benefits of our resource decisions might have produced a future different than the present, a future that better reconciled the energy demands for increasing productivity with environmental protection and preservation.

For example, events such as the pollution-associated deaths of the late 1940s and early 1950s in the United States and England had the effect of shifting the national fuel mix away from coal and of reinforcing the price and convenience advantages of oil and gas. In 1948 coal supplied a 45 percent share of U.S. primary energy consumption. That figure dropped to 17.8 percent in 1973, where it remained fairly steadily until 1978. During this period, however, the technological problems associated with coal burning were not addressed with rapid short-term solutions in mind. Instead, the nation substituted oil and gas for coal; decision makers counted on continued low cost and ready availability for the midterm and placed their confidence in nuclear power and other unconventional sources over the longer term. These alternatives to coal were viewed as less potent environmental hazards and also as more convenient and fully capable of meeting growing consumption needs.

However, an array of social, political, and economic forces distorted the resource substitution process. Federal wellhead price controls on natural gas, aimed at keeping residential heating costs low, actually encouraged consumption and discouraged exploration for new gas supplies. Huge supplies of low-cost foreign oil had a similar effect on the nation's demand for and domestic supply of liquid fuels. Unfortunately, U.S. citizens were confident that foreign supplies would remain available and were convinced that existing oil import quotas were merely devices to guarantee excess profits for U.S. oil companies. The results were analyses, such as the one produced in 1970 by the Cabinet Task Force on Oil Import Control, that underestimated the national security implications of importing more oil.[5]

During the 1960s and early 1970s, total energy consumption rose at the very rapid average rate of 4.2 percent per year, propelled by low prices, plentiful supplies, rapid economic growth, and specific technical factors (for example, the spread of air conditioning, rapid increases in the motor vehicle fleet, and decreasing average mileage ratings). This overall growth rate caught the nation by surprise, since the preceding decade had registered growth in consumption of only 2.7 percent annually.

Demand for oil grew even faster, averaging 4.4 percent per year during the 1960s and early 1970s. This burst in demand occurred just as economic, political, and geological restraints combined to limit new discoveries. Thus, the nation's excess production capacity quietly disappeared sometime between the Arab-Israeli wars of 1967 and 1973 and with it our ability to prevent sudden shocks to our economic system.

By 1973 import dependency on insecure foreign sources permitted the OPEC cartel to create just such a shock. In 1973 and again in 1979, political turmoil in the Middle East created severe fuel shortages resulting in skyrocketing prices and long gasoline lines. The focus on the availability of clean water, clean air, and unblemished land shifted somewhat belatedly to the consequences of being vulnerable to international politics. Moreover, nuclear power, initially received as the great energy hope for the future, fell prey to regulation as people began to question its safety. The Three Mile Island incident made the problem worse and left nuclear energy's future even more uncertain.

Ten years ago, energy use projections for the year 2000 were 50 to 100 percent higher than experts now envision. The U.S. Department of the Interior Dupree-West study and the National Petroleum Council's *U.S. Energy Outlook* testify to these false consumption expectations.[6] Not surprisingly, they assumed similarly high estimates of domestic oil and gas availability for the same year. As the 1970s progressed, it became obvious that not only would the economy not support as much economic and energy growth as anticipated, but also that the short-term substitution of one fuel for another had been mismanaged badly.

In the public's eyes, government had bungled both energy and environmental issues and, as a consequence, U.S. citizens were paying the price—literally. The rising cost of energy and the mounting cost of regulation and clean-up translated into prices, both for fuel and for the consumer goods an energy-intensive economy produces, that were much higher than ever before. In the past, technological fixes always served to hedge against the Malthusian threat of too many people and inadequate resources; but the United States foreclosed some of its options during the 1970s, postponing another cycle of possible resource substitutions.

Moreover, from the public's perspective, business became less a benefactor of prosperity and more a conspirator in the exploitation of material resources and the degradation of the environment. At the same time, industry blamed government for the end of guaranteed cheap and abundant energy. It further viewed government's growing regulatory interference as counterproductive to continuing expansion, and it perceived the public and government as seeking an impossibly risk-free society with costs out of proportion to the benefits. The net result: a series of contradictory signals blocking a consensus about the direction in which policy choices should move.

Summary

Although currently it is difficult to assess the relative status of energy and environmental concerns in the public's mind, there are growing indications that a balance is emerging. Polls show that a majority of citizens now recognize the existence of an energy problem, if not a crisis. The federal government finally has allowed oil prices to reach world levels and is permitting natural gas prices to head in the same direction. Responsible energy studies are acknowledging that there are no world or U.S. energy shortages—only social and political constraints that restrict the use of available supplies. New techniques are being developed for burning coal with less damage to the environment and other technologies for changing coal into liquid and gaseous fuels are being applied in prototype plants. Foreign countries are proceeding to develop advanced nuclear technologies, even though the United States has given up its once-dominant technological position.

Today attention is being devoted to the concept of "productive conservation," which substitutes capital, labor, and materials for energy wherever possible and whenever doing so proves economically prudent. To many people conservation still elicits pejorative associations of doing without or of rationing; but conservation need not equate with deprivation. Prior to the Arab oil embargo, the United States used low-priced energy more lavishly than many other nations. Now, responding to higher-priced energy, people are using energy more sparingly; thus, conservation is granting the nation more time to develop economically feasible alternatives without demanding radical changes in its citizens' styles of living.

Nevertheless, the potential for larger energy contributions from solar power, coal-based synthetics, oil shale, unconventional sources of natural gas, and low-head hydropower installations, to name but a few of the options, has renewed many individuals' belief in technology as a hedge against resource depletion or unpredictable political events. People no longer await the single technological fix that will remedy our energy problems overnight. Simultaneously, some of the fervor that characterized the burst of interest in environmental protection during the 1960s and 1970s has mellowed; now even the most extreme debators accept the fact that trade-offs may be necessary to balance economic, energy, and environmental needs. The answers to our energy and environmental policy questions may not lie in our energy history; but certain trends reinforce our hopes for a manageable resource situation and a clean environment while, at the same time, cautioning against unrealistic expectations.

The International Sector

A philosophical shift from isolationism to interdependence has shaped the postwar nature of the international relations sector. The United States emerged from World War II with decided military and economic advantages over the other participants. Not only was the United States the only nuclear-armed state, but its cities and industries had escaped destruction. Most importantly, it had managed an unparalleled burst of economic growth during the war years. This combination of military and economic power brought with it enormous international political influence. Almost immediately the postwar era came to be characterized by closer links between nations, deeper integration of policy, and unprecedented interdependence. The United States, thrust into a position of Western leadership, found itself the first among equals.

The force of interdependence, which often took the form of negotiations and agreements between free and politically independent nations, was responsible for two significant wartime events: the founding of the United Nations and the signing of the Bretton Woods agreements in 1944. The Bretton Woods conference, which established the World Bank, the International Monetary Fund (IMF), and the General Agreement on Tariffs and Trade (GATT) was, in part, a reaction against U.S. economic self-sufficiency during the war years. These agreements were international efforts to prevent events like the 1932 failure of Creditanstalt, an obscure Austrian bank that plunged the world into a financial panic. In the spirit to which these bonds testify, the United States devised and strongly supported the Marshall Plan to help Europe reestablish itself, industrially and economically. In the same vein, the United States also negotiated a 1951 peace treaty with Japan designed to shelter Japan's industries against foreign competition and, thereby, to enable it to regain economic health.

With the cold war between the West and the Soviet Union as a motivation, the United States pushed to create the North Atlantic Treaty Organization (NATO), an alliance that for more than 30 years has succeeded in stabilizing European frontiers. In Europe itself, the tide of interdependence resulted initially in the formation of the European Coal and Steel Community and, later, the European Economic Community, which eliminated border tariffs and duties on the commerce of member states. In addition to establishing these organizations, Europe also instituted a variety of less formal multilateral plans for developing and producing a wide range of sophisticated commercial and military products, such as the A300 European Airbus and the Tornado Interceptor.

One desirable consequence of Western interdependence has been a dramatic growth in postwar international commerce. The United States itself experienced a fivefold current-dollar increase in foreign commerce between 1960 and 1975, and other trading nations, like West Germany and Japan, have experienced roughly a tenfold increase over the same period. In addition to providing other benefits, this burst of international commerce has enabled newly industrialized states, like South Korea, Taiwan, Singapore, Hong Kong, Malaysia, Brazil, and Mexico, to achieve export-led economic growth rates rivaling the 12 percent averaged by resource-poor Japan between 1957 and 1962, the peak years of its postwar growth.

Politics and Money

The distribution of global power and influence between the United States and the Soviet Union has remained remarkably stable throughout the postwar period, despite wars between the United States and two Soviet proxies, North Korea and North Vietnam, and despite probes by each side (the abortive invasion of Cuba in 1961, and the equally abortive attempt by the Soviet Union to establish nuclear missile forces in Cuba the following year). It is almost ironic, in fact, that the seemingly delicate East-West power balance has proven to be one of the most stable and enduring bequests of World War II. The global instabilities that have emerged since the late 1960s stem from quite different sources than the East-West rivalry itself.

One of these instabilities clearly resulted from the success of the measures created after the war to stimulate the recovery of devastated Western economies. The U.S. current accounts, one measure of the nation's trade balance, suffered during the 1960s in part because dollar-denominated goods were judged to be increasingly overvalued relative to goods denominated in yen, Deutschmarks, and other European currencies. But the deterioration was caused primarily by the flood of low-priced, generally high-quality goods that supplanted U.S. goods in markets abroad and at home.

With the 1967 devaluation of the British pound, the dollar's first line of defense, the dollar came under increasing pressure. As the dollar price of gold was bid upward beyond the established level of $35 an ounce in the private gold market, the United States engineered a gentleman's agreement with its major financial partners restricting gold transactions to governments. These stopgap measures failed to stabilize the situation, and on August 15, 1971, the United States suspended the gold exchange standard and dollar convertibility into gold. That drastic action was the death knell for the fixed exchange standards negotiated in 1944 in the Bretton Woods agreements. Although efforts, notably the Smithsonian agreements of late 1971, were mounted to restore fixed exchange parities, they were unsuccessful. By early 1973 the attempt was abandoned and the world entered a new era of floating currencies without gold convertibility. Although this transition period was marked by severe currency fluctuations, other international devices, such as the Eurodollar market and the government currency swaps, were able to absorb and dampen the impact of speculative surges. More importantly, it seems that the trading community's overriding fear that floating parities would threaten the continued growth of world trade was almost entirely groundless.

The dollar, a more battered and humble exchange unit than it was a decade ago, remains the principal unit of international exchange and likely will remain so for some time. To be sure, several major currencies are stronger than the dollar, but the nations that issue them are not willing to assume the reverse-currency role that the pound sterling and the dollar have filled. The sheer size of the Eurodollar market (hundreds of billions of U.S. dollars held abroad looking to be invested) also supports the dollar's international role. Furthermore, the dollar and dollar-denominated instruments dominate in official reserves as well as in dollar-denominated foreign public and private debt.

Influence of the Oil Shock

Doubtless the severest test of postwar Western interdependence and its stabilizing influence in international commercial and financial dealings came from a source nobody could have imagined at the time of Bretton Woods: the oil price shock of 1973–74. At that time the world price of oil approximately quadrupled. In October 1973 a barrel of Arabian light cost $3.01. Two years later the price was $12.38.

When World War II ended, the world oil price (at U.S. Gulf ports) was $1.28 and Aramco was marketing Saudi crude for about 90 cents a barrel. Its aggregate cost—development, production, and royalty payment—was estimated at 33 cents a barrel. Then, as in the prewar years, the problem for the major international oil companies was one of oversupply. The famous Red Line Agreement and many other restrictive exploration, leasing, production, and marketing arrangements testified to the efforts of the major oil companies to prevent low-cost Saudi, Kuwaiti, Iraqi, and Iranian crude from disrupting established patterns of production and marketing.

These cartel-like arrangements attracted congressional investigations and anti-trust proceedings in the United States but they were never threatened seriously. Despite the large profits the international oil companies reaped from their Persian Gulf operations, it was an era of singularly low-cost energy, and one in which the real cost of pumpable fuels edged downward continuously. The availability of this low-cost oil and gas was a major factor in the remarkable burst of economic growth that Western economies enjoyed during the 1950–70 period.

In retrospect, it is apparent that the multinational oil companies developed agree-ments that had much the same stabilizing effect as the government-to-government agreements that formally established GATT, the World Bank, the IMF, and so on after World War II. Many people argue that the agreements between companies were created simply to increase profits rather than to reduce the price of oil to the lowest possible level that competition would sustain. It seems clear, however, that the interdependence among the major oil companies was a primary factor in insulating the world oil market from massive supply shocks during most of the postwar period.

Two of the most serious of the early energy crises occurred in 1957 and 1967, both involving a cutoff in shipments of Middle Eastern oil. The first took place when Egypt closed the Suez Canal to traffic, blocking about two-thirds of Europe's oil supply (about 2.2 million barrels per day). By means of sharply increased production in other areas, heavy stock withdrawals, and other unusual operations, particularly in the United States, the international oil companies were able to deliver to Europe more than 90 percent of the oil lost as a result of the Suez closure. In 1967, at the time of the third Arab-Israeli War, the Organization of Arab Petroleum Exporting Countries (OAPEC) imposed a boycott on shipments to the United States, Britain, the Nether-lands, and West Germany. Again the international oil companies were able to insulate these markets, primarily by a dramatic increase of more than 1 million barrels a day in U.S. domestic output and by diverting oil intended for the United States to the others.

Unfortunately, the policies and practices of the international oil companies contained the seed of their own destruction. They achieved the steadily expanding markets they sought, particularly as Western and other economies grew at an unprecedented rate in the 1950–70 period, but in the process, the excess capacity that seemed so threatening to orderly marketing in earlier times dried up completely. When the 17-day fourth Arab-Israeli War broke out in October 1973, there was no margin left. The United States, the primary target of the Arab oil boycott, no longer could offset this loss by importing increased supplies from Venezuelan and other non-Arab sources. The shortfall hit U.S. motorists the hardest as they intermittently experienced gasoline lines characterizing a strange new period of oil scarcity.

One of the burning questions of that period was whether the international financial system could cope with the vast balance-of-trade deficits that Western countries would accumulate if they continued their heavy reliance on imported oil. Certainly, they have coped for eight years, but it is still a major issue. Another was whether the growth of international commerce might slow or even be reversed by oil that was enormously more costly. Nightmare scenarios abounded, for example, Paul Erdman's *The Crash of '79.* [7] Interestingly, Erdman, a former banker, found it necessary to stage a war among the Persian Gulf states and to posit the destruction of most of the world's oil production facilities in order to undermine the Western industrial world.

In fact, the West has been able to cope surprisingly well with the oil price shock. The petrodollars have been recycled with surprising ease into government instruments and short-term private bank obligations. Production from new oil fields in Alaska, the North Sea and Mexico, has reduced somewhat Western reliance on imports from insecure sources. The growth of oil demand has been arrested by the sharply higher price level (relative to alternative energy sources), and several nations are pursuing the nuclear and coal options with great determination. For its part, the United States is expected to use less imported oil in the next few years by pursuing all of these options as well as by permitting price-driven conservation measures to take effect.

Over the short term, the most dangerous threat the oil situation holds for the West is the possibility that the impulse to protect domestic manufacturers against foreign competition will get out of hand. Some countries, Japan and West Germany, for example, have been able to offset most or all of their foreign oil import burden by increasing manufacturing exports to the rest of the world. Understandably, political pressure from business and labor in some of these importing nations for drastic countermeasures is strong and increasing.

Summary

Over the longer term, the problem of the third world's increasingly urgent demand for a new international economic order must be considered. Many commentators believe that this new order eventually will emerge. Norman Macrae, deputy editor of the *Economist,* and others argue that manufacturing industries involving mid-level technology (steel, automobiles, ships, and so on) will move from the developed to the developing world because of the more attractive economics of third world production. These observers also contend that the place of industry devoted to mid-level technology in the developed world will be taken over by high-technology industries and "knowledge" activities. Obviously, such a major shift—already apparent in the pattern of industrial development now under way in Brazil, South Korea, Taiwan, and other developing countries—implies an increasingly interdependent world along the lines that the West already has experienced. Such a shift implies a significant reduction in Western demand for Arab and other foreign oil so that the developing world can pursue more energy-intensive industrial activities.

Interdependence obviously has brought great benefits to the Western postwar world, benefits that can be extended far more widely in the future. Interdependence exacts a price, however. In such a world, everything moves much more deliberately. As the British and French found in their abortive invasion of Suez in 1956, individual actions seem to be less effective than they used to be. The United States experienced much the same thing when it intervened in Vietnam a decade later with only a handful of fighting allies. Despite these drawbacks, interdependence has become a major international economic and political force in the postwar era, one that will continue to play a large role in shaping the modern world.

Conclusion

The kinds of questions U.S. citizens are asking at the dawn of the 1980s suggest they have begun to recognize the larger implications of making choices in a democratic society. U.S. citizens no longer see economic and social progress as mutually exclusive. The point of debate now is not whether Americans should strive to make the economy more productive, but how. How active a role should government play? What contributions can labor make and what compromises will it find acceptable? Likewise, what kind of short-term sacrifices are the American people willing to make as consumers? How can we see the best returns from our investments? Can we afford to exclude any presently available resource option or to preclude any future option? Should sunset industries be refurbished or should all of our attention be concentrated on high-technology industries? Does the service sector's growing use of computers foreshadow the direction of our economy's evolution? Is reindustrialization the path to our future or will future economic growth be spurred largely by the emergence of both new technologies and new applications of existing ones, a phenomenon better described as "neoindustrialization"? No future, of course, will enjoy the starting conditions of the United States in 1945: large pent-up demand, substantial accumulated savings, a rapidly expanding and mobile industrial labor force, cheap and abundant resources, unchallengeable military power, and overwhelming international preeminence. That was a United States supercharged for growth; today's United States is quite different, and it is obvious from our historical perspective that our future growth will come slower and harder than in the immediate postwar period.

This perspective on the forces that have dominated society's evolution comprises, in one sense, a qualitative modeling system, a system that presents the elements of economic growth in their relevant social context. The translation of these qualitative forces and their relationships into quantitative inputs for computer modeling allows our history to be linked to a broad range of possible futures. If mixes of policy choices and chance occurrences that reflect both historical continuity and rationality are assumed, resulting alternative futures or scenarios can be simulated. After analyzing the consequences of various choices, a preferred set of policy choices that lead to a preferred future can be identified. This volume presents just such a preferred policy portfolio in Chapter 5. As William Jennings Bryan wrote in 1899, "destiny is not a matter of chance; it is a matter of choice. It is not a thing to be waited for; it is a thing to be achieved."[8]

Notes

1. Pat Choate, *As Time Goes By: The Costs and Consequences of Delay* (Columbus, Ohio: Academy for Contemporary Problems, 1980), pp. V, 9–11.

2. Amitai Etzioni, "Choose We Must," *The Individual and the Future of Organizations*, Vol. 9 of the Franklin Foundation Lecture Series, ed. Carl A. Bramlette, Jr. and Michael H. Mescon (Atlanta: Business Publishing Division, College of Business Administration, Georgia State University, 1980), pp. 25–39.

3. Fairfield Osborne, *Our Plundered Planet* (Boston: Little, Brown, 1948); Paul Bigelow Sears, *Deserts on the March* (Norman: University of Oklahoma Press, 1935); William Vogt, *Road to Survival* (New York: W. Sloane Associates, 1948).

4. Rachel Carson, *Silent Spring* (Boston: Houghton Mifflin, 1962).

5. U.S. Cabinet Task Force on Oil Import Control, *The Oil Import Question,* a report to the President on the relationship of oil imports to national security (Washington, D.C.: U.S. Government Printing Office, 1970).

6. Walter G. Dupree, Jr. and James A. West, *United States Energy Through the Year 2000* (Washington, D.C.: U.S. Department of the Interior, 1972); National Petroleum Council, *U.S. Energy Outlook*, a report prepared for the U.S. Department of the Interior (Washington, D.C.: National Petroleum Council, 1972).

7. Paul E. Erdman, *The Crash of '79* (New York: Simon and Schuster, 1976).

8. Quoted in Paul W. Glad, *The Trumpet Soundeth: William Jennings Bryan and His Democracy, 1896–1912* (Lincoln: University of Nebraska Press, 1960), p. 77.

Chapter 2

DESIGNING ECONOMIC AND ENERGY FUTURES

Modeling Scenarios

To estimate the effect that today's policy decisions will have on tomorrow's economic and energy growth, it is necessary to quantify a description of the economy. Because no one knows precisely how the economy works, any description of it— verbal or mathematical—is reductive. Consequently, the tendency of econometric modeling to simplify the system must be weighed against its advantages. Models account for basic variables and approximate their relationships in mathematical terms. Their use allows the consequences of national decisions to be estimated more precisely by testing specific hypotheses in carefully managed and controlled simulations. Obviously, the resulting figures assume meaning only when they are interpreted within a larger, social context, such as the one discussed in Chapter 1; thus, it was necessary to exercise judgmental analysis both in designing the modeling systems and in interpreting their results. This chapter describes the analytical approach used for this task, including the models employed, the resulting set of alternative scenarios, and the roles that choice and chance play in creating different futures.

The Flow of the Economy

Figure 2.1 depicts a theoretical conception of the U.S. economic system. It presents forces and variables pertinent to each social sector, and the relationships between them. The three principal components of this economic system are labor, capital, and resources. Business combines them to produce the goods and services people need and want. Output, a function of the quantity, quality, and efficiency with which these components are combined, is consumed primarily in two ways: some to sustain or enhance our lives and some to renew or expand our productive capacity. In this way the flow of the economy is self-perpetuating.

The most commonly used quantitative description of output is GNP, the money value of goods and services consumed, private and government expenditures, investment, and net exports. Unfortunately, GNP emphasizes our material standard of living at the expense of the quality of our lives. Over the entire postwar era, for example, the average length of the workweek gradually has been shrinking. We spend relatively less time engaged in work and relatively more time in leisure activities. As measured by GNP, increased leisure could translate into less economic growth, but

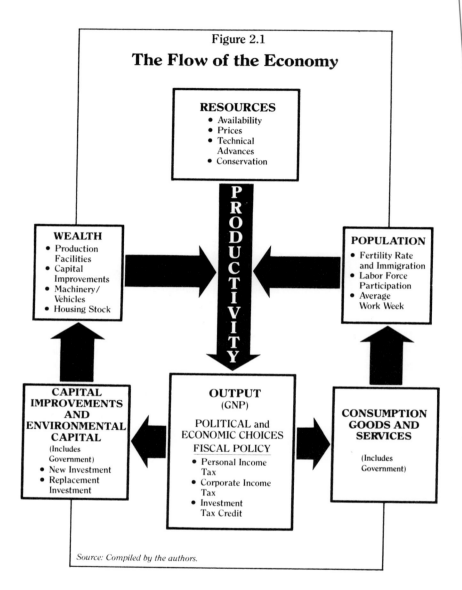

Figure 2.1

The Flow of the Economy

RESOURCES
- Availability
- Prices
- Technical
  Advances
- Conservation

P R O D U C T I V I T Y

WEALTH
- Production
  Facilities
- Capital
  Improvements
- Machinery/
  Vehicles
- Housing Stock

POPULATION
- Fertility Rate
  and Immigration
- Labor Force
  Participation
- Average
  Work Week

CAPITAL IMPROVEMENTS AND ENVIRONMENTAL CAPITAL
(Includes Government)
- New Investment
- Replacement Investment

OUTPUT
(GNP)

POLITICAL and ECONOMIC CHOICES
FISCAL POLICY
- Personal Income
  Tax
- Corporate Income
  Tax
- Investment
  Tax Credit

CONSUMPTION GOODS AND SERVICES
(Includes Government)

Source: Compiled by the authors.

only Scrooge would argue that there are no compensations. Alternatively, GNP overstates our standard of living because the costs of certain modern industrial disadvantages (for example, noise pollution) are partially or totally hidden.[1] Nevertheless, GNP and its various components are the most practical indexes to macroeconomic concepts such as productivity, technological change, the trade-off between consumption and investment, and other major determinants of our standard of living.

Figure 2.1 graphically suggests the sectoral relationships discussed in Chapter 1. The resource sector provides the raw materials of production, including the energy sources that power the production process. The people sector influences the flow at several points—as consumers, as workers, as savers, and as voters. Government-sector policy decisions—primarily fiscal and regulatory but also monetary, social, and international—largely determine first what part of the output flows to consumption and what part to investment, and second the proportions of investment allocated to productive and nonproductive improvements. Central to the economic flow chart, the business sector is where capital, labor, and resources converge. Finally, the international sector affects our economic system in many ways, but perhaps most critically through the resource sector and through foreign economic competition.

Economic and Energy Models

Models essentially are collections of mathematical relationships composed of variables for which the states or values are either calculated by the model (output or endogenous variables) or supplied by judgmental analysis or other models (input or exogenous variables). To measure the impact of hypothetical changes in each social sector, state-of-the-art models were employed that reduce our economic system to quantifiable variables. These models incorporate the overriding reality of uncertainty through the interplay of input variables, some largely determined by conscious choices within the society and others largely the result of chance occurrences — developments over which the nation has little or no control. Time also influences a variable's impact on the economy. For example, the baby bust of the 1960s and 1970s is just now translating into slower labor force growth. Because of such changes in a variable's significance, this book's focus shifts to different variables as different segments of the future are considered, thus necessitating different models to examine the short-, mid-, and long-term futures.

Midterm: 1985–2000

Central to this undertaking, the Hudson-Jorgenson (H-J) equilibrium model focuses on the midterm, combining an interindustry model with a macroeconomic model to project energy and economic growth patterns and energy-economy interactions. The interindustry model relates the gross output of ten industrial sectors, six of which are energy producing, to the final demands for that output in all other sectors. This component of the H-J model offers a significant innovation: the interactions between these ten sectors are functions of the prices of all products, of labor, of capital, and of imports, and these prices are determined endogenously (internally) rather than fixed exogenously (externally). This flexibility simulates the price-induced substitution of inputs that undoubtedly will occur in the economy throughout the midterm. The model's method of projecting growth in energy demand illustrates its flexibility: energy demand is not merely a function of GNP growth, but also demonstrates sensitivity to productivity growth. Gains in energy use efficiency dampen the growth in energy demand. The macroeconomic component of the H-J model differs from that of many other models by balancing supply and demand for labor and capital rather than by focusing exclusively on demand. Hence, capital and labor constraints can be simulated more fully, and supply and demand are allowed to achieve more realistic price-induced market balances.[2]

Linked to the midterm model, a version of the Baughman-Joskow (B-J) model supplements the analysis of the electric utility sector with a wealth of technological, behavioral, and financial-regulatory detail. Within the B-J model, a regional supply model determines both utilization rates for nine different types of plants (coal-fired thermal, light water uranium reactors, and so forth) and the capital outlays necessary for capacity expansion of each. Recognizing that lead times differ for different kinds of plants, the model calculates the most economical plant mix necessary to meet demand in future periods. Using equations estimated from state cross-sectional data of 1968–72, a demand model estimates national demand for electricity, splitting the total into residential/commercial demand and industrial demand. The regional supply component also feeds information to the B-J model's financial-regulatory component. This component determines the price of electricity used as an input to the demand model by simulating the actions of state regulatory commissions and accounting for such factors as distribution and operation costs.[3]

By linking the B-J model to the H-J model, the midterm analysis can simulate more explicitly the electric utility industry's decision-making process as well as the feedback effects on overall economic growth. These combined features make the augmented H-J model particularly appropriate for analyzing the fairly broad, mid-range policies most critical to our midterm future. Supplies, demands, and prices continually shift, maintaining the economy's equilibrium path or balance. These very same features, however, make the model less applicable to short-run disaggregated problems. The H-J is a true growth model and, therefore, does not accommodate disequilibrium situations easily, such as responses to near-term energy or fiscal policy changes.

Short Term: 1980–90

The Wharton Annual Model, a demand-oriented model, is well-suited for short-range analysis. It explores the conditions necessary to direct the economy onto those midterm economic-energy growth paths projected by the H-J model. The short-term or transition period links the present to the 1985–90 time frame. The model uses fiscal measures to allocate GNP among several uses: personal consumption, government spending, and investment. The Wharton model simulates economic disequilibria and determines the impact of government policies on the economy with a fine-grained input-output matrix involving 63 sectors.[4]

To supplement the Wharton model projections of the near-term future, the authors reviewed published results from the Evans Economics supply-oriented model developed for the Senate Finance Committee as well as simulations performed exclusively for this study. Supply-side models, such as the Evans model, are designed to account explicitly for the effects of fiscal and monetary policy on productivity and on incentives to produce. Consequently, this model incorporates somewhat different equations aimed at representing those factors that determine the economy's ability to produce as well as to consume goods and services.[5]

Long Term: 2000–30

Looking at futures past the year 2000 is, obviously, a speculative venture. Techno-logical innovations, demographic trends, resource depletion, shifting international relationships, and other changes in combination will alter dramatically the world we know today. Consequently, the authors selected ETA-Macro, a long-term model that relates the economy and the energy sector, to assess these patterns.

ETA-Macro simulates future markets through an optimization procedure. A simplified macroeconomic growth submodel (Macro) provides for optimal substitu-tion of capital, labor, and energy inputs. Interindustry detail and endogenously determined technological changes are sacrificed in this highly aggregated description of the economy in order to focus on the long-term issues of energy-economy interac-tions. The ETA (Energy Technology Assessment) submodel is linked to the Macro model so that each registers feedback effects. This detailed simulation of the energy sector permits a fuller analysis of the U.S. transition from oil and gas to coal and nuclear power than is possible with the H-J model. The ETA submodel explicitly accounts for the impact that cost-effective conservation, interfuel substitution, and new supply technologies may have on future capital accumulation and economic growth. Both the growth of energy conversion technologies (such as solar electricity plants and coal-based synthetic fuels) and the depletion of natural resources (such as oil, natural gas, and sites suitable for hydroelectric plants) are modeled in order to supply the electric and nonelectric energy inputs for the Macro submodel.[6]

The Modeling Variables

The principal variables that guide these models in their simulations of future economic and energy growth divide into five categories: demographic, labor force, productivity, fiscal policy, and energy. The first two groups of variables relate most directly to the people sector, the third to the business sector, the fourth to the government sector, and the last to the resource and international sectors.

The pertinent demographic variables—fertility and immigration rates—determine the population's growth rate. The size and age structure of the population influences the investment/consumption split and in large part determines the level of demand. On the supply side, fertility and immigration rates determine the number of potential workers, and labor force variables then determine the number of actual workers and hours worked. The participation rates of males and females and the average length of the workweek for both measure the labor force quantitatively; the unemployment rate provides the link between labor force and actual workers.

Four variables largely determine the overall productivity or output potential of the economy. Gross labor productivity or output per employee-hour is influenced by a host of factors—some affecting technological potential and some affecting demography—such as the median age of members of the work force, their level of educational attainment, the nature of their work, and so on. However, because labor productivity, in turn, is influenced by all the other variables, the actual rate of its growth projected by a modeling system will differ from the assumed rate used as an input to the system. The three other variables in the productivity assumption are the percentage of GNP devoted to capital investment, the percentage accounted for by government expenditures for goods and services, and the average annual real rate of investment in environmental protection.

Without productive investment to replace, expand, and improve plants and equipment, the potential for progress is greatly reduced. Fiscal policy variables function as the predominant determinants of the investment/consumption ratio and also influence the incentive to work and save. Personal and corporate income tax rates, depreciation lives, and investment tax credit rates control the amount of capital available for investment and, in effect, establish the rate of return needed to encourage it.

The most important of the energy variables the authors selected is the real rate of increase in world oil prices. That variable, in turn, strongly influences the other energy variables—the real rate of increase in the price of coal and natural gas as well as the quantities of solar, synthetics, and nuclear power available in the year 2000. The cost and availability of alternate energy sources will depend largely upon the cost and availability of oil.

It is impossible to predict how the specific value of any one of these variables will change. For example, the surprise with which demographers greeted the postwar baby boom was equaled only by the surprise with which they observed the ensuing baby bust. Likewise, the economy adjusted vigorously and rapidly from the World War II years, amazing economists and politicians alike. However, its disappointing performance during the 1970s has alarmed not only these experts but lay people as well. Significant changes in our economic system in the last 15 to 20 years have expanded the spectrum of possible futures and given rise to greater uncertainties. In 1980 a special *Newsweek* cover depicted the shattering of a rainbow, the traditional emblem of people's hopes and expectations. Today, the proverbial pot of gold and the better tomorrow historically symbolized by this rainbow seem elusive to many people.

Despite the pervasiveness of uncertainty, particular combinations of change appear to be unlikely. For example, it is difficult to imagine how gross labor productivity could improve rapidly and significantly without a corresponding increase in the percentage of GNP devoted to capital investment. Similarly, the amount of energy available from synthetic fuels largely depends upon the cost of oil.

The Interplay of Choice and Chance

The 1973 oil embargo, the rise of the OPEC cartel, and the fivefold increase in world oil prices during the 1970s are partially responsible for a general social malaise. Many U.S. citizens believe that the future has been taken out of their hands. Commentators often refer to the sense of helplessness to which President Carter

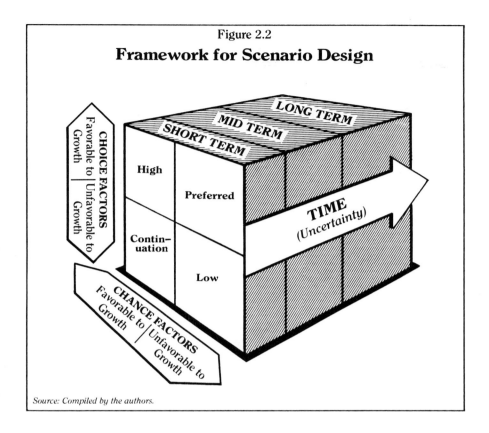

Figure 2.2

Framework for Scenario Design

Source: Compiled by the authors.

referred in a July 1979 speech when he spoke about a "crisis of the American spirit—a crisis of confidence. It is a crisis that strikes at the very heart, soul, and spirit of our national will [and] is threatening to destroy the social and political fabric of America."[7] A rash of recent books offering strategies for dealing with an economic downturn, such as Howard Ruff's *How to Prosper During the Coming Bad Years,* Geoffrey F. Abert's *After the Crash,* and Douglas Casey's *Crisis Investing,* [8] suggests a widespread pessimism about this country's economic outlook. This climate fosters fears that we lack the power to improve the situation.

The question of uncertainty, the relative importance of the choices we can make as opposed to uncontrollable chance factors, obviously is crucial to the nation's future. To translate the interactions among choices and chances into alternative futures, the authors constructed a matrix with government and social choice variations on one axis and variations involving chance or luck on the other axis. In each case the variations range from growth-favoring to growth-inhibiting. Figure 2.2 illustrates the interaction of the variables and the resulting scenarios. With the addition of a third dimension to the chart, it illustrates not only uncertainty expanding over time but three separate horizons considered by the study: the short term, through the next decade; the midterm, through the 1990s; and the long term, after 2000.

The values of choice variables depend primarily upon the social and political decisions of the American people, individually and collectively. The odds on accurately predicting how many immigrants will cross our borders in the year 2000 may be as high as the odds on accurately predicting how many quads of solar energy will be available that year, but one is more within our control, if we choose to exercise it rigorously, and the other is primarily dependent upon luck—new fuel discoveries, the rate of scientific breakthroughs, and the world price of oil. U.S. policy decisions do have some impact on the pace of technological progress and may have some impact on world oil prices, but both are essentially beyond our control.

It is important to remember that the distinction between choice and chance variables is obviously not absolute and elements of both choice and chance influence all variables. For example, unless we decide literally to wall up our borders, immigration cannot be controlled absolutely. Nevertheless, the distinction is generally valid and provides a useful analytical framework for scenario design. Chance dominates only five of the principal variables—the five energy variables. The values of demographic, labor force, productivity, and fiscal policy variables are almost wholly the result of U.S. social and public choices. Distinguishing between choice and chance variables or inputs allows the different scenario results to be attributed to either choice or chance factors. Hence, from the range of plausible values for each choice variable, a growth-favoring or growth-inhibiting value can be determined and, based upon it, economic growth implications can be inferred.

The Influence of Public Opinion

The individual beliefs and attitudes of the American people underlie all social and governmental decisions. These beliefs and attitudes are the ultimate source of legitimacy for any action. For instance, the move toward censorship rarely gains any ground in the United States because it violates the majority belief in freedom of the press. Likewise, the belief that taxation without representation is an illegitimate practice has shaped our society's evolution. Over the long run, beliefs and attitudes about economic and energy growth will determine the future direction of our economy.

The traditional view that economic growth and increasing individual prosperity are unqualified blessings came under sharp question in the 1970s. Citing environmental damage, risks to personal safety, the centralization of large-scale economic activity and power, and increasing individual alienation, growth skeptics argued that the price of prosperity had become too dear and that prosperity itself is a false and unworthy goal. Such skeptics rightly contend that quality of life is not solely a function of per capita income or consumption. They further argue that simplicity and autonomy are preferable to the sophisticated interdependence and mass production methods of modern industry, and that society on the whole would be healthier and happier if individuals were to pursue nonmaterial goals.

Those dubious about the need for growth or hostile to its undeniable costs have enjoyed many individual successes influencing regulatory bodies and the courts, as well as in shaping legislation. While they have succeeded in canceling or delaying many large-scale energy and industrial ventures, they have yet to convince the majority of their fellow citizens that cottage industry and the ascetic life are inherently desirable or even feasible.

In a survey completed in 1980 for this project to determine beliefs and attitudes behind no-growth and pro-growth views in the U.S. population, Dr. Edward Hyman of the University of San Francisco found that approximately 50 percent of the respondents favored growth and 25 percent favored no growth. Of the balance, 14 percent had mixed views, and 11 percent were undecided.[9]

While the antigrowth view does not seem to be prevailing, it must be emphasized that the growth debate itself remains unresolved. There is evidence, however, that the extreme polarization characterizing this debate in the early 1970s is weakening. In view of mounting evidence that the world population growth rate is declining and that world food supplies are improving, the Club of Rome has abandoned its 1972 call for an immediate institution of no-growth policies and now proposes selective growth with emphasis on the developing world. Recent studies, such as the Ford Foundation's *Energy: The Next Twenty Years*, Resources for the Future's *Energy in America's Future,* and the National Academy of Sciences' CONAES Study, *Energy in Transition,* conclude that the world is "not running out of energy."[10] As the doomsday scenarios of seven years ago recede, there are grounds for hope that the growth debate finally is becoming a manageable issue for the democratic process and the legal system. Whether and how this debate eventually is resolved is pivotal for each of the scenarios, and its current status helped shape this book's input assumptions.

Decision Tree Analysis

The specific parameters assumed for the exogenous choice and chance variables for each scenario are based on historical experience, current trends, and the informed opinions of a group of recognized authorities. Chapter 3 presents detailed justifications for the assumed values of these variables.

Figure 2.3 illustrates the decision tree structure applied to each variable. The upper branch emerging from each node indicates a choice or chance occurrence favorable to growth while the lower branch represents a growth-inhibiting choice or chance occurrence. Although this structure implies that contradictory government and social decisions can exist simultaneously and thus would suggest the need for at least eight scenarios, it was assumed that these types of decisions generally work in concert. For this reason, the analysis is restricted to the four futures resulting from complementary government and social decisions. This abridged structure is simple and it captures the extreme range of possible economic growth paths while it considers the impacts of government and social choices relative to each other and to chance occurrences.

For example, the outer bounds of annual gross labor productivity were assumed to be 2.86 percent and 1.23 percent. The higher figure reflects the historic rate achieved

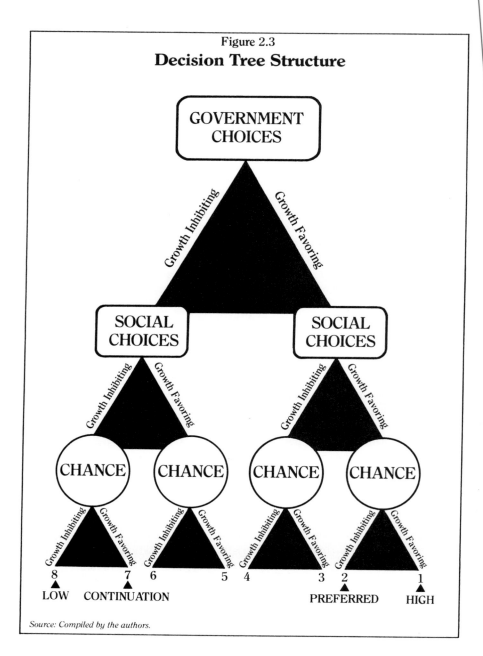

Figure 2.3
Decision Tree Structure

Source: Compiled by the authors.

from 1960 to 1969, a period during which conditions heavily favored growth, and the low figure matches the rate actually achieved from 1973 to 1977, a period during which a number of factors combined to inhibit growth. This range then was split into components corresponding to the influence of government and social decisions and chance occurrences. Judgmental analysis was employed to specify that fraction of the difference attributable to each, thus providing the figures for the tree's interior branches. Figure 2.4 illustrates the results. The correspondence of the middle figures, 2.24 percent and 1.85 percent, to the rates actually achieved from 1970 to 1978 and from 1969 to 1976, respectively, lends credence to their plausibility.

Because the range of gross labor productivity growth in effect defines the potential equilibrium path for total economic growth, these input assumptions are particularly crucial ones. Embodied within them are assumptions about the rate of technological advancement, which increases labor's efficiency. Together with increased man-hours, it is the ultimate source of midterm growth. The potential equilibrium path — 2.04 percent average annual gross labor productivity growth — imputed by the productivity bounds employed for this book reflects the potential for technological change that was determined to be inherent in contemporary U.S. society. Even if choices made and chance events interacted in such a way that each neutralized the other's impact on the economy, technological progress would not grind to a complete halt. To that extent, this analysis assumes a certain growth potential and the initial dominance of choice over chance in determining our future. Formal decision analysis entails assigning probabilities to each branch of the tree but, in the authors' judgment, each point on the range of possible productivity growth is equally probable. Establishing two realistic outer technological targets and working inward made it possible to model four relatively distinct futures. Starting with the imputed growth rate and working outward, the variant scenarios of the future would have been just that — variations of one central scenario, which, it must be emphasized again, is no more probable than any of the others. A certain potential for technological change is built into this scenario design, but the design does more than model the sensitivities of one potential equilibrium path for economic growth.

Scenario Descriptions

During the scenario design process, the authors tried to develop an integrated physical, economic, and psychological view for each scenario to assure that its particular set of assumptions were internally consistent. This endeavor illustrates how judgmental analysis can complement economic modeling, their combination offsetting inherent weaknesses of either technique for examining possible futures.

Using the decision tree procedure, input assumptions were generated for each variable in each of the four scenarios shown in Figure 2.2. The high-growth scenario results from the combination of growth-favoring decisions and good luck. More people choose to work than is the case in the other scenarios, and capital investment is encouraged by fiscal policy least biased toward consumption. Hence, gross labor productivity rises more rapidly than in other scenarios. This overall climate stimu-

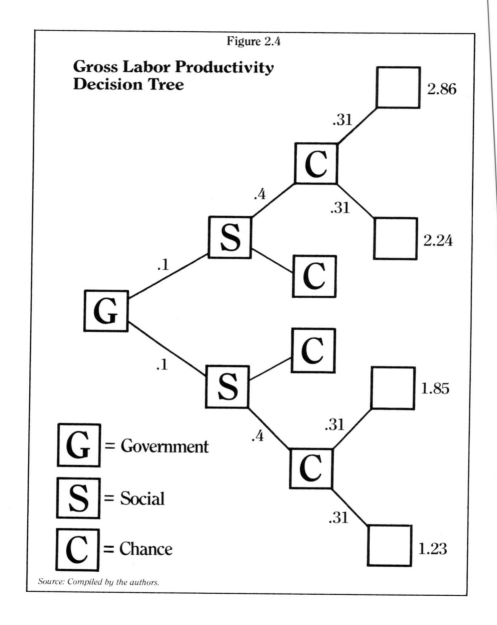

Figure 2.4

Gross Labor Productivity Decision Tree

G = Government

S = Social

C = Chance

Source: Compiled by the authors.

lates fertility rates and immigration and not only accommodates the fastest population growth of all scenarios but also benefits from the correlative labor force growth.
Good luck brings the most moderate rate of increase in world oil prices, which, in turn,
holds down the price of coal and the need for alternative energy sources.

The low-growth scenario represents the opposite combination of choices and chance occurrences. Public policy, in fact if not in intention, limits economic expansion by depressing investment and productivity. Individual family and job decisions favor fewer children and more leisure. Chance occurrences further dampen growth: oil prices escalate more rapidly, the rate of resource discovery falters, and technological advancements are fewer and farther between. Thus, even though the liability of our reliance on oil and coal is greatest in this scenario, alternative energy sources are available in quantities no larger than those of the preferred scenario.

The preferred scenario is so designated for a variety of reasons. It results from the interaction of growth-favoring choices and growth-inhibiting chance factors. Given the overriding reality of uncertainty, the authors believe that the most prudent strategy is to foster growth-encouraging social and public policies that are flexible enough to accommodate the worst of luck. Then, if good fortune brings lower oil prices or rapid breakthroughs in the production of synthetic fuel, for instance, so much the better.

The history of evolution has shown that adaptability is the key to survival. Choices made today should foster multiple options so that a setback in one area can be offset by extra margin elsewhere. Contingency planning is redundant and wasteful only if we presume certainty. For example, the uncertainty associated with every form of energy currently known—oil, gas, coal, synthetics, nuclear, solar, geothermal, wind, biomass, and other exotic technologies — makes the "wasteful" pursuit of all options, in fact, prudent. Although bad luck in the preferred scenario means world oil prices equal to those in the low-growth scenario, alternative energy sources are pursued more vigorously by choice and, consequently, are more readily available. The alternative options, in turn, keep coal prices from rising as rapidly as they do in the low-growth scenario.

In the preferred scenario choices available to individuals and to society at large are expanded and flexibility is encouraged and accommodated. Fewer people than in the high-growth scenario choose to participate in the labor force, but those who do work have basically the same amount of leisure time. The fiscal policy embodied in personal and corporate tax rates and investment tax credit rates favors growth much as in the case of the high-growth scenario, but the overall slower growth due to higher energy prices and a smaller labor force means that a slightly smaller percentage of GNP is devoted to capital investment. Consequently, gross labor productivity does not advance as rapidly as is assumed possible in the high-growth scenario. Still, economic growth is strong and steady, much closer to the rate of growth averaged over the entire postwar era than that experienced in the last decade. Our ability to guarantee all U.S. citizens an acceptable living standard is assured, our physical environment is safeguarded, and our vulnerability to the shocks of imported oil price hikes and supply interruptions is decreased.

The fourth scenario couples government and social choices averse to economic growth with favorable chance occurrences. Because this combination of economic variables generally has characterized the last 15 years (only during the last half of the period have energy prices surged ahead of inflation), this scenario has been termed the continuation scenario. Government intervention continues to curtail rather than to expand free-market options. Fiscal policy depresses labor force participation rates and the portion of GNP devoted to capital investment. Gross labor productivity advances no faster than it did during the early 1970s. Fertility rates remain below replacement level. Chance factors, such as the weather and the rate of resource discoveries, remain generally favorable. Good fortune means oil prices rise less rapidly than in the preferred or low-growth scenarios but, consequently, alternative sources are not pursued as actively and coal prices therefore exceed those in the preferred scenario. Projecting a combination of growth-inhibiting decisions and good luck suggests the best that can be expected if the policies of the last 15 years continue.

In addition to the four core scenarios, the authors explored a variation on the high-growth scenario that assumes more rapid escalation of world oil prices. This price increase is assumed to accelerate solar and synthetic fuels production and to stimulate the expansion of both our nuclear power capacity and price-induced conservation. This independence scenario, in which prices induce greater energy self-sufficiency, emphasizes our ability to overcome adverse chance occurrences given prudent social and government choices. Our economic vitality depends upon the flexibility with which we can adapt to sudden and unpredictable chance developments.

Finally, the authors contemplated futures that lie outside the probable range and thus outside the designed purpose and capabilities of the econometric models employed in this analysis. Drawing when possible from the results of the quantitative modeling work completed for the other scenarios, these alternative scenarios were developed by qualitative analyses. Like the independence scenario, they illustrate the critical importance of the choices we face concerning economic and energy growth. The decisions we make today can be the basis for our economic undoing as well as our economic salvation.

Conclusion

The importance of the decisions we make in determining our future economic well-being cannot be overemphasized. Econometric modeling helps us anticipate the likely consequences of our actions. However, the authors' perspective on contemporary U.S. society indicates that a wide range of equally plausible values exists for each particular variable. It also suggests the oversimplification necessary to reduce the economy's flow through the five social sectors into a discrete system composed of relatively discrete variables. The judgmental analysis employed here to specify the required input assumptions partially offsets this reductiveness. Assigning quantities to the variables is neither less critical nor less complex than designing modeling systems because each variable influences other variables. Chapter 3 traces the rationale for the range of each input assumption. When the resulting span of plausible scenarios is interpreted in Chapter 4 within the broad social context developed in Chapter 1, the desirable ramifications of the preferred scenario policy choices become fully apparent.

Notes

1. A definitive attempt to develop a more accurate measure of economic welfare (MEW) was undertaken by William Nordhaus and James Tobin. They adjusted GNP by adding and subtracting the estimated value of these and other changes in the quality of our lives. Their measure has not been widely adopted, however. See their study, "Is Growth Obsolete?" In *Fiftieth Anniversary Colloquium*, Vol. 5, National Bureau of Economic Research (New York: Columbia University Press, 1972).

2. Further documentation for the H-J model may be found in Edward A. Hudson and Dale Jorgenson, *The Long Term Interindustry Transactions Model: A Simulation Model for Energy and Economic Analysis*, a report prepared for the Mathematics and Computation Laboratory of the General Services Administration and the Department of the Interior (GSA/FPA/MCL TR109), July 1979.

3. Further documentation for the B-J regionalized electricity model (REM) may be found in Martin L. Baughman, Paul L. Joskow, and Dilip P. Kamat, *Electric Power in the United States: Models and Policy Analysis* (Cambridge, Mass.: MIT Press, 1979).

4. Further documentation for the Wharton model may be found in William W. Hogan et al., *Energy and the Economy*, 2 vols. (EA620), a report prepared by Energy Modeling Forum of the Institute for Energy Studies at Stanford University for the Electric Power Research Institute (Palo Alto: EPRI, 1978).

5. Further documentation for the Evans model may be found in "Investigation of Supply-Side Economics," a report prepared for the U.S. Senate Finance Committee by Michael K. Evans, completed March 1980.

6. Further documentation for the ETA-Macro model may be found in Alan S. Manne, *ETA-Macro: A Model of Energy-Economy Transactions* (EA592), a report prepared by the Stanford University Department of Operations Research for the Electric Power Research Institute (Palo Alto: EPRI, 1977).

7. Goldman et al., "To Lift a Nation's Spirit," *Newsweek*, July 23, 1979, p. 20.

8. Howard J. Ruff, *How to Prosper During the Coming Bad Years* (New York: Times Books, 1979); Geoffrey Abert, *After the Crash: How to Survive and Prosper During the Depression of the 1980's* (Atlanta: Bradford Press, 1979); Douglas R. Casey, *Crisis Investing: Your Profits and Opportunities in the Coming Great Depression* (Atlanta: '76 Press, 1979).

9. Edward J. Hyman, *Attitudes Toward Economic Growth and the Environment* (Berkeley: The Center for Social Research, 1980). Available from EEI upon request.

10. Hans H. Landsberg et al., *Energy: The Next Twenty Years* (Cambridge, Mass.: Ballinger, 1979), a report sponsored by the Ford Foundation and administered by Resources for the Future; Sam H. Schurr et al., *Energy in America's Future: The Choices Before Us* (Baltimore: Johns Hopkins University Press, 1979), a report prepared by the staff of Resources for the Future; National Research Council, Committee on Nuclear and Alternative Energy Systems (CONAES), *Energy in Transition: 1985–2010* (San Francisco: Freeman, 1980).

Chapter 3

ASSUMPTIONS ABOUT
ALTERNATIVE FUTURES

Introduction to Scenarios

Some energy-economy studies compress their input assumptions into a table of growth rates and a paragraph or two explaining that they were chosen and tested for "reasonableness." Often this material is relegated to an appendix. Other studies deemphasize their assumptions by stating that they were drawn or adapted from other sources, which in many cases are not readily accessible to the general public. The normal justification for these approaches is to speed the reader more directly to the results and recommendations.

The authors have avoided these approaches for two reasons. First, the input assumptions either determine directly, or influence significantly, the final results. Simply, good input is necessary for good output. Second, preparing a detailed exposition of the assumptions requires a close examination of the interrelationships among key input assumptions, the awareness of which is so crucial to interpreting the present volume's results. Further, placing the assumptions ahead of the results and the recommendations provides the readers with a sensible flow of information that allows them to evaluate critically the policy portfolio of Chapter 5.

The variables introduced in Chapter 2 will determine in large part the economy's future performance. These variables are grouped into five categories—demographic, labor force, fiscal policy, productivity, and energy. The relative impact of each variable changes over time; that is, variables assume greater or lesser significance depending on whether their context is the short, mid-, or long term. This study concentrates on the midterm simulation of the Hudson-Jorgenson Model. Most of the social choices that U.S. citizens make today—such as how many children to have or what energy sources to develop—will not begin to produce significantly measurable economic effects until sometime during the mid-1990s, given birth cycles, lead times, and other factors. Hence, the midterm projections were used as the foundation for this book, providing targets for the Evans and Wharton Models and anchors for the ETA-Macro Model. During the 1980s those social choices that can have immediate and significant economic impacts are the ones that are reflected in this volume's fiscal and monetary variables. Therefore the short-term modeling focuses rather exclusively on these variables to explore the available alternative paths that will link the economy to the growth paths described by the H-J Model. Assuming that the economy achieves an equilibrium path during the midterm, the availability and price of various energy sources become the pivotal long-term variables. This chapter's summary juxtaposes the book's three sets of assumptions — discussed here in terms of the short-, mid-, and long-term frames they influence — and illustrates how certain combinations of assumptions lead to distinct scenarios depicting different futures.

Short-Term Assumptions: 1980–90

The short-term models employed require hundreds of input assumptions, but for the purposes of this project, the most critical variables are those determined primarily by fiscal and monetary policy. In contrast, the demographic variables that will affect labor force growth between now and 1990 are primarily the historic birth rates of the 1960s. Variables that affect productivity are influenced strongly by the quantity and quality of investment. Fiscal and monetary policy, in turn, can be manipulated to alter the nation's propensity and ability to invest.

How such policies can be used most effectively to foster growth is currently the topic of national debate. The crux of the argument arises out of two opposing theories of short-term growth: one characteristic of the traditional Keynesian school of economic thought, and the other characteristic of the newly emerging theory of economics known as supply-side economics. In order to stipulate a sufficient range of fiscal policy assumptions for this book, both theories were examined and representative sets of input assumptions were developed.

Keynesian versus Supply-Side Economics

Immediately following World War II, U.S. citizens widely feared that the economy would collapse again into the depressed state of the 1930s. Heeding John Maynard Keynes' warning that industrially advanced capitalistic countries naturally tended to such conditions, Congress passed the Full Employment Act of 1946, specifically authorizing the federal government to stabilize the economy at the level of "maximum employment, production and purchasing power." Keynesian theory became the basis for postwar fiscal and monetary policy.

The central proposition of Keynesian theory is that aggregate demand determines employment and output. Although Keynes identified instability and unemployment as chronic diseases of capitalism, his theory — developed during the Depression — is most concerned with short-term remedies, not long-term reforms. Because changes in technology, in the quantity and quality of the labor force, and in other factors that affect aggregate supply are generally negligible over short periods, Keynes assumed supply to be unchanging. He reasoned that the level of employment depends on what firms expect the most profitable volume of output to be. Assuming costs of production (supply) to be constant, employment and output depend, then, on the anticipated level of demand. Figure 3.1 shows where these initial assumptions led him and his followers.

For Keynesians, controlling aggregate demand, composed of consumption and investment expenditures, becomes the key to economic stability and growth. Consumption depends on income and on individuals' propensity to consume. Of course,

Figure 3.1
Determinants of Growth

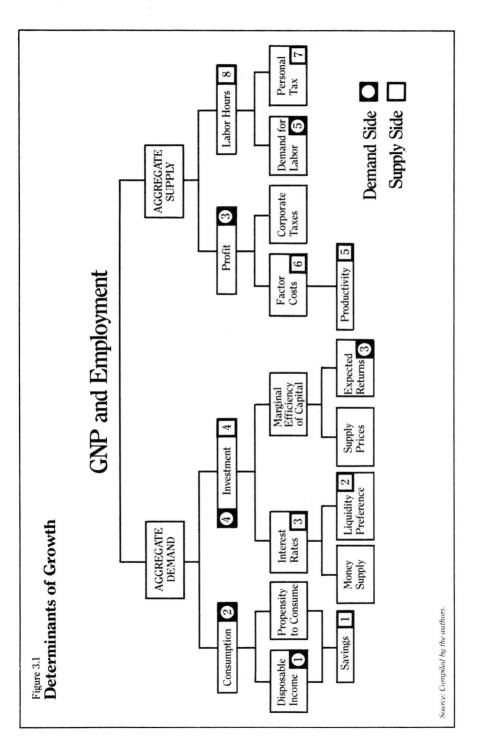

GNP and Employment

Source: Compiled by the authors.

how to influence income, that is, how to avoid economic stagnation, is the question that prompted Keynes' analysis. In mature industrialized countries like the United States, the propensity to consume tends to be relatively low. Because lower and middle income groups spend a greater portion of their income than higher income groups, the propensity to consume can be, and has been, altered to a limited degree by redistributing income to these groups through progressive tax rates. Nevertheless, the propensity to consume is basically stable over the short term.

Thus, in Keynesian economics, the potentially unstable component of aggregate demand is investment. Because the existing stock of capital goods is already large, investment opportunities may be insufficient to absorb the economy's potential output. If the gap between potential output and consumption is not filled by investment, actual output must fall until the gap closes. Hence, to realize maximum growth, aggregate demand must be stimulated to expand the economy's productive capacity.

To solve this dilemma, Keynes focused on investment. He identified its determinants as the marginal efficiency of capital and the rate of interest. The marginal efficiency of capital, in turn, depends on supply prices, which were assumed to be constant, and the expected returns yielded by capital assets, a psychological factor not readily susceptible to direct manipulation. Of course, interest rates can be manipulated by a central bank. Unless they are relatively high, however, Keynes found investment to be generally insensitive to interest rates. Furthermore, no matter how low interest rates are forced, if business expectations are extremely depressed, investment will be sluggish.

This reasoning, sequenced in Figure 3.1,[1] led Keynes to conclude that the most effective way to boost aggregate demand was through increased government spending. Whether these public expenditures take the form of transfer payments or payments for goods and services, they eventually translate into increased consumer income ① and demand ②. The spending can be financed by additional tax revenues or by incurring budget deficits. Increased taxes, however, reduce the income available to the private sector and, therefore, reduce aggregate demand — while deficit spending does not. Moreover, a given amount of deficit spending increases output by a multiple of that amount. A rise in consumer demand ② increases the returns expected on capital assets ③ and, thus, encourages investment ④. Investment, in turn, whether publicly or privately financed, has a magnified impact on national income. If a company decides to expand its capacity by upgrading its equipment, for instance, the supplier of that equipment may hire additional workers ⑤ to meet that demand. Their income then increases ① and, consequently, so does demand for consumption goods ②. The initial investment's impact ripples outward, increasing income by a multiple of the original expenditure. Because people save some of their new income, however, the ripple fades as the increase in demand transferred through the economy grows smaller and smaller.

Although Keynes' theory is concerned primarily with recessions, by extension the theory also implies cures for the opposite ailment to which the economy is susceptible — inflation. Inflationary gaps occur when aggregate demand exceeds full-employment output. Again, assuming aggregate supply remedies for closing the gap to be unavailable, such as increasing either the labor supply or productivity, fiscal and monetary policy must be used to dampen aggregate demand. A tight money policy that drastically raises interest rates will discourage investment to some extent and, through the investment multiplier, depress consumer demand accordingly. The more effective weapon, given Keynes' reasoning that investment is relatively inelastic with respect to interest rates, is fiscal policy. By spending less than it takes in, the government can bring aggregate demand back in line with full-employment output.

Thus, only when the economy is at full-employment equilibrium should the federal budget be balanced. Under this condition, growth can be achieved only if resources currently allocated to consumption are shifted to investment. If the economy's full resources are being employed already, by definition output cannot be expanded faster than supply-side changes permit — which in Keynes' analysis means negligibly over the short term. No matter how slow, this equilibrium growth is infinitely preferable to chronic unemployment. As postwar history has shown, however, the full-employment equilibrium, a precarious balance, almost inevitably begins to oscillate between recessionary and inflationary states.

Having explained why a tendency toward instability is inherent in mature capitalistic systems, Keynes' theory then suggested how appropriate combinations of fiscal and monetary policy could be used to counter that instability. Expansionary policies — easy money, low taxes, and higher government spending — can push the economy to the full employment of its resources, but they also raise prices. Contractionary policies — tight money, higher taxes, and reduced government spending — can retard inflation, but they also increase unemployment. Through the early 1960s the inverse relationship between unemployment and inflation seemed to hold, and the application of Keynesian policies seemed to achieve admirable results.

In recent years, however, the supposedly inverse relationship between the two phenomena appears to have undergone a metamorphosis. Both inflation and unemployment rates have exceeded those of any other period in the postwar era — and simultaneously. During the 1950s the average unemployment rate was 4.5 percent, but during the 1970s it was significantly higher: 6.2 percent. Paradoxically, so was inflation, averaging 2.6 percent annually over the 1950s and 6.7 percent during the 1970s. The balance between stability and economic growth, inflation and unemployment, and budget surpluses and deficits began to shift in the mid- to late 1960s. At no time since 1951 has a surplus exceeded $1 billion. Beginning with the 1960s, the government began to use deficit spending not only to cut off recessions but also to stimulate an already growing economy. By the middle of the decade the combination of funding a war in Vietnam and the most sizable and prolonged economic expansion in history — without an adequate tax increase — set the federal deficit on an exponentially rising curve.

Part of the explanation for this inflation-unemployment paradox lies within certain assumptions Keynes made in order to focus most sharply on private-sector employment. It is assumed, for example, that all workers are employed by business firms in quest of profit. Naturally, the determinants of employment in nonprofit and for-profit organizations are not the same. Furthermore, Keynes assumed a closed economy. Yet, world economic interdependence and competition have been growing forces over the postwar era — with increasing consequences for the U.S. economy. Equally significant, since the late 1970s interest rates have climbed to such heights that even Keynes would agree that they have severely depressed investment. Perhaps most importantly, Keynes' theory neglects the economy's aggregate supply side. Although his reasons for doing so made sense at the time, the magnitude of supply-side changes that have occurred in recent years merits consideration. As the labor force explosion of the 1970s demonstrates, labor supply can fluctuate markedly, even over the short term. The cost and availability of other factors of production — such as energy — can change rapidly as well. Keynes, however, tended to equate factor costs solely with wages and assumed supply to be constant. Likewise, he assumed all workers to be equally productive and labor productivity to be constant. He also assumed all investments to be profit-inspired and, therefore, maximally productive. Of course, as Keynesian theory has evolved, it has been modified to increase its applicability to the economy's present state, but the fundamental tenet remains: aggregate demand is the key to economic growth and stability.

Increasingly, the combination of high inflation and unemployment in the 1970s pointed to a fundamental weakness in Keynesian theory as it has been interpreted and applied. Not surprisingly, both economists and politicians are examining the supply side of the economy in an attempt to solve this puzzle. Supply-side proponents argue that the dominance of consumption in demand-oriented fiscal and monetary policies over the last decade and a half has caused the ratio of investment to output not merely to stagnate, but to shrink. Consequently, the economy's total productive capacity has grown more slowly than total demand, resulting in bottlenecks, shortages, and higher inflation. However, instead of closing the inflationary gap by reducing aggregate demand and causing even higher unemployment, supply-side champions argue that the most effective means to battle the current woes of inflation *and* unemployment is to increase aggregate supply. According to this theory, the production possibility curve of the economy can be raised, and jobs and output increased at the same time that inflation is being lowered.

Instead of fanning the inflationary fires as demand logic implies, supply-side reasoning suggests that corporate and individual income tax reductions would trigger the following chain of events. As Figure 3.1 shows, both reductions stimulate savings [1] by increasing their after-tax rate of return. Because increased savings means greater liquidity [2] and less loan demand, interest rates [3] fall, stimulating both business and residential investment [4]. The rise in the ratio of investment to GNP leads to greater productivity [5]. Productivity growth, in turn, dampens the rise in factor costs [6], including wage gains, which have already been slowed by the rise in disposable income occasioned by the personal tax cut. The personal tax cut [7] also stimulates labor force participation [8]. Thus, lower tax rates increase labor supply, capital stock, and productivity, thereby expanding the productive capacity of the U.S. economy and improving its competitive position in the world economy. The effects of these tax reductions on inflation are equally wide-reaching. The economy's increased productive capacity reduces the inflationary gap; productivity growth lowers factor costs;

wages rise more slowly; the improved trade balance strengthens the dollar and causes less inflation to be imported. Lower inflation then lessens bracket creep and increases real disposable income, stimulating consumption, output, and employment. Lower inflation also stimulates investment by lowering interest rates. This increase in aggregate demand, however, is matched by the rise of the economy's maximum potential capacity. The result is balanced, noninflationary growth.

Figure 3.1 illustrates the similarities and differences between Keynesian and supply-side theories. Both agree that investment is a crucial element of growth, that the marginal efficiency of capital and the rate of interest determine whether or not investments are made, and that fiscal and monetary policy can influence those two determinants of investment. Both theories seek to achieve the same ultimate goal: stable, noninflationary growth.

Their approaches to that goal differ, however. In situations of less-than-full employment, demand theorists hold that the most effective way to encourage investment is to increase individuals' incomes through deficit spending so that consumption will rise. Once consumption demand rises, the return that business expects capital assets to yield will rise and business will expand productive capacity. In somewhat oversimplified terms, demand creates its own supply. Supply-side proponents argue that no such automatic mechanism exists to equilibrate demand and supply. To be sure, an increase in demand does raise the rate of return, other things being equal — but it does not in and of itself guarantee an adequate rate of return no matter what the equilibrium state of the economy. Fiscal and monetary policy also must take into account the supply prices of capital goods, which entails considering factor costs and corporate profits as well. Therefore, the impacts of policy on labor supply and productivity merit explicit recognition.

Furthermore, in a full-employment or inflated economy, labor supply and productivity are the sole sources of growth. Fiscal and monetary policy should be designed to encourage both the most productive investments and labor force participation. In contrast, the single-minded goal of demand-oriented policy during times of full employment is to trade off a decrease in consumption for an increase in investment. Otherwise, inflationary pressures will build, and policy will have to be employed to dampen aggregate demand — investment as well as consumption.

Thus, although proponents of both theories agree that fiscal and monetary policy can impinge upon the economy at several points, they disagree on which points can be manipulated with greatest effect. Consequently, they differ on which policies are most appropriate.

Model Assumptions

Two models were employed to explore the short-term policies necessary to move the economy onto the projected midterm growth tracks. The Wharton Model's construction incorporates a Keynesian economic perspective, and the Evans Model's construction incorporates a supply-oriented economic perspective. Despite variations in their approaches, the models concur that policies encouraging investment and discouraging consumption will be required to align the U.S. economy to the higher midterm growth paths. To accomplish this linkage, investment as a share of GNP had to be increased. Fiscal policy assumptions are the chief means of adjusting the investment ratio in both models, but the particular policy tools manipulated in each differ because supply- and demand-side theories differ on how this necessary reallocation of resources can best be accomplished. The investment tax credit rate was altered significantly and personal and corporate income tax rates were refined slightly in the Wharton Model assumptions. In the Evans Model, corporate and personal tax rates and depreciation lifetimes were adjusted. The impact of monetary policy on investment also is recognized in both models, but in different ways. Interest rates had to be

TABLE 3.1
Wharton Model Assumptions, 1980–90

	Preferred	Continuation	Low
GNP and Productivity Targets (1990)			
GNP target (billion $ 1972)	1,961.00	1,872.00	1,689.00
Productivity target (GNP/employment)	19,160	17,970	16,800
Personal Income Tax percent, (first bracket $0–500)			
1980	11.39	11.39	11.39
1981	13.56	12.53	11.62
1982	13.86	12.53	11.62
1983	13.86	12.53	11.62
1984	12.80	12.53	11.62
1985	12.20	12.81	11.62
1986	12.05	13.10	12.53
1987	12.80	13.10	13.10
1988	12.80	13.10	13.10
1989	12.80	13.10	13.10
1990	12.80	13.10	13.10
Investment Tax Credit (percent)			
1980	15.00	15.00	15.00
1981–90	30.00	10.00	1.00
Corporate Tax Rate (percent)			
1980	46.00	46.00	46.00
1981–90	46.00	46.00	50.00

Source: Compiled by the authors.

set exogenously to complement the fiscal assumptions in the demand model. In the supply-side model they are determined internally.

Each Wharton scenario was calibrated to its midterm counterpart by altering fiscal variables until 1990 targets of GNP and labor productivity were matched most closely. Table 3.1 shows these targets and the fiscal policy assumptions made to achieve them. The high growth and independence scenarios become distinct sometime between 1990 and 1995 if the policies that lead to the preferred scenario are continued. The investment tax credit was the primary tool used to manipulate the investment/GNP ratio. To prevent the economy from becoming inflationary, personal income taxes were raised; then, to boost aggregate demand at mid-decade, they were reduced temporarily. Corporate income tax rate increases were required to further depress investment in the low-growth scenario.

The calibration process for the Evans Model was reduced to matching its GNP range to that of the midterm model because the Evans Model specifies labor productivity endogenously. The supply-side model achieves the full range of midterm targets by 1990, but because of the vastly different internal dynamics of the Evans Model and of the inputs it requires, its scenarios should not be directly correlated with the four

TABLE 3.2
Evans Model Assumptions, 1980–90

	High (large deficit)	Preferred (no deficit)	Continuation	Low
Real GNP[a]	3.80	3.64	2.90	1.57
Average personal income tax rate (percent)	24.9– 12.3	24.9– 11.0	24.9– 23.5	24.9– 38.3
Corporate income tax rate (percent)	46.0– 20.0	46.0– 20.0	46.0– 46.0	46.0– 46.0
Investment tax credit (percent)	10.0– 10.0	10.0– 10.0	10.0– 10.0	10.0– 0.0
Accounting life structures (years)	23.0– 10.0	23.0– 10.0	23.0– 18.4	23.0– 23.0
Accounting life equipment (years)	10.5– 5.0	10.5– 5.0	10.5– 8.4	10.5– 10.5
Transfer payments[a]	11.4	2.2	11.4	15.6
Government regulation[b]	5.96– 7.0	5.96– 7.0	5.96– 7.0	5.96– 11.4

[a] Annual percent growth rates.
[b] Billions of current dollars.
Source: Compiled by the authors.

core midterm scenarios. Table 3.2 presents the GNP growth rates modeled and summarizes the assumptions upon which they depend. The large-deficit high-growth scenario largely results from dramatic personal and corporate income tax rate reductions and liberalized depreciation allowances. Because of the questionable political feasibility of the sizable deficit that results from such changes, a second scenario was run with identical assumptions except that the growth in transfer payments was reduced sufficiently to balance the budget. Growth is moderated in the base scenario by less liberal depreciation allowances (although they are increased relative to 1980 levels) and smaller personal income tax reductions. The low-growth scenario is distinguished by sharper increases in the costs of energy and government regulation and greater growth in transfer payments. The bulk of the decline in GNP growth is attributable to these changes and their impacts on labor force growth and labor productivity. Also contributing, but less significantly, are changes in fiscal variables. The average personal income tax rate rises, but this rise is due entirely to bracket creep. Statutory rates remain at 1980 levels. Corporate taxes and depreciable lives also are held at 1980 levels, but the investment tax credit is canceled.

These input assumptions simply reflect a range of social and economic possibilities based on different kinds of choices available to U.S. citizens. The fiscal and monetary policy options selected for the preferred scenario suppose a decision on the part of the U.S. public to pursue a path of economic revitalization and economic growth; the policies that characterize the continuation scenario suggest a choice, whether conscious or by default, to maintain the status quo. However, a decision to pursue either option must reflect a consensus of the American people.

Midterm Assumptions: 1985–2000

Introduction

The acronym KLEM—the combination of capital, labor, energy, and materials—summarizes the driving forces that determine the quantity and kind of output the economy produces.[2] As the relative cost and availability of each of these factors change, its contribution to the production equation changes. Because the first three factors have been particularly volatile since the mid-1960s and probably will continue to be so for some time, this book concentrates on them. However, presumably the economy will adjust to these fluctuations, eventually arriving at a new KLEM formula. The equilibrium growth path that emerges in the midterm will depend both on the future states of the factor inputs and on how the nation chooses to prepare for them.

This book's midterm analysis simulates a wide range of future states for capital, labor, and energy. It does so by assuming an equally wide range of values for both the major variables that influence those inputs and the efficiency with which they are combined. The cost and availability of capital, for instance, are affected directly by fiscal and monetary policy variables, which are assumed to retain their short-term values. The efficiency of capital input is influenced by government regulation, especially environmental protection regulation, by demographic and labor force variables that govern the economy's capital/labor force mix, by technical progress, and by chance factors that determine the efficiency of energy input relative to capital. Thus, although the input assumptions for the midterm modeling are presented here in four separate categories — demography, labor force, productivity, and energy — the state of each variable has some impact on the others. These assumptions were derived from detailed reviews of historical trends and current conditions and from careful consideration of the collective views of the book's authors, consultants, and advisers.

Demographic Assumptions

Demographic variables — birth, death, and immigration rates — figure prominently in both the demand and supply sides of the economy; they largely determine the demand for the economy's output and they dictate the labor force's size and age profile.

Birth Rates

Birth rates generally have decreased throughout U.S. history. Births per year per thousand women 15 to 44 years of age (BYT) dropped from 55 in the early 1800s to 15 in the late 1970s. Only once — between 1935 and 1955 — has that decreasing trend been reversed. If one plots BYT data since the turn of the century, the resulting graph would reveal a cyclical pattern superimposed over a declining curve that appears to be leveling off at about 14 BYT. These cycles, about 40 years from peak to peak, underlie an interesting but still disputed theory of birth rate fluctuations. Richard Easterlin and others have argued that children born in periods of low birth rates face less competition for jobs, improve their economic positions faster, marry earlier, have less need for a spouse's second income, and raise larger families.[3] Conversely, members of baby-boom generations face greater competition in their early careers, experience lower incomes relative to more senior members of the labor force, and consequently defer both marriage and having children.

Easterlin believes this relative income effect has been a principal reason for the sharp decrease in birth rates since the mid-1950s. Figure 3.2, adapted from data published by Easterlin, illustrates the income and employment experience of young males. This figure suggests that birth rates can be correlated with the income and employment experience of young males relative to those of typical male breadwinners, and that this experience, in turn, is related to the size of the young male population relative to the size of the older male population. The figure also shows sharply falling numbers of this segment of the population during the 1980s and early 1990s as the baby-bust generation of the 1960s and 1970s matures and enters the labor force. Easterlin suggests that the birth rate could rise sharply as these young adults find comparatively smooth sailing in their early careers and earn relatively higher incomes in proportion to their employment experience than do more senior members of the work force.

Nevertheless, many demographers dispute the relative income thesis. They cite the postwar economic and social recovery to explain the sudden increase in birth rates

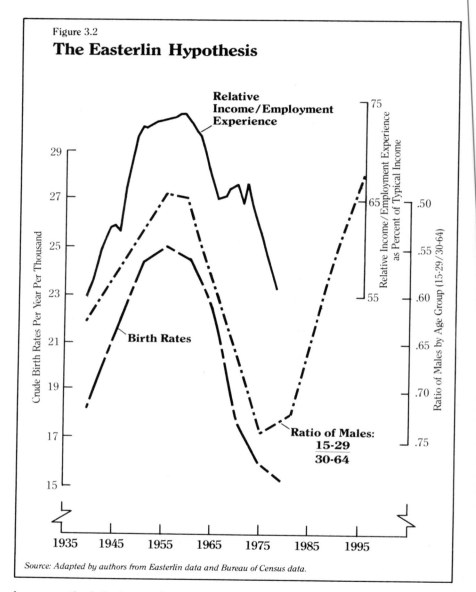

Figure 3.2

The Easterlin Hypothesis

Source: Adapted by authors from Easterlin data and Bureau of Census data.

known as the baby boom. Similarly, they point to social changes in the 1960s and 1970s as causes of the birth rate decreases since 1957. These sociological explanations of this decrease in birth rates do stand up to close scrutiny; for example, today more women actively are pursuing careers. Furthermore, the incompatibility of large families and modern styles of living seems both to delay the beginning of families and to reduce their ultimate size. For the first time in U.S. history, fertility is greater among women 25 to 29 years of age than among the younger age groups. In addition to such planned reductions or postponements in births, some overall reduction of unplanned births accompanied this trend as improved techniques, accessibility, and knowledge of contraception and abortion countered the effects of increasing sexual activity in our society.

If crude birth rates follow the pattern described in Figure 3.2, then it is likely that members of the baby-bust generation soon will begin to have larger families. What Figure 3.2 cannot tell us conclusively is whether economic or social factors will dominate future birth rate trends. This book reflects the Easterlin income thesis only to the extent that a higher birth rate is assumed in the higher-growth scenarios than in the lower-growth scenarios — 2.1 versus 1.7 births per average woman over her entire child-bearing years (total fertility rate). The Easterlin thesis implies even faster population growth rates are possible over the next 20 years. Consequently, it would presume more pressure for economic growth — particularly after the year 2000 — than this book foresees, even in the high-growth scenario.

Regardless of the reason, in countries as technologically and educationally advanced as the United States, birth rates seem to be predominantly a matter of social choice. This book attributes some of the variation in birth rates to government choices, but social choice is seen to be the principal cause of the fluctuation. The changing role of women exemplifies this kind of social choice. Economic factors obviously influence social decisions, and many of these factors reflect government's hand in its citizens' lives, such as tax and transfer payment policies. Since economic conditions reflect a complex mix of social decisions and government actions, the authors attributed all of the birth rate variations between scenarios to choices — either socially or governmentally inspired — and accorded no weight to chance.

Death Rates

Of the three factors influencing the nation's population growth, death rates have demonstrated the most stability over much of the post-World War II period, declining from 9.9 deaths per year per 1,000 population in 1948 to 9.5 in 1970. Since then, however, the rate has dropped as much as it did in the preceding 25 years, reaching 8.8 in 1977 and reflecting the combined effects of changing age distribution in the population and changing life expectancies. Life expectancy at birth, in general, has mirrored these trends, rising only modestly from 68.2 years in 1950 to 70.9 in 1970, and then increasing to 73.2 by 1977. Conventional projections, such as those of the Census Bureau, combine continued increases in longevity with the effects of a gradually aging population to yield only modest changes in death rates. This book employs those projections. However, there is a possibility that longevity may increase dramatically over the next 20 years as the result of medical breakthroughs predicted with confidence by some biologists and experts in the field of geriatrics. If this happens, death rates will drop, health will improve, working life will lengthen, and population will grow somewhat faster. Here then, is a second possibility that suggests that even this book's high-growth scenario may underestimate the future, both in terms of population and economic growth.

Immigration

Because immigrants include a broad spectrum of age groups, immigration levels can affect the labor force and, thus, the level of aggregate economic output more rapidly than changes in birth rates. The amazing influx from Cuba in early 1980 and the slower but persistent flow from Haiti demonstrate their potential impact. Population pressures in Mexico, its common border with the United States, the traditionally friendly relations between the two countries, and a growing U.S. need for Mexican oil and gas suggest that many Mexicans will move north in future years. As populations explode in parts of Asia, Africa, and South America, the United States may continue to attract the world's immigrants and refugees. The desire to foster good international relations may well force the United States into accepting significant numbers of potential citizens year after year.

The Census Bureau's practice of basing most of its population projections on the standard annual limit of 400,000 immigrants is inadequate for this volume. Some informal estimates of illegal immigration from Mexico alone recently exceed 500,000 per year.[4] Obviously, no accurate figures on illegal immigration exist, but the Census Bureau recently estimated past illegal immigrations at about 3.5 million persons — mostly Mexicans. Others have estimated the total number of illegal aliens now living in the United States as high as 12 million.[5] Therefore, in the high-growth scenario, an annual immigration of 1 million persons is assumed. As time passes, laws probably will be altered to allow more of the additional 600,000 to enter legally. In fact, more than 700,000 were expected to have gained legal admission in 1980.[6] The preferred and continuation scenarios assume an annual immigration of 700,000 persons, and the low-growth case employs the Census Bureau figure of 400,000. Theoretically, the poorer economic conditions of the lower-growth scenarios will reduce immigrants' desire to enter the United States and reinforce national efforts to limit newcomers. For the purposes of this work, the variation between the high- and low-growth scenario immigration estimates is seen to be influenced equally by government policy actions and chance factors.

Significantly, the difference in birth rates and immigration assumptions from scenario to scenario can dictate a rather wide potential population spread for the United States in the year 2000. The lower birth rate of 1.7 employed in the low-growth scenario, coupled with the modest Census Bureau immigration figure of 400,000, yields a total population figure in 2000 of 245.9 million people. At the other end of the scenario spectrum, both the high-growth and independence scenarios use a 2.1 birth rate figure and 600,000 additional immigrants above the base estimate of 400,000 for a total population figure of 274.5 million. The high-growth to low-growth difference of 28.6 million people by the year 2000 illustrates the potential importance of demographic assumption variations. The effects of these variations on economic growth begin to increase around the turn of the century when the additional youngsters born in the 1980s begin to move into the labor force.

Labor Force Assumptions

The second set of variables that bears directly on the labor component of the

KLEM equation is composed of participation rates, the length of the workweek, and unemployment rates. Whether one focuses on the relationship between employment and aggregate demand, as Keynesians do, or on the relationship between labor supply and the economy's productive capacity, as supply-side proponents do, labor force variables are critical determinants of the nation's future.

Participation Rates

Participation rates have changed greatly since World War II: female participation rose rapidly while that of males declined slowly. From 1950 to 1978, the fraction of all females 16 years of age and older in the civilian labor force rose from one-third to one-half. Over the same period, male participation rates dropped from roughly 87 percent to about 78 percent. Well over two-thirds of the increase in female participation occurred after 1964. In contrast, not much more than 40 percent of the decrease in male participation occurred after that time. The net effect has been a particularly rapid boost in the labor force since 1964.

Some analysts would attribute these recent shifts in participation rate trends primarily to changing styles of living. Others maintain that efforts to sustain past rates of improvement in living standards are the cause. Because the change in the female rate has been the most dramatic, much of the controversy hinges on why women have entered the labor force in increasing numbers. Have they gone to work in order to maintain an expected and desired rate of improvement in family living standards? Or have more women decided that the rewards of motherhood and homemaking are less desirable than the rewards of other careers?

Regardless of their motivation, the increase in real GNP per capita testifies to the effect of increased female participation in the labor market. From 1964 to 1978, GNP per capita growth averaged about 2.5 percent per year while, from 1950 to 1964, it

TABLE 3.3
Comparison of Real GNP Growth Rates and Civilian
Labor Force Participation Rates, 1950–78

Years	Real GNP Per Capita (1972 dollars)	Labor Force Participation		
		Female (percent)	Male (percent)	Total (percent)
1950	3,503	33.9	86.4	59.2
1964	4,557	38.7	81.0	58.7
1978	6,404	50.0	77.9	63.2
	Average Growth (percent/year)	Percentage Point Changes		
1950–64	1.9	+ 4.8	−5.4	−0.5
1964–78	2.5	+11.3	−3.1	+4.5

Source: Economic Report to the President, *1979.*

averaged only 1.9 percent per year. In fact, the 1.9 percent annual growth probably could have continued through 1978 with the same labor force participation rate recorded in 1964 and with some 7 million fewer employed persons in 1978 than the 94.4 million who actually were working. Table 3.3 shows the supporting statistics.

These statistics suggest that, in recent years, factors other than, or in addition to, family or per capita income have stimulated the increase in female labor force participation. Consequently it is assumed that the recent upward trend in female participation rates will continue. However, because job opportunities expand more rapidly in a high-growth society than they do in a low-growth society, the rise in female participation rates is assumed to slacken in each successively lower-growth scenario. Similarly, the recent slowing of the decline in male participation is assumed to continue in all scenarios, but most noticeably in the higher-growth futures.

Both of these significant changes in participation-rate trends — the quickening of the increase in female rates and the slowing of the decline in male rates — have occurred since the mid-1960s when the apparently growing numbers of "small is beautiful" advocates attracted so much publicity. Only if the no-growth syndrome were to penetrate our society much more deeply in the future would trends in labor force participation likely shift in a major way.

Thus, in this study, higher growth is connected with higher labor force participation and vice versa. In the high-growth scenario the female participation rate is assumed to rise to 60 percent by the year 2000, while the male rate drops to 76 percent. In each successively lower-growth scenario, the rise in female participation is slower and the decrease in male participation is more rapid. The participation rates for the low-growth scenario in 2000 are 53 percent for females and 68 percent for males. The male and female rates rise to 75 percent and 58 percent, respectively, by 2000 in the preferred scenario and to 69 percent and 55 percent, respectively, in the continuation scenario. An extension of these trends would achieve equal rates for men and women by the middle of the twenty-first century.

Social choices — such as those regarding the proper roles of men and women, birth rate decisions, and divorce trends — and government choices — such as those embodied in tax policies, minimum wage and maximum hour laws, abortion laws, and pension eligibility age changes — are accorded considerably more influence than chance factors in determining labor force participation rates.

Length of the Workweek

The length of the average workweek, a second factor determining labor input to the economy, displays an irregular, historical downward trend. The manufacturing workweek, for example, decreased from about 60 hours in 1890 to 40 a half century later, but since then it has remained relatively stable except for fluctuations corresponding to business cycles. After World War II the length of the manufacturing workweek diverged from that of other industries, some of which maintained the downward trend. From 1950 to 1979 the length of retail trade and services workweeks sharply declined, reaching the vicinity of 30 to 32 hours by 1979. A review of the 1979 workweeks for other industries shows three clustered around manufacturing (mining at 43 hours, transportation and public utilities at 40 hours, and wholesale trade at 39 hours), and the remainder close to the average for all private, nonagricultural jobs (construction at 37 hours; finance, insurance, and real estate at 36 hours; and government estimated at 35 hours).

In addition to the variations among industries, the lengths of the average male and female workweeks also differ. To some degree the shorter female workweek results from the traditional concentration of women in retail trades and services. This concentration has been decreasing slowly. The female workweek also has been characterized by the relatively high proportion of women who work part-time. The average female workweek has ranged from 33 to 31 hours since production wound down as World War II ended. During this same period, the male workweek gradually dropped from 41 hours in 1948 to 36 hours in 1977. However, during the next 20 years, as women continue to move vigorously into work areas that still remain largely male preserves and as changing social ethics, more flexible work rules, and an increase in older workers likely boost the fraction of part-time male participants, the difference in the length of female and male workweeks should lessen.

The male-female split is only one of many social and economic factors influencing each scenario. However, the high-growth scenario is not likely to be realized unless both males and females hold labor and the fruits of labor in relatively high regard. The incremental need for goods and services that results from the higher birth and immigration rates assumed in the high-growth scenario tends to reinforce this emphasis on labor. In contrast, the low-growth scenario includes both a lower demand for economic output (fewer persons) and lower supply of job opportunities (lower investment in productive facilities, different public policy decisions, and unfavorable resource availability). Table 3.4 highlights the postwar history of male and female workweeks and presents the midterm assumptions.

TABLE 3.4
Workweek: Past and Future
(hours per week)

	Female		Male		Difference
1948	35.1		41.1		6.0
1960	31.0		40.1		9.0
1969	31.9		37.8		5.9
1977	30.7		36.2		5.5
	L & C[a]	**P & H**[b]	**L & C**	**P & H**	
1990	29.0	31.0	33.2	34.5	
2000	28.0	31.0	31.0	33.0	

[a]L & C = low and continuation scenarios.
[b]P & H = preferred and high scenarios.
Source: Compiled by the authors.

Social choices and government choices have virtually equal importance in determining the total variation in workweeks across scenarios; chance events influence the total minimally. In an absolute sense, each of the three categories of factors are accorded twice as large an impact on the female workweek as on the male workweek. The greater variation across scenarios assumed for the female workweek (four hours versus two hours) reflects the greater uncertainty about how government actions, social choices, and chance events have influenced the female workweek in the recent past and are likely to influence it in the future.

Unemployment

In addition to participation rates and workweeks, the unemployment rate also bears on labor input to the economy. Between 1948 and 1968 U.S. unemployment rates averaged just under 4.7 percent. From 1970 through 1978 the unemployment rate average increased to 6.2 percent. Several reasons have been advanced for the abrupt change in the late 1960s: there was no war-related economic boom such as those that had created additional employment opportunities in the early 1950s and again in the mid-1960s; the combined surge of women and young adults into the labor force from 1960 through 1978 far exceeded the pace of earlier increases; finally, the rate at which industry has expanded its productive facilities — and thus its job opportunities — in recent years has lagged badly when compared, on a constant dollar basis, to the earlier rates of increase.

The midterm assumptions do not anticipate the return of wartime environments, but they do reflect a slackening of labor force growth because the task of absorbing the young adults of the baby boom essentially is completed. Additionally, a gradual reduction in the rate at which women will enter the labor force is expected. Teenage and female unemployment rates have increased since the late 1950s as these two segments of the labor force grew. As the relative size of the teenage population decreases in the 1980s, teenage unemployment should drop rapidly, reaching a level much the same as that of the early 1950s. In the early 1950s, when only about 11 percent of the labor force was composed of teenagers, their unemployment rate was a little better than 6 percentage points higher than the rate for adult males. In the 1970s, however, teenagers constituted nearly 16 percent of the labor force and their unemployment rate was 12 to 13 percentage points higher than the figure for adult males.

Within the next decade or so, the population's changing age distribution will act to bring the teenage fraction of the labor force back close to the levels of the early 1950s, causing a major decline in teenage unemployment. This decline may be even more dramatic if teenagers are exempted to some degree from the minimum wage laws. Similarly, the difference between male and female unemployment rates likely will shrink, if not disappear completely, as a result of women's full integration into the labor force. Consequently, unemployment rates should drop significantly over the next decade. In fact, some labor market analysts predict labor force scarcities during this period.

It is assumed in this book that unemployment rates will follow a cyclic pattern to 1985, reaching 7.3 percent at that time, and then decrease steadily to 5.2 percent by

1990 where they will remain through 2000. A variety of offsetting factors are assumed in each scenario. In the higher-growth societies, the larger numbers of young adults and immigrants will tend to boost unemployment rates, but government and social choices should combine to increase employment opportunities and therefore depress unemployment rates. In the lower-growth societies, job opportunities will be fewer, but there will be fewer people and a greater desire for leisure. Therefore, the same unemployment rates were assumed for all scenarios.

Productivity Assumptions

The remarkably steady improvement in per capita living standards achieved in the United States over the postwar era can be attributed to the growth of factor inputs of the KLEM equation and the efficiency with which they are combined. According to productivity expert Dale Jorgenson, capital input, labor input, and productivity growth all made significant contributions "and must be considered in analyzing future growth potential. For the postwar period capital input has made the most important contribution to the growth of output, productivity growth has been next most important, and labor input has been least important."[7]

Since the late 1960s, however, economic growth has lagged, dropping off the trend rate in the 1974–75 recession to an extent most economists find alarming. Statistics from the past several years indicate that the drop was not a fluke; in fact, the trend rate itself appears to be slowing significantly. Experts can account for part of the drop by a combination of specific one-time and ongoing shifts in the contributions of capital, labor, and energy inputs. Most of the fall, however, has been due to a dramatic decline in productivity growth, the efficiency with which the inputs are combined. Although some of the decline can be attributed to those changing contributions of factor inputs, the relationships are difficult to quantify and much of the productivity slowdown remains to be completely understood. Thus, productivity growth assumptions are particularly difficult to formulate and the major source of uncertainty in projecting future economic growth.

This volume's tactic has been to use two measures of productivity—total factor and gross labor—to estimate future productivity growth trends. Initially, the major determinants of total factor productivity, the ratio of total output to total input, were examined and values assigned to them. They are the efficiency of energy input, the quantity and quality of investment, and the quantity and quality of labor. With these as background assumptions, the assumed gross labor productivity growth rates were developed. These growth rates reflect underlying assumptions about the potential for technological advancement that translates into greater economic efficiency. Adding the labor productivity growth rate employed in a scenario to the growth of labor supply implied by the demographic and labor force assumptions yields an approximate measure of potential GNP growth.

The Efficiency of Energy Input

Soaring energy prices have contributed significantly to the productivity slowdown of the 1970s. The standard explanation of how higher energy costs reduce productivity in the short run is usually confined to the manufacturing sector. When energy prices increase relative to other factor prices, firms use less energy and more capital, labor, and materials. The mix of production factors becomes less efficient, a reality testified to by the experience of 1979. Employment increased throughout the year, but output was virtually stagnant. Although the recession of 1980–81 has caused the unemployment rate to rise slowly, the demand for labor still has shifted to a higher plane.

This shift toward increased labor intensity is an important change and one that cannot be treated lightly. Yet, an analysis by Michael Evans suggests that in the longer run it will probably turn out to be less important than the productivity changes that affect the transportation and distribution network.[8] Some of these changes are already obvious, such as the 1974–75 productivity decline in the transportation industry when higher fuel prices led airlines to lower speeds voluntarily and the trucking industry to do so according to federal mandate. However, longer-term changes brought about by higher energy prices will affect the entire economy's production and distribution system.

The negative impact of higher energy prices on productivity becomes apparent if one presumes an economy in which the cost of the transportation and distribution of goods is negligible. The location of manufacturing plants would be largely independent of markets except for those products that gain weight or bulk during manufacturing or those processes that utilize large quantities of raw materials. Competition would thrive because one firm could not obtain an advantage merely by accident of location. Most important, all plants would be large enough to take full advantage of economies of scale. Thus, cheap transportation and distribution aid productivity and retard inflation.

The higher cost of energy, by reducing the amount of transportation utilized, raises prices by much more than the cost of the more expensive fuel alone—in fact, it reduces the efficiency of the whole production and distribution process. Although existing plants do not shrink when energy costs rise, they often run at a lower rate of capacity utilization. And, although consumers do not change their driving or living habits overnight, they eventually do. Over time these gradual changes, almost imperceptible within the time frame of a year, cumulate and eventually represent a potent force affecting productivity.

Recent energy/productivity research by Jorgenson, commissioned for this study, empirically supports Evans' speculations.[9] After concluding that the post-1973 slowdown in U.S. economic growth was caused largely by a dramatic decline in total factor productivity growth and, less importantly, by declines in capital and labor inputs, Jorgenson extended his analysis beyond that of other experts by using a model that disaggregated the economy into 35 industrial sectors.[10] This disaggregation permitted an examination of the effects on productivity of the intermediate factors of production—that is, energy and materials—as well as the primary factors—capital and labor. The use of a 35-industry sectoral model revealed more than aggregate productivity analyses in which the production and consumption of the intermediate factors cancel out, leaving capital and labor as the only visible inputs.

Jorgenson's sectoral analysis shows that major slowdowns in productivity growth rates occurred for nearly all of the 35 industries after 1973. It also suggests that the reduction in energy inputs that accompanied rapid energy price increases was a major cause of the slowdown for at least 29 industries, including agriculture, mining, machinery, motor vehicles, fabricated metals, petroleum refining, electrical and gas utilities, paper, chemicals, textiles, food, services, trade, and others. Together those industries accounted for nearly 80 percent of the nation's total industry output in 1978.

Jorgenson's results also suggest a way to counter the adverse productivity effects of high energy prices in the future. The modeling equations show that over the entire postwar period the rate of productivity growth improved for 25 of the 35 industries whenever the price of capital fell relative to the price of the other inputs in the KLEM equation. Thus, Jorgenson concludes that policy changes that reduce the relative price of capital through tax abatement, increased depreciation rates, or other means can help to offset the adverse effects of high energy prices and return productivity growth to a more nearly normal rate by increasing the rate at which old capital stock is replaced by more energy-efficient capital stock. Similarly, productivity growth improved for 31 industries whenever the relative price of labor fell, suggesting that other fiscal changes, such as decreased personal tax rates, that lower the relative price of labor also will remove some of the productivity drag caused by higher energy prices.

The Quantity and Quality of Capital Investment

Total factor productivity depends in large part on how much of current output, measured as a fraction of GNP, the nation chooses to save and invest in renewing or expanding the economy's productive capacity. As Figure 2.1, "The Flow of the Economy," illustrates, a certain investment level is required for stable growth. If it drops below that level, output in the future gradually will decrease, and obviously the reverse holds true. Furthermore, if the efficiency with which today's investment can be translated into tomorrow's output decreases, the ratio of investment to GNP, in effect, must rise. To offset this decreased efficiency the nation either must trade some consumption growth for higher growth in investment or accept slower increases in standards of living. The consumption-investment trade-off is one of the most distinctive features of each scenario and defines to a great extent its growth potential.

The postwar range of investment ratios was reviewed to determine a feasible range of future ratios. That part of total investment most obviously related to the business sector is fixed nonresidential investment. It excludes savings invested in home building and business inventories, neither of which directly increases the nation's productivity. As Figure 3.3 demonstrates, a cursory review of the historical data would suggest that the ratio of fixed business investment to GNP has remained roughly constant over the postwar period and, in fact, registered an above-average value for 1979. A closer examination of recent investment trends, however, reveals that this ratio is misleading and must be adjusted.

First, the ratio should be calculated in constant rather than current dollars. Just because the price of capital goods has increased faster than other prices does not

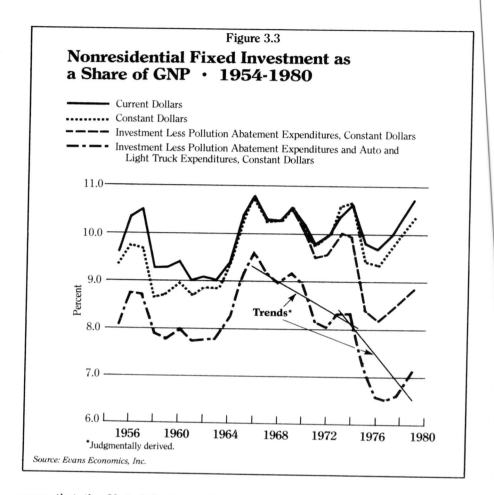

Figure 3.3

Nonresidential Fixed Investment as a Share of GNP • 1954-1980

——————— Current Dollars

·············· Constant Dollars

— — — — Investment Less Pollution Abatement Expenditures, Constant Dollars

— · — · — Investment Less Pollution Abatement Expenditures and Auto and
          Light Truck Expenditures, Constant Dollars

*Judgmentally derived.

Source: Evans Economics, Inc.

mean that the United States is devoting more of its real resources to capital formation. Changes in the quality of investment necessitate two other adjustments. Next, the investment figure should exclude capital spending to meet government mandated standards, for it does not expand the economy's productive capacity. Because data on such mandatory expenditures are not readily available, Figure 3.3 excludes spending only for pollution abatement and control. Consequently, the adjusted ratio understates the impact of government standards on the investment ratio although the deduction makes a noticeable difference. Second, investment in cars and light trucks, most of which are purchased for personal or quasi-business reasons, should be excluded because in many cases they do not represent productive business investments. Although the nominal ratio may have remained fairly constant, the real ratio of capital spending to GNP, once properly adjusted, exhibits a striking decline since the peak in the mid-1960s. On a trend-line basis, the real ratio dropped 13 percent during the first eight years after 1966 and experienced an equally severe drop over the next four years. In actual percentage terms the real ratio decreased from 9.6 percent of GNP in 1966 to 6.7 percent in 1978.

A parallel decline in the capital/labor ratio—the amount of capital available to support each unit of labor—demonstrates the declining investment ratio's impact on productivity. If one deducts the stock of environmental capital included in constant dollar net stocks of fixed nonresidential capital, it appears that the average worker had no more "productive" capital at his disposal in 1978 than in 1971. Part of the decline in the capital/labor ratio, of course, must be attributed to the wave of new workers that flooded the labor market in the late 1960s and 1970s. This surge in the labor force and the burgeoning capital requirements for meeting federal standards, in effect, have increased the level of fixed business investment necessary to maintain stable economic growth.

Over the last 15 years government spending has had a significant impact on investment as more and more of its total budget has been allocated to consumption and ever-smaller fractions to the construction of public physical facilities, or "gross capital formation" as it is termed in official statistics. Total government expenditures rose a dramatic 176 percent from 1955 to 1978, even though real GNP rose only 114 percent and population 32 percent. Table 3.5 reveals some significant changes in government spending patterns over this period. Defense, space, and foreign spending

TABLE 3.5
Real Government Expenditures by Function, 1955—78
(total of federal, state, and local)

	Percent Growth 1955—78	
National defense and space, foreign aid, and other international expenses	16	
General government, civilian safety, public utilities, postal service, and sanitation expenses	382	
Interest paid	113	
Highways, other transportation, communications, natural resources, and agricultural expenses	103	
Average Growth: Basic Functions		85
Health and hospitals, education, and housing	326	
Public assistance, old age, welfare, and veterans benefits	426	
Average Growth: Human Services		377
Total Average Growth	176	

Source: Survey of Current Business.

rose only 16 percent. At the other extreme, expenditures for direct transfer payments, such as public assistance and welfare, rose 426 percent. A division of these total expenditures into basic functions and human services shows that spending for basic functions rose about 85 percent while spending for human services rose 377 percent.

As a result, gross capital formation as a percentage of total government spending began to decline in the mid-1960s. Prior to that, fixed capital formation's share of total government expenditures for goods and services (exclusive of military spending) was remarkably stable, averaging more than 17 percent from 1955 to 1966. Since 1967, however, the ratio has been declining. In 1977 it actually was less than 12 percent of total government purchases for goods and services. The ratio's decline is even more dramatic when calculated in terms of total government expenditures—spending for goods and services plus transfer payments, military expenditures, net interest payments, and subsidies for government enterprise. This emphasis on present consumption over investing for the future parallels the government-induced behavior of the private economy, which also has emphasized consumption at investment's expense.

Certainly, continued reductions in government spending for capital goods in some areas, such as new schools, can be expected. However, other national needs may press the government to reverse some of its recent emphasis on consumption goods and services. Many analysts consider large public capital expenditures to be just as critical as private investment in any sensible national reindustrialization program.[11] It has been projected, for instance, that trucks will carry 50 percent more ton-miles in the year 2000 than they do today and that autos and buses combined will account for 25 percent more passenger-miles.[12] However, expenditures for building and repairing roads actually declined during the 1970s. In the late 1960s the government spent $13 billion a year in real dollars on roads but 1979's expenditures were only $6 billion, exactly what was spent in 1953 on roads. However, in the intervening period, the number of drivers increased 2.5 times, the number of autos doubled, and the number of trucks trebled. Furthermore, most of current road spending is localized in the growing areas of our country—the South and the Southwest. In the older, more established parts of the nation, roads and other public capital facilities are deteriorating rapidly. Clearly, the capital being devoted to the nation's roads is insufficient to maintain them, much less to expand them.

The financing of all government expenditures affects overall investment. Aside from very minor revenues from government enterprises that provide goods and services for purchase, everything the government spends comes from its citizens through taxing, borrowing, or inflating the currency. Only during 12 years since World War II have taxes been sufficient to cover all government expenses. Since state and local governments generally have been in a surplus position on the National Income and Products Account (NIPA) basis, the deficit-causing agent nearly always has been the federal government. In recent years, U.S. deficits often seem to result from Congress' reluctance to ask the voters to pay directly for all the spending programs that government has enacted, rather than from efforts to blunt the effect of recessions. From 1950 to 1960 the combined government deficit grew by some $10 billion.

During the 1960s it grew by almost $60 billion, and during the 1970s by some $360 billion.

The negative impacts on the investment process of this deficit spending depend as much on *how* the deficit is financed as on the *size* of the deficit. If the deficit is financed by money creation, via the Treasury and the Federal Reserve System, the effect is more inflationary than if it is financed through sales of debt securities to the private sector. However, if the deficit is large, debt sales to the private sector in amounts sufficient to avoid inflationary impacts will tend to crowd out new corporate financing efforts, since the level of savings is relatively inflexible over the short term given constant tax policies. This crowding-out can be offset to some degree if the state and local government surpluses can be directed to new corporate financing efforts. Unfortunately, these surpluses are primarily pension fund and other assets that typically are invested in very conservative securities—often, in fact, in government securities that finance housing, transportation, sanitation, and other public improvements. Thus, one part of the federal deficit generally ends up aggravating inflation and much of the rest tends to hinder private investment.

The midterm assumptions eliminated government deficits of any significance and fixed total government expenditures for goods and services (on a National Income and Products Account basis) at 20 percent of real GNP for all scenarios after 1990. The assignment of a fixed share of GNP reflects a judgment that the higher-growth scenarios will require—and revenue generation will permit—large public expenditures on streets, roads, mass transportation systems, sewage systems, and other infrastructure roughly proportional, in real physical terms, to the size of the economy. The lower-growth scenarios will experience similar needs but will have less revenue-generation capabilities because of slower growth of GNP and, thus, will be able to do less public rebuilding—in an absolute sense—than the higher-growth scenarios. The lower-growth scenarios are expected to shoulder a heavier burden of transfer payments to individuals than the higher-growth scenarios, but in the NIPA scheme, these payments show up as increased private consumption, not government spending.

Another integral part of total investment, particularly important to total factor productivity growth, is research and development spending (R&D). That small part of investment aims to make future output bigger or better or different—or all three. Although no single relationship between R&D expenditures and increases in economic output or productivity applies across all industries, most analysts generally agree that the decline in R&D spending trends since the mid-1960s has contributed to the recent slowdown in productivity growth.

Much of the decline has been due to a cutback in federally funded space and defense R&D. Although some observers argue that such research has little applicability to private output and productivity, others maintain that the by-products were often significant. For example, "from it we can now trace the electronics revolution; medical advances such as the pacemaker, which can be recharged through the skin; the laser for cutting, measuring, and communications; nuclear power; fuel cells; space satellites for weather, agricultural, and geological studies." [13] Thus, the drop in federal funding for basic research affects the private economy both directly and indirectly.

Many fear that R&D quality has changed as well. The President's Council of Economic Advisers and others have suggested that "the direction of industry's research and development activity may have shifted away from basic research and new product development in response to such influences as the changed regulatory environment." [14] As the economic uncertainties accompanying inflation and regulation have grown, R&D spending has shifted away from long-term, basic research programs, with their unknown pay-offs, to less innovative short-term applied research projects.

The changing distribution of private savings, especially since the mid-1960s, is also probably responsible for some of the recent changes in the quantity and quality of investment. True savings—personal savings and retained corporate earnings—have been decreasing for a number of years, while corporate depreciation has grown in importance. This shift toward depreciation accruals may have slowed the pace at which investment funds are channeled toward new, growing industries and away from old, static, or declining industries. A low-visibility source of investment funds, depreciation accruals are completely at the disposal of corporate management. Some managers almost automatically invest them in the corporation's current lines of business rather than first examining other and perhaps better growth and profit potentials.

Government regulation also has affected both the quantity and the quality of investment. Since the mid-1960s, private investment has been slowed by the uncertainties resulting from rapidly changing regulations. Businesses have been understandably reluctant to invest in expensive facilities with useful lives of 10 or 20 years when regulatory changes might render the facilities useless by the time they could be put in service. During this same period more and more of the investment dollars that were expended have been devoted to meeting pollution, health and safety, and other regulatory requirements. In 1978 private investment for environmental improvement was 4.7 percent of total outlays by all business and 8.7 percent of outlays by public utilities. In absolute terms, the utility industry spent approximately $3 billion for environmental capital and other industries spent $5 billion. Although the objectives of such investments are most often laudable, the investments do not produce marketable goods and services and, thus, their results generally are not reflected in GNP figures. In a market sense, they have decreased the efficiency with which today's investment can be translated into tomorrow's output. Therefore, unless total investment is increased, future GNP will be reduced below the level it would attain without environmental investment.

In the past, government choices embodied in fiscal and monetary policies, regulatory policies, and government spending and deficit policies have been predominant in influencing incentives to invest: in the recent past these policies increasingly have combined to *reduce* incentives. Government choices will continue to dominate in the future, but the calls for reindustrialization and economic rejuvenation are multiplying in and out of government and are beginning to change government's role from reducing to increasing investment incentives. Such change could increase the investment ratio substantially in the near future. Indeed, the ratio of fixed nonresidential investment to GNP most probably will have to increase just to sustain even a minimal level of economic growth. The postwar investment range, exclusive of expenditures for pollution abatement and control, is bounded by the 1966 high of 9.6 percent and the 1978 low of 6.7 percent. The future range deemed both necessary and feasible is from 8 to 10 percent. Of course, the nation's ability to attain these investment ratios by 1990 depends on the fiscal and monetary policies employed in the 1980s. The upper part of this range, in particular, is feasible only if it is assumed that tax and interest rates are altered to encourage greater investment. These assumed percentages exclude all spending for environmental capital other than that undertaken by the electric utility industry. This range of fixed business investment translates into a range of gross private investment ratios bounded by 17 percent in the high-growth scenario and 13 percent in the low-growth scenario. The preferred scenario employs an investment ratio of 16 percent and the continuation scenario a ratio of 14 percent.

Some reindustrialization proponents, such as Amitai Etzioni, have estimated that a serious reindustrialization effort would require the dedication of some 19 percent of GNP to investment spending over the next ten years, with most of it to be used for private productive facilities.[15] Such an abrupt increase might foster economic growth more quickly but would be impractical politically because it would cause an actual *drop* in consumption. More gradual increases in investment's share of GNP are assumed in this book because they result only in a slightly slower *growth* of consumption.

Because these assumed investment ratios exclude nonelectricity spending for environmental capital, it was necessary to develop input spending assumptions for all other industries. In keeping with the belief that low-growth societies will be more concerned about environmental cleanliness and less concerned about slower growth in material output than high-growth societies will be, it is assumed that environmental capital spending will constitute a larger fraction of total capital investment in lower-growth futures than in higher-growth futures. This volume assumes that in all scenarios these other industries will increase their expenditures at 3 percent per year in real terms, starting from a base of $5 billion.

The Efficiency of Labor Input

Both the inherent quality of the labor force and the allocation of that input throughout the economy are significant contributors to total factor productivity. Recent changes in both factors have contributed to the productivity decline.

The most sudden and dramatic of these changes was in the age-sex composition of the labor force. Members of the baby-boom generation began to enter the labor force in the late 1960s just as the major surge in female participation rates also began. Over 80 percent of the entire postwar increase in the 16- to 34-year-old labor force and about 70 percent of the increase in the female labor force occurred after 1965. This wave of inexperienced workers boosted training requirements rather suddenly and, in many occupations, forced major adjustments in traditional work patterns. The negative impact on the capital/labor ratio already has been noted. During these same years U.S. productivity growth rates first began to slip.

However, the adverse effects of these age-sex changes on U.S. productivity are largely behind us. In fact, as members of the baby-boom generation move into their most productive and heavily consuming years, and, later, into their most affluent and heavily saving and investing years, their impact on productivity should be positive. From 1960 to 1978 the ratio of primary workers—people 25 through 64 years of age—to the rest of the population shifted very little. In the 1980s, however, the significant shifts will be to a higher proportion of the most productive persons and a lower proportion of children, young adults just entering the labor force, and elderly persons. This shift augurs well for productivity growth over the rest of the century.

Another universally recognized shift coming to an end is the movement of labor out of the farm sector into nonfarm industry. This gradual reallocation of labor contributed to productivity growth up through the late 1960s because the agricultural sector traditionally has been less productive than the industrial and service sectors. However, as farming has been transformed technologically, the gap between farm and nonfarm productivity levels has narrowed. Furthermore, the percentage of the labor force engaged in farming reached 4 percent in 1978, with the consequence that the shift out of agriculture virtually has stopped. The boost that this long-term migration has given to the productivity of the overall economy for more than a century finally has come to an end.

Most experts agree on the impact of these first two trends on productivity growth. The range of opinion is much wider concerning another often-mentioned trend—the shift away from industry into services. Broadly defined, the service sector is that part of the economy that produces intangible output. While conventional wisdom sees the shift as a significant cause of the slowdown, its impact on total factor productivity growth is difficult to quantify because methods of measuring productivity are often less certain in the service sector than in other sectors.

TABLE 3.6
Output per Man-Hour in the Private Service Sector, 1950–77

Industry	Average Annual Percent Change		
	1950–65	1965–73	1973–77
Transportation	3.0	2.9	1.0
Communication	5.3	4.6	6.7
Utilities	6.1	3.5	0.2
Finance, insurance, and real estate	1.6	0.2	2.3
Trade			
Wholesale	2.6	3.4	−0.8
Retail	2.3	2.1	0.8
Other services	1.0	1.6	0.7

Source: American Productivity Center, Incorporated.

Table 3.6 presents the labor productivity trends for several service-sector industries. The range of growth rates, −0.8 to 6.7 percent, experienced by individual
service industries since 1973 suggests why generalizations about the impact of labor's
gradual shift to the service sector are difficult to make. Most experts attribute only a
small but continuing part of the productivity slowdown to this trend.

Gross Labor Productivity

This brief review of influences on total factor productivity growth suggests the
major uncertainties surrounding the causes of the recent slowdown; but it also
suggests the general consensus that investment, government spending and regulation, energy prices, and labor force trends all have contributed to this slowdown. All of
these trends will continue to be influenced to a significant degree by social and
government choices. The American people, as consumers, savers, and voters, have a
large measure of control over capital input and government regulation. Although
energy is a factor over which near-term control is limited, the United States can exert
some control over it in the mid- and long term. Admittedly, control over the shifting
allocation of labor among the agricultural, industrial, and service sectors is significantly limited; but the changing age-sex composition of the labor force is on the verge
of reversing and well may provide as sharp a boost to productivity in the 1980s and
1990s as it provided a brake in the 1970s. Despite the predominance of choice in many
of the productivity determinants, chance does play a significant role, particularly with
regard to resource availability (U.S. geology and international developments for
imported resources) and technology (effectiveness of R&D). Even though there are no
precise quantitative relationships between total factor productivity growth and its
determinants, the assumptions regarding the labor force, investment, government
spending, the cost of complying with environmental regulations, and energy prices
imply certain bounds for future gross labor productivity trends.

After analyzing past periods when conditions were favorable and unfavorable for
productivity growth and reviewing others' analyses, labor productivity assumptions
were developed for each scenario that are consonant with the economic environment
described by these other total factor productivity determinants. Table 3.7 presents

TABLE 3.7
Labor Productivity
Assumptions

Scenarios	Percent Annual Growth	Matching Period
High and Independence	2.86	1960−69
Preferred	2.24	1970−78
Continuation	1.85	1960−76
Low	1.23	1973−77

Source: Compiled by the authors.

these assumptions and the historical periods in which those growth rates actually were achieved.

The 2.86 percent average annual growth of the high-growth scenario corresponds to the growth of labor productivity experienced from 1960 to 1969 when real energy prices were declining, investment was peaking, and the full impacts of the changing composition of the work force and the changing regulatory environment were yet to be felt. Still, it is lower than the 3.2 percent annual rate of increase averaged from 1947 to 1967 when the labor force composition was more stable and less investment was diverted to environmental capital. The rate assumed for the low-growth scenario matches the 1973–77 period when energy price hikes repeatedly shocked the economy, the level of productive investment hit postwar lows, the total federal debt escalated at an unprecedented pace, and the composition of the labor force continued to shift dramatically. The continuation scenario employs an average annual labor productivity growth rate of 1.85 percent; this rate equals that achieved from 1960 to 1976, a mixed period in which real oil prices declined for 13 years and then rose sharply, while fixed nonresidential and R&D investment rose for the first 4 years and then dropped for the next 12. Thus, most of this period was characterized by good luck and growth-inhibiting policies. The preferred scenario's 2.24 percent growth rate is matched by the period 1970–78, which includes two periods of strong economic growth straddling the recession after the Arab oil embargo. Strong Keynesian growth policies dominated the years on either side of the recession, first to secure the presidential election of 1972 and second to assure recovery from the recession. Thus, the United States had a period of strong, if ill-advised growth policies coupled with bad luck. Although these numbers were used as modeling inputs, other assumptions related to total factor productivity reflect future conditions different from those that prevailed during past periods. These other assumptions alter labor productivity somewhat so that the final output from the models shows different productivity growth rates than were assumed as inputs.

Energy Assumptions

A society that evolves to make maximum use of abundant and cheap energy is particularly vulnerable to changes in energy availability and price. This condition both describes the recent energy history of the United States and, in part, explains its energy problems. Because the United States was forced to adjust to rapidly changing energy use patterns from a position of energy affluence, the effects were even more pronounced. The United States faced rapid and turbulent changes in energy supply and price in the 1970s, rendering an efficient conversion to a less energy-intensive society more difficult. Delays coupled with certain unfortunate decisions by government and business alike impeded a gradual shift from capital-intensive, energy-using equipment to more efficient replacements. In the final analysis, the cost has been borne by consumers and producers alike.

In 1970 the U.S. energy per capita consumption, like its GNP per capita, far and away outdistanced that of most other developed nations. Since that time, countries such as Japan and West Germany have enjoyed substantial productivity increases and, therefore, GNP growth, while using considerably less energy per capita than the U.S. record implies is necessary. Several factors mitigate the impression that the United States easily could have matched the rapid GNP advances of other industrialized nations over the same time period with reduced energy consumption. First, there is a substantial difference between refurbishing plants and equipment, as the United States has continued to do, and rebuilding economies devastated by war. Postwar recovery for countries like West Germany and Japan often allowed for—in fact, necessitated—installing equipment more modern than, and technologically superior to, that used in the United States. Additionally, the room for productivity improvements in these countries currently is much greater than in the United States, which registered such improvements far earlier and more extensively.

World Oil: A Chance Factor

The kind of transition the United States eventually will make to a less-energy-intensive economy and the speed with which that transition is accomplished relates directly to the world oil market. The availability and price of imported oil largely determines the costs of conventional alternatives, the intensity of U.S. conservation efforts, the rate at which synthetic fuels are developed, and many other energy-related issues. World oil prices, in turn, depend largely on two things: geologic and technological factors, and economic and political factors. Both determine production levels, especially in the Middle East, and the Middle East has become the focus of the world oil market. Its preeminent position is likely to be maintained, at least for the foreseeable future, given the fact that it produces 40 percent and has proved reserves equaling 60 percent of the world's crude oil.[16]

Such was not always the case. Not until 1965 did the Middle East replace the United States as the world's largest oil producer and, as recently as 1973, it supplied less than 15 percent of U.S. imports. Prior to 1973, oil prices were set by the international oil companies. Profits were shared, in effect, with producing countries through income taxes levied against the companies. As demand and production grew during the early postwar years, so did host governments' revenues. By 1959, however, supply exceeded demand, and the oil companies reduced their posted prices that year and the next. Consequently, revenues per barrel collected by the Middle East governments fell. Middle East governments responded by founding OPEC in the fall of 1960.

Initially, OPEC's objective was only to protect governmental revenues from such fluctuations. The member nations resolved to "study and formulate a system to ensure the stabilization of price by, among other means, the regulation of production. . . ."[17] However, the changes OPEC effected during the 1960s were confined to alterations in the methods of computing tax revenues. The international oil companies retained ultimate control over production and held prices fairly stable throughout the decade. Operating costs were declining, but the average per barrel revenue to Middle East governments was rising to the pre-1959 level.

Partly because of the stable prices and partly because of the continuing economic recovery of Western Europe and Japan, during the 1960s the industrialized world

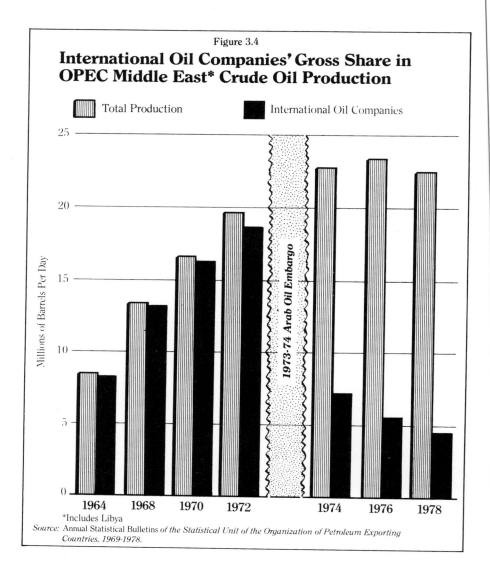

Figure 3.4

International Oil Companies' Gross Share in OPEC Middle East* Crude Oil Production

*Includes Libya

Source: Annual Statistical Bulletins *of the Statistical Unit of the Organization of Petroleum Exporting Countries, 1969-1978.*

became more and more dependent upon the Middle East as its primary energy supplier. By 1970 OPEC supplied over 85 percent of the world's crude oil exports.[18]

In 1971 OPEC, realizing its market strength, resolved to "establish negotiations with the oil companies . . . with a view to achieving effective participation in setting production and price levels."[19] As Figure 3.4 illustrates, by 1974 the OPEC countries had acquired majority interest in the producing properties. Between October 1973 and January 1974 the price of OPEC crude oil quadrupled; about the same time Arab governments ordered production cutbacks and embargoed shipments to the United States. Price and supply were no longer solely a function of demand, a fact further proved by the doubling of prices since 1974 and by the recent Iranian embargo. The international and domestic political, economic, and social concerns of producing countries influence both price and availability. What net importers once valued as a cheap, efficient input to their economies, net exporters now value as a powerful, yet depletable resource. Producing at maximum levels is not always consistent with optimum economic development: oil in the ground can be a good investment for the future.

Thus, the erratic price increases for Middle Eastern crude in the last decade reflect not only the strength of OPEC's position but also the world economy's current state of disequilibrium and the uncertainty surrounding both future supply and demand. The Middle East's and, more broadly, OPEC's political and economic concerns are tied to the world economy and, thus, are beyond the absolute control of a single nation or group of nations. Nonetheless, OPEC's strategy for addressing those concerns remains the overwhelming determinant of price and availability for the United States and Western Europe. The trend is clear and the principal conclusion to which it leads is even clearer: the United States now has very little choice about the availability and price of world oil. Therefore, this book's midterm assumptions treat oil and its influence on other energy options as predominantly chance factors.

In designing scenarios, conservation of energy, substitution of fuels, and the rates of new discoveries and technological advancements all play a role. This volume assumes that no mid- or long-term resource or technology constraints will render substitution impossible in the United States, but the nation's ability to substitute fuels is limited sharply in the short term. In some cases, such as that of motor gasoline, conservation is the only U.S. short-term option for lessening the impacts of shortages and price increases. Therefore, in this book domestic energy production, with the exception of nuclear plant construction, is restrained politically and socially only to insure environmental protection. Because the midterm model requires only price inputs for conventional fuels, the authors defer further discussion of their supply potentials until Chapter 5 and instead concentrate here on the production of energy from new sources, on installed nuclear capacity, and on prices, all of which were set exogenously.

Oil Prices

This volume projected world oil prices and then tied domestic oil prices to them. The authors solicited the expert advice of ICF, Inc., a Washington, D.C., consulting firm, to arrive at the world oil price projections. These assumptions incorporate ICF's views about possible political developments, ranges of world oil demand, the world oil resource base, and various technological developments relating to oil recovery.

The high-growth and continuation scenarios assumed good luck with regard to prices and supply availability—specifically, a 2 percent per year increase in real prices of world oil. Conversely, the preferred and low-growth scenarios assumed relatively bad luck on prices and supply availability—a 4 percent per year increase in real world oil prices. The differences between scenarios are attributed to chance factors: the state of international relationships, the unknown size of the world resource base, and the pace of technological advancements.

A variation of the high-growth scenario, the independence scenario, further examined the consequences of a 4 percent per year rise in real world oil prices. All of its other assumptions, except for installed nuclear capacity by the year 2000, replicate those of the high-growth scenario.

For all scenarios, decontrol of domestic oil prices was assumed. This book equates the average price of domestic oil in the United States in 1981 with the price of imported oil. This equality is maintained in future years across all scenarios, regardless of the size of the domestic resource base. The pace at which that resource base becomes economically recoverable, and thus can be translated into proven reserves, does vary with price, of course, and therefore does vary across scenarios. A refining markup of $2.08 per million Btus in constant (1978) dollars was assumed for all crude oil—across all scenarios. These refining costs were assumed to be fixed in real terms, regardless of crude oil price changes.

Natural Gas

The issue of decontrol is as important for natural gas as it is for oil, and the pricing of each is influenced by the other. Because oil and gas often can be used interchangeably, especially for industrial purposes, the deregulation of natural gas wellhead prices likely will push their prices to parity eventually. The desirability of natural gas, which both burns more cleanly than oil and offers a buffer against the U.S. oil import burden, argues for its near- and midterm significance. These factors suggest that natural gas prices could even rise above world oil prices, prompting the federal government to extend gas price controls into the late 1980s. For the purpose of deriving modeling assumptions for this project, pricing issues dominated.

Natural gas prices (measured at the wellhead) rose at an average rate of 2.4 percent per year from 1950 through 1973, and then climbed more rapidly as wellhead price controls of interstate gas rose to reflect the increasing values of all energy sources, especially oil.

In the present volume, all scenarios assumed complete decontrol of natural gas prices by 1985, with decontrol phased in gradually until that date. From then on, the price of natural gas was calculated as a function of the price of oil set for that scenario. The calculation links the prices per Btu of gas and petroleum first by equating the price of crude oil per Btu to the price of natural gas per Btu and, then, by decreasing the price of unprocessed natural gas 20 cents per thousand cubic feet because of the differences in transportation costs. Differences in refining costs mean that the delivered price of natural gas is not related directly to the delivered price of oil. The refining markup for natural gas, estimated in constant (1978) dollars per thousand cubic feet, decreases from 54 cents in 1985 to 52 cents in 1990 to 51 cents in 2000.

Coal Prices

Because of the abundant coal reserves of the United States, coal is not subject to the vagaries associated with imported resources that render them chance-dominated.

If the effects of mining and burning coal can be made more environmentally benign and if costs of transporting coal can be lowered, it will continue to gain the competitive advantage over other fossil fuels, particularly oil and gas.

Coal prices decreased at a rate of about 2.3 percent per year from 1948 until 1968, after which time mine safety regulations and the effects of the 1974 oil price increases combined to push coal prices upward. In this book coal prices are assumed to rise at different rates for each scenario, partly because of luck and partly because of policy. Technological developments are assumed to have a more significant impact than resource availability in determining what kind of luck the future holds for coal prices. Public policy related to mining and transporting coal also is expected to influence price measurably. Social and governmental choices are equally important in determining that policy. Coal price increases in real terms are assumed to range from a low of 0.5 percent per year in the high-growth scenario (with good luck and favorable policy) to a high of 2.0 percent per year in the low-growth scenario (with bad luck and growth-inhibiting policies). The rates assumed for the preferred and continuation scenarios are 1.0 and 1.5 percent, respectively.

Synthetic Fuels
The economics of synthetic fuels production depends on its cost relative to traditional alternatives. Thus, the world price of oil and the rate of technological advance will determine potential contributions from synthetics in future energy mixes. Rapidly rising oil prices stimulate the production of synthetic energy. With slowly rising oil prices, price inducements for synthetic developments are small, and government policies to encourage its development are of much greater consequence.

The capital and labor costs for synthetic oil and synthetic gas are the same for all scenarios. The synthetic oil costs are based on plans by Texaco for a synthetic oil plant—capital costs equal $18.1 billion (1978) per quadrillion Btus of capacity. Annualizing this at 18 percent gives a capital services cost of $3.3 billion per year per quadrillion Btus. A corresponding estimate for labor costs yields $774 million (1978) per quadrillion Btus. A comparison of three gasification plans shows gasification costs to be approximately 1.2 times liquefaction costs for equivalent Btu production. By the year 2000, these costs translate into a dollar per barrel price for synthetic fuel that will be at parity with the world oil price in the continuation scenario. This price will be slightly higher or lower depending on the coal price assumptions in the other scenarios.

In this book synthetics in the year 2000 contribute only one-half and one quad in the continuation and high scenarios, respectively, because of their lack of competitiveness with the world oil price; but in the independence, preferred, and low cases—with very high oil prices—synthetics make their maximum penetration, providing 5 quads in each scenario.

Solar Energy
The future production of solar energy, like that of synthetics, is assumed to depend primarily on the price of oil and secondarily on the rate of technological advancement.

Currently, economic and technological barriers inhibit the contribution solar energy can make to U.S. near- and midterm futures. Almost all of the 4.2 quad contribution that solar energy presently makes is from high-head hydro and biomass. Financial and institutional barriers to solar technologies are beginning to relax, however, and increasing contributions in residential and commercial systems (active and passive hot water heating and space conditioning) are becoming measurable. Low-head hydro turbines now are being imported from Switzerland and are expected to make increasing contributions.

For the purposes of this book, solar energy excludes hydroelectric power but includes all other energy forms, such as water and active space heating, winds, tides, solar electricity, and biomass. Passive solar heating is defined as conservation. The capital and labor costs for solar energy are identical for all scenarios. Figures supplied by the Solar Energy Research Institute give total capital and labor costs for solar energy of $10.06 million (1978) per trillion Btus. For input to the models, this cost is divided into 60 percent capital and 40 percent labor. It does not include the cost of back-up capital and labor needed to insure generation. Therefore, a barrel equivalent of solar energy will be priced slightly higher than the world oil price in the preferred case.

Because of the dominance of chance factors, the development of solar energy varies across scenarios. This book assumes a maximum contribution, excluding hydro, of 5 quads by 2000 in the independence, preferred, and low scenarios. Production is stimulated by the 4 percent increase in world oil prices. The lower oil price in the continuation scenario combined with the absence of government incentives to develop solar energy leads to the assumption that solar energy will contribute only 1 quad by 2000 in that scenario. In contrast, even though real oil prices rise at the same rate in the high and continuation scenarios, 2 quads of solar energy are assumed to be available in the high-growth scenario because public policy is more favorable to growth.

Nuclear Power

Nuclear power growth projections of the early 1970s presumed the electric utility industry's continuing rapid growth; but the pace of such growth has slowed, and nuclear penetration with it. As recently as the mid-1970s, electricity growth projections averaged 5.5 percent. The actual rate ranged from 6.3 percent in 1976 to 3.0 percent in 1979, a progressive downward shift.

Slower electricity growth, however, is not the sole cause for actual capacity's falling short of past projections. In the wake of Three Mile Island, a variety of barriers to nuclear power have evolved. In addition, financial constraints on many utilities have made it difficult if not impossible for them to raise funds in the amounts needed to support the on-going construction of capital-intensive nuclear facilities, let alone order new ones. These already severe financial problems consistently have been aggravated by social and political barriers. Since 1977 only two new nuclear reactor units have been announced and additionally a substantial number of reactor units on order or with construction permits pending have been canceled or delayed.

Slow growth, the effects of Three Mile Island, and current financial constraints have combined to induce a de facto moratorium on orders that could last through the mid-1980s. If at that time utilities start ordering plants with up to 12-year lead times, the first of these facilities could come on line in 1994, leaving only six years until the target date, 2000. Four companies now manufacture nuclear reactors. In order for competition to exist, at least two of these must remain in business; and they will remain so only if demand is sufficient. Each manufacturer probably can start five 1-gigawatt (gw) reactors a year. Thus, 10−20 reactors (depending on whether two or four manufacturers remain in business) might be expected to go on line every year from 1994 to 2000. Combining this 60−120 gw range with this book's estimate of the 150−175 gw of planned capacity (as of midyear 1978) provides a range of 210−295 gw by 2000. If the moratorium on orders extends longer, the range will shift downward; if it ends sooner, if plant lead times shrink, or demand allows the manufacturing industry to increase its output capacity in the 1990s, the range will shift upward. If sufficient nuclear capacity is not available, it is assumed that baseload coal generation will supply the difference. An upper limit of 300 gw of installed nuclear capacity in the year 2000 is assumed for all but the independence scenario, in which a 400 gw limit is employed. In that case, the combination of growth-favoring policies, high oil prices, and high energy demand act to reduce construction lead times and to increase manufacturing capacity.

Conservation

For the purposes of this book, conservation is defined as the price-induced process whereby capital and labor, and to a lesser extent materials, are substituted for energy in the KLEM equation. Thus, before settling upon energy supply and price input assumptions, a review of the current status and future potentials for conservation was needed. Particular attention was paid to energy markets in which regulation and other nonprice effects might be significant, since the present volume's models could not capture their effects.

Federal mileage standards will result in gradually increased annual petroleum savings over and above the amounts that would be saved if price restraints acted alone. By 2000 this incremental savings was calculated to be some 3 quads, or about one-third of the expected consumption without federal standards. The calculated effects of these standards were introduced into the midterm model projections for the preferred scenario as an adjustment to the model's price-based motor gasoline forecasts. The reduced consumption was achieved by introducing higher-than-market prices for petroleum in the transportation market. These higher prices then were used as a reference point in applying similar higher prices and lower motor gasoline forecasts in the other scenarios.

Long-Term Assumptions: 1995−2030

The long-term model focuses primarily on the energy-economy interactions that will characterize the equilibrium state emerging during the twenty-first century. To simulate alternative equilibrium states, the long-term modeling required three groups of input assumptions: those dealing with energy price, supply, and capital requirement relationships that do not change from one scenario to another; those concerning energy and economic factors that vary across scenarios; and those reflecting energy and economic measures that calibrate the ETA-Macro long-term model to the Hudson-Jorgenson and Baughman-Joskow models. The price and availability of various energy sources that distinguish each scenario are largely attributable to chance; the population and productivity growth rates, choice-dominated variables, also significantly influence the rate of economic growth achieved.

The first group of assumptions defines each of 16 energy supply or conversion technologies by their operating expenses and by the investment costs needed for each unit of output. These assumptions relate to both conventional and new fuel sources. In addition to existing fossil-fired generation (coal, oil, and gas), the long-term analysis considers several types of nuclear generation (light-water reactors with and without plutonium recycle, and breeder reactors), advanced solar electric and fusion generation, and hydroelectric, geothermal, wind, and other generation fueled by renewables. The long-term analysis also considers nonelectric energy supply technologies such as petroleum and natural gas, coal-based synthetic fuels, shale oil, direct uses of coal, electrolytic hydrogen, and nonelectric advanced energy systems that are identified only in terms of their cost and availability. The technical characteristics for this first class of assumptions were assumed to change from year to year.[20] The assumptions relating to electricity generation for the period after 2000 were calibrated to the assumptions required for the midterm modeling.[21]

After 2000 the second group of assumptions varys from one scenario to the next. The prices and quantities of coal, oil, and natural gas were projected to continue increasing at the same rates used in the midterm analysis. In addition, midterm assumptions about the availability of synthetic fuel and solar energy in 2000 were used as starting points. The 300 and 400 gigawatt limitations on installed nuclear capacity in 2000 imposed on the midterm analysis were eliminated from the long-term modeling assumptions. Instead, installed capacity after 2000 was allowed to grow in response to demand, limited only by the technical and capital constraints on construction that are part of the first group of assumptions. An additional nuclear limit was imposed, however, in the form of the maximum cumulative uranium reserves available at $135 per pound or less. This limit was set at 10 million short tons for the high-growth and independence scenarios and 4.5 million for the other scenarios.

This second group of assumptions also includes some important macroeconomic variables that enable the long-term model to project real GNP. The values for labor input depend on changes in the working-age population, labor force participation rates, the unemployment rate, and the average length of the workweek. While all of these variables were assumed to follow different trends for each scenario in the years prior to 2000, all but the working-age population were assumed to level off and remain unchanged at their 2000 levels in the twenty-first century. Thus, the only source of labor input growth in the long term is assumed to be increases in the working-age population.

These working-age population increases were adjusted from Census Bureau projections to the year 2030 to reflect varying immigration rates.[22] The immigration rates for each scenario were assumed to be the same as those used for the midterm analysis. The resulting figures for working-age population are shown on Table 3.8, which demonstrates the cumulative impact of these demographic assumptions. A comparison across scenarios reveals that the working-age population may differ by about 16 million people between the high- and low-growth scenarios in 2000, but by 2030 that gap widened to approximately 65 million people.

TABLE 3.8
Working-Age Population Assumptions, 2000–30
(millions of persons 16 years of age or over)

Year	High-Growth or Independence	Preferred	Continuation	Low-Growth
		Scenario		
2000	211.8	205.5	202.0	195.9
2010	235.1	225.2	214.7	205.4
2020	253.5	239.9	221.0	208.4
2030	271.9	254.1	223.3	207.3

Source: Compiled by the authors.

In addition to the labor input projections, the long-term modeling requires estimates of labor productivity growth in the years after 2000. To develop these estimates, this book compared the U.S. productivity record for the post-World War II era (which provided the target figures for the midterm future) with productivity growth over long stretches of U.S. history. The longer record showed generally smaller growth rates: about 1.8 percent annually over the 70 years prior to 1947 compared to 2.6 percent in the 30 years after 1947. This finding supplemented the authors' and their consultants' judgments that a combination of social constraints and physical resource limitations would tend to restrain growth after 2000. Thus, productivity growth assumptions for the long-term analysis were reduced to the figures shown in Table 3.9. Note that the targeted growth rate for the high-growth and independence scenarios after 2000 was reduced by nearly 40 percent compared to the 1978–2000 target for those scenarios. Targets after 2000 for lower-growth scenarios were reduced by lesser amounts and left unchanged for the low-growth scenario.

The third group of input assumptions was used to calibrate or link the long-term to the midterm analysis. Three inputs were used in this calibration process: the potential GNP growth rate, the elasticity of substitution between energy and capital and labor, and the elasticity of substitution between electric and nonelectric energy consumption. The potential GNP growth rate is the rate at which the economy would grow in

TABLE 3.9
Productivity Growth Rate Targets
(percent per year)

Scenario	1978–2000	2000–30
High-growth	2.86	1.80
Independence	2.86	1.80
Preferred	2.24	1.68
Continuation	1.85	1.48
Low-growth	1.23	1.23

Source: Compiled by the authors.

real terms if energy prices remain constant—again in real terms. These rates were derived by combining the estimates of the growth in labor input with the estimates of growth in labor productivity. The energy versus capital and labor elasticity is a measure of the ease with which capital and labor can be substituted for energy. With a given potential GNP growth and an increase in relative energy prices, for example, a lower value of this elasticity will lead to lower realized GNP and higher energy consumption. The electric versus nonelectric energy elasticity characterizes the ease with which electric energy can be substituted for nonelectric forms of energy. A higher value of this parameter will raise electricity generation as well as total energy consumption, but it will have only a secondary effect on realized GNP. Table 3.10 lists the values of these calibration assumptions that best matched the long-term model output to the midterm model output for the year 2000. These values were chosen by

TABLE 3.10
Calibration Assumptions for ETA-Macro

	Variables		
Scenario	Potential Real GNP Growth Rate 2000–30 (percent per year)	Energy versus Capital/Labor Elasticity of Substitution	Electric versus Nonelectric Energy Elasticity of Substitution
High-growth	2.49	0.35	0.40
Independence	2.49	0.35	0.40
Preferred	2.26	0.35	0.30
Continuation	1.58	0.35	0.30
Low-growth	1.20	1.20	0.40

Source: Compiled by the authors.

adjusting the three parameters iteratively and running the model until a satisfactory approximation was obtained.

The long-term model and the model systems used in the midterm analysis have vastly different structures and levels of detail. Because of these differences, the three parameters chosen for the calibration task can only act as approximate compensating devices. Variation of the three parameters permits the long-term results to be linked with the five sets of midterm scenario output but cannot provide for exact duplication of the two modeling systems' results. The calibration values that were chosen for the energy versus capital and labor elasticities illustrate the limits of such duplicating efforts. As seen in Table 3.10, a value of .35 for the energy versus labor and capital elasticity provided a good fit for four of the five scenarios, while in the low-growth case, the elasticity value had to be raised significantly to allow for greater substitution. This variation is due to a fundamental difference in the way the long-term and the midterm modeling systems treat technical progress. In the long-term model, the change in energy demand associated with economic growth depends only on the changes in GNP and energy price. In the midterm modeling systems, however, the growth in energy demand is sensitive to growth in the inputs of capital and labor and growth in productivity. When economic growth is due to productivity growth, less energy is required per unit of output because all inputs, including energy, are used more efficiently. In the midterm low-growth scenario, the sole source of growth is increased productivity—the greater energy needs to produce a higher GNP are almost exactly offset by gains in the efficiency of energy use. However, the long-term model must attribute all of the reduction in energy use per unit of GNP to price-induced conservation, because it uses aggregate primary energy to drive the economy. Thus, in the low-growth scenario, a very large amount of price responsiveness must be assumed.

The highly aggregate structure of the long-term economic model and the simplicity with which it treats energy-economy interactions prevents it from examining a number of likely long-term changes in the United States. It cannot consider, for example, the consequences of a change in the composition of GNP that decreases the relative consumption of goods and increases the use of services. It also cannot evaluate the changes in energy and other mineral consumption patterns that may be caused by international pressures from an increasingly crowded world. Nor can it reflect changing U.S. social and political trends. The model's limited ability to accommodate these and other changes biases it toward economic and energy growth. Therefore, as a supplementary assumption, the study has adjusted the raw long-term results to impose continuing gradual downtrends in energy-GNP ratios through the end of the long-term period. These decreases are assumed to average 1.0 percent per year for the low-growth scenario, and about 0.2–0.4 percent for the continuation and preferred scenarios, while in the high-growth scenario the energy-GNP ratio remains essentially constant after 2000. The relationship between these energy-GNP assumptions and those projected by the raw long-term results are discussed at greater length in Chapter 4.

	High	Inde-pen-dence	Pre-ferred	Con-tinuation	Low
TABLE 3.11 Summary of Scenario Assumptions					
			Demographic		
Fertility rate (1980–2030)	2.1	2.1	2.1	1.7	1.7
Immigration (1980–2030) (millions persons above 400,000)	0.6	0.6	0.3	0.3	0.0
			Labor Force		
Participation rates (percent in 2000–30)					
Male	76	76	75	69	68
Female	60	60	58	55	53
Hours per week (2000–30)					
Male	33	33	33	31	31
Female	31	31	31	28	28
			Productivity		
Gross labor productivity (AAGR)					
1980–2000	2.86	2.86	2.24	1.85	1.23
2000–30	1.80	1.80	1.68	1.48	1.23
Investment (percent of GNP)					
2000–30	17	17	16	14	13
Government spending (percent of GNP) 2000–30	20	20	20	20	20
Environmental capital (AAGR)					
1980–2030	3	3	3	3	3
			Fiscal Policy		
Wharton					
Personal income tax[a] (percent)					
First bracket (1980 and 1990)	[b]	[b]	11.4–12.8	11.4–13.1	11.4–13.1
Corporate income tax (percent)					
1980 and 1990			46.0–46.0	46.0–46.0	46.0–50.0
Investment tax credit (percent)					
1980 and 1990			15.0–30.0	15.0–10.0	15.0– 1.0
Evans					
Personal income tax (percent)					
Average rate 1980 and 1990	[b]	[b]	24.9–11.0	24.9–23.5	24.9–38.3
Corporate income tax (percent)					
1980 and 1990			46.0–20.0	46.0–46.0	46.0–46.0
Accelerated cost recovery (years)					
Structures 1980 and 1990			23.0–10.0	23.0–18.4	23.0–23.0
Equipment 1980 and 1990			10.5– 5.0	10.5– 8.4	10.5–10.5
			Energy		
Real coal price (AAGR)	0.5	0.5	1.0	1.5	2.0
Real world oil price (AAGR)	2.0	4.0	4.0	2.0	4.0
Solar quads in 2000	2	5	5	1	5
Synthetic quads in 2000	1	5	5	0.5	5
Nuclear gw in 2000	300	400	300	300	300

[a]Other tax brackets change in same proportion.
[b]This scenario was not specifically examined by the short-term models on the grounds that the fiscal assumptions employed in the preferred scenario would lead to this scenario sometime in the 1990s, given its other assumptions.
Source: Compiled by the authors.

Summary

This book's modeling assumptions divide into five groups: fiscal policy, demographic, labor force, productivity, and energy assumptions. Table 3.11 juxtaposes the principal assumptions employed. Reading across each row makes it possible to compare the values of individual assumptions in each scenario, thereby illustrating which variables were held constant (such as environmental capital expenditures) and which changed demonstrably across scenarios (such as immigration). Reading down each column yields a distinct characterization of the policy choices made and the luck encountered in each scenario.

For example, the lower birth rates, decreasing labor participation, and shorter workweeks of the low-growth scenario reflect that society's emphasis on leisure. Since government's share of GNP as well as environmental capital expenditures remain constant, and since overall investment is lower, workers have less productive capital with which to work. Therefore, gross labor productivity advances less rapidly. Fiscal policy further dampens the incentive to invest. The energy scene is equally restrained. High oil and coal prices make all energy prices higher and encourage a greater reliance on synthetics and solar technologies. Thus, the low-growth scenario assumptions for 2000 reflect the combination of bad luck and choices unfavorable to economic growth.

Comparing that future and the one described by the preferred scenario assumptions highlights the growth-favoring choices made by that society. The preferred scenario encourages higher fertility and immigration rates. More people elect to work, and those who do work longer hours; thus, labor dominates in this scenario, just as leisure did in the low-growth future. Fiscal policy encourages work, savings, and investment. The greater percentage of GNP directed toward investment translates into increased gross labor productivity. These growth-favoring economic policy choices combine to partly offset the bad luck of higher energy prices.

Good luck and policies favorable to growth characterize the high-growth scenario in 2000. It employs the same fertility rate and workweek as the preferred case, but higher immigration and participation rates. Both investment and gross labor productivity are at their highest in this society, and coupled with good luck on energy prices, they lead to greater economic growth than is experienced in the other scenarios.

The continuation scenario projects trends of the 1970s into the future. Fertility and immigration rates eventually slow the growth of the working-age population. Leisure and consumption—choices reinforced by government policy—continue to be favored at the expense of labor and investment. Despite its good luck regarding energy prices, these growth-inhibiting choices of the continuation scenario stunt gross labor productivity advancement and, consequently, the potential to expand the economy. Thus, as Table 3.11 illustrates, the range of potential futures that the United States might expect by 2030 is wide, as choices and chance events either offset or reinforce one another.

Notes

1. The numbers in the figure are keyed to the discussion in the text.

2. Capital and labor refer to capital and labor services, the primary inputs to the producing sectors of the economy. Energy represents the intermediate inputs produced by the coal mining, crude petroleum extraction, petroleum refining, electric utilities, natural gas utilities, and natural gas extraction industries. Materials represent the intermediate goods provided by the agriculture, nonfuel mining, construction, manufacturing (excluding petroleum refining), transportation, communications, trade, and service industries.

3. Richard Ainley Easterlin, "What Will 1984 Be Like?: Socioeconomic Implications of Recent Twists in Age Structure," presidential address to the Population Association of America, Atlanta, April 1978; Richard Ainley Easterlin, *Birth and Fortune: the Impact of Numbers on Personal Welfare* (New York: Basic Books, 1980).

4. "Desperate Ones," *Time*, October 8, 1979, p. 51.

5. David J. Blum and Sonja Steptoe, "The Immigrants," *Wall Street Journal,* September 17, 1980.

6. Ibid.

7. Dale W. Jorgenson, "Energy Prices and Productivity Growth," a report prepared for Edison Electric Institute, 1980, p. 1. Available from EEI upon request.

8. Evans Economics, Inc., "Supply-Side Economics for the 1980's," a report prepared for Edison Electric Institute, 1980. Available from EEI upon request.

9. Jorgenson, "Energy Prices."

10. For development of the model, see Dale W. Jorgenson and Barbara Fraumeni, "Substitution and Technical Change in Production," in *The Economics of Substitution in Production*, ed. Ernest R. Berndt and Barry Fields (Cambridge, Mass.: Ballinger, forthcoming).

11. See, for example, Amitai Etzioni, "Choose We Must," in *The Individual and the Future of Organizations*, Vol. 9 of the Franklin Foundation Lecture Series, ed. Carl A. Bramlette, Jr. and Michael H. Mescon (Atlanta: Business Publishing Division, College of Business Administration, Georgia State University, 1980), pp. 25–39.

12. U.S. Department of Transportation, "National Transportation Trends and Choices to the Year 2000" (Washington, D.C.: U.S. Government Printing Office, 1976); The Pace Co., "Energy and Petrochemicals in the U.S. to 1990," 4 vols. (Houston: Pace Co., 1976).

13. Perry Pascarella, "Our Technological Recession," *Across the Board*, December 1979, p. 61.

14. President's Council of Economic Advisors, "Annual Report 1979" in *Economic Report of the President* (Washington, D.C.: U.S. Government Printing Office, 1979), p. 70.

15. Etzioni, "Choose We Must."

16. Public Affairs Department, Exxon Corporation, *Middle East Oil*, 2d, ed., Exxon Background Series, September 1980, p. 2.

17. September 1960 OPEC resolution as quoted in *Middle East Oil*, p. 28.

18. *Middle East Oil*, p. 28.

19. September 1971 OPEC resolution as quoted in *Middle East Oil*, p. 30.

20. These energy price, supply, and capital requirement assumptions are the same as those outlined by the Technical Assessment Group of the Electric Power Research Institute's Planning Staff in *Technical Assessment Guide* (PS-1201-SR) (Palo Alto: EPRI, 1979).

21. These assumptions are based on those provided by the Electric Power Research Institute's Planning Staff in *Overview and Strategy: 1980–1984 Research and Development Plan* (PS-1141-SR) (Palo Alto: EPRI, 1979).

22. U.S. Bureau of the Census, *Current Population Reports*, series P-25, no. 704 (Washington, D.C.: U.S. Government Printing Office, 1977).

Chapter 4

SCENARIO RESULTS

Given the range of input variables assumed, it is not surprising that this book's modeling systems projected a range of alternative futures that expands significantly over the next half century. Figure 4.1 displays the broadest, simplest indicators of this range, the core scenarios' GNP growth paths. The differences between them are substantial: by the year 2000 real output in the high-growth scenario is almost 1.6 times larger than output in the low-growth scenario, and by 2030 it is more than 2.0 times larger.

This difference reflects the extent to which the KLEM equation—capital + labor + energy + materials = output—may reasonably be expected to shift. However, to construct detailed representations of the possible equilibrium states to which the economy may evolve requires examining other less aggregative indicators on both sides of the equation, such as the supply and demand for energy and the components of GNP. Also, like the input variables, different output variables are more enlightening in different time periods.

The challenge of the 1980s is to conquer the stagflation that has characterized much of the 1970s. Thus, in Figure 4.1 the short term is designated a recovery period. Because society can exercise more immediate control over capital-related choices— how much output should be allocated to consumption, to investment, and to government spending, and how that allocation should be achieved—than it can exercise over the size of the work force or the price and availability of energy supplies, the authors focus the discussion of short-term results primarily on the K variable of the KLEM equation. The Wharton and Evans models provide separate but similar statistical pictures of how the capital-formation process might shift in response to changes in fiscal policy and what the impact of those changes might be on productivity growth and economic recovery. The models also suggest how the economy may react to its current dependence on imported oil and to the decontrol of domestic energy prices.

The midterm results highlight the substitution processes that the KLEM formula may undergo as a new equilibrium state emerges. During this transition period, the relative contributions of the factor inputs to total output shift. The impact of those changes in the capital formation process instituted in the 1980s grows stronger, labor force composition and growth become relatively stable, and the availability of

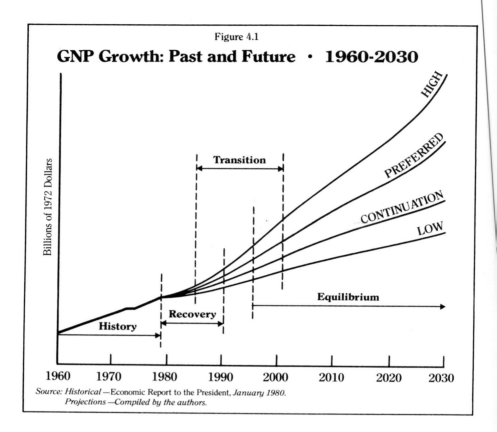

Figure 4.1

GNP Growth: Past and Future · 1960-2030

Source: Historical —Economic Report to the President, January 1980.
Projections —Compiled by the authors.

alternative energy sources becomes significant. Thus, this chapter examines in detail selected modeling results related to all three factors — capital, labor, and energy.

During the long term, when the economy has matured into a new equilibrium or steady state, the labor component of the KLEM equation becomes a progressively more significant determinant of GNP growth. The further one peers into the twenty-first century, the greater the cumulative impact of demographic assumptions. ETA-Macro results also anticipate significant variations, not only between scenarios but also within a given scenario, in the composition and price of the energy component. The substitution process occurring over the midterm—greater capital intensity, lessened energy intensity—may be reversed over the long term. If technological innovations provide reliable energy supplies at relatively stable costs, the economy may evolve once again, as it did prior to the early 1970s, toward greater use of energy inputs. Therefore, the discussion of the long-term results concentrates on a few broad economic indicators, especially those tied to population, and on the crucial role of energy technology.

Economic Recovery: 1980–90

Introduction

Since the early 1970s the economy has been mired in stagflation. Real GNP advanced on average 2.3 percent per year from 1973 to 1978, more slowly than the postwar average.[1] The recession of 1979–80 and the economy's laggard recovery from the 1973–74 recession indicate that the economy is suffering from chronic inertia exacerbated by temporary external stresses such as oil supply disruptions and price shocks. Productivity growth remains stagnant and inflation remains at unacceptably high levels.

Figure 4.2 displays the actual GNP growth path of the past two decades and those projected for the 1980s by the Evans and Wharton models. It also depicts the midterm preferred and continuation scenarios, which served as short-term modeling targets. As the figure suggests, the stagflation that has plagued the economy in recent years cannot be overcome easily or quickly. Not until the mid-1980s do the preferred scenarios emerge as futures significantly distinct from a continuation of the recent trend. Low-growth futures, however, are identifiable as early as 1982. The high-growth scenarios develop early in the midterm if the fiscal policies employed in the preferred scenarios are continued and real energy prices increase only 2 percent annually. The uppermost average annual GNP growth rates projected by the demand- and supply-side models, 3.2 percent and 3.6 percent, respectively, both fall far short of the 4.3 percent average annual growth experienced from 1960 to 1969. In fact, both models' continuation cases average 2.8 percent annual growth, somewhat better than the 2.3 percent of the 1973–78 period, a low point in our postwar economic history. The models suggest that even slower growth is entirely feasible. The Wharton low-growth case averages 1.8 percent average annual growth and the Evans low-growth case averages 1.6 percent. The general story told by Figure 4.2 is that, even in the best of probable futures, economic recovery will come more slowly and with greater difficulty than in any other part of the postwar era.

TABLE 4.1
Real GNP
Average Annual Growth Rates, 1980–90

	Preferred	Continuation	Low
Evans	3.6	2.9	1.6
Wharton	3.2	2.8	1.8

Source: Compiled by the authors.

The figure tells a second story as well, one important for interpreting the policy implications of the modeling analyses. The spectrum of possible futures projected by the supply-side model envelopes the range projected by the demand-oriented model. Table 4.1, which presents the GNP growth rates averaged in each model, highlights the difference between the ranges. The greater variation in the Evans model is

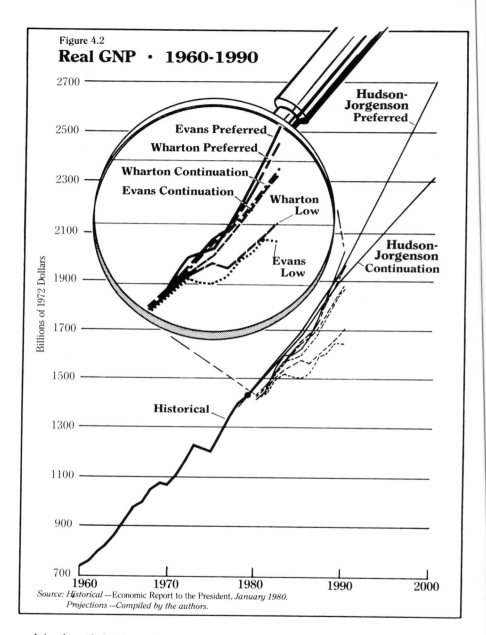

Figure 4.2
Real GNP • 1960-1990

Source: Historical —Economic Report to the President, *January 1980.*
Projections —Compiled by the authors.

explained partly by the wider range of fiscal policy assumptions it employs. Although the Evans model explores changes in tax rates and government spending patterns that are inappropriate to traditional Keynesian theory, they are entirely reasonable from the perspective of supply-side growth theory. Supply-siders argue that the fiscal policy employed since World War II, especially since the mid-1960s, has been one of the most significant causes of stagflation and must now be counteracted with policies that more directly stimulate the economy's supply side.

TABLE 4.2
Productivity Growth
(AAGR, 1980–90)

	Preferred	Continuation	Low
Evans (output per man-hour)	2.0	0.9	0.3
Wharton (output per employed person)	1.9	1.3	0.7

Source: Compiled by the authors.

Related to this belief and also contributing to the disparity between the model projections are the differences in the labor productivity measures they employ. Although the growth rates, provided in Table 4.2, suggest that the two modeling systems treat productivity identically, there are substantial dissimilarities. Because productivity in the supply-side model is more directly related to investment and the model's wider range of tax policies produces a wider range of investment ratios, the contribution of productivity to GNP growth is also greater in the Evans model than in the Wharton model. Other differences also make the two sets of scenarios less than absolutely comparable. For instance, oil prices in the Wharton model are slightly lower than they are in the Evans model. Also, the projections almost always begin at slightly different 1980 starting points. Still, the two models' outputs exhibit dissimilarities primarily because of the differences in their fiscal policy assumptions and internal dynamics, differences attributable to the dissimilarities between the two growth theories associated with them.

The Investment Prerequisite

Although both models identify the chief cause of stagflation as a chronic investment deficiency, their prognoses for the economy's recovery differ. As Figure 4.3 reveals, the supply-side fiscal prescriptions effect more rapid and dramatic changes in investment's share of GNP than the demand-oriented tax assumptions. Because the models employed different 1980 starting points, the average annual growth rates given in Table 4.3 are a more valid basis for comparison. The most striking conclusion is that both models suggest that the investment ratio must increase merely to reach the relatively modest growth path of the continuation scenario.

The average annual growth rates (AAGR) of real private, nonresidential fixed investment expenditures projected in the continuation scenarios are substantially higher than the 2.7 percent averaged from 1969 to 1979. In fact, to reach the preferred scenario growth track by the end of the decade required that such spending increase

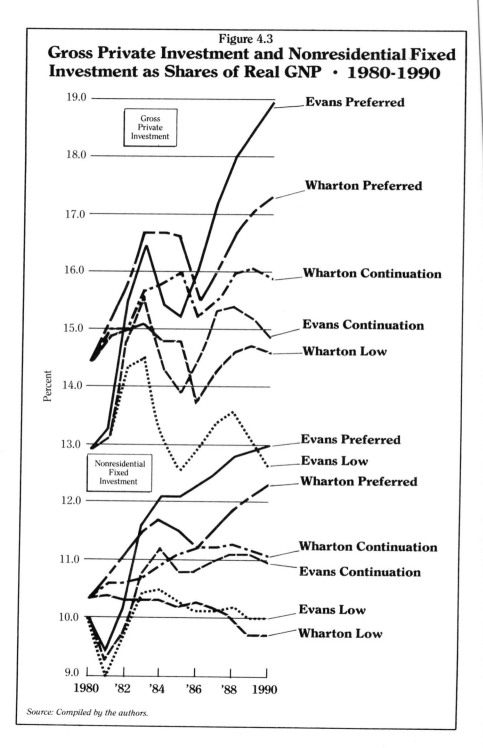

Figure 4.3
Gross Private Investment and Nonresidential Fixed Investment as Shares of Real GNP • 1980-1990

Source: Compiled by the authors.

TABLE 4.3
Real Private Nonresidential Fixed Investment
(AAGR, 1980–90)

	Preferred	Continuation	Low
Evans	6.45	3.96	1.54
Wharton	5.04	3.57	1.16

Source: Compiled by the authors.

more rapidly than the 4.7 percent (AAGR) achieved from 1957 to 1969 during the postwar investment boom. Although the absolute level of private, nonresidential fixed investment is increasing in the low-growth scenarios, the ratio of these expenditures to real GNP remains at or below its 1980 value. In all other scenarios investment grows more rapidly than GNP.

The Investment-Consumption Trade-Off

The increase in the investment ratio is paid for partially by a decrease in the consumption ratio. Figure 4.4 illustrates that the demand-side model relies more heavily on this trade-off than the supply-side model. In the Wharton results, consumption's GNP share increases only in the low-growth scenario, and even then the increase is only one percentage point. The Wharton preferred scenario requires the most severe drop in consumption ratio, a decline of 3.4 percentage points over the ten-year period. The Evans scenarios require somewhat less short-term sacrifice. In the Evans preferred scenario, the consumption ratio does decline 3.2 percentage points, but in the continuation scenario its share increases slightly, 0.7 percentage points, and in the low scenario it rises 3.0 percentage points. Table 4.4 presents these short-term consumption ratio trends.

TABLE 4.4
Consumption as a Share of Real GNP
(AAGR, 1980–90)

	Preferred	Continuation	Low
Evans	−0.50	0.11	0.45
Wharton	−0.54	−0.28	0.15

Source: Compiled by the authors.

An examination of the scenario's real levels of consumption expenditures more fully reveals the choices characteristic of each society. In no case does consumption spending decrease in absolute terms; rather, the pace of its growth relative to GNP growth varies. In the Evans preferred scenario, for example, GNP grows on average 3.64 percent each year over the decade while consumption growth averages only 3.13 percent each year. Subtracting the second from the first yields a useful approximation

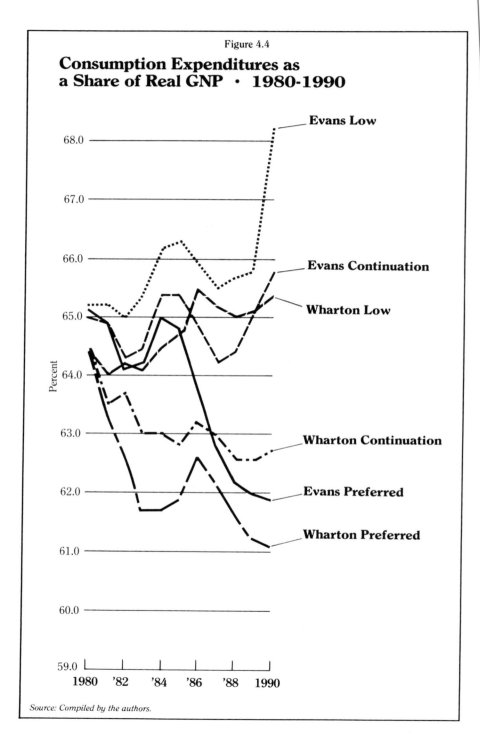

Figure 4.4

Consumption Expenditures as a Share of Real GNP · 1980-1990

Evans Low

Evans Continuation

Wharton Low

Wharton Continuation

Evans Preferred

Wharton Preferred

Percent

Source: Compiled by the authors.

of the average annual percentage rate of the decline in consumption's share of GNP: 0.51 percent. The growth in consumption expenditures experienced in each scenario is given in Table 4.5. The higher-growth societies choose to consume relatively smaller shares of their economic output than the other societies. In absolute terms, however, those shares are substantially larger than the ones consumed in the lower-growth societies because higher-growth societies produce greater output. This distinctive trade-off between consumption and investment chosen by each society sets them on diverging GNP growth paths.

TABLE 4.5
Real Consumption
(AAGR, 1980–90)

	Preferred	Continuation	Low
Evans	3.13	3.02	2.03
Wharton	2.64	2.47	1.95

Source: Compiled by the authors.

How each society chooses to distribute its consumption expenditures among durable goods (automobiles, appliances, books, and so on), nondurable goods (food, clothing, drugs, gasoline, and so on), and services (dry cleaning, medical care, television repair, music lessons, and so on) further distinguishes it from other societies. Both models' results suggest a continuation of a long-standing trend: a slowing of growth in spending for nondurable goods offset largely by a quickening of growth in spending for services with relatively less change in durable goods spending. Output from the Evans model scenarios, presented in Table 4.6, illustrates this trend in terms of real dollar consumption.

TABLE 4.6
The Changing Distribution of Real Personal Consumption,
1980 and 1990
(percent of total personal consumption)

	1980*	1990		
		Preferred	Continuation	Low
Durable goods	14.8	17.4	15.5	14.7
Nondurable goods	37.8	32.1	32.7	29.9
Services	47.4	50.5	51.8	55.4

*From Evans low-growth scenario.
Source: Compiled by the authors.

More interesting, however, is the increasing emphasis on durables at the expense of services in higher-growth scenarios. Because upper income groups generally have adequate stocks of durables and nondurables, when income rises, as it does in the

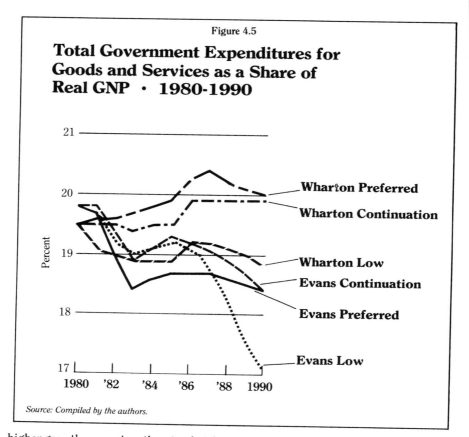

Figure 4.5

Total Government Expenditures for Goods and Services as a Share of Real GNP · 1980-1990

Source: Compiled by the authors.

higher-growth scenarios, they tend either to save more or spend more on services. Given sufficient savings incentives, they devote more of their increased income to savings and less to services. Lower-income groups, on the other hand, respond to the high-growth environment by concentrating on the purchase of durables. In the lower-growth scenarios, societywide purchases of durables are markedly lower because of the reduced purchasing power of the lower income groups. Limited savings opportunities and lower rates of returns cause the higher income groups to concentrate more heavily on services—the only form of consumption spending that holds significant attraction for them.

The Public Sector's Role

Projections of the growth of combined government expenditures for goods and services as a percentage of GNP epitomize the fundamental difference between supply-side and demand-side economic theories. As evident in Figure 4.5, the supply-side model consistently reduced government's share of GNP in order to stimulate growth. In contrast, the greater the economic growth projected in the demand model, the greater the share of government spending. Each phenomenon is the logical consequence of the growth theory embodied in its particular model.

In the Wharton model, the public sector is the conduit through which the flow of income in the private economy is redirected from consumption to investment. By altering investment tax credits and adjusting personal income tax rates to offset resulting revenue changes, the government controls the trade-off made. The greater the trade-off—that is, the higher investment and the lower consumption—the greater the flow of income through the public sector. Real government spending grows slightly faster than real GNP in the higher-growth scenarios and slightly lower in the low-growth scenario. The actual share averages 0.25 percent annual growth in the preferred scenario, 0.20 percent in the continuation scenario, and −0.37 percent in the low-growth scenario.

In the Evans model, on the other hand, the capital formation process is most efficient when less income is siphoned through the public sector. Indeed, reducing federal government revenues as a percentage of GNP was a conscious objective of the fiscal policy assumptions employed in that model. As a result of investment-stimulating tax reductions, the economy expands faster than government revenues in the Evans preferred and continuation scenarios, although, in absolute terms, they too are growing. For both scenarios, the average annual growth of the government spending/GNP share is −.74 percent. The fact that the ratio declines fastest in the low-growth scenario, −1.48 percent (AAGR), is not anomalous to supply-side theory. Because statutory tax rates are held at 1980 levels in that scenario, real government revenues remain virtually constant. Without investment incentives, the economy expands much more slowly, but, primarily because the labor force continues to grow,

TABLE 4.7
Total Federal Government Expenditures as a Share of Real GNP, 1980 and 1990

		1990		
	1980[a]	Preferred	Continuation	Low
Wharton model projections				
Goods and services[b]	9.9	8.9	9.1	8.8
Transfer payments[c]	12.8	14.4	14.5	15.5
Total	22.7	23.3	23.6	24.3
Evans model projections				
Goods and services[b]		11.1	11.3	10.4
Transfer payments[c]		5.7	13.0	17.2
Total		16.8	24.3	27.6

[a] Averages of slightly different Wharton and Evans model figures for 1980.

[b] Goods, services, net interest payments, and subsidies less surplus of government enterprises.

[c] Transfer payments and grants-in-aid.

Source: Compiled by the authors.

GNP does increase; since tax revenues do not, the ratio of government spending to GNP is lowest in the low-growth scenario.

The impact of federal government spending on economic growth is clearer if federal outlays for goods and services are isolated from the state and local government spending data and combined with all other federal expenditures, such as interest and transfer payments. Table 4.7 presents these data in terms of GNP percentage.

In all three Wharton scenarios, the federal government controls a slightly larger share of national income in 1990 than it does in 1980, although in no case is the increase greater than 1.6 percentage points. The composition of federal expenditures changes significantly, however. Spending for goods and services grows more slowly than GNP, while transfer payments grow significantly faster than GNP in all scenarios. Both trends are strongest in the low-growth scenario, but because these shifts offset one another, total federal expenditures as a percentage of total output are only 1 percentage point higher in the low-growth scenario than in the preferred scenario.

In contrast, the supply-side model's projections vary by almost 11 percentage points. The greater variation results primarily from the exogenously set differences in transfer payments growth rates. Thus, in all six scenarios, transfer payments and total federal spending (as GNP percentages) decrease as the economy's growth rate increases, while federal purchases of goods and services retain a relatively constant share of GNP regardless of the growth rate. The Evans preferred scenario best typifies these trends.

An alternative Evans run suggests, however, that GNP growth on or above the preferred path can be achieved even if federal spending increases at a rate nearly equal to that in the continuation scenario. In the Evans continuation scenario, federally funded transfer payments increase 11.6 percent annually (current dollar). Taking into account inflation and population growth, this growth rate is necessary to keep benefits at current levels. Not surprisingly, this assumption, when combined with tax assumptions identical to those of the preferred case, generates a variant preferred scenario in which GNP growth approximates the preferred scenario and government spending approximates the continuation scenario. Of course, by 1990 the combination also results in a budget deficit of some $500 billion in current-dollar terms. Although this deficit amounts to nearly 7 percent of the GNP in 1990, and thus is even larger than the postwar record of 4.6 percent in 1975, it is economically feasible. Because of the tax reductions, much of the dissaving by government is funneled into saving and investment in the private sector, thus boosting economic output and efficiency and keeping inflation within bounds, although at higher levels than in the preferred case.

In the Evans preferred case, the $500 billion deficit was eliminated wholly by a reduction in the real level of federally funded transfer payments and their inflationary impact. Specifically, $75 billion was saved through lower inflation; $115 billion was eliminated by tying Social Security and other government retirement benefits to the personal consumption deflator rather than the consumer price index; $200 billion was erased by raising the retirement age in one-half year increments each year over the next decade; $50 billion was saved by instituting deductible and "co-pay" provisions for medicare benefits, under which patients would pay the first $100 of their annual medical expenses plus a portion of the remainder, but with an absolute maximum of 10 percent of their income; and $70 billion was saved by slowing the growth of other programs such as food stamps and welfare programs.

Although some of these changes seem sharp at first glance, it is important to note that benefits sponsored by state and local governments grow faster than inflation; the increased retirement age does not fully offset longevity increases gained since 65 was established as the official retirement age; the changes will take place over a 10-year period during which the economy will be moving from a labor-surplus to a labor-shortage condition; the Medicare and other benefit programs still will be increasing at about 5 percent per year, and the entire process will take place in a rapidly growing economy with expanding employment opportunities.

Of course, other government spending categories also could be called upon to help erase the $500 billion deficit. The lower inflation in the no-deficit case, for example, would permit a $100 billion reduction in federal, state, and local spending on goods and services without any reduction in real terms. Another $125 billion could be saved by paring the growth rate for these goods and services from 10.7 to 9.7 percent per year. The first of these effects could offset half of the increase in retirement age assumed and the second could eliminate fully the need for the medicare and other welfare program savings.

Based on traditional multiplier analysis, one might expect that the $500 billion current-dollar decrease in government spending would slow the rate of GNP growth because of the resulting decline in consumption, and initially it does. However, that is not all that happens. The reduction in the federal government budget deficit lowers interest rates, thereby stimulating capital formation. The lowered cost of capital induces higher productivity growth. Higher productivity, in turn, lowers the rate of inflation and again reduces interest rates. Lower inflation and lower personal income taxes slow wage gains, thereby lowering the cost of labor. Additionally, since income is redistributed to those who are working away from those who are not, labor force participation rises, which provides the additional labor inputs needed to complement increased capital spending. Thus, although real GNP growth is about 0.5 percent per year higher for the large-deficit alternative in the early 1980s, the pattern reverses in the second half of the decade as these supply-side changes work through the economy.

Both of these high-growth scenarios are economically feasible futures. However, given the current social and political mood of the nation, the large-deficit alternative does not seem likely. Furthermore, even though this analysis indicates that high growth and a balanced budget can be achieved simultaneously over the next decade, it also indicates that doing so will not be easy. In fact, both the demand- and supply-oriented models tend to rely on government deficits to spark the economy's recovery and to show that government surpluses will prolong its inertia. Thus, when the ten-year average federal government surplus or deficit positions projected by Wharton are expressed in 1980 dollar terms, they range from a $28 billion surplus in the low-growth scenario to a $27 billion deficit in the preferred scenario. Similarly, the

Evans projections range from a $12 billion surplus in the low-growth scenario to an $8 billion deficit in the preferred scenario.

The Energy Factor

In all scenarios the real cost of energy increases relative to the costs of the other principal factor inputs—capital and labor. The economy responds by turning to cheaper inputs and becoming less energy intensive, as evidenced by the decline in the energy/GNP ratios projected by the Wharton model. Table 4.8 presents 1980 and 1990 end-year levels of real GNP, primary energy consumption, the economy's primary energy intensity, and the imported oil needed to supplement domestic oil and gas supplies in order to sustain that relationship. The continuation case employed "good-luck" energy prices—oil increasing annually 2 percent above inflation, natural gas increasing at that same rate after full decontrol in 1986, and coal prices growing 1.5 percent annually. Therefore, the energy/GNP ratio declines at a slightly slower pace in that scenario than in the preferred and low-growth scenarios. The preferred scenario has considerably less favorable energy prices: although the real rate of growth of coal prices does decline to 1 percent, both oil and natural gas are assumed to grow at an average annual rate of 4 percent. As a result, even though GNP in the preferred scenario is higher than in the continuation case, energy consumption in the preferred case does not exceed that of the continuation scenario until late 1989, as shown in Figure 4.6. Thus, the energy/GNP ratio reduction is larger in the preferred scenario. The low-growth scenario also assumes 4 percent annual increases in the prices of oil and natural gas, but, in addition, it assumes a 2 percent annual increase in the price of coal. Energy as a result becomes somewhat more expensive than in the preferred scenario and energy consumption actually dips below current levels, driving the energy/GNP ratio down further a fraction of a percent. Energy consumption in this scenario is considerably lower than in the other two because of the lower level of economic activity. In fact, as Figure 4.6 makes apparent, even in the preferred and continuation cases, energy consumption grows very little during the early 1980s. The economy does not gain substantial ground against stagflation in either scenario until the second half of the decade; thus, energy prices rise more rapidly than real income. Until the economy begins to recover its equilibrium, GNP growth is stunted and little growth in energy consumption is required. Consequently, the midterm energy consumption trends are not foreshadowed until 1990.

What these projected energy/GNP ratios mean in terms of each economy's dependence on imported oil depends, of course, on domestic supply assumptions. Based on price assumptions provided by the authors and ICF, Inc., the Wharton modelers assumed domestic oil production to be constant across scenarios through 1990. The natural gas supply/demand balance, on the other hand, is assumed to vary in response to the price assumptions. The authors believe the domestic oil and natural gas supply assumptions to be unduly pessimistic. The United States probably has greater short-term supply potential than was modeled; consequently, import requirements probably are overstated in all scenarios. Nonetheless, an examination of Table 4.8 reveals that even if 1990 domestic oil and gas supply has been underestimated by

TABLE 4.8
The Changing Energy Factor, 1980 and 1990
(Wharton scenarios)

	1980	1990		
	(preferred case)	Preferred	Continuation	Low
GNP (billion 1972 dollars)	1,430.90	1,960.60	1,878.70	1,707.50
Primary energy consumption (quads)	78.56	87.46	86.80	75.89
Primary energy intensity				
(thousand Btus/1972 dollar)	54.90	44.61	46.20	44.44
Petroleum				
Domestic (quads)	19.11	16.83	16.83	16.83
Imports	18.27	19.47	18.56	13.27
Exports	.57	.39	.39	.39
Total petroleum domestic supply	36.80	35.90	35.00	29.71
Natural Gas				
Domestic (quads)	18.68	14.94	16.07	12.85
Imports	.83	.06	.14	.03
Exports	.06	.06	.06	.06
Total natural gas domestic supply	19.44	14.94	16.15	12.82

Note: Columns may not yield totals due to rounding.
Source: Compiled by the authors.

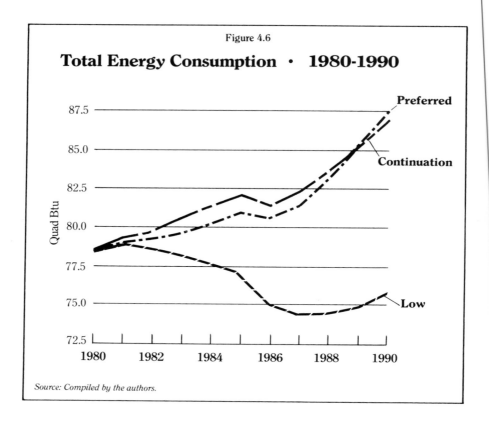

Figure 4.6

Total Energy Consumption • 1980-1990

Source: Compiled by the authors.

as much as 10 quads, the U.S. economy will not be rid of its dependence on imported oil in any likely short-term future. In relative terms, the dependence on oil is similar for all scenarios because of the temporal mismatch between domestic primary energy supply and end-use demand. Only in the low-growth scenario is the import requirement significantly reduced by 1990, but only because of the much lower rate of GNP growth. The energy intensity of the low-growth economy nearly matches that of the preferred scenario's economy. Thus, the low-growth society's economy is almost as dependent on oil imports as the preferred society's. In the low-growth scenario 17.5 percent of total energy consumption is derived from imported oil, while 22 percent is derived from imported oil in the preferred scenario.

In all scenarios, the rising cost of world oil induces an expansion of the domestic energy sector's capacity to produce coal and coal-generated electricity, but the utilization of these energy sources on the demand side of the economy initially lags far behind. The combination of inflation and long lead times makes the task of retrofitting or replacing capital stock in order to convert to alternative fuels slow and costly. Hence, domestic energy capacity is not utilized fully and the economy's dependence on imported oil and oil in general does not begin to vary greatly across scenarios until early in the midterm. A similar imbalance has occurred recently in the automobile industry, although in that case the domestic capacity to supply small fuel-efficient vehicles is lagging behind consumer demand. However, the net impact has been the same — dependence on imports.

The substitution process — away from oil to other energy sources — is sensitive to income, prices, and investment. As Figure 4.6 demonstrates, total energy consumption grows most slowly during the early 1980s in those scenarios generated with the highest price assumptions. However, the investment-stimulating fiscal policy employed in the preferred scenario enables the energy sector to expand its capacity to supply energy other than oil. This supply capacity shift anticipates the shift in end-use demand that occurs as the total economy's underlying capital stock evolves toward greater use of less-expensive coal and electricity generated from both coal and uranium. This conversion's impact begins to be apparent on the demand side in the late 1980s when total energy consumption in the preferred scenario surpasses the level projected for the continuation scenario, despite the fact that oil is cheaper in the continuation scenario. Because the investment ratio in the continuation case is lower, the turnover of capital stock is slower. The lower investment ratio and the lower world oil prices inhibit the substitution process, and the continuation scenario's economy requires almost as much imported oil (18.56 quads) to maintain its modest rate of growth as the preferred scenario's economy needs (19.47 quads) to produce its much larger GNP. In both the preferred and low-growth scenarios, an upswing in energy consumption occurs at the end of the decade as the substitution process begins to alleviate this dependence on oil, although, of course, the temporal lag between supply and demand is exacerbated in the low-growth society by the low investment ratio. To varying degrees this imbalance remains in all scenarios throughout the short term. A fuller discussion of energy results, therefore, is reserved for the midterm.

The Productivity Pay-Off

The critical impact of the current decade's investment decisions on the economy's recovery from stagflation is evident in Figures 4.7 and 4.8. The increased investment in the preferred scenarios translates into increased productivity, which, in turn, translates into lowered inflation. Without increases in investment, productivity growth continues its recent disappointing performance and inflation continues to climb, as they do in the low-growth scenario. Both the supply- and demand-oriented model projections illustrate this inverse relationship between productivity and inflation. This inflationary spiral, whether characterized as demand-pull or cost-push, can be broken only by reducing demand and/or increasing supply. The two must be balanced to achieve stable, noninflationary growth.

The fiscal policy assumptions for the Wharton model act on both demand and supply simultaneously. In the preferred scenario, the investment tax credit encourages the business sector to expand its productive capacity, while personal income tax rate increases slow consumer demand. The combination begins to bring the two into balance, especially during the last half of the decade. In the low-growth case, corporate as well as personal tax rates are increased and the investment tax credit

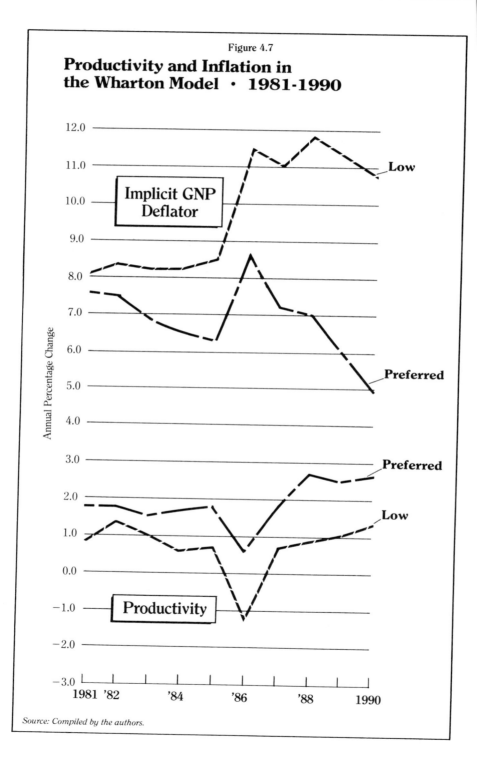

Figure 4.7

**Productivity and Inflation in
the Wharton Model · 1981-1990**

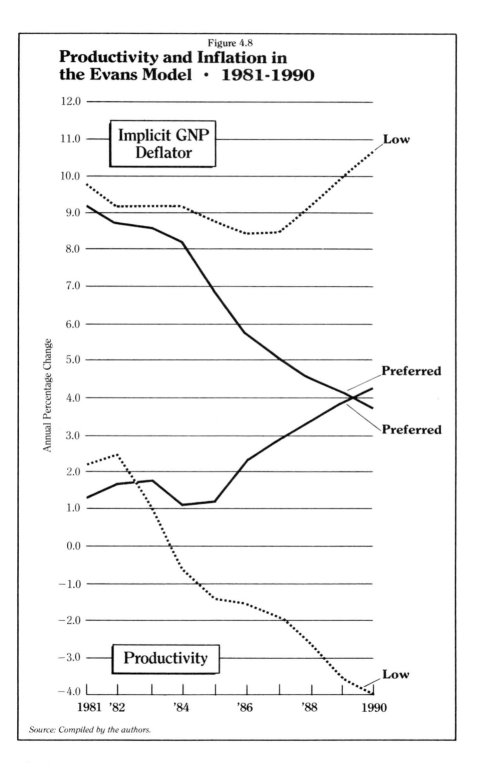

Figure 4.8
Productivity and Inflation in the Evans Model · 1981-1990

Source: Compiled by the authors.

canceled, thereby reducing not only consumer demand but also the economy's ability to expand its output. Yet, inflationary expectations and institutionalized rigidities insure that wage rates rise simultaneously with a decline in labor productivity. Rising unit labor costs and energy prices elevate production costs; consequently, retail prices rise. The rise in prices supports inflationary expectations and both phenomena feed back into the production process, exerting upward pressure on factor prices.

The mid-decade inflation-rate bubble projected by the Wharton model corresponds to the large increase in the price of natural gas (assumed to be completely deregulated in 1986). However, only about 1 percentage point of the rate increase is the direct consequence of the price increase. The indirect effects have a greater impact. As the economy adjusts to the increase in the relative cost of energy, the mix of factor inputs becomes less efficient. Labor productivity suffers, and, as a result, the inflationary spiral spins even higher. The indirect effects of deregulation on the GNP deflator are weakest in the preferred scenario because its stronger productivity gains in the early 1980s have reduced inflation consistently and weakened inflationary expectations. Furthermore, investment- and growth-encouraging public policy have worked to increase the efficiency with which natural gas can be supplanted by other energy sources. Thus, in the preferred scenario, this bubble in the inflation rate reduces the growth in GNP from an average of 3.0 percent in 1985 to 1.4 percent in 1986, while in the low-growth case the level of activity is hit much harder—real GNP, which grew 1.7 percent in 1985, actually drops at a rate of 0.8 percent in 1986.

The Evans results suggest the same general relationship between inflation and productivity, but they also indicate that fiscal policy designed solely to increase supply could conquer inflation and, in fact, do so more quickly than traditional policy prescriptions. Both the supply-side and demand-side models project converging growth paths for the GNP deflator and productivity in their preferred scenarios, but, as a comparison of Figures 4.7 and 4.8 reveals, this critical juncture occurs within the decade in the Evans model while the Wharton results suggest that the economy's struggle to break out of stagflation will continue into the early 1990s. The corporate and personal tax rate reductions and the liberalized depreciation allowances assumed in the Evans preferred case lower the costs of both labor and capital in order to stimulate investment. As the investment ratio rises, productivity growth regains momentum, supply catches up with consumer demand, and the inflationary gap closes. In the Evans low-growth scenario, the lack of work and investment incentives, combined with drags created by the growing costs of energy inputs and regulatory compliance, sap the economy's productive strength. The KLEM inputs become increasingly costly and the production process increasingly sluggish and inefficient; consequently, prices rise. Rising prices further increase production costs and inflationary expectations, and the chase becomes circular, a linkage Albert Sommers, chief economist of the nonprofit economic research institution The Conference Board, aptly describes as a "squirrel-cage."[2] This squirrel-cage behavior is apparent in the markedly accelerated growth of the GNP deflator that occurs after mid-decade in the Evans low-growth case.

Monetary Strategy

The impact of fiscal policy on investment and, thus, on productivity and inflation that is projected in each scenario must be interpreted in light of the monetary policies that are simulated by the models. When money and credit growth exceed the growth of output, prices naturally rise. Bracket creep and inadequate depreciation allowances drain the pool of investment funds on tap. On the other hand, "tight-money" policies can smother the capital formation process with high interest rates. Thus, at any given time, monetary policy can undermine the government's fiscal strategy for stimulating stable economic growth. Since the mid-1960s, the economic policy implications of the government's commitment to a full-employment economy have been complicated by the deteriorating trade-off between unemployment and inflation. The federal deficits incurred to lower unemployment during recessions and the monetary restraint exercised to lower inflation during economic expansions have become progressively more extreme. Because of the higher underlying inflation level during the 1970s, monetary restraint has been applied earlier in expansions than before. The resulting sharp increases in the cost of capital cut off the investment response to the rise in consumption demand—a demand stimulated by "easy-money" policies and deficit spending. Interest rates have become the Achilles' heel of the capital formation process.

In both short-term models monetary policy is manipulated to complement the fiscal policies under examination. Only in the low-growth societies is the growth of money supply significantly asynchronous with productivity growth. However, the easy-money policies at work in these scenarios reflect the economy's disequilibrium state as well as contribute to it. Given the priority of social goals over economic goals —leisure over labor, consumption over investment, equity of income over equity of opportunity, environmental sanctification over environmental utilization—and the bad luck embodied in energy prices, labor productivity stagnates or declines and inflation soars. The application of fiscal and monetary policies in such a society becomes increasingly complex, as recent history has shown. In both low-growth scenarios, particularly during the latter half of the decade when inflation is highest, the money supply growth rate far exceeds the output growth rate—more and more dollars chase each good. Monetary policy makers are caught between a rock and a hard place: monetary restraint—high interest rates—merely would shrink further the investment ratio and stunt productivity growth, the principal antidote for stagflation.

In the preferred and, to a lesser extent, in the continuation scenario, however, fiscal policies—the investment tax credit in the Wharton model and the corporate income tax reductions and depreciation liberalizations in the Evans model—raise corporate profits. The business sector's greater liquidity lowers loan demand and exerts downward pressure on interest rates that counterbalances the upward pressure of greater monetary restraint. Paradoxically, both interest rates and the money supply growth rate are lower in each successively higher-growth scenario. The coordination of fiscal and monetary policies strengthens their effectiveness in battling inflation, especially in the preferred scenarios. Fiscal policy lowers the cost of capital, thereby encouraging the investment needed to expand the economy's productive capacity and to reduce

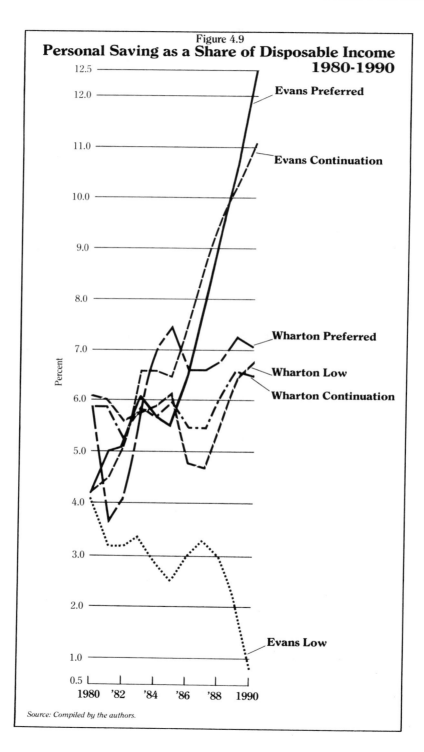

Figure 4.9
**Personal Saving as a Share of Disposable Income
1980-1990**

Evans Preferred

Evans Continuation

Wharton Preferred

Wharton Low

Wharton Continuation

Evans Low

Percent

1980   '82   '84   '86   '88   1990

Source: Compiled by the authors.

the inflationary gap between supply and demand. In this environment, monetary policy can restrain the growth of money supply to levels appropriate to productivity growth without resulting in exorbitant interest rates.

Getting Ahead of Inflation

The resulting reduction in inflation encourages personal as well as corporate savings in both models, although to vastly different extents, as Figure 4.9 makes obvious. The personal income tax increases assumed in the Wharton scenarios (to offset the loss in federal revenues incurred by the investment tax credits assumed and to dampen consumer demand) at first cause a decline in the ratio of personal savings to net personal income (personal income less personal income taxes). The decline is sharpest in the preferred scenario because taxes are highest. As the impact of increased investment credits begins to move the economy out of stagflation, however, the rates begin to rise. The shock of natural gas deregulation causes a temporary mid-decade dip in all scenarios. Savings recover most slowly in the low-growth case because the corresponding bubble in the inflation rate is largest. The continuation scenario is affected least because of the lower energy prices assumed.

Given the personal tax cuts assumed, it is not surprising that the Evans model projects much greater variation in the personal savings rate. In the low-growth scenario, which was generated assuming no change in personal tax rates other than the increase effected by bracket creep, the personal savings rate continues its recent downward trend. In the higher-growth scenarios, however, savings react immediately to the tax reductions, and as inflation and inflationary expectations are lessened progressively, the real and expected after-tax rate of return on savings steadily improves, making saving once again profitable—even though interest rates are lower. The increased personal savings, combined with the greater corporate savings and lessened government dissavings, channel resources from consumption to investment, the critical trade-off that permits output to expand, inflation to subside, and real living standards to improve.

Standards of Living

The political viability of these fiscal and monetary policies depends largely on their implications for the future material well-being of individual U.S. citizens. Although no single aggregate economic indicator of material well-being exists, real GNP per capita and real disposable income per capita serve as useful proxies from which the net impact of these short-term choices on living standards can be inferred. For each indicator, the difference between scenarios grows progressively wider as the decade unfolds and the rewards of foregoing present consumption are compounded.

The ultimate price paid for maintaining or expanding consumption's current share of GNP is indicated best by the small increase in GNP per capita experienced in the low-growth societies. The real dollar increases attained in 1990 over the 1980 GNP per capita ratio of about $6400 per person are displayed in Table 4.9.

The low-growth societies achieve a smaller increase over the entire decade than actually was achieved from 1973 to 1979 ($621 in 1972 dollars) when the combination

TABLE 4.9
Increase in Real GNP per Capita, 1980– 90
(1972 dollars)

	Preferred	Continuation	Low
Evans	2,000	1,442	477
Wharton	1,509	1,180	579

Source: Compiled by the authors.

of energy supply and price shocks, radical shifts in labor force composition, deeper and more costly government intervention, and other factors leeched the economy's productive strength and fattened the inflationary gap between supply and demand. Because no greater a percentage of economic output is devoted to investment than was allocated during the 1970s, material living standards improve even more slowly than they did then. The modest increases in the investment ratio modeled in the continuation scenarios merely sustain the recent rate of improvement in living standards. The growth rate in GNP per capita projected in the Evans continuation scenario (2.07 AAGR) equals that experienced from 1969 to 1979 while the rate in the Wharton continuation case (1.70 AAGR) matches the rate averaged from 1973 to 1979. Because GNP grows at the same rate in both continuation scenarios, most of the difference between their GNP per capita growth rates (0.37 percentage points) must be traced to the difference between their population growth rates. Population grows 0.20 percentage points faster in both the Wharton preferred and continuation scenarios than it does in the Evans counterparts. In fact, the population growth rate assumption in the Evans model is constant across scenarios. Fiscal policy assumptions, on the other hand, are responsible for most of the difference between the growth rates of GNP per capita in the preferred scenarios. Because the fiscal assumptions in the supply-side model translate more quickly into increased investment and thus into faster productivity growth, the growth rate of GNP per capita in the Evans preferred scenario (2.78 AAGR) far exceeds that projected in the Wharton preferred scenario (2.13 AAGR). The Wharton preferred scenario does not break away from the continuation path until mid-decade, while the Evans preferred scenario distinguishes itself almost immediately. The basic connection between productive investment in the early 1980s and standards of living in the late 1980s is the same in the supply-side and demand-side models, but the timing differs.

A more fundamental difference between the scenarios projected by the two models emerges from a comparison of the growth rates of GNP per capita and of disposable income per capita given in Table 4.10. Real disposable income per capita, the after-tax gain people derive from their own labor and/or capital plus transfer payments to them, grows substantially faster than GNP per capita in both the Evans preferred and continuation scenarios. However, in the Wharton counterparts, it grows substantially slower than GNP per capita. As with real GNP growth, the Evans model projects a wider range for disposable income partly because supply-side theory holds that fiscal

TABLE 4.10
Standards of Living, 1980–90
(AAGR 1972 dollars)

	Preferred	Continuation	Low
GNP per capita			
Evans	2.78	2.07	0.73
Wharton	2.13	1.70	0.87
Disposable income per capita			
Evans	3.15	2.84	0.79
Wharton	1.54	1.38	0.99

Source: Compiled by the authors.

policies, such as those simulated, can affect productivity growth more rapidly and dramatically than traditional prescriptions. More important, however, is the trade-off made in each model to increase the investment ratio. Most of the increase in investment expenditures prompted by the fiscal policies assumed in the supply-side model's preferred and continuation cases occurs at the expense of government spending. Because taxes are reduced, disposable income grows faster than GNP. In contrast, the trade-off effected by the demand-oriented model is between investment expenditures and consumption expenditures. In accordance with traditional Keynesian theory, consumer demand must be lowered in order to quell inflation; thus taxes are increased. Hence, in the Wharton preferred scenario, disposable income grows more slowly than GNP. In fact, until mid-decade, disposable income per capita is actually lower in the Wharton preferred scenario than it is in either the Wharton continuation or low-growth scenarios because personal income taxes are higher. Only in 1985 when the investment-stimulated increases in labor productivity begin to depress the ratio of employee compensation to national income, and tax rates are lowered exogenously, does disposable income per capita surpass continuation and low-growth levels.

Conclusion

In both the Wharton and Evans models, the public policy initiatives employed determine in large part the economic growth and stability attainable by 1990. The three scenarios projected by each model are represented by the statistics presented in Table 4.11. The results are organized into three groups—growth and allocation of real GNP, energy input, and standards of living—but the interplay between the groups is crucial to economic recovery.

Investment grows fastest in the preferred scenarios, both in absolute terms and in relationship to the other components of GNP. As seen in the growth rates of the shares, the supply-side model trades consumption and government spending for this increase in the investment ratio, while the demand-side model actually increases the government's share of GNP slightly and reduces the portion allocated to consumption. Despite the differences between the particular trade-offs simulated by each

TABLE 4.11
Economic Recovery: Short-Term Possibilities

Growth and Allocation of Real GNP
(AAGR)

Components	Evans			Wharton		
	Pref.	Cont.	Low	Pref.	Cont.	Low
Gross Private						
Invest.	7.68	4.38	1.29	5.09	3.78	1.92
Nonresid. Fixed	6.45	3.96	1.54	5.04	3.57	1.16
Consumption	3.13	3.02	2.03	2.64	2.47	1.95
Gov't Expenditures[1]	2.87	2.16	0.09	3.46	2.97	1.40
GNP	3.64	2.93	1.58	3.20	2.76	1.80
Ratios to GNP						
Gross Private						
Invest.	3.89	1.45	−0.31	1.85	0.99	0.07
Nonresid. Fixed	2.65	0.96	0.0	1.79	0.75	−0.60
Consumption	−0.50	0.11	0.45	−0.54	−0.28	0.15
Gov't Expenditures	−0.74	−0.74	−1.48	0.25	0.20	−0.37

Energy Input
(AAGR)

Energy Consumption				1.08	1.00	−0.35
Energy/GNP Ratio				−2.09	−1.74	−2.13

Standard of Living
(AAGR)

Indicators	Evans			Wharton		
	Pref.	Cont.	Low	Pref.	Cont.	Low
GNP/Capita	2.78	2.07	0.73	2.13	1.70	0.87
Disposable Inc./ Capita[2]	3.15	2.84	0.79	1.54	1.38	0.99
Personal Savings Rate	11.52	10.21	−17.75	1.87	0.97	1.09
Implicit GNP Deflator Rate	−9.24	−2.92	2.23	−5.79	−1.67	2.30

[1] Total federal, state, and local government purchases of goods and services.
[2] Personal income plus transfer payments and less employee contributions to social security and personal taxes.

Source: Compiled by the authors.

model, both models indicate that the more favorable fiscal policy is to investment, the faster the economy recovers from its present state of disequilibrium and expands its productive capacity. As a result, even though the consumption ratio declines in both preferred scenarios, they achieve the fastest growth in the absolute level of consumption and the greatest reduction in inflation. Consequently, standards of living improve more rapidly than they do in the other scenarios.

A comparison of these indicators of material well-being in the two preferred scenarios highlights again the different means by which economic recovery is simulated by the two models. Because of the personal income tax reductions assumed for the Evans model, disposable income per capita grows significantly faster than GNP per capita. With more income at their disposal and a lessening of the difference between real and nominal interest rates as inflation begins to subside, people save more. This sharp rise in the personal savings rate contributes significantly to the nation's ability to undertake greater investment. In the Wharton preferred scenario, on the other hand, GNP per capita grows significantly faster than disposable income per capita. In order to stimulate investment demand without simultaneously widening the inflationary gap between aggregate demand and aggregate supply, consumer demand is moderated by increases in personal income tax rates and fiscal stimulants are targeted specifically on business investment. Because of these assumptions and differences in productivity and population growth rates, the indicators rise more slowly in the Wharton preferred scenario than they do in the Evans scenario. Regardless of how the trade-off is effected, however, both models indicate that fiscal policy that allocates a substantially greater share of GNP to investment eventually results in faster overall economic expansion and higher living standards.

This growth also requires the greatest consumption of energy, of course, but the economy does become less energy-intensive. In fact, in all scenarios, the output produced for each unit of energy input increases over the short term. World oil prices and the investment ratio both play critical roles in determining how energy-efficient each society becomes, but, because it takes time to turn over the economy's capital stock, the energy intensities of these scenarios just begin to become distinctive as the decade closes. Chance brings the least rapid price increases in the continuation case, weakening the impetus for improving energy efficiency. Consequently, the growth of energy consumption in that scenario nearly equals the growth rate projected for the preferred scenario, even though GNP growth is substantially lower. The energy/GNP ratio declines at virtually the same pace in the preferred and low-growth scenarios because real oil prices increase at the same pace. The distinctive drop in consumption experienced in the low case is attributable to the slow rate of overall economic growth.

The low-growth scenarios also are distinguished by the absence of any growth in the investment ratio. In fact, gross private investment's share of GNP actually declines in the Evans low case, as does fixed nonresidential's share in Wharton's low case. The trade-off is reversed — consumption grows at the expense of government and investment expenditures. GNP growth is stunted, consequently, and inflation persists. Because they choose not to allocate a greater share of present output to investment, the low-growth societies limit their midterm growth options. By 1990 standards of living improve so slowly that in order to increase the investment ratio substantially, they would likely have to remain static temporarily, or perhaps even register an absolute decline.

The continuation scenarios, predicated on investment's growing about 1.3 percentage points faster than consumption, achieve more rapid improvements in standards of living. The impact of the investment ratio's growth slowly but steadily works through the economy, and the resulting productivity growth retards inflation. By the late 1980s recovery is within sight. Even in the preferred scenarios, with their greater investment ratios, economic recovery is a slow, gradual process. Most of the changes on the input side of the KLEM equation that are affected by the assumed fiscal policies are not reflected clearly on the output side until the second half of the decade. Then the range of projected GNP growth paths begins to broaden significantly.

Although the short-term models could not reach the high-growth track by 1990 or stabilize the low-growth economies, the combinations of modeled choice and chance variables lead early in the 1990s to four distinct stable growth paths for the economy. The exact timing of the recovery varies across scenarios primarily according to the impact that fiscal and monetary policies have on the prices of capital and labor. In all cases, however, the economy eventually arrives at that critical juncture when productivity growth retards the acceleration of inflation and stable growth is initiated.

The Economy in Transition: 1985–2000

Introduction

The consensus reached by the nation during the short term about the proper allocation of output to its various uses largely determines the initial level and slope of each scenario's midterm growth path. Once the critical juncture is reached and economic growth stabilized, the GNP ratios, that is the percentages of GNP devoted to consumption, investment, and government functions, become fixed and prices replace public policies as the principal directors of the economy's evolution. The emergence and stabilization of these secular trends mark the beginning of the midterm.

This stability on the output side of the KLEM equation contrasts sharply with the dynamics underlying it—each factor input's contribution to growth fluctuates significantly. As the impacts of chance events and social and government choices cumulate, the relative costs of capital, labor, and energy shift, altering the economic efficiency of the resource mix utilized in the production process. Thus, although the midterm scenarios are distinguished from their short-term predecessors by the lack of wide swings in output and inflation, dynamic changes do occur. The flexibility with which the economy can react to these changes by substituting factor inputs for one another is the story of the midterm. The choices society makes over the next 20 years will determine both the resiliency with which the economy can adapt to factor changes and the degree to which those changes — and the nation's economic future — can be controlled.

Economic Progress

The GNP growth rates projected for the midterm, which are presented in Table 4.12, indicate the broad economic impact of these factor changes. The Hudson-Jorgenson model estimated equilibrium growth paths from 1978 to 2000. Throughout the short term the economy remains in a state of disequilibrium, a state more fully and accurately simulated by the Wharton and Evans models. The 1978–90 Hudson-Jorgenson data, therefore, should be analyzed in light of the short-term results. However, in general both the short-term and the midterm modeling suggest that the probable range within which future GNP growth will fall is wider and lower than that actually experienced thus far in the postwar period.

TABLE 4.12
Real GNP, 1978–2000
(AAGR)

Scenario	1978–90	1990–2000	1978–2000
High	3.8	3.8	3.8
Independence	3.6	3.7	3.7
Preferred	2.9	3.3	3.1
Continuation	2.6	2.1	2.4
Low	1.8	1.5	1.7

Source: Compiled by the authors.

Even in the high-growth scenario, the economy expands at a pace significantly slower than the 4.3 percent annual growth averaged from 1960 to 1969. In fact, the center of the projected range matches the 2.8 percent growth experienced from 1969 to 1978 when the economy was growing more slowly than at almost any other period of comparable length in the postwar era. From 1948 to 1978 GNP increased 3.5 percent each year on average, a rate likely to be equalled in the future only if all conditions simultaneously favor growth, as they do in the high-growth scenario, or if choices regarding investment and nuclear power are made that counteract the impact of "bad-luck" world oil prices, as in the independence scenario. The substantial impact that choice-dominated variables have on the economy is demonstrated further by the fact that those societies assumed to be committed to growth experience a gradual quickening of GNP growth, regardless of the luck they encounter, while the continuation society, despite its good luck, experiences a gradual slowing of economic expansion, as does the low-growth society. The choices made by the three growth-oriented societies enable them to exert more control over the costs of KLEM inputs, first capital and labor, but eventually energy as well. With greater control comes greater economic flexibility.

The growth orientation of each scenario is apparent in the way GNP is allocated among its components. Table 4.13 presents the 1978–2000 growth rates of real GNP and its components along with their historical rates. Throughout the midterm proper the GNP ratios within a scenario are constant and each component, therefore, grows at the same rate as GNP. The distinctive ratio trade-offs are made in the short term, but the consequences of those choices define in large part the midterm growth possibilities. Those short-term choices are reflected in the 1978–2000 average annual growth rates. The general relationship between consumption, investment, and GNP growth is apparent in both the historical and projected data. The economy expands most quickly when investment grows faster than GNP and consumption grows slightly slower than GNP. Such was the case from 1960 to 1969 and such is the case in the high, independence, and preferred scenarios. The opposite is true of the continuation and low-growth scenarios. In those societies, investment grows substantially slower than GNP while consumption grows slightly faster than GNP. Similar statistical relationships describe the 1969–78 period when GNP growth was at its postwar nadir. The projected import/export balances are also consistent with postwar history. The higher the level of economic activity, the faster both of these GNP components grow. In all cases, however, the U.S. economy becomes increasingly intertwined with the larger world economy. Another similarity between scenarios exists in government spending growth rates. Historically, government purchases of goods and services have grown faster than GNP, although only slightly faster during the economy's 1960–69 peak, despite the demands of the Vietnam War. From 1969 to 1978 such spending declined precipitously, but it should be emphasized that transfer payments, which then absorbed record-breaking portions of the federal budget, are classified as consumption expenditures rather than government expenditures. In the midterm model, the ratio of government spending to GNP does fluctuate slightly up into 1990, but not dramatically enough to be reflected in the 1978–2000 averages. The growth rate of government purchases for goods and services is held virtually equal to the GNP growth rate in all scenarios. Thus, the most distinctive characteristic of each scenario —and the most critical determinant of its GNP growth rate—remains the investment/consumption trade-off. In the higher-growth societies the composition of spending moves toward investment and slightly away from consumption. In the lower-growth societies the opposite pattern emerges: consumption spending grows as a percentage of GNP while investment spending declines.

Material Standards of Living

These macroeconomic statistics are only important, of course, for what they imply about the economic welfare of individual U.S. citizens, and, in fact, that is why the present volume was undertaken—to discover the ongoing socioeconomic consequences of the policy decisions confronting U.S. society today. In all modeled scenarios, living standards, as measured by real GNP per capita, rise, even in the low-growth case. However, like the GNP range itself, the projected growth range, presented in Table 4.14, is both lower and wider than that experienced thus far in the postwar era.

TABLE 4.13
Real GNP and Its Components
(AAGR)

	HISTORIC			PROJECTED 1978–2000				
	Historic Low (1969–78)	Historic Average (1948–78)	Historic High (1960–69)	High	Independence	Preferred	Continuation	Low
Real GNP	2.8	3.5	4.3	3.8	3.7	3.1	2.4	1.7
Consumption	3.5	3.6	4.2	3.7	3.5	3.0	2.5	1.8
Investment	2.5	3.2	5.3	4.3	4.2	3.3	2.0	0.9
Government	0.8	4.0	4.5	3.8	3.7	3.1	2.4	1.7
Exports	3.3	4.2	6.3	6.1	5.8	5.1	4.1	2.7
Imports	1.9	5.4	8.6	6.5	6.3	5.5	4.5	3.1

Source: Compiled by the authors.

TABLE 4.14
Real GNP Per Capita Growth
(AAGR)

HISTORIC				PROJECTED 1978–2000			
Low 1969–78	Average 1948–78	High 1960–69	High	Indepen- dence	Pre- ferred	Continu- ation	Low
1.96	2.2	3.0	2.7	2.6	2.2	1.7	1.1

Source: Compiled by the authors.

At the higher bound, real GNP per capita is 80 percent higher in 2000 than in 1978. At the lower bound it increases only 27 percent, even though the total population is smaller. Naturally, part of the difference is attributable to the high priority accorded to leisure time in the lower-growth scenarios, but most of the difference results from choices regarding the investment/consumption trade-off rather than the labor/leisure trade-off. As shown in Table 4.15, the projected range of real GNP growth per working-age person is more than double the range of leisure time per working-age person.

More significant, given the traditional consensus that society must strive to assure modestly comfortable living standards for all of its citizens, is each scenario's potential for income redistribution. According to Census Bureau estimates, in constant-dollar terms the average money income of the poorest 20 percent of the nation's households in 1980 was about $7,000, while that of the next higher income grouping was about $13,000. In contrast, the income of the highest 20 percent was 6.8 times as large as that of the lowest. Of course, the multiple is larger still for the top 1, 2, or 5 percent.

In the low-growth scenario, and to a lesser degree in the continuation scenario, significant improvements in the lot of our poorest households can come only at the expense of the middle and upper income families. As the experience in Britain and

TABLE 4.15
Labor/Leisure Trade-Off
(AAGR, 1978–2000)

	Real GNP/Population, over 16	Leisure/Population, over 16
High	2.6	−0.1
Independence	2.5	−0.1
Preferred	2.0	0.0
Continuation	1.3	0.6
Low	0.7	0.8

Source: Compiled by the authors.

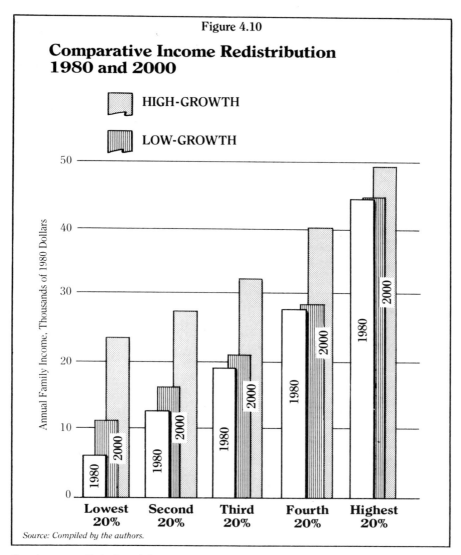

Figure 4.10

Comparative Income Redistribution 1980 and 2000

HIGH-GROWTH

LOW-GROWTH

Source: Compiled by the authors.

other low-growth industrial economies suggests, income redistribution of this sort, which is achieved through the tax system, can produce considerable political and social strife. In contrast, the three growth-oriented scenarios permit a major income distribution to the low income sector of society without exacting the kind of toll on middle and upper income groups that would impair their economic performance through the creation of disincentives. Figure 4.10 shows a range of income distribution derived from the high- and low-growth scenarios. Although the midterm model does not project income distribution trends, it does provide aggregate income estimates from which the potentials for income distribution improvements can be derived. Without reducing the absolute income levels of the top groups, the high-growth society could reduce the high-to-low ratio from 6.8 to 2.1, increasing the lowest income group's average household income to $23,500. Under the same restriction, the low-growth society could reduce the ratio to only 3.9, raising the lowest group's family income to $11,500 and providing even smaller gains for the middle groups. The derived income distribution for both the preferred and continuation scenarios falls within this range, with the preferred scenario having a potential for almost doubling the continuation scenario's incremental contribution to future incomes for the lowest and the second lowest 20 percent of the nation's families.

Sectoral Evolution

The sectoral composition of the economy's gross output, which includes the intermediate goods and services absorbed during production as well as the final demand goods and services measured by GNP, also distinguishes the higher-growth societies from the lower-growth societies. Table 4.16 shows both the share of total output accounted for and the growth rate of output produced by each of five broad sectors of the economy: agriculture, nonfuel mining, and construction; manufacturing; commercial transportation; services, trade, and communications; and energy extraction and processing. Current-dollar measurements indicate the contemporary value of sectoral outputs in terms of the total spending occurring within the economy. Constant-dollar measurements indicate the real value of sectoral outputs and, thus, indirectly measure the physical volume of sectoral outputs. The amount by which the growth rate of spending exceeds the growth rate of quantity indicates the rate at which prices are increasing.

In all cases the value of spending shifts toward manufacturing and away from agriculture and services. Spending for the agriculture sector's output grows about 0.5 percentage points slower than total spending in all scenarios; consequently, agriculture's share of the total value of gross output declines consistently across scenarios. The shift toward manufacturing and away from services varies more distinctively. In each successively higher growth scenario the manufacturing sector's output commands a greater share of total spending and the service sector's output yields more ground. The relative value of the transportation sector's output remains virtually unchanged and that of the energy sector fluctuates very little.

However, in terms of quantity of output, a different pattern emerges. The transportation sector's share of total production rises significantly in all cases, meaning that the lack of growth in its value share is due to its output prices rising substantially less rapidly than average prices because of strong productivity growth. In the preferred scenario, for example, the transportation sector's gross output grows 3.6 percent on average each year in real terms while the economy's combined production grows at a rate of only 2.4 percent. Yet the nominal value of that sector's output grows at the average rate. Hence, prices for its output grow more slowly than the average price level—5.2 percent yearly versus 6.4 percent yearly. Likewise, improvements in efficiency permit a steady expansion of the service sector's share of output (except in the

TABLE 4.16
Gross Output: Sectoral Composition and Growth Rates, 1978–2000

	1978	High		Preferred		Continuation		Low	
	Share Percent	Share Percent	AAGR	Share Percent	AAGR	Share Percent	AAGR	Share Percent	AAGR
Value (current $)									
Agriculture	13.0	11.5	9.2	11.5	8.2	11.5	6.8	12.0	5.4
Manufacturing	35.2	40.9	10.6	40.2	9.4	39.2	7.9	38.6	6.2
Transportation	3.6	3.6	9.8	3.6	8.8	3.6	7.4	3.7	5.9
Services	41.6	37.9	9.4	38.3	8.4	39.0	7.1	39.3	5.5
Energy	6.6	6.2	9.5	6.4	8.6	6.7	7.5	6.3	5.6
Total	100.0	100.0	9.8	100.0	8.8	100.0	7.4	100.0	5.8
Quantity (1972 dollars)									
Agriculture	12.6	8.5	1.3	8.5	0.6	8.3	−0.2	8.5	−0.8
Manufacturing	35.4	38.6	3.5	38.1	2.8	36.9	1.9	36.7	1.2
Transportation	4.1	5.1	4.2	5.2	3.6	5.4	3.0	5.6	2.5
Services	42.5	42.3	3.1	43.4	2.5	44.4	2.0	45.4	1.4
Energy	5.4	5.5	3.2	4.8	1.9	5.0	1.4	3.9	−0.4
Total	100.0	100.0	3.1	100.0	2.4	100.0	1.8	100.0	1.1
Price (difference)									
Agriculture			7.9		7.6		7.0		6.2
Manufacturing			7.1		6.6		6.0		5.0
Transportation			5.6		5.2		4.4		3.4
Services			6.3		5.9		5.1		4.1
Energy			6.3		6.7		6.1		6.0
Total			6.7		6.4		5.6		4.7

Note: Due to rounding, sectoral-composition percentages do not always yield 100 percent.

Source: Compiled by the authors.

high case) despite the steady decline in its share of total spending. Consequently, prices for services rise 0.4– 0.6 percentage points more slowly than average prices in all scenarios. As with the trend in value of total spending, the agriculture sector's reduced share of output fluctuates very little across scenarios, and, in all cases, its prices rise most rapidly. The book's productivity assumptions allowed less room for productivity improvement in the agricultural, nonfuel mining, and construction industries than in most other industries: the agricultural industry, which registered phenomenal productivity gains earlier in the postwar era, reaches its maturity; all mining enterprises naturally become more costly as the materials sought become more remote and/or dispersed; and because construction remains a very labor-intensive industry and wage rates exhibit little if any downward flexibility, those costs ultimately are passed through the system as higher prices.

The biggest gainer in terms of its share of the total quantity of production is the manufacturing sector. In the higher-growth scenarios only the transportation sector's output grows faster than manufacturing's. However, in keeping with the value trends, its growth, although significant, is slower in the lower-growth scenarios, in which the service sector as well as the transportation sector outpaces manufacturing. These trends are related directly to the investment choices assumed for each scenario. Most investment goods are produced by the manufacturing sector. Because of the greater investment demand in the high-growth and preferred scenarios, the manufacturing sector's output grows significantly faster than combined output, while in the continuation and low-growth cases its output expands only 0.1 percentage point faster than total gross output.

The energy sector's share of output declines in all cases except the high-growth scenario, in which good luck and strong productivity growth combine to hold the price of energy below the general price level. Relative to other prices within the economy, energy is most costly in the low-growth scenario, and consequently, that sector's gross production as measured in 1972 dollar terms actually drops at a rate of 0.4 percent yearly on average. However, this drop is misleading. Primary energy consumption does drop in the low-growth case, but only at the negligible average annual rate of .04 percent. Two factors explain the much larger drop in the quantity of gross energy output. Solar energy, which supplies over 6 percent of the low-growth society's energy needs in the year 2000, is not supplied by any of the six industries that compose the energy sector—coal mining, crude petroleum, petroleum refining, electric utilities, gas utilities, and natural gas extraction. The link between the consumer and the sun actually is the manufacturing sector, which produces the hardware necessary to capture this resource. The nation's fuel mix shifts in another way as well, away from expensive oil and gas to less costly coal and nuclear power. Thus, the negative growth rate of the energy sector's quantity of output in the low case is exaggerated somewhat by the constant-dollar measure. Still, the results do confirm the probability that unless all conditions simultaneously favor growth, future energy prices will outpace the general price level.

Perhaps more revealing than the comparative performance of any single sector in terms of gross output is the relationship between the growth of total output and the

TABLE 4.17
Final Demand: Sectoral Composition and Growth Rates, 1978–2000

| | 1978 | 2000 | | | | | | | |
| | | High | | Preferred | | Continuation | | Low | |
	Share Percent	Share Percent	AAGR	Share Percent	AAGR	Share Percent	AAGR	Share Percent	AAGR
Value (current $)									
Agriculture	12.9	13.3	9.4	13.0	8.3	12.6	6.7	12.6	5.3
Manufacturing	30.3	31.1	9.3	30.6	8.3	29.5	6.7	28.9	5.2
Transportation	2.6	2.5	8.9	2.6	8.2	2.8	7.2	3.1	6.1
Services	50.9	50.0	9.1	50.7	8.2	52.0	7.0	52.4	5.5
Energy	3.2	3.2	9.1	3.2	8.2	3.2	6.7	3.0	5.0
Total	100.0	100.0	9.2	100.0	8.2	100.0	6.9	100.0	5.4
Quantity (1972 dollars)									
Agriculture	12.0	9.5	2.6	9.3	1.8	8.8	0.9	8.6	0.2
Manufacturing	31.0	33.2	4.0	32.7	3.3	31.4	2.4	31.1	1.7
Transportation	2.8	3.7	5.1	3.8	4.6	4.2	4.3	4.6	4.1
Services	51.2	50.0	3.6	51.2	3.0	52.5	2.5	53.4	1.9
Energy	3.1	3.7	4.6	3.0	2.9	3.1	2.4	2.2	0.2
Total	100.0	100.0	3.7	100.0	3.0	100.0	2.4	100.0	1.7
Price (difference)									
Agriculture			6.8		6.5		5.8		5.1
Manufacturing			5.3		5.0		4.3		3.5
Transportation			3.8		3.6		2.9		2.0
Services			5.5		5.2		4.5		3.6
Energy			4.5		5.3		4.3		4.8
Total			5.5		5.2		4.5		3.7

Note: Due to rounding, sectoral-composition percentages do not always yield 100 percent.
Source: Compiled by the authors.

growth of GNP. As stated earlier, gross output equals the intermediate goods and services required to produce GNP plus the final demand goods and services that GNP itself measures. Table 4.17 presents the growth rate of the final demand portion of gross output produced by each sector from 1978 to 2000 along with the sectoral composition of GNP in those years. Interestingly, in all scenarios, real GNP grows 0.6 to 0.7 percentage points faster than gross output. In other words, the quantity of goods and services produced for final purchase is growing faster than the quantity of intermediate goods and services needed to produce them; that is, more GNP is being produced for each unit of input. Table 4.18 highlights this salient feature of the midterm results.

In all scenarios, less of any sectors' gross output is required by the other sectors' production processes. In 1978, for example, less than 55 percent of the agriculture, nonfuel mining, and construction sector's gross output was purchased as final demand. Over 45 percent of it was absorbed by interindustry transactions. In the year 2000, however, total factor productivity in the other sectors has increased to the extent that intermediate purchases claim only 27 to 33 percent of the agriculture sector's gross output, leaving between 73 and 67 percent for final demand. The increase in the final demand/gross output ratio is smallest in the manufacturing sector, indicating the vital role it plays throughout the economy in boosting the efficiency of production or total factor productivity. The other sectors continue to depend heavily on its products for their own production processes. Interindustry transactions claim a larger share of gross output only from the energy sector, but even those needs are reduced to a greater extent than their needs for manufactured goods. This gap projected between the growth rates of real gross output and real final demand will lessen as the most efficient mix of inputs is approximated and the KLEM equation stabilizes late in the 1990s. This stabilization likely will trigger a slow-down

TABLE 4.18
Final Demand for Sectoral Output
as a Share of Gross Sectoral Output, 1978 and 2000

	1978	2000			
		High	Pre-ferred	Continu-ation	Low
Agriculture, nonfuel mining, construction	54.7	72.6	71.4	69.5	67.4
Manufacturing	50.4	56.0	55.9	55.6	56.0
Commercial transportation	38.8	46.7	48.2	51.1	54.3
Service, trade, communications	69.2	76.9	77.2	77.3	77.6
Energy	32.4	43.7	40.5	40.4	37.5
Total	57.5	65.1	65.3	65.4	66.0

Source: Compiled by the authors.

in GNP growth, marking the emergence of an equilibrium state to which the midterm transition has led. Beyond this point GNP will grow approximately at the same rate as gross output.

Sources of Growth

As shown in Table 4.19, labor, capital, and total factor productivity all contribute to the economy's expansion, but productivity is the most important source of GNP growth, particularly in the continuation and low-growth societies; these cases describe societies that place less emphasis on work and investment than the higher-growth societies. These data are derived from the model's projection of labor hours, capital stock, and GNP growth. The contributions of labor and capital are weighted according to their historical contributions to growth (67 percent labor, 33 percent capital), and total factor productivity's contribution is obtained as a residual, a productivity measure that also includes the additional contributions made by the improved quality of capital and labor.

The absence of a wide range of total factor productivity growth rates can be explained by the substantial flexibility of final demand and production patterns incorporated in the H-J model, one of the features that makes it particularly appropriate for the midterm analysis. The model explicitly, simultaneously, and consistently simulates the bidirectional interactions among all parts of the economy. Within the H-J model, for example, given a reduced energy availability, final demand patterns can shift at rates dependent on the historic experience that has been incorporated in the model. Thus, in a macroeconomic way, the model approximates a whole complex of microeconomic changes: commercial transport can be substituted for automobile travel; insulation of homes can be substituted for fuel oil; a stereo system can be substituted for going to the movies; and, on a more general level, consumers can substitute between quite unrelated goods, for example, switching some spending away from personal services toward food purchases, or away from automobiles and toward clothing. Within production, there are also significant possibilities for substitution between inputs. The substitutions can occur in the production process—for example, away from energy and capital and toward labor-intensive operations—or between the types of products used—for example, away from plastic and toward paper or metal containers. The widespread possibilities for substitution within production mean the economy, given time to adjust, can adapt to reductions in the availability of particular inputs without incurring a loss in output proportional to the reduction in the input supply.

However, many of the decisions and chance events of the last several years have combined to throw the economy into a state of disequilibrium and to curtail sharply the rapidity and efficiency of the substitution process. Also, as the short-term analysis indicates, to restore the economy's balance and flexibility will take time. Thus, the midterm model's simulation, especially through the early 1990s, very well may overestimate total factor productivity advancements by systematically underestimating the drag on the substitution process in all scenarios. If so, real GNP growth from now until the century's end may be more heavily dependent on the projected capital and labor growth; in fact, it might be somewhat closer to the real gross output growth rates shown in Table 4.16 than the midterm model results suggest. The likelihood is particularly strong in the lower-growth scenarios because their lower investment ratios and population growth limit their substitution options. Yet, for the same reasons, these are the very scenarios that depend most heavily on total factor productivity's contribution to growth.

Because of the flexibility bestowed upon the economy by the midterm model, it projects average annual GNP growth to fall within a range of 1.7–3.8 percent through 2000. The short-term models project a lower range: 1.6–3.6 percent. Just as the midterm model probably overestimates the near-term potential for efficient substitution, given the economy's current state of disequilibrium, the short-term models probably underestimate that potential. Within the Wharton and Evans models, final demand and production patterns remain rather rigid, and appropriately so given the present constraints and imbalances in the system. However, this rigidity, which hampers total factor productivity growth, probably is exaggerated during the late 1980s, especially in the preferred scenario and to a lesser extent in the continuation scenario. In both of these cases, the investment ratio rises, which should enhance the flexibility of final demand and production patterns. In other words, the bridge between the short and midterm probably lies somewhere between the paths projected by the midterm and short-term models. Achieving the total factor productivity growth simulated by the midterm model probably will require greater investment than actually was modeled. The Wharton model projects, for example, GNP growth to average 1.8 percent annually until 1990 in the low-growth scenario, as does the midterm model. In the Wharton model, however, that growth is predicated upon gross private investment's growing 1.9 percent each year, almost four times the increase simulated by the H-J model. The short-term models, on the other hand, may overstate the capital requirements for achieving the higher-growth scenarios, or at least exaggerate the temporal lag between changes in factor costs and the shifts in final demand and production trends that those changes induce.

These qualifications to the modeling results suggest that the probable range within which total factor productivity growth will fall between now and the turn of the century may be somewhat wider than the range actually projected by the midterm model, with most of the expansion occurring at the lower bound. Reduced productivity growth in the lower-growth societies would mean, of course, that more of gross output would be absorbed within the production process. Consequently, labor and capital's contributions to growth would have to be increased to achieve the GNP growth modeled. The implications for the third component of the KLEM equation, energy, are likewise significant. A reduction in GNP caused by a reduction in productivity would not accommodate a proportional reduction in the energy sector's gross output and, in fact, could increase the nation's energy needs.

Energy Balances

Even though historically it has accounted for a very small portion of the economy's real gross output—5.4 percent in 1978 and an even smaller figure prior to the Arab oil

TABLE 4.19
Sources of Real GNP Growth
(AAGR)

	Historic			Projected 1978–2000			
	Low 1969–78	Average 1948–78	High 1960–69	High	Independence	Preferred	Continuation	Low
Labor hours	1.05	0.74	0.96	0.9	0.9	0.7	0.3	0.1
Capital	0.8	1.0	1.1	1.1	1.1	0.9	0.6	0.2
Total factor productivity	0.97	1.8	2.27	1.8	1.7	1.6	1.5	1.4
Real GNP	2.82	3.54	4.33	3.8	3.7	3.1	2.4	1.7

Source: Compiled by the authors.

embargo of 1973—energy plays a vital role in the KLEM equation. In fact, the United States has enjoyed such rapid postwar economic growth largely because energy's constant-dollar share has been so small. As explained in the justification of the midterm productivity assumptions, the declining energy prices of the 1950s and 1960s fostered total factor productivity growth throughout all sectors of the economy by permitting greater energy input use to complement or substitute for the two other primary production factors, capital and labor.

The rapid turnabout of energy prices experienced since the early 1970s has disturbed the integral relationship between energy and capital and labor. In order to restore productivity, growth strategies must be designed to contain energy's cost to the economy, or, in other words, to keep its share of gross output small. Two avenues lead to this destination. One path is to lower the cost of capital and labor and to improve their quality so that they either require less energy input or may be substituted more readily for it. Greater energy efficiency—more gross output per unit of energy input—in effect lowers energy's costs, thereby keeping its share of gross output relatively small. The second route to maintaining the traditional balance between total gross output and the energy sector's output involves substituting one energy product for another rather than substituting capital and labor for energy in general. By altering the fuel mix consumed, the nation can minimize energy's cost to the economy. Within the limits defined by the assumed choice and chance variables, both of these avenues are pursued in each scenario over the midterm.

How successfully they are pursued can be inferred broadly from the gross sectoral output results displayed in Table 4.16. Not surprisingly, the cost of energy relative to the general price level rises progressively from the high-growth scenario to the low-growth scenario. What is surprising at first is that energy prices are not higher across all scenarios, given the input assumptions. The linkage between the H-J model and the B-J model, which projects electricity prices, provides room for some statistical error, but more importantly, the H-J prices are apparent rather than real. They are adjusted downward to compensate for the model's limited ability to simulate technical change in the final demand sectors, a limitation especially strong in the residential/commercial sector and further complicated by the fact that energy composes such a small portion of GNP. Because consumption is a function of both energy prices and investment, the consumer response captured is approximately the same as if all improvements in end-use energy processes were modeled directly. Thus, although the absolute values of the energy prices given in Table 4.16 are understated, the trend across scenarios that is projected—the relative cost of energy to the economy increases in each successively lower growth scenario—remains valid. In order to understand why, both the energy efficiency and the fuel mix of each scenario must be examined.

The enhanced energy efficiency of the economy is evident in Figure 4.11, which exhibits the historic relationship between energy consumption growth and GNP growth and the evolution of the relationship as projected by the midterm model. Prior to 1973 GNP growth was locked into a relatively stable 1.0-to-0.9 correlation with growth in energy consumption. Until the mid-1970s most of the deviations from the

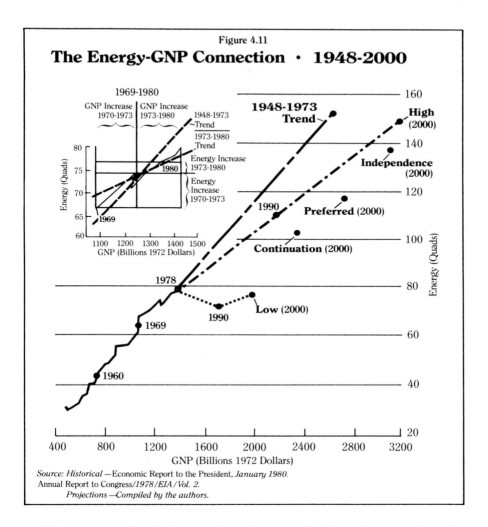

Figure 4.11
The Energy-GNP Connection · 1948-2000

Source: Historical — Economic Report to the President, January 1980.
Annual Report to Congress/1978/EIA/Vol. 2.
Projections — Compiled by the authors.

trend line correspond to business cycle peaks or troughs. From that point forward to 1980 both the growth of energy consumption and the growth of GNP become compressed, a phenomenon highlighted by the inset in Figure 4.11. GNP expanded almost as much between 1970 and 1973 as it did during the remainder of the decade. The contrast between the increase in energy consumption over the same two periods is even more striking, suggesting a shift in the relationship between energy use and economic growth. Since the Arab oil embargo the ratio between energy consumption and GNP consistently has fallen below the postwar trend line. To what degree recent U.S. experience reflects the emergence of a permanent new trend line and to what degree it reflects a temporary aberration induced by the economy's current state of disequilibrium cannot be known with certainty.

Nevertheless, this book's analysis indicates that under any probable set of circumstances the economy will be more energy efficient than it has been in the past. In fact, the midterm projections neatly bound the trend line suggested by the 1970– 80 data. The low-growth economy, which encounters the fastest escalation of energy prices and the slowest increase of capital and labor, is forced to be most energy efficient; the high-growth economy, which experiences the slowest rise in energy prices and the strongest growth of capital and labor, can afford to reduce its energy intensity the least. The dominance of choice variables over chance variables becomes apparent by comparing the paths projected for the continuation and preferred scenarios. Although the continuation scenario's good-luck prices allow for a steeper rise in energy consumption than the preferred scenario's bad-luck prices permit, the preferred scenario's choices overcome this handicap and yield greater GNP growth.

This generalized decoupling of aggregate energy consumption and aggregate net output occurs in all scenarios, but the changing energy supply and demand patterns that prompt it are scenario specific. The primary supply mix, the composition of delivered energy, the role of conservation, and the sectoral consumption of energy all vary across scenarios and play a part in determining the interaction between the energy sector and the economy as a whole. Thus, all four factors are examined here in turn.

Primary Supplies

The economy's primary energy composition shifts away from petroleum and natural gas toward coal and nuclear power in all cases, although the magnitude of the shift varies greatly. Table 4.20 shows the amount of each fuel available in 2000 and the percentage of total supply for which it accounts. The nation's fuel mix shifts in response to both price and the level of general economic activity. Additions to hydro and geothermal capacity, for example—the two primary components of the "hydro and other" category—are limited strictly by physical and economic constraints. Consequently, no more than 3.4 quads of energy are supplied by such means in the year 2000, and the lion's share of that is generated by facilities already in place. The variation across scenarios in those resources' relative contribution to the nation's primary energy supply reflects the economic growth range projected, a range determined predominantly by choices made rather than by chance factors encountered. Nuclear capacity likewise is limited by assumption, and, thus, its contribution also reveals more about the economic growth level achieved than it reveals about world oil prices. The contribution that petroleum makes, on the other hand, is more sensitive to price—or chance. Its share of total supply drops in all cases but much more drastically in those scenarios that experience the higher rate of increase in world oil prices. So, too, with natural gas. Conversely, solar energy's contribution rises most sharply in the high-price cases. Coal supply grows substantially in all scenarios, almost doubling in the low-growth and continuation cases and more than tripling in the higher-growth cases.

Not surprisingly, most of the differences in the petroleum and natural gas supplies available to each scenario are a function of how much of those fuels each society is

TABLE 4.20
Primary Energy Supply and Composition, 1978 and 2000

	1978		High		Independence		2000 Preferred		Continuation		Low	
	Quads	Percent of Total	Quads	Percent of Total	Quads	Percent of Total	Quads	Percent of Total	Quads	Percent of Total	Quads	Percent of Total
Petroleum	37.7	48.3	47.8	32.5	35.3	25.9	29.4	25.1	32.9	31.6	16.9	21.9
Natural gas	20.2	25.9	26.7	18.2	20.7	15.2	16.9	14.4	21.9	21.0	11.5	14.9
Coal	14.1	18.1	49.1	33.4	48.1	35.2	44.5	38.0	27.0	25.9	24.7	32.0
Nuclear	2.9	3.7	18.0	12.2	24.0	17.6	18.0	15.3	18.0	17.3	15.8	20.4
Hydro and other	3.1	4.0	3.4	2.3	3.4	2.5	3.4	2.9	3.4	3.3	3.4	4.4
Solar: displacing fossil fuel and electricity	—	—	2.0	1.4	5.0	3.6	5.0	4.3	1.0	0.9	5.0	6.4
Total	78.0	100.0	147.0	100.0	136.5	100.0	117.2	100.0	104.2	100.0	77.3	100.0

Source: Compiled by the authors.

willing to import. As Table 4.21 shows, traditionally produced domestic supplies vary little across scenarios, except in the low-growth case. Slow overall economic growth, coupled with greater energy efficiency, reduces substantially the low-growth society's demand for both fuels and eliminates entirely its dependence on imports. Within the other scenarios, however, supply-side constraints limit production. The amount of oil and gas produced by traditional means varies little in these scenarios. Oil supply falls within a 2.4 quad range and gas supply within a 1.5 quad range. The much wider range in consumption—16.4 quads for oil and 8.7 quads for gas—reflects the variance in the availability of supplies produced by alternative means and the amount of oil and gas imported. The 4 percent annual rise in real world oil prices experienced in the independence, preferred, and low-growth scenarios encourages the development of alternative methods of boosting domestic production. In those scenarios, shale oil and synthetic oil and gas together contribute 5 quads of primary energy to the economy, almost five times the contribution they make in the high-growth case and ten times the contribution they make in the continuation case. Enhanced oil recovery techniques also become viable in the independence and preferred scenarios, further increasing domestic production. The net supply-side effect is that the combined domestic supply of oil and gas in the independence and preferred scenarios exceeds domestic supply in the high-growth and continuation scenarios by 5 or 6 quads.

The higher prices also affect the economy's demand side. Even though GNP is growing much more rapidly in the preferred scenario than it is in the continuation scenario, consumption of both fuels is lower in the preferred scenario. The electric utility sector's demand for oil and gas declines much more rapidly, industrial demand for natural gas increases less rapidly, and the commercial/residential sector's demand for that fuel declines slightly while it actually grows in the continuation scenario. Because world oil prices are higher in the preferred scenario, the economic liability of the nation's traditional reliance on oil and gas is greater than it is in the continuation scenario. Consequently, the transition to coal and electricity, a transition facilitated by the higher investment ratio and the more rapid turnover of capital stock, is accomplished more rapidly in the preferred scenario. Likewise, the demand for oil and gas in the independence scenario is just 4.8 quads greater than it is in the continuation case. Only in the high-growth scenario does the combined demand grow substantially above 1978 consumption levels. However, as shown in Table 4.20, even in this case oil and natural gas make up a smaller portion of total primary supply than they do in the continuation case. The high investment level assumed for the high-growth case allows the substitution process to proceed more rapidly than it does in the continuation scenario.

The net result of these shifting production and consumption trends can be seen in each scenario's import requirements. Because of the physical, economic, and time constraints facing domestic energy producers, oil supply falls short of demand in all but the low-growth scenario, and natural gas supply falls short in all but the preferred and low-growth scenarios. Imports must make up the balance. Good-luck world oil prices and low capital growth slow the substitution process in the continuation scenario. Consequently, its economy requires more imported fuel to produce its

TABLE 4.21
U.S. Oil and Gas Production and Consumption, 1978 and 2000
(Quads)

	1978	2000				
		High	Indepen-dence	Pre-ferred	Continu-ation	Low
Domestic Supply						
Oil						
Petroleum	19.6	19.7	22.0	21.6	19.6	15.9
Shale oil	—	0.2	1.0	1.0	0.1	1.0
Synoil[a]	—	0.5	2.5	2.5	0.2	2.5
Total	19.6	20.4	25.5	25.1	19.9	19.4
Natural Gas						
Gas	19.2	16.5	16.0	16.9	17.5	11.5
Syngas[a]	—	0.4	1.5	1.5	0.2	1.5
Total	19.2	16.9	17.5	18.4	17.7	13.0
Domestic Consumption[b]						
Oil						
Commercial/residential	6.2	9.8	7.0	5.8	6.0	3.1
Industrial	7.7	10.1	7.3	6.1	6.1	3.3
Transportation	20.0	26.1	20.6	17.2	17.4	10.7
Electricity	3.8	2.3	2.8	2.8	3.6	2.3
Total	37.7	48.3	37.8	31.9	33.1	19.4
Natural gas						
Commercial/residential	7.5	10.9	8.8	7.3	8.6	4.7
Industrial	9.4	14.4	11.9	9.8	11.6	7.4
Transportation	0.5	1.0	0.6	0.5	0.7	0.2
Electricity	2.8	0.7	0.8	0.8	1.2	0.7
Total	20.2	27.1	22.2	18.4	22.1	13.0
Shortfall						
Oil						
Consumption	37.7	48.3	37.8	31.9	33.1	19.4
Production	19.6	20.4	25.5	25.1	19.9	19.4
Imports	18.1	27.9	12.3	6.8	13.2	—
Gas						
Consumption	20.2	27.1	22.2	18.4	22.1	13.0
Production	19.2	16.9	17.5	18.4	17.7	13.0
Imports	1.0	10.2	4.7	—	4.4	—

[a]Coal-derived synthetics net of conversion losses.
[b]Columns may not yield totals when added due to rounding.

Source: Compiled by the authors.

relatively moderate GNP than the independence scenario's economy requires to produce its much larger GNP. Imports rise above 1978 levels only in the high-growth scenario, and there they rise substantially. Even though the economy's energy intensity is declining in this case, the high-growth scenario's rapid rate of economic expansion requires more energy than the nation itself can produce. The difference between its import requirements and those of the independence scenario's economy, which also expands rapidly, reflects the latter's greater nuclear capacity and the fact that coal's price advantage is much greater in the independence scenario. The choices made in the preferred scenario enable the economy to expand significantly even though world oil prices are rising rapidly. By 2000 the nation imports only 6.8 quads of oil, less than 38 percent of the total foreign energy supplies imported in 1978.

A critical relationship exists between the diminished role played by oil and gas and the enlarged role projected for U.S. coal. In each scenario, coal consumption grows between 2.6 and 3.5 percentage points faster than primary energy use in general. In all but the continuation scenario, in which growth-inhibiting choices combine with good-luck world oil prices to slow the transition away from oil and gas, coal ascends to the dominant position in the nation's fuel mix. Furthermore, as shown in Table 4.22, U.S. coal's significance as an international commodity increases in all cases, reaching the equivalent of 1 + million barrels of oil per day by 2000.

In the high-growth and continuation scenarios, in which world oil prices escalate most slowly, petroleum and natural gas retain more of their traditional share of the energy market, and, consequently, less than 10 quads of coal are used domestically for purposes other than generating electricity. In the bad-luck cases, between 13 and 17 quads are so used. Not surprisingly, industrial coal use grows fastest in the scenario assumed to be committed most strongly to achieving energy self-sufficiency, the

TABLE 4.22
U.S. Coal Consumption and Production, 1978 and 2000
(Quads)

	1978	2000				
		High	Indepen-dence	Pre-ferred	Continu-ation	Low
Domestic Consumption						
Commercial/Residential	0.3	0.4	0.7	0.5	0.5	0.4
Synthetics industry	—	1.2	6.0	6.0	0.6	6.0
Other industry	3.7	7.8	10.1	8.9	8.7	7.2
Electricity	10.1	39.7	31.3	29.1	17.2	11.1
Total	14.1	49.1	48.1	44.5	27.0	24.7
Domestic production	14.5	51.6	50.7	46.9	29.8	26.9
Exports	0.4	2.5	2.6	2.4	2.8	2.2

Source: Compiled by the authors.

independence scenario, and most slowly in the scenario with the lowest level of economic activity and lowest energy intensity, the low-growth scenario. In keeping with the modeling assumptions, coal input into the production of synthetic liquids and gas varies across scenarios according to the price of oil and natural gas, the fuels that synthetics displace. The bulk of the variation in total consumption occurs in electricity utility use.

This growing reliance on coal reverses the substitution process that has characterized coal production and use over most of the postwar era. Although real coal prices declined steadily through the 1960s, so too did the prices of oil and gas; consequently, the economy evolved toward greater use of the cleaner, more convenient liquid and gaseous fuels and coal consumption actually dropped. Even when oil prices skyrocketed in the early 1970s, coal failed to gain a clear competitive edge. Environmental, health, and safety regulations combined to push the costs of both mining and burning coal sharply upward over the 1970s, while federal regulations held the price of natural gas below its true marketplace value. In 1948 coal supplied 14.9 quads of energy to the U.S. economy, 44 percent of the primary energy consumed that year. Thirty years later, only 14.1 quads were consumed, accounting for only 18.1 percent of total energy consumption. The logistics and costs of transporting coal and controlling its environmental impacts have confined its use today largely to the electric utility industry, and the bulk of 1978 coal supply, 10.1 quads, was used in that sector. Only 4.0 quads were used for other purposes, mainly to fuel large industrial boilers and furnaces, as opposed to the 12.5 quads used outside of utilities in 1948.

Reversing this historical trend to utilize fully coal's potential contribution to the economy will take concerted public policies, time, and capital. Even though the sharp real price increases of the 1970s—an average of 12 percent annually from 1969 to 1978—are not expected to continue because most of the additional costs imposed by federal mining regulations have been internalized, uncertainty remains high at the user end of the coal fuel cycle, particularly for the industrial user. Future prices of alternative fuels, availability of suitable technologies, costs of complying with future air quality standards, severance taxes, and transportation costs taken together could reduce coal's price advantage over oil and gas. Furthermore, oil and gas conversions to coal are technically infeasible in some industries and costly in all cases.

Thus, demand rather than supply could limit coal's increased penetration in the nation's fuel mix throughout the short term. U.S. coal production capacity currently exceeds actual output by 15 to 20 percent and could continue to do so through the 1980s. However, under the midterm price assumptions, as capital stock is turned over and coal-based synthetics become available, demand for coal rises quickly, absorbing this excess capacity and tightening the coal market considerably. All scenarios show the nation's dependence on petroleum and natural gas—for firing industrial boilers and generating electricity—abating as coal displaces these less abundant, more expensive energy sources.

How tight the coal market becomes depends on how fast demand for electricity grows. Additions to the nation's primary energy supply from other sources—nuclear, hydro and other, and solar—are constrained by geography, costs, and time. As seen in

Table 4.20, solar energy's displacement of fossil fuels and electricity does vary across scenarios according to world oil prices, but the other two primary supplies are nearly identical across scenarios. Because other supplies are limited, coal becomes the swing fuel in electricity generation. It is the input over which the utilities have the most control.

Energy Conversion: The Electric Utility Sector

The share of total primary supply committed to electric generation grows substantially in all scenarios over the midterm, reflecting electricity's continuing penetration into the energy market. In 1978, 29 percent of total primary energy supply was used to generate electricity. The present volume's modeling results suggest that by 2000 that share will rise to somewhere between 41 and 46 percent. As seen in Table 4.23, over the whole postwar period electricity has grown historically at twice the pace of the overall economy and 2.5 times as fast as general primary energy consumption. Because economies of scale were present, conversion technologies were improving, and energy input costs were declining, electricity prices declined steadily until the 1970s. The flexibility of its use and its cleanliness and easy availability combined with its declining price to encourage electricity consumption. For many of the same reasons its growth is projected to continue outpacing real GNP growth over the midterm, although not at the 2-to-1 ratio averaged from 1948 to 1978.

The midterm model projects average annual electricity generation growth to fall within a range of 2.0 to 5.1 percent, far below the 7 to 8 percent averaged until the 1970s when soaring energy prices shocked the entire economy, and real GNP, primary energy consumption, and electric generation growth rates all plummeted to their postwar nadirs. As seen in Figure 4.12, the 2-to-1 ratio that characterized the general relationship between electricity growth and GNP growth since 1948 in all likelihood will not describe the future. In fact, the relationship began shifting gradually in the late 1960s. The ratio averaged over both the low historic period (1969–78) and the high historic period (1960–69) was closer to 1.7-to-1.0 than to the 2-to-1 postwar average. This slowdown in electricity's growth relative to GNP growth is traceable to the changing trend in the costs of building new plant equipment. Real costs were declining in the 1950s and 1960s because of advances in boiler technology and economies of scale. Over the 1970s, however, costs began to rise for a variety of reasons: increasing pollution control requirements, increasing construction delays, changes in the structure of the economy that led to real increases in the costs of construction labor and materials, and increasingly high rates of inflation. Although the decline in the electricity growth/GNP growth ratio is projected to continue, electricity generation does grow one-third faster than GNP in all scenarios except the low-growth scenario, which embarks on a path of zero growth in primary energy consumption. Significantly, even in the zero energy growth case the ratio rises, a fact that emphasizes the vital role electricity will play in freeing the nation of its import dependence.

The electric utility industry continues to penetrate the energy market for two reasons. It is virtually the only industry able to capture uranium's potential contribu-

TABLE 4.23
GNP—Primary Energy—Electricity
(AAGR)

	Historic			Projected 1978–2000				
	Low 1969–78	Average 1948–78	High 1960–69	High	Independence	Preferred	Continuation	Low
Real GNP	2.8	3.5	4.3	3.8	3.7	3.1	2.4	1.7
Primary Energy	2.0	2.8	4.4	2.9	2.6	1.9	1.3	0.0
Electricity generation	4.8	7.1	7.5	5.1	4.9	4.3	3.2	2.0

Source: Compiled by the authors.

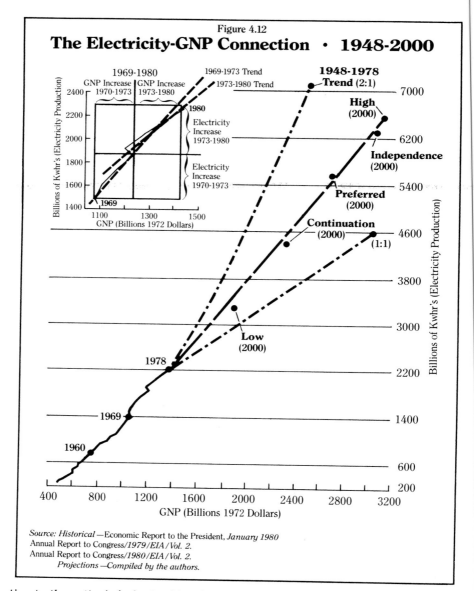

Figure 4.12
The Electricity-GNP Connection • 1948-2000

Source: Historical—Economic Report to the President, *January 1980*
Annual Report to Congress/1979/EIA/Vol. 2.
Annual Report to Congress/1980/EIA/Vol. 2.
    Projections—Compiled by the authors.

tion to the nation's fuel mix. Also, for the same reasons that coal consumption has been confined largely to the electric utility sector, it is best able to step up its utilization of that resource. Fortunately, both of these fuels are in good domestic supply. Furthermore, coal prices escalate significantly below the rate of oil and gas prices, and fuel costs constitute only a very small percentage of the cost of power from nuclear facilities. By transforming coal and uranium into a safe, clean, reliable source of energy that can be utilized by all sectors, the electric utility sector distributes the cost advantage of these domestic resources throughout the economy. Electricity's flexibility makes it particularly well-suited for use in the economy's largest producing sector, the service sector, and part of the strong productivity advancements achieved by service industries over the midterm can be traced to their growing utilization of electricity.

Two nonfuel factors also contribute to holding electricity prices down, thereby encouraging consumers to substitute electricity for the scarcer, more expensive fuels, oil and gas. First, as the nation recovers from stagflation, capacity utilization rates rise throughout the economy, increasing the demand for electricity and allowing the electric utility industry to make fuller, more productive use of its own existing facilities. Second, as electricity pricing methods are adopted that more accurately reflect the actual costs of generating electricity at any given time, load variability decreases, reducing the excess capacity utilities must carry to meet peak demand periods (diurnal and seasonal). The changeover of end-use capital stock, for example, from air conditioners to electric heat pumps that both heat and cool homes, also will help to smooth out variations in seasonal demand.

Thus, the determinants of electricity's future price fall into two major categories: the variable cost of energy inputs to the utility industry, and the fixed cost of its capital. Table 4.24 displays the amount and composition of primary energy inputs committed to electric generation in each scenario for the year 2000. Coal and nuclear power play a critical role in all futures, contributing together between 80 and 90 percent of the total energy consumed by utilities in contrast to the 57 percent they supplied in 1978. The shift toward these lower-priced domestic fuels permits utilities to cut their requirements for oil and gas by 27 to 55 percent across scenarios and helps restrain electricity price increases.

Enhanced recovery techniques and synthetic production of oil and gas allow utilities to consume about half a quad more of these traditional fuels in the preferred and independence scenarios than in the high-growth scenario. In the continuation case, the low investment ratio and slow productivity growth, which combine to reduce coal's relative price advantage, hamper the utility sector's transition from oil and gas. Nuclear power's price advantage is highlighted by the fact that utilities use that resource to the maximum extent feasible in all cases. Long lead times constrain nuclear's expansion in the high, independence, preferred, and continuation cases, while slow capital growth, zero energy growth, and peaking capacity requirements constrain its expansion in the low-growth case. All in all, oil and gas inputs, nuclear inputs, and hydro and other inputs vary little across scenarios. In combination they contribute between 22.2 and 31.1 quads in each scenario, and the range narrows even more — to between 24.5 and 26.2 — if the rather exceptional independence and zero energy growth cases are excluded. Supply-side constraints limit the utility sector's ability to utilize each of these energy inputs, leaving coal as the input that adjusts to meet the level of electricity demanded across scenarios.

Consequently, the nation's willingness and ability to expand coal production at the rate projected for the three higher-growth scenarios—between 5 and 6 percent average annual growth from 1978 to 2000 — while holding average real price increases to no more than 1.0 percent per year is particularly crucial to the electric utility industry. These potential production levels depend on access to coal deposits on federal lands, on adequate and cost-competitive transportation, and on cost-effective control of environmental hazards of burning coal. These contingencies and others are discussed in Chapter 5, but the fact remains that by and large public policies rather than chance will determine the future availability and cost of coal. In the high-growth, independence, and preferred scenarios, growth-favoring choices allow utilities to triple or quadruple their coal consumption from 1978 levels in order to satisfy the nation's rapidly growing demand for electricity. In these higher-growth scenarios coal provides between 50 and 60 percent of the utility sector's primary energy requirements.

Naturally, the utility sector's growing utilization of coal and uranium inputs requires a parallel shift in its mix of generating facilities, and, consequently, the installed capacity data presented in Table 4.25 mirror the energy input trends. Additional coal and nuclear capacity account for almost all expansion. In the three higher-growth scenarios, generating capacity doubles or triples over the 1978–2000 period, and even in the low-growth case it expands by almost 50 percent.

Given the financial problems besetting the electric utility industry today, its ability to attract the large sums of money required to construct this new capacity while continuing to replace worn-out and economically obsolete capacity is one of the greatest uncertainties surrounding future electricity growth. Historically, the electric utility sector has been the economy's most capital-intensive; the midterm transition to coal-fired and nuclear plants further will increase its capital needs. Because coal does not burn as cleanly as oil or gas, coal-fired plants require more extensive environmental protection devices. For this reason and due to other engineering differences, coal-fired plants cost between 60 and 80 percent more to build than oil- or gas-fired ones. Nuclear plants are even more expensive to build; on a kilowatt basis they usually cost 20 to 30 percent more than coal-fired plants. Once installed, however, their markedly lower fuel costs offset this difference. Still, the move toward coal and nuclear plants, which, in many cases, is mandated indirectly by federal regulations on future oil and gas use, already is placing severe financial demands on the electric utility industry, and at a time when its attractiveness to investors has been impaired by pricing regulations.

For the last 10 to 15 years utilities have earned only 11 to 12 percent return on common stock equity, primarily because of the typical 18- to 24-month lag between requests for rate increases and public utility commissions' responses to them. Prices of utility common stock have eroded as a result and, combined with low earnings, have hampered the industry's ability to raise the capital necessary to finance large construction programs. Lengthy nuclear licensing procedures have aggravated these financing problems by delaying or slowing construction and thereby allowing inflation to escalate nuclear plant cost.

Thus, the flexibility with which the electric utility sector responds to the changing energy scene in the midterm model is predicated not only upon public energy policies

TABLE 4.24
Energy Inputs, 1978 and 2000

| | 1978 | | 2000 | | | | | | | | | | | |
| | | | High | | Independence | | Preferred | | Continuation | | Low | |
	Quads	Percent of Total	Quads	Percent of Total	Quads	Percent of Total	Quads	Percent of Total	Quads	Percent of Total	Quads	Percent of Total
Coal	10.1	44.5	39.7	61.8	31.3	50.2	29.1	53.8	17.2	39.6	11.1	33.3
Oil and gas	6.6	29.1	3.1	4.8	3.7	5.9	3.6	6.6	4.8	11.1	3.0	9.0
Nuclear	2.9	12.8	18.0	28.1	24.0	38.5	18.0	33.3	18.0	41.5	15.8	47.5
Hydro and other	3.1	13.6	3.4	5.3	3.4	5.4	3.4	6.3	3.4	7.8	3.4	10.2
Total	22.7	100.0	64.2	100.0	62.4	100.0	54.1	100.0	43.4	100.0	33.3	100.0

Source: Compiled by the authors.

making coal readily available at modest prices and exploiting the nation's nuclear option, but also upon public economic and regulatory policies allowing utilities to earn a return on capital expenditures that will attract the investment capital needed to finance capacity additions. Under these conditions, the utility sector's variable and fixed costs combine to keep average real electricity price increases modest in all scenarios—between 0.7 and 1.0 percent annually. Of course, these average growth rates hide significant regional differences. Electricity prices rise most rapidly in those areas that face major shifts in the energy input mix, experience most rapid growth in demand, and currently have low reserve capacity—for utilities in these regions must undertake the most ambitious construction programs. The rapidly growing areas of the Sunbelt region, for example, particularly those central southern states that traditionally have used natural gas as a primary input for generation, experience higher than average electricity price increases over the midterm. On the other hand, prices rise less rapidly than average where smaller shifts in fuel mix are required, where demand grows more slowly, and where generous levels of reserve capacity currently are available. In many parts of the central northern, northeastern, and midatlantic states, more modest construction programs adequately will meet future demand because population grows more slowly and because these areas traditionally have burned coal and began installing nuclear plants some years ago.

Throughout the nation, however, electricity's price advantage over oil and gas remains substantial, especially when coupled with its flexibility, reliability, and cleanliness, thus encouraging all sectors to substitute electricity for oil and gas when possible. Table 4.26 displays the sectoral electricity consumption data projected for the year 2000. The total economy demands between 1.5 and 3.0 times the electricity consumed in 1978. Industrial consumption increases most markedly, almost equalling the residential/commercial sector's consumption by 2000 in each case.

In 1978 roughly one-quarter of the energy consumed by the residential/commercial sector was electricity; by 2000, electricity meets almost one-half of that sector's total energy demands. The utility industry claims a greater share of the energy market partly because of the service industries' growing demand for electricity (for example, for computerized inventory and billing systems). More generally, electricity displaces oil and gas for space heating in both residential and commercial structures. Electricity makes similar inroads into the industrial sectors. In 1978, it accounted for less than one-eighth of the energy that sector consumed. By 2000 its share rises to about one-fourth. Electricity's further penetration into manufacturing industries accounts for much of this shift in the industrial sector's fuel mix. The precision with which it can be controlled renders it a particularly useful source of energy in production processes and enhances the manufacturing sector's total factor productivity.

This economywide transition to greater electrification in part explains the lessened energy intensity of each scenario's economy. From the point of consumption forward, electricity users experience very small energy losses such as dissipated heat. In fact, today's electric heat pumps, by extracting some of the heat in ambient air, actually deliver more than two units of heat for every single unit of electric energy they consume, and that efficiency could improve to as much as 3-to-1 by the late 1980s.

TABLE 4.25
Installed Electric Generating Capacity, 1978 and 2000
(Gigawatts/percent share)

	1978		High		Independence		Preferred		Continuation		Low	
							2000					
	GW	percent	GW	percent	GW	percent	GW	percent	GW	percent	GW	percent
Coal	224	40	806	52	626	43	582	45	355	35	245	30
Oil and gas (steam)	161	29	170	11	170	12	170	13	170	17	170	21
Turbines	50	9	183	12	188	13	146	11	100	10	50	6
Nuclear	52	9	300	19	400	27	300	23	300	30	270	33
Hydro and other	74	13	86	6	86	6	86	7	86	8	86	10
Total*	561	100	1,545	100	1,470	100	1,284	100	1,011	100	821	100

*Columns may not add to totals due to rounding.
Source: Compiled by the authors.

TABLE 4.26
Sectoral Electricity Consumption, 1978 and 2000

| | 1978 | 2000 | | | | | | | | | |
| | | High | | Independence | | Preferred | | Continuation | | Low | |
	Quads	Quads	AAGR	Quads	AAGR	Quads	AAGR	Quads	AAGR	Quads	AAGR
Residential/commercial	4.5	11.2	4.2	10.8	4.1	9.4	3.4	7.5	2.3	5.8	1.2
Industrial	2.9	11.1	6.3	10.7	6.1	9.3	5.4	7.4	4.4	5.7	3.1
Transportation	0.1	0.1	—	0.1	—	0.1	—	0.1	—	0.1	—
Total	7.5	22.4	5.1	21.6	4.9	18.8	4.3	14.9	3.2	11.6	2.0

Source: Compiled by the authors.

TABLE 4.27
Electricity Generation and Consumption, 1978–2000

| | 1978 | | 2000 | | | | | | | | | |
| | | | High | | Independence | | Preferred | | Continuation | | Low | |
		AAGR percent[a]		AAGR percent[b]		AAGR percent[b]		AAGR percent[b]		AAGR percent[b]		AAGR percent[b]
Installed capacity (gigawatts)	561	6.7	1,545	4.7	1,470	4.5	1,284	3.8	1,011	2.7	821	1.7
Energy input (quads)	22.7	4.5	64.2	4.8	62.4	4.7	54.1	4.0	43.4	3.0	33.3	1.7
Consumption (trillions of Kwh)	2.2	4.8	6.6	5.1	6.3	4.9	5.5	4.3	4.4	3.2	3.4	2.0
System heat rates (Btus/Kwh)	10,318		9,727		9,905		9,836		9,863		9,794	

[a]1969–78 growth rates.
[b]Average annual growth rates 1978–2000.
Source: Compiled by the authors.

Because of electricity's high end-use efficiency, the end-use intensity of the economy declines as the utility sector penetrates deeper into the energy market.

The overall productivity with which the electric utility sector operates also improves over the midterm, as seen in Table 4.27. The electricity generated and consumed grows faster than installed capacity in all scenarios, reversing the trend of the 1970s. Potential supply and actual demand come into a productive balance. Furthermore, the efficiency with which power plants convert primary inputs into electricity improves. In 1978, 10,318 Btus produced one kilowatthour, but, according to this book's modeling results, the heat rate should drop to somewhere between 9,727 and 9,905 Btus by the end of the century. Thus, the electric utility sector contributes to the reduction of the economy's primary-energy intensity as well as its end-use intensity.

Energy Consumption and Conservation

Projected shifts in the nation's mix of primary and converted energy supplies correlate with the projected end-use energy consumption trends. Table 4.28 displays the consumption data by sector and energy type—primary fuels and electricity—for the years 1978 and 2000. Total end-use energy ranges widely, from less than 54 quads in the zero energy growth case to almost 105 quads in the high-growth scenario, a difference of nearly 100 percent. In all scenarios, however, the economy becomes more energy efficient, as evidenced by the lowered energy intensities.

Electricity penetrates into the nontransportation sectors substantially, as noted earlier, and in fact accounts for over 50 percent of the additional end-use consumption in all scenarios. Even in the low-growth scenario, in which total end-use consumption actually drops, electricity consumption grows 2.0 percent on average every year — further evidence of electricity's price and end-use efficiency advantages. Solar energy contributes 5 quads when world oil prices rise rapidly, but supplies only 1 or 2 quads when chance is favorable. Although the midterm model does not distribute this total among sectors, solar's contribution will be strongest in the residential/commercial sector where its cost competitiveness with other energy sources already is being demonstrated. The transportation sector's end-use consumption drops in all but the high-growth case, in large part because improved automobile fuel efficiencies conserve energy.

In fact, conservation plays a significant role in all sectors. Although this book's scope precluded a detailed end-use analysis to determine conservation's impact on each sector's energy requirements, its potential aggregate contribution to the economy over the midterm can be captured in two ways: first, by imposing the nation's actual energy intensity in 1978 on the preferred scenario's economy and then by imposing the high-growth scenario's energy intensity in 2000. If the preferred scenario in 2000 required today's current energy intensity, primary energy use would be 35 quads higher. Viewed in terms of variations across scenarios in 2000, if the preferred scenario had required the high growth scenario's 47,000 Btus to produce each real dollar of its GNP in 2000 rather than the 43,000 actually required, its primary energy needs would have been 10 quads greater, as Figure 4.13 graphically

TABLE 4.28
End-Use Consumption, End-Use Intensity, and Primary Energy Consumption, 1978 and 2000 (Quads)

Sectors	1978 General	Elec-tricity	Total	High General	Elec-tricity	Total	Preferred General	Elec-tricity	Total	Continuation General	Elec-tricity	Total	Low General	Elec-tricity	Total
Consumption															
Residential/commercial	14.4	4.5	18.9	21.1	11.2	32.3	13.6	9.4	23.0	15.1	7.5	22.6	8.2	5.8	14.0
Industrial	20.6	2.9	23.5	32.3	11.1	43.4	24.8	9.3	34.1	26.4	7.4	33.8	17.9	5.7	23.6
Transportation	20.3	0.1	20.4	27.1	0.1	27.2	17.7	0.1	17.8	18.0	0.1	18.1	10.9	0.1	11.0
Solar						2.0			5.0			1.0			5.0
Total (quads)*		7.5	62.8		22.4	104.8		18.8	79.9		14.9	75.5		11.6	53.6
AAGR (percent)					5.1	2.4		4.3	1.1		3.2	0.8		2.0	−0.7
Intensity															
1,000 Btus per $1972			45			34			30			32			27
AAGR (percent)						1.3			−1.9			−1.5			−2.4
Primary Energy															
Use (quads)			78.0			147.0			117.2			104.2			77.3
Intensity (1,000 Btus per $1972)			56			47			43			45			39
AAGR (percent)						−0.8			−1.2			−1.0			−1.7

*Columns may not add to totals due to rounding.

Source: Compiled by the authors.

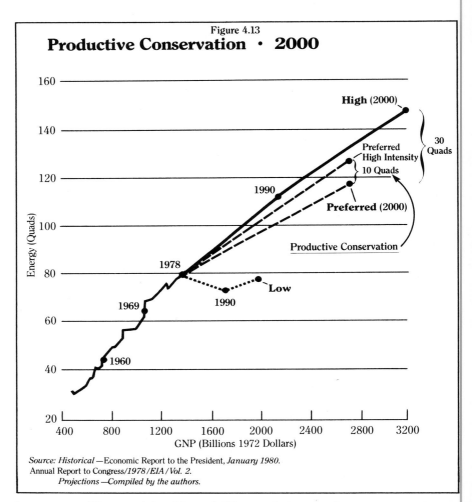

Figure 4.13
Productive Conservation • 2000

Source: Historical—Economic Report to the President, *January 1980.*
Annual Report to Congress/*1978/EIA/Vol. 2.*
Projections —Compiled by the authors.

demonstrates. The remaining 20-quad difference between primary energy consumption in the high-growth and preferred scenarios relates to their GNP differences. Although it is difficult to distribute the 10 quads of productive conservation between primary and end-use energy supplies, the sheer magnitude of this contribution testifies to conservation's important and growing role within the economy.

Its impact is strongest in the low-growth and preferred scenarios because their higher energy prices cause a greater realignment of the KLEM equation. The interaction between conservation and the economy is bidirectional, however. The extent to which energy can be conserved depends not only on consumers' willingness "to do without," as may be the case in the low-growth scenario, but also on their ability to replace existing capital stock—heating systems, manufacturing equipment, automobiles—with more energy-efficient ones.

The Changing KLEM Equation

A quantity or quality change in one KLEM input, whether induced by choice or chance, causes a corollary change in the relative economic contribution of the other inputs. The KLEM input mix used to produce GNP in 1978 consisted of 14.1 percent capital services, 22.9 percent labor services, 3.4 percent energy, and 59.5 percent nonenergy materials. As seen in Table 4.29, unless all conditions simultaneously favor growth, as they do in the high-growth scenario, energy's relative contribution will drop between now and 2000. The flexibility and speed with which the economy can adapt to this probable change will determine the nation's future material well-being.

By and large in the high-growth and preferred scenarios, the KLEM equation's evolution is being directed by investment-stimulating policies that enable all the economy's producing sectors to utilize significantly more capital services to complement labor services. The resulting productivity growth helps to hold down output prices from both energy-producing industries and nonenergy- or materials-producing industries. Consequently, even though world oil prices rise rapidly in the preferred scenario, energy's relative contribution drops rather mildly — 0.37 of a percentage point — and material's share actually rises by 0.46 of a percentage point. With good luck, GNP growth averages 3.8 percent annually, and even with bad luck, it grows 3.1 percent each year.

In the continuation and low-growth scenarios, on the other hand, investment-retarding policies dampen the growth of capital and productivity. Consequently, despite the continuation scenario's better luck, energy's relative contribution drops almost as much as it does in the preferred scenario, and materials' contribution drops as well. As a result, GNP grows at 2.4 percent on average each year. When slow capital and productivity growth are aggravated by rapidly escalating world oil prices, as they are in the low-growth case, GNP growth declines even further to 1.7 percent each year. Producers can do little more than hold energy consumption at 1978 levels. The resulting 1.0 percentage point decline in energy's relative contribution to the economy of necessity induces some small changes in the other factor inputs' contributions, but these changes occur, more or less, by default.

In fact, within the limits defined by the modeling input assumptions, the mix of primary production factors projected for each scenario is the most efficient one possible. Prices have balanced supply and demand. Moreover, the most dramatic changes occur by 1990. The policies adopted in the lower-growth scenarios offer the economy little flexibility. In both cases the KLEM equation divides into shares not vastly different from those of 1978. The policies employed in the higher-growth scenarios effect more dramatic changes, stabilizing the KLEM equation in a shape that reduces vulnerability to chance-dominated factors.

Economic Equilibrium: 1995–2030

The long-term results appear anticlimactic when compared with the earlier time periods. By the year 2000, the economy has long since regained its vitality and has entered an equilibrium growth state for each scenario. The KLEM equation is essentially in balance. Even the transition away from oil and gas, particularly imports, toward coal, nuclear, and renewables is well underway in all but the high-growth scenario. For the most part, aggregate energy prices have stabilized, slowing the need for increased substitution of capital and labor for energy. Furthermore, from a statistical point of view, the post-2000 results are highly aggregative and sketchy, especially with respect to the structure of the economy and the composition of its output. In a more telling way, however, the long-term results are indeed climactic: they provide a strategic vantage point from which to assess not only the long-term economic and energy growth potentials underlying each scenario's policy choices, but also the precipitous vulnerability associated with some of those scenarios' too heavy reliance on a favorable chance factor.

Table 4.30 combines five key variables — working population, GNP, capital stock, energy, and electricity—to capture the scenarios' dimensions. The sheer magnitude of the high-growth scenario all but precludes it from further consideration. The likelihood of GNP surging forward by 367 percent while working population increases by only 67 percent is extremely small, especially when that expansion is prompted by energy and electricity growth rates that return to their historical relationship with GNP growth. Even without the high-growth scenario, the remaining scenarios exhibit a considerable range across variables, with population playing an increasingly important role after 2000.

Economic Results

ETA-Macro combines the working-age population and productivity assumptions with labor force participation rates, hours per workweek, and energy prices to project GNP growth through the year 2030. As shown in Table 4.31, the span between the continuation scenario's and the independence scenario's real GNP growth rate narrows and shifts downward after 2000, reflecting similar changes in the growth of labor productivity and labor hours. The reduced productivity growth rates offer few surprises: they simply reflect the impact of slowing capital and labor quality gains on total factor productivity growth. The fact that labor hours grow at half the population growth rate in the preferred and independence scenarios, however, does signal a fundamental long-term change in work force participation rates and the length of the workweek. In combination these trends cause the two higher scenarios to take on economic growth characteristics similar to the midterm's continuation case, while the continuation scenario itself assumes the characteristics of the midterm's low-growth scenario.

Adjusting the Energy/GNP Ratio

In Chapter 3 the authors argued that the highly aggregate structure of the ETA-Macro model and the simplicity with which it treats energy-economy interactions tend to bias its results toward increased energy consumption per dollar of real GNP. Because the near-, mid-, and long-term results only served to strengthen this argument, the authors adjusted the long-term results by imposing a continuing but gradual downward trend on the energy-GNP ratios.

TABLE 4.29
The Composition of KLEM, 1978 and 2000

	1978	High		Preferred		Continuation		Low	
	Percent Share	Percent Share	Percent Change	Percent Share	Percent Change	Percent Share	Percent Change	Percent Share	Percent Change
Capital services	14.14	18.24	29.0	17.68	25.0	17.23	21.9	15.38	8.8
Labor services	22.90	18.03	−21.3	19.27	−15.8	20.96	−8.5	22.72	−0.8
Energy	3.42	3.51	2.6	3.05	−10.8	3.09	−9.6	2.41	−29.5
Materials	59.54	60.22	1.1	60.00	0.8	58.72	−1.4	59.49	−0.1

Source: Compiled by the authors.

TABLE 4.30
Scenario Dimensions[a], 2000 and 2030
(Percent of 1978)

	High		Independence		Preferred		Continuation		Low	
	2000	2030	2000	2030	2000	2030	2000	2030	2000	2030
Population, working-age	130	167	130	167	126	156	124	137	120	127
GNP	225	467	220	426	195	357	168	264	144	213
Capital stock[b]	204	386	204	370	176	293	148	208	114	131
Energy	188	385	175	311	150	244	134	190	99	106
Electricity	300	882	287	600	251	432	199	323	155	186

[a]Adjusted ETA-Macro results.
[b]Authors' estimate.
Source: Compiled by the authors.

TABLE 4.31
Generating GNP
(AAGR)

	Independence		Preferred		Continuation	
	1978– 2000	2000– 30	1978– 2000	2000– 30	1978– 2000	2000– 30
GNP	3.7	2.2	3.1	2.0	2.4	1.5
Labor productivity	2.4	1.8	2.1	1.7	2.0	1.5
Labor hours	1.3	0.4	1.0	0.3	0.4	*
Population (16 and over)	1.2	0.8	1.1	0.7	1.0	0.3

*Negligible increase.
Source: Compiled by the authors.

Table 4.32 contrasts the modeled energy-GNP ratios with the adjusted ones (ADJ). In all three scenarios, ETA-Macro results reverse the midterm trend of decreasing ratios so that by 2030 they revert back to 1990 levels. The adjusted ratios continue to decline but at a slower pace than in the midterm.

Of course, the adjusted energy-GNP ratios substantially change each scenario's primary energy requirement and mix. Obtaining the adjusted primary energy totals poses no problem; they are derived simply by multiplying the new energy-GNP ratios by the ETA-Macro GNP values. Changing the energy mix, however, is not quite so straightforward. An energy source's absolute contribution and penetration rate depend, in large part, on total energy requirements, alternative sources, and time. Merely compressing the ETA-Macro results to yield an energy mix associated with an earlier time would tend to favor existing energy sources over promising new ones. Con-

TABLE 4.32
Adjusted Primary Energy Intensities

	Independence		Preferred		Continuation	
	MR[a]	ADJ[b]	MR	ADJ	MR	ADJ
1978	56	56	56	56	56	56
1990	47.5	47.5	46.8	46.8	46.8	46.8
2000	44.8	44.8	43.4	43.4	44.8	44.8
2010	44.8	43.0	44.7	41.0	43.3	43.0
2020	46.9	42.0	48.1	39.5	45.3	41.5
2030	47.2	41.0	48.4	38.5	46.5	40.5

[a]Modeling results.
[b]Adjusted judgmentally.
Source: Compiled by the authors.

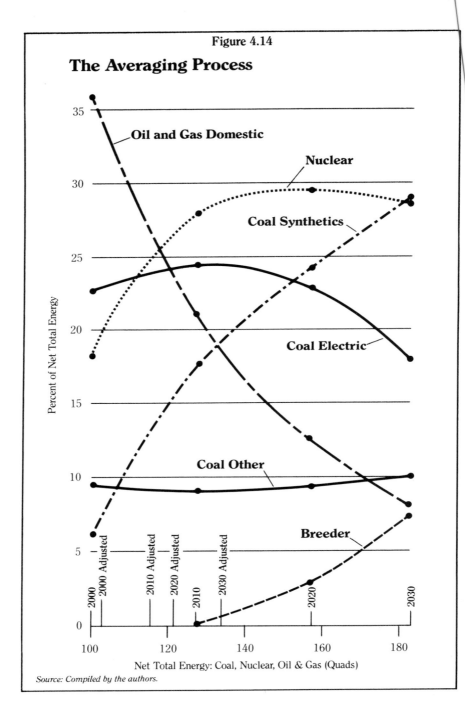

Figure 4.14

The Averaging Process

sequently, averaging was employed to balance the selections from both sources. It was assumed, moreover, that contributions from advanced electric, shale, hydro, geothermal, solar, and other new or renewable sources would remain the same in both the adjusted and unadjusted energy totals. Although this assumption leaves much to be desired from a forecasting point of view, it does limit needless debate over new energy sources without significantly altering the implications for energy policy.

Figure 4.14 highlights the key step in the averaging process. Six trajectories were constructed from data on the remaining energy sources with coal subdivided by end use. The vertical and horizontal axes are measured in percent share of net total energy and quads (10^{15} Btus), respectively. Each trajectory is drawn by interpolating between the four points corresponding to ETA-Macro's (EM) long-term results. At 2030 EM, for example, coal electric accounts for 17.8 percent of net energy requirements. The point 2030 ADJ, derived from the energy-GNP ratios, corresponds to coal electric's share of 24.3 percent. In terms of quads, 2030 EM and 2030 ADJ coal electric percentages call for 23.8 and 32.5 quads, respectively. The average of the two, 28.2 quads, is selected for coal electric's contribution to the adjusted energy mix in the year 2030. Averaging is particularly important in the case of breeder technology. Taken separately, the 2030 EM and 2030 ADJ results have different implications for breeder research and development. The 2030 EM result gives the breeder a 7.3 percent share of net total energy, a share that clearly requires breeder availability by 2010 and an aggressive R&D program today. The 2030 ADJ results assign breeder only a 0.08 percent share — a share that suggests breeder development could be slowed without posing significant problems for the energy sector.

Primary Energy Results

By 2030 the major sources of primary energy are coal, nuclear power, and renewables. Domestic oil and gas supply play a much smaller role because of declining reserves, an irreversible trend unless major technological breakthroughs make available massive new sources of "unconventional" gas, such as geopressured methane. In fact, as Table 4.33 shows, domestic oil and gas production falls by about 50 percent in the preferred and independence scenarios, even though high prices keep production at a maximum, and by about 70 percent in the continuation case, in which low prices limit production. Imports are completely phased out of the economy. Shale oil, geothermal, and various forms of solar energy make major contributions, but in no case do they provide more than 35 percent of the total. The increasing dominance of coal and nuclear power over the period is self-evident. By 2030 coal holds the major primary fuel share in all scenarios. Coal use by electric utilities levels off in the preferred and continuation scenarios and accounts for less than half of total coal consumption in all scenarios, reflecting coal's shift to its fastest-growing market, coal-based synthetics. Once free of midterm constraints, nuclear begins to shoulder the industry's increasing need for base-load generation.

Electricity Results

Table 4.34 shows the trend toward increased electrification continuing over the long term for the three central scenarios. By the end of the long term, total generation

TABLE 4.33
Energy Supply, 1978, 2000, and 2030
(Quads)

	1978	Independence		Preferred		Continuation	
		2000	2030	2000	2030	2000	2030
Petroleum and gas supply							
Domestic	38.8	38.0	16.3	38.5	17.5	37.1	9.8
Imports	19.1	17.0	—	6.8	—	17.6	—
Shale oil	—	1.0	12.6	1.0	12.6	0.1	6.3
Coal Supply							
Electricity	10.1	31.3	41.2	29.1	28.2	17.2	18.0
Synthetics	—	6.0	39.2	6.0	25.3	0.6	19.5
Other	4.0	10.8	15.0	9.4	12.7	9.2	14.9
Nuclear	2.9	24.0	73.7	18.0	50.0	18.0	35.6
Hydro, geothermal and advanced electricity	3.1	3.4	14.3	3.4	14.3	3.4	14.3
Solar, other	—	5.0	30.0	5.0	30.0	1.0	30.0
Total	78.0	136.5	242.3	117.2	190.6	104.2	148.4

Source: Compiled by the authors.

TABLE 4.34
Electricity Generation, 2000–30
(Quads)

	Independence				Preferred				Continuation			
	2000	2010	2020	2030	2000	2010	2020	2030	2000	2010	2020	2030
Energy inputs												
Coal	31.3	37.5	39.4	41.2	29.1	28.1	29.1	28.2	17.2	19.2	19.2	18.0
Nuclear	24.0	39.7	52.6	73.7	18.0	29.1	35.7	50.0	18.0	25.4	26.7	35.6
Petroleum and gas	3.7	2.5	1.5	1.6	3.6	2.5	2.5	1.8	4.8	3.6	2.5	1.9
Hydro, geothermal and advanced electricity	3.4	12.9	15.2	14.3	3.4	12.9	15.2	14.3	3.4	8.9	11.2	14.3
Total	62.4	92.6	108.7	130.8	54.1	72.6	82.5	94.3	43.4	57.1	59.6	69.8
Percent coal	50.2	40.5	36.2	31.5	53.8	38.7	35.3	29.9	39.6	33.6	32.2	25.8
Percent nuclear	38.5	42.9	48.4	56.3	33.3	40.1	43.3	53.0	41.5	44.5	44.8	51.0
Generation												
Trillion KWH	6.3	9.4	11.0	13.2	5.5	7.3	8.3	9.5	4.4	5.8	6.0	7.1
Percent of delivered energy	22.9	31.9	32.0	31.5	23.5	28.8	28.2	27.1	19.7	24.6	22.7	25.1
KWH per dollar of real GNP	2.07	2.40	2.33	2.24	2.04	2.14	2.03	1.93	1.89	2.06	1.85	1.93

Source: Compiled by the authors.

ranges from approximately 3 to 6 times the 1978 level of 2.2 trillion kilowatthours. Nuclear power becomes increasingly important to the industry's fuel mix, overtaking coal as the prime generating source by 2010 in all scenarios. By 2030 coal and nuclear power generation together account for more than 75 percent of total generation in all cases. Coal use by utilities ranges from about 0.8 to 2 billion tons, the maximum practical limit given the demand for coal-based synthetic fuels. Nuclear capacity ranges from 600 to 1,200 gw. The breeder, which can utilize uranium much more efficiently, begins to supplement light-water reactors by the middle of the second decade of the new century.

Long-Term Implications

Although sketchy, the adjusted ETA-Macro results do accent a theme that has emerged throughout this study—flexibility. The high- and low-growth projections for 2030 reinforce the finding that the nation's economic and energy policies must be designed to keep options open. Even with its strong commitment to growth, the society represented by the high-growth scenario in all likelihood would not be able to avoid the reality of resource depletion before 2030. That electricity growth and energy growth could return to their pre-1970 relationships seems all but impossible. Likewise, that in 2030 the low-growth scenario's economy could produce over twice the GNP produced in 1978 while using only 6 percent more energy seems equally improbable. Because such worlds are so remote and unlike the world we live in today, these two scenarios have not been examined closely. Although the economy may evolve along a growth path similar to that projected for either of these cases, its equilibrium likely would not be maintained throughout the long term unless policies were revised to foster more moderate growth, particularly in energy consumption.

Alternative Futures

Even though the high- and low-growth scenarios bound the probable range within which the economy will grow, the existence of other less probable, yet possible, growth paths cannot be denied. However, because they are extreme, these alternative scenarios are difficult to envision and impossible to model econometrically. Still, they must be considered in order to realize the possible ramifications of today's public policy decisions.

Ultrahigh Growth

Several circumstances could drive the economy to growth rates even higher than those projected for the high-growth scenario: higher birth and immigration rates; sharper increases in labor force participation; workweeks that remain stable rather than grow shorter; much higher saving and investment rates; significantly greater productivity improvements; elimination of many pollution control requirements; major reductions in government regulations; and significant decreases in real energy prices, including stable or decreasing real world oil prices. Some of these forces, such as the sharp increases in labor force participation, would have only a temporary effect, reaching a saturation level after a few years. Those that might persist more or less permanently, such as significant decreases in energy prices, have a low probability of occurring independently and an even lower probability of occurring in combination.

With the exclusion of higher birth and immigration rates, the ultrahigh-growth scenario would lead to higher average living standards much sooner than in the present volume's other scenarios, but they likely would be achieved at the expense of greater pollution, less consumer and worker protection, less leisure, and more re-source depletion. Depending on the rate of productivity improvements and the choice of fiscal and monetary policies, inflation either could be aggravated or improved. Over the near term (1980–90) none of these consequences likely would be severe; but in the longer term (1990–2030) the risks associated with this scenario are extremely high.

Negative Growth

Risks associated with negative growth are equally high. A negative-growth scenario could come about episodically or gradually. The episodic scenario's economy would experience almost instantaneous major discontinuities: sudden changes in styles of living, wildly fluctuating employment, cascading business failures, and peaceful or violent disruptions that permanently change society. Such episodic events have occurred in the past and cannot be taken lightly. For the United States the cataclysmic episodic event that comes readily to mind, aside from wars, is the stock market crash of 1929 and the subsequent Depression of the 1930s—nearly a decade of economic and social trauma. However, a negative-growth scenario could unfold in a more gradual manner. Prolonged economic stagnation, under the right set of circumstances, could evolve into a spiraling economic downturn. The U.S. economy's performance in the late 1970s has served to increase the recognition that such a future is distinctly possible.

Episodic Negative Growth

Two potential episodic events that could lead to negative economic growth scenarios seem possible within this century: one triggered by a massive, runaway inflation, and a second triggered by a total, sustained cutoff of Middle East-North African oil supplies. Either event would be unique to U.S. experience, precluding direct historical comparison.

While inflation has not yet approached hyperinflationary levels in the United States, our society is becoming accustomed at least superficially to two-digit infla-tion. Interest rates of 25 percent per year are accepted routinely by segments of our population who anticipate the eventual indexing of wages, taxes, and prices. The overwhelming popularity of books on how to survive "financial collapse" and the "coming bad times" suggests that the possibility of runaway inflation is being taken much more seriously in the United States today than it was a decade or two ago. To understand this growing concern, one need only extend into the future the post-1965 trends of investment, government spending, deficit accumulation, money supply growth, interest rates, and inflation.

The general socioeconomic implication of such a scenario can be inferred from hyperinflationary episodes in other economies. The most telling example occurred in Germany in the 1920s. That long-term episode brought about the almost total collapse of the nation's industrial and financial institutions, the virtual elimination of the middle class, enormous human suffering, and political anarchy, setting the scene for Adolph Hitler's eventual rise to power. More recently, a number of South American and third world countries have experienced inflation rates well above 100 percent per year. Even Israel, with its relatively sophisticated economic and financial institutions, recently has approached a 200 percent annual inflation rate. Some of these countries have accommodated their very high rates by indexing nearly all financial transactions, but a fear exists that indexing only can postpone the eventual day of reckoning.

A scenario reflecting an episodic cutoff of Middle East and North African oil supplies is more difficult to conceptualize because never before in its peacetime history has the United States been so dependent on foreign sources for a primary resource. If the cutoff included Western Europe and Japan, a severe and prolonged depression probably would extend throughout the developed world. Such a situation could be brought about by greater Soviet domination in the Middle East or by a change or reunification of Arab policies that focuses on a hard-line anti-Israeli stance and perpetuates the recent divergence between U.S. and West European policies toward the Arab-Israeli dispute.

The United States probably would be somewhat less severely affected than its trading partners by such an episode because it is less dependent on both imported energy and world-export trade. Even if the oil-sharing provision in the current International Energy Agency agreements initially were honored, sooner or later that commitment might be withdrawn, given the severity of the economic and human consequences of the shortage. Still, styles of living would change abruptly. Regulations and prohibitions would sprout as fast as they do in wartime. Gasoline would be rationed. Heavy-energy-using industries' production would be constrained severely and the resulting shortages could cause sporadic localized civil disturbances. Wartime controls would be directed at exploiting domestic energy supplies, notably coal, gas, and nuclear power, and at developing alternative energy sources. In all likelihood environmental considerations would be set aside.

If the cutoff did not include Western Europe and Japan, and growth continued in the rest of the world at a more nearly normal pace, the consequences for the United States would be even more severe. Even in this scenario, however, the disruption would have worldwide effects. Those nations most heavily dependent on U.S. trade probably would experience moderate economic depression as the United States turned inevitably inward. Gradually, they would adjust to the much smaller U.S. role in the world, an adjustment helped almost certainly by trade increases with the communist bloc nations. The possibility of such cutoff episodes occurring is small. No long-term complete shut-off of Persian Gulf and North African oil could be sustained without a major breakdown in international relationships. A long-term shutoff that applied only to the U.S. is even less likely, since oil is a fungible commodity, easily resold and retransported around the world. Only in a situation where the Soviet Union controlled the oil fields and, through this control, dominated Western Europe could the United States alone be made to suffer. However, such situations are not impossible; in fact the possibility of their occurring is far from minuscule. In fact, a cutoff scenario is somewhat more likely than a hyperinflation scenario. More likely than either of these, however, is a partial breakdown in the oil supply from the turbulent regions of the world. One need not look far for probable causes: the continuation of the Arab-Israeli conflict, the spread of orthodox Muslim movements typified by the theocracy in Iran, an expansion of intraregional struggles such as the Iran-Iraq War, or internal political breakdowns due to the inadequacy of existing institutions to cope with cultural stresses and economic problems brought on by the immense new oil revenues. Any of these events could be aggravated by major world powers seeking to extend their influence or to protect their economy and world-trade position as competition for energy resources grows. Certainly, the record to date of the International Energy Agency, established specifically to deal with emergency supply situations among importing nations, provides little reason for optimism regarding effective cooperation of the user nations.[3]

The consequences of such breakdowns depend, of course, on their frequency and extent, neither of which can be estimated. Given that the United States takes over 30 percent of its imports from the Persian Gulf alone, however, and that Western Europe and Japan take 60 to 70 percent of their imports from the same region, any breakdown would shock the world economy. The likelihood of such an episode occurring will increase as world demand strains current supply capabilities, forcing producing regions either to increase their production capacity or to restrict supplies. If world demand continues to grow at its current pace, supply limits may be reached early in the 1990s. Under these conditions, oil disruptions in the 1980s could have economic impacts far more severe than they had in the 1970s. Although not all of the post-1973 falloff in economic growth can be attributed to the energy price hikes of the 1970s, those disruptions surely caused a substantial part of the decline. Before the 1973 Arab oil embargo, U.S. GNP was growing 4 percent annually. After that episode GNP growth dropped to 2 percent. Total free world economic growth dropped from 5.1 to 3.5 percent. If the frequency and severity of disruptions increase, and domestic and foreign policies remain unchanged, the United States could experience stagnant GNP growth during the 1980s.

Spiraling Downturn

A negative-growth scenario could emerge as a spiraling downturn, the aftermath of hyperinflation, or, more likely, the combination of low-growth policies and extremely bad luck. Significant and prolonged underinvestment is the most likely prompter of a spiraling economic downturn. If public policies consistently were to squelch incentives to save and invest, the investment ratio would fall far below the level needed for economic stability. Because of the long life of most existing capital stock, underinvestment could continue for a number of years. When the resulting decline in GNP growth finally turned into an actual drop in GNP, the nation might be unable to summon the collective willpower necessary to remedy the situation. If inadequate investment is coupled with sporadic oil supply interruptions and repeated sharp price increases, such as were experienced in 1974 and 1979, the nation's material living standards could slide in the last 20 years of the century as rapidly as they rose in the 20 years after World War II.

Notes

1. For consistency, throughout Chapter 4 computations are based on the preliminary 1978 GNP number employed in the H-J model: $1,385.7 billion (1972 dollars), except in the long-term results, which use ETA-Macro numbers, and in the figures. The 1978 GNP reported in the *1980 Economic Report of the President* is $1,399.2.

2. Albert T. Sommers, "Inflation: The Crucial Challenge in the 1980's," in *The Economy and the President: 1980 and Beyond*, ed. W. E. Hoadley (Englewood Cliffs, N.J.: Prentice-Hall, 1980), pp. 34–73.

3. See Walter J. Levy, "Oil and the Decline of the West," *Foreign Affairs* 58 (Summer 1980): 999–1015.

Chapter 5

POLICY PORTFOLIO

Seeking Flexibility

In fashioning a policy portfolio for the highly uncertain 1980s, the United States will have to employ a strategy long familiar to security analysts: "A good portfolio is more than a long list of stocks and bonds. It is a balanced whole, providing the investor with protections and opportunities with respect to a wide range of contingencies. The investor should build toward an integrated portfolio which best suits his needs."[1] Such a philosophy clearly extends beyond economic planning to all aspects of national life, and its wisdom lies in its emphasis on balance and flexibility. In the past decade the United States has experienced more than one object lesson in the effect of limiting its options: certainly, the 1973 Arab oil embargo springs to mind.

If modern decision makers were gifted with oracular insight they could plan confidently and single-mindedly for the future; but the only contemporary phenomenon as inevitable as death and taxes seems to be uncertainty. With uncertainty growing with the complexity of modern life, the need to plan for the unexpected constantly grows. Thus, balance and flexibility afford decision makers, indeed all citizens, a means of dealing with a world more technologically sophisticated, more politically interdependent, and more rapidly changing than it has been at any time in its history. Balance simply dictates that social choices should not be made arbitrarily, but instead with an eye toward the relationship of one policy to others and of the present to the future, and flexibility counters those factors beyond human control with multiple choices that U.S. citizens can make to hedge against potentially misguided bets.

Mutually supportive and consistent policies, carefully integrated to approach the same goal from multiple perspectives, can serve to offset the debilitating effects that chance events can have on national and international affairs. A policy portfolio that fits such a description is like a national insurance policy providing social, environmental, economic, and energy security in the face of most reasonable futures.

The idea of reasonable futures, *plural*, which is central to this book, distinguishes it from a forecast. A single forecast—one scenario of the future—cannot hope to pinpoint all social, economic, and energy developments accurately. It would be virtually impossible to predict changes in either the direction, magnitude, or potential combinations of those forces that can influence the shape of the future. Instead, this book presents a range of conditional projections, a series of plausible futures that when juxtaposed allow decision makers to see the spectrum from which the future might develop. Once that range has been defined, policy makers can use it to establish realistic objectives. If, for example, a moderate level of economic growth is deemed desirable, then a GNP growth target that allows for the adverse influence of potential chance events makes more sense than a target unachievable in the wake of any undesirable contingency.

This book presents five distinct scenarios that combine the techniques of economic and energy modeling with judgmental analysis. The nation's real economic growth rate varies significantly among these scenarios, but in all five there is at least a modest positive and continuing improvement in average living standards. The distinctions between these scenarios result from various combinations of chance events, to which the economic system reacts with varying degrees of success, and conscious policies that are either continuations of past policies or planned deviations from them. All scenarios reveal how central economic policy is to all aspects of U.S. life — particularly the energy sector.

In addition, two types of qualitatively developed scenarios are presented, although as less likely futures. These scenarios are triggered by either shocks or episodic events for which the nation is unprepared or by a continuing sequence of poor policy choices resulting in economic stagnation or in long periods of negative real growth.

When this study was in its design stage, the authors decided that labeling the different scenarios by numbers or letters would make it difficult for readers to remember their distinguishing characteristics when comparisons were being made. Consequently, they elected to label each senario with a descriptive name that also reveals the economic growth potential of that particular future. Obviously, this decision means that the individual scenarios carry highly connotative and therefore potentially judgmental names.

The Preferred Scenario: The Economic Picture

As its name implies, the preferred scenario appears to offer more advantages and fewer disadvantages to the nation, its citizens, and their descendants than the other four modeled alternatives. The study does not maintain that, of all possible futures, the preferred is *exactly* the optimum. Rather, the preferred scenario, or any number of futures with similar characteristics, would be markedly superior to any of the even larger variety of futures that cluster around the other four scenarios.

To approximate the preferred scenario's economic growth rates, the nation must improve its productivity growth dramatically, which can be achieved only by sharp boosts in spending for investment — particularly for research and development. These boosts, in turn, will show us how to use resources more efficiently and in more environmentally acceptable ways and how to substitute plentiful resources for scarce ones at a faster rate.

Faster productivity growth also will require improved levels of understanding and cooperation among business, labor, and government. These improvements will have strong positive implications for individual liberty in both social and economic spheres, reducing the need for government-imposed sanctions and promoting the spirit of compromise.

Moreover, productivity improvements will help to reestablish our competitiveness in international markets, to strengthen the dollar, and to provide us a firmer basis on which to pursue effective foreign policies. If our international trade and currency positions become less precarious, we will be in a better position to help our foreign allies and those third world nations who need assistance so desperately. A strong, productive, competitive United States can help other nations as well as itself.

Labor productivity growth provides one convenient index to the nation's economic well-being. The preferred scenario requires a 2.1 percent average annual labor productivity growth rate between 1978 and 2000, a figure that takes on meaning when compared to the historic low of 1.2 percent between 1969 and 1978, and the historic high of 2.9 percent between 1960 and 1969. At first glance, the difference between the labor productivity growth rate modeled for the continuation scenario—2.0 percent average annual growth between 1978 and 2000—and the preferred scenario's slightly higher rate of 2.1 percent appears insignificant. To a great extent, however, the continuation scenario's projected labor productivity growth is fueled—literally—by good luck on world oil prices, which increase at a rate of 2 percent as opposed to 4 percent in the preferred.

Another important by-product of the preferred scenario will be the reduction of inflationary pressures. While it can be argued that rapid money supply growth is one of the most direct causes of inflation, it is apparent that unfulfilled economic expectations are the primary source of domestic pressures on the federal government —and these pressures eventually erupt in the form of rapid money supply growth. A continual jockeying among the societal sectors for a larger share of our national output is a closely related source of inflationary pressure. As the nation's economic growth rate recedes, each sector realizes its only chance for improvement is actually to take a piece of another sector's share.

Once it is generally recognized that total output is rising, even though the growth rate may be modest by former standards, the severity of these struggles—which often pit the government and the other social sectors against one another—decreases. Thus, the need for continuing government intervention in the form of rules, regulations, and prohibitions also will decrease.

By far the most important consequence of the preferred scenario's moderate economic growth is the improved average living standard and the enhanced quality of life that it offers U.S. citizens. As Chapter 4 makes clear, the nation is still rather far from being able to provide a modestly pleasant and secure standard of living for all citizens—even if incomes were redistributed to suit the strictest egalitarian principles. Because any income distribution scheme that even approaches absolute equality is impractical given a democracy's guarantee of economic and political liberty, the only viable avenue to improved living standards for the underprivileged is through a combination of moderate economic growth and modest income redistribution. With such a combination, incentives to excel and to take risks can be preserved, extreme income differences can be reduced and their adverse effects minimized, and living standards can be improved in ways that are reasonably equitable for all. Chapter 4 suggests that such objectives are more likely to be achieved in the preferred scenario than in the two lower-growth alternatives.

Moderate economic growth also will allow for the continuation of environmental programs designed to provide cleaner water, clearer air, and more acres of pristine wilderness. Only after the population's basic near-term economic needs are met will average citizens be willing to concern themselves with the environment. Especially now, U.S. citizens seem unwilling to spend more on the environment at a time when inflation and slow growth are reducing the purchasing power of their average hourly wage. Moderate economic growth, however, will produce an economic surplus that can be distributed for environmental purposes and for other desirable public activities.

Of course, even faster progress in all of these areas is possible under the high-growth scenario, but it assumes that chance factors will turn out more favorably than they do in the preferred alternative. While hoping for favorable chance factors and working to make them come to pass are good psychological strategies, it seems unwise to plan on them. If the components of real GNP growth are examined, the preferred scenario argues eloquently for itself. The preferred scenario's average annual labor hours growth of 1.0 percent more than doubles the growth rate of the continuation scenario. Similarly, capital spending grows at a rate of 2.7 percent in the preferred future, but at only 1.8 percent in the continuation. When these factors are weighted and combined with respective total factor productivity growth rates of 1.6 and 1.5 percent for the preferred and continuation scenarios, they yield considerably different GNP growth rates. Clearly, however, at 3.1 percent, the real GNP growth of the preferred scenario offers a target that potentially affords a greater degree of flexibility and security than the 2.4 percent growth registered in the continuation future. The continuation scenario depends on good luck for a substantial part of its growth; without that luck, the growth rate would shift toward the 1.7 percent of the low-growth scenario. The independence scenario combines unfortunate chance factors affecting energy prices with the labor force participation, capital investment, productivity growth, and immigration rates assumed for the high-growth scenario. This combination yields economic growth rates, in terms of both real GNP and real GNP per capita, that are significantly higher than those that occur in the preferred scenario and nearly as high as those in the high-growth. It is certainly appropriate to set high investment objectives and to anticipate high labor participation rates and substantial productivity growth as in the independence scenario, but it is no wiser to expect all growth policies to be fully effective than it is to be overly optimistic regarding chance factors. Therefore, this book does not advocate a pursuit of the independence scenario but, instead, suggests a concentration on the preferred scenario. However, the independence scenario is important for its confirmation that high energy prices need not seriously hamper our future if sensible growth-favoring policies are implemented.

The Preferred Scenario: The Energy Picture

There is no credible evidence that the nation or the world is running out of energy. The authors of this book found none and, in this conclusion, they agree with those who have produced other recent, scientifically respectable studies.[2]

There are, however, three crucial energy questions currently faced by this nation: how rapidly can we reduce our dependence on unreliable and expensive foreign oil; how much energy will the country need 10, 20, and 50 years from now; and what mix of raw energy supplies can best meet the country's needs while granting full consideration to the needs of other nations? Although complete energy independence may be achieved someday, it need not be a primary objective now. The principal objective of the United States should be to reduce imported oil to maximums of 25 to 30 percent of total oil consumption and 10 to 12 percent of total primary energy consumption. The nation probably will consume 40 to 80 percent more energy in the year 2000 than it does today — and further increases are likely in the twenty-first century — if reasonable economic growth rates are sustained. Although coal and nuclear energy appear to be the major new contributors to supply over the next 20 to 30 years, other resources such as unconventional sources of gas and various solar technologies also can contribute to the national energy mix, particularly in the later years. In addition, over the near term conservation must be considered a form of energy.

Given the answers to these energy questions, a review of the five scenarios confirms the present volume's judgment for the preferred scenario. In the preferred scenario, oil imports decline to 11 percent of total primary energy use and 30 percent of total oil consumption by 1990. Further major progress is made in the next two decades: by 2000 oil imports are less than 6 percent of total energy use and by 2010 the need for them has disappeared completely. This schedule is about a decade ahead of the independence scenario and much more rapid than the high-growth or continuation alternatives. Table 5.1 compares these statistical measures for all scenarios, showing that only the low-growth scenario achieves a faster reduction in imports, but it is a reduction resulting from a combination of unacceptably low economic growth rates and exceptionally high energy efficiency growth rates.

This study also advocates the preferred scenario because it makes provision for substantial—but not huge—increases in energy consumption. The preferred scenario, for example, aims at boosting coal consumption by 5.4 percent per year and nuclear energy by 8.7 percent per year over the remainder of the century. While these increases may not match precisely the rates that ultimately will be necessary, they do require that major social and political uncertainties be resolved promptly concerning the utilization of these energy sources. Similarly, the preferred scenario is relatively restrained in its planned consumption levels for oil and natural gas, contemplating a 20 percent reduction in the combined use of these energy forms. Once again, although the exact rate of decrease ultimately may differ, and even though the projected oil and gas mix likely will change, the preparations for significantly lowered use are sensible and necessary. Potentially large unconventional gas supplies, such as are thought to be available from geopressured methane deposits, eventually may prove to be economically recoverable. If that happens, they either may replace some of the planned coal and nuclear facilities or may be used to hasten the phase-out of imported oil. If the nation plans on large future unconventional gas supplies and they do not become available when expected, the resulting energy supply shortfall can be offset only by increased oil imports — or by doing without.

The relatively rapid increases in energy prices projected for the preferred scenario have an effect analogous to the preparations for relatively high energy consumption. However, the high prices serve both to accelerate the search for new oil and gas supplies and to encourage expansion of synthetic fuels, shale oil, and various forms of solar energy and to promote productive conservation. Thus, planning for adverse chance factors in the nation's and the world's energy economies accelerates the effort to shift our own energy economy away from oil and gas and toward substitutes for energy and toward energy sources for which ample domestic reserves are available. At the same time it enables us to keep all reasonable energy options open, to pursue promising research and development leads, and to sustain our flexibility. Although

TABLE 5.1
Trends in Oil Imports, 1990–2010

Scenario	Oil Imports (quads)	Percentage of Total	
		Oil Use	Energy Use
Actual 1978	18.1	48.0	23.2
High-growth			
1990	21.7	49.2	19.3
2000	27.9	58.4	19.0
2010*	23.7	50.1	12.2
Independence			
1990	17.6	45.4	17.4
2000	12.3	34.8	9.0
2010	2.5	7.7	1.5
Preferred			
1990	10.2	30.3	11.1
2000	6.8	23.1	5.8
2010	—	—	—
Continuation			
1990	12.1	35.2	13.7
2000	13.2	40.1	12.7
2010	12.0	34.6	9.8
Low-growth			
1990	1.8	7.1	2.5
2000	0.0	—	—
2010	—	—	—

*Numbers for 2010 combine oil and gas.
Source: Compiled by the authors.

some of this effort ultimately may prove to have been unnecessary, the costs to the nation will be small compared to the international and domestic costs of not only underestimating but of underpreparing and underdeveloping our energy system.

In all scenarios except the low-growth, there is a need for significant and growing amounts of installed commercial breeder reactor capacity beginning somewhere between 2010 and 2030. The preferred scenario's adjusted results require 2.0 quads of primary energy from breeders by 2020 and 5.3 quads 10 years later. A constant and consistent commitment to the nation's breeder program will be necessary if development and precommercial phases of this new technology are to be completed in time to permit the commercialization schedule implied by these projections.

Prompt support for the breeder program also is strongly suggested by the study's coal consumption trends for the early twenty-first century. By that time coal production well may be approaching maximum practical rates, with increasing proportions of the output being allocated to the production of synfuels or coal-based plastics. This period likely will see increasing demands from the rest of the world for the export of U.S. coal. Of course, by this time renewable energy supplies and fusion energy may make major contributions to the energy supply picture; however, the uncertainties are very large, and an emphasis on resource flexibility is appropriate. At the very least, today's planning should incorporate multiple options, pursuing them with "all deliberate speed" until the shape of the nation's and the world's energy futures becomes clearer.

No amount of capital investment, no breakthroughs as a result of research and development, no increases in labor productivity — to cite only three of the many areas of national concern ripe for improvement — can launch the United States into a new era of moderate but sustained economic growth without refinements in this country's regulatory processes and climate. The unjustifiable delays occasioned by the current regulatory system of the United States, for example, can add untenable costs to new energy system construction and thereby postpone the viability of necessary energy projects — from nuclear to novel energy sources. The economic and energy recommendations that follow stand a greater chance of gearing the United States to the preferred course if the benefits of regulation more closely align with its cost.

Policy Portfolio Structure

Assuming that such regulatory changes come about in the near term, the preferred scenario's combined economic and energy choices should result in potential futures for this nation that will sustain and improve our current standard of living and allow for inevitable but as yet undefined national needs. Consequently, the recommendations presented in this chapter are designed to yield the preferred scenario results.

These recommendations have been divided into two general categories: economic vitality and energy security. Both groups of recommendations are divided further into sections that treat specific issues. The general heading of economic vitality, for example, presents separate but mutually reinforcing recommendations concerning productivity, investment, government spending, and government regulation of business. Similarly, the volume's energy security section, comprised mainly of individual discussions about fuel sources and productive conservation, is a carefully conceived set of interrelated policies designed to meet U.S. energy needs in the short, mid-, and long terms. Because the consumer ultimately pays for the cost of regulation, regulatory equity is an important aspect of both economic and energy policy. Consequently, two additional regulatory policy studies are presented. Each of the policy studies that constitute this portfolio is divided into three segments: a statement of the problem, the background, and recommendations. Since most readers of this volume are not energy experts or economists, sufficient detail is given to provide a context for the recommendations.

Economic Vitality

Of the five social sectors described in Chapter 1 and depicted in Figure 1.1, business forms the focal point of our economic system, serving as the sector directly responsible for the flow of material benefits to the U.S. citizens. In performing this function, business operates through relationships with the other four sectors: people, government, resources, and international. Although the nature of these relationships is changing continually, the last 10 to 15 years have been a period of unusual turmoil, punctuated by shifts so abrupt that they might better be described as discontinuities than trends.

These near-discontinuities included the surge in the labor force caused by increased female participation and by the maturing of the baby-boom generation; the explosion of government spending that resulted from the Great Society's open-ended social programs and their offshoots; the shift from energy abundance to energy scarcity following the Arab oil embargo; and the burst of productivity by our major international trade competitors. It is possible, although not clearly probable, that the 1980s will hold fewer surprises.

Therefore, as the nation faces the last 20 years of the century, its efforts to regain economic vitality must focus on completing the adjustment process forced upon it by past changes and on preparing to meet future changes more efficiently. In discharging these responsibilities, it will be necessary to focus on the ends, the means, and the available catalysts. The ends, of course, are to improve living standards for all citizens, with special attention to the lowest-income segments of society, while assuring that the economic interests of future generations are protected. The means are the factors of production: capital, labor, and resources. The catalysts are investment, productivity, and government.

This section of the policy portfolio deals with the catalysts and, through them, with the uses of capital and labor. To revitalize the U.S. economy so that it eventually approximates the conditions of the preferred scenario, six economic policy objectives and a list of recommendations that would make them feasible have been established. These objectives, summarized in Table 5.2, and their related recommendations are presented in discrete sections — productivity, investment, and government fiscal and monetary actions—although it is in combination and through a concerted program of action that they can have a positive effect on the economy.

In some cases—for example, average personal income tax rates for the short term—subsidiary quantitative objectives are presented, but both the primary and subsidiary policy objectives should be understood to be approximations. The preferred scenario's combined objectives and recommendations constitute an overall program that is internally consistent, but the actual year-to-year consequences of instituting this particular program or any other series of choices would require close and frequent monitoring.

TABLE 5.2
Economic Vitality Policy Objectives

---

1. Maintain an average real GNP growth rate of at least 3.0 percent per year from now until 2000.

2. Improve labor productivity at an average rate of at least 2.0 percent per year from now until 2000.

3. Increase real private domestic investment at an average rate of at least 3.5 percent per year from now until 2000.

4. Reduce government spending as a percent of current dollar GNP so that
   a. federal spending for all purposes declines from 23 percent in 1980 to no more than 17 percent in 1990, and
   b. government spending at all levels for all purposes declines from 33 percent in 1980 to no more than 27 percent in 1990.

5. Reorient spending for goods and services at all levels of government so that by 1990 about 20 percent is allocated to new public capital facilities, rather than the roughly 12 percent of the recent past.

6. Gradually reduce the growth of nominal money supply to rates consistent with potential GNP growth. During the transitional 1980s, an average growth rate of about 4.5 percent per year is proposed for M1B, approximately a percentage point higher than potential GNP growth.

Source: Compiled by the authors.

Productivity

The Problem
Improvements in productivity, defined broadly as the efficiency with which the KLEM factors are combined to produce output, have been an important source of the strong postwar U.S. living standard increases. In the late 1960s, however, productivity

improvement rates began to slow. During the 1974–75 recession they turned negative, and they have recovered only haltingly since then. U.S. national output in 1980 would have been nearly 20 percent higher than it was had pre-1973 productivity rates been maintained. Productivity losses have aggravated inflation seriously and also have altered international trading patterns. If the current productivity growth slowdown persists to the end of the century, it will have enormous effects on the nation's economic condition by 2000. Without reasonably robust productivity growth, the United States will find it difficult, if not impossible, to stop inflation, improve the lot of the poor, continue to improve the environment, compete in international trade, and maintain a satisfactory level of defense. Thus, the productivity problem is twofold: the recent slowdown's causes must be discovered and corrective actions compatible with those socioeconomic conditions anticipated in the 1980s and 1990s must be devised.

Background

Productivity's changing contribution to national economic growth can be visualized best by comparing growth in the private economy with growth in labor productivity (output per man-hour). Table 5.3 presents this information for three post-World War II periods.

TABLE 5.3
Productivity and Output in the Private Economy, 1947–80
(AAGR)

Period	Output Per Man-hour	Man-hours	Output
1947–65	3.45	0.49	3.95
1965–73	2.55	1.45	4.02
1973–80	0.23	1.33	1.58

Source: Compiled by the authors.

Prior to 1965, over 85 percent of private-sector national output growth was derived from labor productivity improvements, while the remainder—less than 15 percent—can be attributed to increased labor input. In the most recent period, the much slower growth in private-sector national output can be traced largely to nearly stagnant productivity coupled with relatively strong increases in labor input; in fact, the proportions essentially have been reversed, with 85 percent coming from labor input and only 15 percent from productivity growth.

Productivity analysts have examined this record, using a variety of economic and statistical techniques to break labor productivity into its many components. Many analysts define three distinct postwar periods, with beginning and ending years roughly equivalent to those used in Table 5.3. Several analysts have noted that the last half of the 1960s marked a variety of conditions unconducive to productivity growth:

the beginning of a more rapid surge of women into the labor force, the maturing and entry into the labor force of the first members of the baby-boom generation, the beginning of government spending for the Great Society programs, the disruptions stemming from Vietnam, the start of exorbitantly large federal budgets, the early push for environmental protection legislation, and the decline in private- and public-sector spending for productive facilities.[3]

It is remarkable that productivity growth held up through the 1960s as well as it did, given the likely adverse impacts of these various developments. By the early 1970s, however, pressures resulting from each of these factors had increased and begun to combine with increasingly desperate government attempts to maintain economic growth through demand incentives. This combination resulted in an outburst of inflation, which when reinforced by the Arab oil embargo, led to the 1974–75 recession.

Analysts agree that each of these developments, from the explosive growth of the labor force to the slow growth in investment in productive facilities, played a measurable part in the near-cessation of post-1973 productivity improvement, but they differ sharply on each factor's relative contribution. Moreover, some analysts offer still other explanations—such as the demise of the work ethic, the growth of the underground economy, the stagnation of research and development spending, the stultifying effect of increased government regulation, the end of labor's shift from agriculture to manufacturing and the continuation of its related shift from manufacturing to services—to explain the decline of modern U.S. productivity rates.

The authors believe the factors listed in Table 5.4 account for the bulk of the productivity growth decline since the mid-1960s. If these five factors indeed are largely responsible, it is reasonable to conclude that intelligent public policy choices can restore an environment that promotes healthy productivity growth. It seems impossible, however, to regain all lost ground and thus return to those productivity

---

TABLE 5.4
Factors Contributing to the Productivity Growth Slowdown
1965 — 80

1. Insufficient productive investment, including lack of R&D and diversion of investment to nonproductive efforts.

2. Stifling of total factor productivity by government regulations, constraints, prohibitions, and economic instabilities.

3. Increased prices, uncertain availability, and ambivalent federal energy supply policies.

4. Changing age-sex mix of the labor force.

5. Growth of the service sector and end of the shift from agriculture.

Source: Compiled by the authors.

levels that would have prevailed had the 3.45 percent improvement in output per man-hour continued after 1965. To regain this lost ground fully would require phenomenally high growth rates of about 6.5 percent per year for the entire next decade.

In fact, given all of these barriers it seems likely that future growth rates will remain significantly below the 3.45 percent figure—even under the most favorable public policies. Nevertheless, there is little doubt that we can improve upon the 0.23 percent figure of the last seven years. Public policies can encourage investment and thereby eliminate the single greatest inhibition to productivity growth rather quickly— perhaps within five years. Next to insufficient productive investment, factors 2, 3, and 4 have been important brakes on productivity growth, with each bearing essentially equal responsibility for the productivity decline of the 1960s and 1970s. Rational regulatory and energy policy programs can reduce significantly the negative impacts of factor 2 within a decade, and can ameliorate the worst effects of factor 3 over the next 10 to 15 years. Time alone, with only minor assistance from public policies, will transform the negative effects of factor 4 into positive effects throughout the next 20 years. Factor 5 is least amenable to human intervention, although many people believe that technological improvements in service jobs, such as the electronic revolution of the office, will improve this sector's productivity markedly over the next 20 years.

Because of these factors, labor productivity growth rate assumptions for each scenario over the next 20 years guided the midterm modeling efforts. The modeling results incorporate implicit productivity growth rates that differed somewhat from the input assumptions but that confirmed two preconceptions inherent in these assumptions: on average, future growth rates would be significantly lower than past rates, and future high-to-low variations would be smaller than in the past. The three sets of figures are compared and then contrasted with the preferred scenario in Table 5.5.

TABLE 5.5
Past and Future Labor Productivity Figures
(percent per year)

	Past Figures		Future Estimates: 1978–2000	
	Period	Growth Rate	Assumed	Modeled
High	1947–65	3.45	2.86	2.50
Low	1973–80	0.23	1.23	1.50
Average	1947–80	2.53	2.05	2.00
Preferred			2.24	2.10

Source: Compiled by the authors.

Recommendations
Many of this book's recommendations that will help to achieve or exceed the productivity growth rate objective of 2.1 percent per year deal with either investment

or regulation. Similarly, several recommendations associated with various energy supply sources also contribute significantly to productivity growth.

Because the influences that impinge on the nation's productivity growth are so disparate, the private sector should perform further analyses into the causes of the post-1965 productivity slowdown. Since productivity is central to the nation's future economic prospects, it is in the interest of all the social sectors to discover what actions are necessary to assure reasonable productivity growth. The private sector should sponsor and perform these analyses to assure that they are objective, focused, and practical.

Jorgenson's analysis indicates the need for industry-by-industry evaluations and suggests that particular attention be given to the relationships between energy use and productivity.[4] His studies show a direct relationship between the two for most industries, thus leading to the tentative conclusion that energy use restrictions since 1973 have been an important contributor to the very low growth in output per man-hour during these years. Thus, renewed productivity growth in the 1980s may be accompanied by a concomitant surge in energy consumption. This surge may be reinforced by the shift to more capital-intensive production methods as labor markets tighten in the coming years.

Productivity analyses should include intercountry evaluations of productivity trends. By answering a variety of questions, these evaluations should assess the long-term capacity of various U.S. industries to compete internationally: can any reasonable capital improvement program offset the wage advantages of third world countries in labor-intensive manufacturing? In contrast, are there industries for which foreign wage and inflation levels are rising so rapidly that the United States may one day hope to regain a competitive position, given a combination of lowered inflation, rejuvenated investment, and wage restraint? Can moderate wage restraint play a significant part in restoring international competitiveness in medium-technology industries such as steel, radio and television manufacturing, and motor vehicles? In the latter industry, for example, adjusting the 1980 employee compensation level so that it equaled the average for all durable goods manufacturing employees in the United States would have reduced the average cost (or increased the quality) of each vehicle manufactured by $600 to $700.[5]

Moreover, such productivity studies must examine management practices as well as labor constraints and government impacts on the productive process. In examining current management performance, it will be necessary to study closely the practices of our foreign competitors. Some analysts argue convincingly that recently the United States seems to have ignored or forgotten much of what it earlier taught the Germans and Japanese about entrepreneurship, management philosophy, quality control, work simplification, worker incentives, and the many other management factors that can contribute to improved productivity.

Government and labor must cooperate with and participate in these business-sector productivity studies, since the three sectors together determine productivity. Each sector must learn to appreciate the others' problems; each must recognize how its own actions help or hinder the common effort; and each must be prepared to compromise if the nation is to rejuvenate its faltering production machine. Much of the nation's productivity problem may result from widespread misinformation and clogged communication channels among these three sectors, which often view each other competitively. Sectoral cooperation will facilitate accomplishing the long-range goal of a healthy, growing economy.

Individual industries and regions should consider establishing productivity councils devoted to productivity improvements. Such councils, under private-sector leadership, could act to enhance communication and reduce misinformation. On a regional basis, similar labor-management committees, such as that in Jamestown, N.Y., should be established.[6]

Such groups could provide objective information and records of actual productivity improvement achievements to aid the nation's reindustrialization efforts. These efforts must be guided by the well-informed and profit-motivated actions of private-sector individuals and organizations. Only the discriminating powers of the profit motive can sidestep the strong pressures to prop up "sunset" industries that have no reasonable potential for long-term profitability.

Business, labor, and government should focus jointly and separately on improving the productivity of the nation's human resources. Substantial numbers of unemployed and underemployed U.S. citizens' economic condition and overall quality of life could be improved greatly if they were trained and educated adequately, and thus could be employed productively. Reducing unemployment and improving the skills of the marginally or only sporadically employed will increase national productivity in two ways: first, by increasing the output per man-hour of those directly affected; and second, by reducing the drag on national output that results from the array of social services and the amount of social service employment now needed to sustain those whom society has judged unable to sustain themselves.

Job training efforts should be based in and run by the private sector so that efficient and well-targeted programs can be developed. The nation's experience with federally sponsored and administered programs generally has not been successful. It is imperative that future programs be adapted to the students' capabilities and backgrounds and that training focus on skills and labor markets with substantial growth potentials in the private economy. Proper attention to growing labor market areas, of course, would require that graduating students be encouraged to migrate from parts of the country with high unemployment to parts with lower unemployment. The programs should involve strong incentives for the student to enroll in and complete the program successfully. Additionally, well-assured prospects for appropriate job openings for graduates and equally strong penalties for unwarranted drop-outs, such as restricting the availability to them of other transfer payment programs, should be stressed.

The federal minimum wage laws should be modified. To enlarge the labor market for young trainees and other low-skill, low-seniority job aspirants, exceptions to the federal minimum wage law should be implemented. These exceptions should be targeted, restricted, and limited so that they restore the first step of the labor market ladder that many studies clearly show has been removed for many young and poorly trained persons, particularly among minorities, by the minimum wage laws. Differential treatment for both the minimum wage and its exceptions in different parts of the country would help to offset major regional differences in living costs, wage rates, and unemployment rates.

Transfer payment programs should be modified to increase incentives for productive employment and to reduce the national economic burden created by income maintenance programs. With the exception of old-age insurance, those transfer payment programs that currently emphasize maintenance in place of human recovery, regeneration, and reclamation should be reoriented to provide stronger incentives for productive employment. Social Security and public pension provisions should be examined with the same objectives. Considering gradual increases in longevity, health improvements, and decreases in the physical demands of many jobs, the present transfer payment programs demand reconsideration.

Investment

The Problem

The nation's total economic output either is consumed or invested. Investment allows for future consumption, just as the farmer sets aside seed corn for the next year's crop from each harvest. A certain level of investment, measured as a fraction of total economic output, is needed simply to maintain stable output from year to year, and only additional investment will allow future output to grow. Furthermore, if the efficiency with which today's investment can be translated into tomorrow's output decreases, then the investment proportion must rise to maintain past output growth rates. Environmental and other types of regulation have had this effect on the economy in recent years. Thus, society must strike a continual balance between its desire to maximize current consumption and its expectation of better future standards of living. Over the last decade, the balance has shifted to current consumption. If the future balance is not shifted toward increased investment, the nation will continue to experience low economic growth and high inflation.

Background

Over the last two decades about 63 percent of GNP was used for personal consumption which includes transfer payments, 21 percent for government purchases of goods and services, 4.5 percent for residential construction, 1 percent for a combination of business inventories and net exports, and the remainder—some 10 percent—for nonresidential private investment. Future output was based on this relatively small 10 percent segment of total economic output. Although the 10 percent fraction was considerably smaller than the investment efforts of our major international trading partners, such as Germany and Japan, it was sufficient to support an average real economic growth rate of 4.1 percent per year during the 1960s. As the 1970s advanced, however, several developments reduced the efficiency of the nation's production apparatus, but without eliciting sharp investment increases to sustain

normal growth. Among these developments were increasingly stringent environmental laws requiring that significant fractions of new investment funds be allocated to
equipment that produced clean air and water, and some jobs, but no increases in
marketable goods. Another factor—spiraling inflation—boosted the prices of investment goods faster than the general price level, thus reducing the real purchasing
power of a given GNP fraction. Together these two developments reduced the GNP
fraction allocated to *real, productive* investment from the 10 percent level to about
8.5 percent by the mid- to late 1970s.[7] Reinforcing these developments, a legion of
miscellaneous government regulations frequently made existing, as well as newly
purchased, equipment less productive. Similarly, the energy price increases of 1974
and 1979 made much existing equipment obsolescent. Finally, the surge of women
and young adults into the labor force called for a matching surge in investment, if
historic trends in the capital/labor ratio were to be maintained, but the call went
unheeded.

Several strong pressures should have been boosting the *demand* for investment
dollars during the decade of the 1970s, but even stronger factors were restricting
savings, the source of *supply* for these investment dollars. In the later 1960s and early
1970s, the baby-boom generation reached adulthood, took jobs, and began to form
households, substantially increasing the proportions of the adult population that are
generally high consumers and very high borrowers, while decreasing the proportions
from which come the bulk of personal savings. At the root of several other factors that
also restricted savings was the unbalanced interpretation of Keynesian economic
theory, which dominated the U.S. political process during much of the post-World
War II period. This interpretation justified government deficit spending as the only
useful means for averting business cycle downturns and called for continuing public
policies that would boost consumption to assure long-term growth. By the 1970s the
nation gradually realized that deficit spending had become endemic. Policies designed to encourage consumption more often than not also discouraged investment.
The growth of government spending at state, local, and national levels was fueled by a
combination of federal deficits and ever-increasing taxes, which absorbed funds that
otherwise would have been invested. Moreover, policies such as those that imposed or
levied capital gains taxes, inadequate depreciation allowances, and double taxation of
dividends acted to discourage investment even more directly.

The effects of inflation further discouraged investment. Inflation made depreciation allowances based on historical costs sadly inadequate to provide for replacement
and modernization. Funds that should have contributed to purchasing high-cost
replacement facilities instead were defined as earnings and then taxed or paid out as
dividends. Companies were forced more heavily into the sale of new debt and equity
securities to raise funds for replacements as well as for the expansion of productive
facilities. Simultaneously, of course, federal deficits were being financed by selling
government securities in the same capital markets to which private companies
increasingly were forced to turn. Equally serious was the tendency for investors faced
by the uncertainties of inflation to turn to shorter-term securities. Prudent investors
saw the dangers that unpredictable inflation rates held for long-term investments—

particularly debt securities—and they responded by shortening their horizons to less than a decade or by shifting from financial assets to tangible assets such as gold, jewels, and fine arts.

Other factors have compounded the uncertainties caused by inflation. The nation's inability to formulate a sensible, comprehensive energy policy has discouraged many new investments and caused delays in replacing equipment made obsolescent by changing energy prices and new energy legislation.

Environmental and other regulations have had similar effects on investment. Legislative challenges to private company actions based on the new regulations often had the potential to—and did—drag out for years, literally destroying many investment opportunities, while inflation added millions to the cost of approved projects. To offset this antiinvestment bias, the nation sought roundabout solutions such as increasing tax depreciation rates and granting investment tax credits. These devices gave corporations more funds over the short term, yet escaped most of the criticism generally directed against higher earnings. Unfortunately, devices such as tax depreciation rates and investment tax credits tend to funnel funds toward existing large, heavily capitalized and profitable industries at the expense of fledgling businesses. Similarly, the rapid growth of private and public pension funds also seeks to offset the slow growth of personal savings, but these funds tend toward a relatively conservative mix of securities. The result is not unlike that of higher depreciation rates and investment tax credits—large, well-established institutions are favored. Other policies used tax incentives to direct investment to activities the government sought to foster, namely residential and public construction. As desirable as activities such as the Housing Construction Act of 1968 might have been, they do not add to the nation's private productive facilities.

Even the strongest adherents of Keynesian economics now recognize the cumulative consequences of ignoring or discouraging the investment side of the economy. Unless economic policy changes to encourage more savings, the United States will be unable to regain a competitive stance at home or abroad. Renewed emphasis on capital formation and savings has led to growing support for supply-side policies. The congressional Joint Economic Committee's (JEC) 1980 study employed a supply-side model, the results of which supported tax cuts to stimulate investment.[8] According to the 1980 study, two modest tax cuts—a small increase in the investment tax credit and a four-year reduction in the average tax lifetime of producers' durable equipment—would reduce the consumer price index by 4 percent by the end of the 1980s. Over the same period they also would increase real business fixed investment by 15.6 percent, productivity by 3.3 percent, and raise the capital stock by 7.2 percent.

This book's results corroborate the JEC analysis by finding that a higher level of investment in capital stock is crucial to achieving a moderate real GNP growth rate of 3.1 percent per year. National output must be reallocated to increase the portion reserved for private investment from the present 14 percent of GNP to at least 15 percent by 1990 and 16 percent by 2000, if future growth patterns are to approach those of the preferred scenario. All of this additional investment must be allocated to productive facilities with the fraction devoted to residential construction dropping slightly and that absorbed by environmental protection equipment remaining unchanged. Such an increase in investment in the United States would result in an increase in the capital stock, thus improving productivity, minimizing increases in unit labor costs, and providing increases in real wages, while reducing the inflation rate. These developments would encourage more saving, which in turn would lessen demand pressures and further reduce the rate of price increases. More saving contributes to higher productivity and thus lowers inflation over the long run.

Recommendations

This study recommends boosting the real investment growth rate to at least 3.5 percent per year from now until 2000. Increasing private investment in the United States is ultimately the responsibility of private citizens and businesses; but this responsibility is discharged only in response to perceived self-interest: that is, individuals and businesses invest in some measure proportionate to the expected return from their investment. The government, an essential partner in this process, can alter incentives and disincentives; it can minimize government competition for investment funds; it can avoid excessive incentives for nonproductive investments; it can concentrate on insuring stable business, economic, regulatory, and monetary conditions; and it can emphasize long-range research and development spending.

These actions focus on changes in government incentives and are included here, rather than in the section on government, to emphasize that encouraging investment is crucial to the nation's future. Certain recommendations dealing with monetary policy, the reduction of inflation, and government spending for capital facilities, which are included under government spending, also will influence investment positively.

The U.S. government should reduce personal income tax rates, thereby increasing incentives to work and save; such an action would serve to offset inflation's effects on our progressive taxing system. A uniform rate reduction across all income brackets will have a positive, but perhaps small, effect on labor force participation rates and the length of the workweek. The Evans model, for example, suggests that a 1 percentage point reduction in average tax rates will raise the work effort of middle and upper-middle income workers by 0.25 percent. Incentives to save can be enhanced measurably by tax changes targeted at reducing taxes on income from saving. The Evans model estimates that a $10 billion reduction in taxes on income from saving would increase saving by some $13 billion.

In an inflationary environment the progressive income tax produces sharp and continuing automatic tax increases as taxpayers are moved into higher and higher tax brackets. The additional revenue derived from this "bracket-creep" is a strong incentive for the federal government to condone, if not actually encourage, inflation. Bracket-creep has been a major source of federal revenues in recent years as individual income taxes rose from 11 percent of adjusted gross income in 1976 to about 14 percent in 1980 and 15.2 percent in 1981 (barring tax decreases).

Based on a judgmental assessment of supply-side results, this book recommends a 1 percentage point reduction per year in the average personal income tax rate for each of the next four or five years, bringing that rate from about 25 percent at present to about 20 percent by mid-decade, a reduction roughly equivalent to the Economic Recovery Tax Act of 1981. Part of the 1 percentage point annual reduction should be applied "across the board" to all income brackets, but a major fraction should be reserved for targeted reductions to increase saving, as suggested in the following two recommendations.

A national priority should be to reorient the federal and state personal income tax systems to encourage saving by reducing the tax on incomes derived from savings. Increasing the tax exclusion on dividend income and extending the exclusion provision to interest income would be one effective technique. Another approach would be to tax income from savings separately from other income (primarily wage and salary), with each segment taxed progressively after excluding a certain basic amount. This approach would permit different degrees of progressivity to be associated with each income stream. All such methods act to encourage savings *indirectly* by increasing the net after-tax income from savings.

The government should increase the ability of the small saver to get a competitive rate of return on his savings. In recent years government policy has aimed at removing restrictions on the small saver at the same time that private institutions have developed new and attractive investment vehicles for this important class of saver. This trend should be continued and, in fact, accelerated by eliminating the interest rate limits on passbook savings and by raising returns on small-denomination government securities to competitive levels.

To spur investment, the U.S. government should reduce federal and state corporate income tax rates to encourage private productive investment. Demand- and supply-side models both have shown that increasing the rate of return on business investment is an effective way to increase capital spending. The Evans model, for example, shows that a $1 billion increase in after-tax corporate profits will raise fixed business investment by about $0.7 billion. Reducing federal and state corporate income tax rates is a simple and direct way to increase the return on investment. Based on a judgmental evaluation of both the Wharton and Evans model results, the authors recommend a 3 percentage point reduction per year in federal corporate income tax rates in each of the next four or five years, along with comparable reductions in state rates. Such a sequence would move the federal rate from the present 46 percent to 31 or 34 percent by mid-decade.

Tax depreciation rates on productive facilities should be increased by decreasing tax lives on structures and equipment. This action also would boost investment by increasing the after-tax profitability of the investment. As such it should be approximately as effective at the national level as a comparable increase in profitability stemming from a reduction in the corporate income tax. The results of these two recommendations may differ somewhat from industry to industry, however, with capital-intensive manufacturing activities benefiting differently than labor-intensive service activities from the two forms of tax reduction. On the basis of the Evans model results, a reduction in the average tax life of structures from 23 years at present to 10 years over a three-year period of approximately equal reductions is recommended. Equipment tax lives should be reduced in a similar three-step process from about 10.5 years at present to 5 years.

A number of other actions, suggested as possible supplements to or substitutes for the decreased income tax rate and increased tax depreciation rates, should be considered to increase investment. Such alternatives include increasing the investment tax credit and extending it to include modernization of old facilities, indexing depreciation accruals to offset the effects of inflation, reducing capital gains taxes, reducing or eliminating double taxation of dividends, and allowing tax-free dividend reinvestment.

Policy actions specifically tailored to increasing research and development expenditures should be considered promptly. Total R&D spending has dropped from nearly 3 percent of GNP in the middle 1960s to barely 2.2 percent in the later 1970s, with most of the decline occurring in federally funded R&D. In addition, the focus of spending has shifted markedly away from long-term basic research toward short-term development activities aimed at responding to environmental and other regulatory restrictions.

Recommended policies should focus on tax or other incentives for private industry to extend its research horizon and should concentrate more heavily on the basic scientific research from which must come the productivity improvements of the late 1980s and 1990s. Although the expected boosts in defense spending probably will immerse the federal government more deeply in long-term basic research activities once again, incentives to expand, extend, and intensify privately administered research clearly are justified.

Focused investment incentives aimed at a specific industry or region should be avoided wherever possible. Instead, broad general incentives should be applied to establish a general national investment climate, with the investment distribution determined ultimately by consumer preferences expressed in a free-market environment. Where unique public policy considerations of overriding importance are judged to demand focused incentives, they should be applied with great caution. In those cases, the special incentives should be self-extinguishing within a relatively short period, for example, three to five years, thereby forcing periodic reexamination of their usefulness.

Among such policies currently under consideration are those providing special tax treatment for industries that locate in depressed inner-city regions, and for industries severely influenced by government regulatory action or unforeseeable foreign developments. Despite the direct and measurable advantages to the favored area or industry, the distortion of investment flows and the resulting loss in national productivity create large but not easily measurable disadvantages to the society as a whole.

Government Spending

The Problem

Including transfer payments, government spending has risen faster than national output through much of the postwar period. Therefore, taxes needed to support a growing number of government programs have consumed ever larger fractions of the average wage earner's income. This growth reflects citizens' and political leaders' gradually expanding view of government's capabilities and responsibilities. Much of the legislation has been formulated so that costs associated with government programs escalate automatically each succeeding year. In recent years the increasing cost burden from old programs has combined with the costs of new programs to yield total spending requirements that outstrip the nation's willingness to be taxed. Deficit spending has been called upon with increasing frequency to bridge the gap between tax revenues and expenditures.

Deficit spending, initially justified as the appropriate fiscal policy for boosting the economy out of a recession, gradually has come to dominate good times as well as bad. This deficit spending has focused on encouraging consumption, while generally ignoring, if not actively discouraging, savings and investment. The deficits have been financed through the sale of government securities, for which ready markets have been assured by the Federal Reserve System's monetary policy actions. At times this combination of fiscal and monetary policies could be seen to overheat the economy and inflation rates worsened; consequently, a more stringent monetary policy was invoked and the economy was plunged into recession. Complicating the efforts to coordinate fiscal and monetary policies were changing interpretations of the independence of the Federal Reserve System and diverse views as to whether interest rates or money supply growth rates were to be the primary target of monetary policy.

Background

Federal government spending, including transfer payments, has risen much more rapidly than national output and now accounts for about 24 percent of nominal dollar GNP, double the proportion at the end of World War II. State and local government spending has risen even more rapidly, reaching about 13 percent of GNP at present, compared to about 5.5 percent at the end of the war. Thus, government now takes about two dollars from every five (or 40 percent of tax payers' incomes), uses about 50 cents to purchase things it needs, uses another 50 cents to pay its employees, and transfers the remaining dollar to other individuals through social security, welfare, and so on. In the years just after World War II, however, it managed on only one dollar of every five generated, dividing that dollar into 35 cents for purchased items, 35 cents for wages, and 30 cents for transfer payments.

Although government spending increases have disturbed U.S. taxpayers for 200 years, the level of concern has grown sharply since the mid-1960s. Many who voice this concern now focus not only on the rising fraction of their incomes that government takes, but also on the apparent inefficiency and ineffectiveness of many government programs using those funds. Growing taxpayer dissatisfaction with government at all levels is apparent from frequent voter rejection of new municipal bond proposals at the local level, from Proposition 13 in California and similar tax limitation proposals in many other states, and from the 23-state approval for a constitutional amendment prohibiting an unbalanced federal budget. More and more people are no longer joking when they say that the last successful government program was World War II.

Yet, political pressures for ever-larger government spending are almost irresistible. Each new program is almost certain to offer major advantages to the special interest group that advocates it, while the program's cost generally can be described as only a tiny addition to the total government budget. Thus, special interest groups eagerly mount concerted efforts to have their programs enacted into law, while the taxpayers who will be forced to pay the cost have no similarly strong incentive to oppose each new program.

In addition, many programs are formulated so the initial-year costs are relatively low, thus improving chances for enactment and pushing the major cost burdens into the future. Often the accumulation of these future cost burdens occurs automatically, without the need for further legislative action, as benefits gradually are extended to more and more citizens, as environmental standards are broadened and stiffened, or as escalation provisions respond to inflation. In this way the fraction of the budget defined as "uncontrollable" has risen from 67 percent of the total a decade ago to 75 percent at present. Of course, every uncontrollable program can be controlled by legislation, just as originally it was created by legislation.

The U.S. taxpayer's informed and growing resistance began in the second half of the 1960s with the combined expenses of the Vietnam War and President Johnson's Great Society programs. Continuing through the 1970s, this resistance convinced political leaders that government's full costs could not be collected directly in the form of taxes. Thus, the federal budget has been in deficit for 14 of the last 15 years, a period during which cumulative revenues were sufficient to cover only 91 percent of total expenditures. The other 9 percent—over $400 billion—has been obtained through deficits. Even these figures do not tell the full story, however, since they ignore the off-budget borrowing by a variety of federal agencies—borrowing not included in the official deficit calculations.

A convenient justification for the deficit spending was available in Keynesian fiscal policy as interpreted in the 1960s to include "fine-tuning," a technique which uses deficit spending to keep a growing economy from entering a recession. The concept of a "full-employment" economy was developed to justify deficits throughout all parts of the business cycle—as long as the economy gave signs of remaining below the calculated full-employment level. As economic growth rates slowed and the labor force exploded in the 1970s, a deficit could be justified every year. In fact, the last budget surplus was achieved in 1969. This application of Keynesian policies, however, encouraged consumption and neglected investment. As suggested by University of Pennsylvania economist Lawrence Klein, "We have lived high on the hog and failed to modernize our plant and equipment. We must go from being a high-consumption economy to being a high-saving economy if we are to reindustrialize and improve our standard of living."[9] Otto Eckstein, president of Data Resources, Inc., spoke in a similar vein when he identified the 1980 economic downturn as "the first genuine supply recession in modern U.S. history." Eckstein believes the slump began when the economy came up against the limits of industrial capacity, which he calls, "a supply problem 10 years in the making." He argues that because the recession was generated on the supply side, "we won't get out of it by a simple-minded stimulation of demand."[10]

A necessary complement to a successful fiscal policy is a properly accommodative monetary policy. By adjusting the economy's supply of money and credit, Federal Reserve System monetary policies can act to support or to undermine fiscal policy. Proper Keynesian monetary policy support is achieved by assuring adequate money supplies and credit at reasonable interest rates. If the nation pursues an expansionary fiscal policy and the federal budget is in deficit, the Federal Reserve System must monetize at least a part of the debt by buying government securities and assuring adequately available credit supplies to permit the private economy to absorb the remainder. This tactic generally has the consequence of increasing the money supply growth rate, which, in turn, likely will increase inflationary pressures. Historic relationships between money supply growth and inflation demonstrate that while the correlation between the two is not perfect, it is rather impressive. Throughout most of the postwar period, while claiming to act independently, the Federal Reserve System's role generally has supported a Keynesian economic philosophy. As several of our past business cycles approached peaks with no signs that the legislative or executive branches of government would institute a properly restrictive fiscal policy, the Federal Reserve System did attempt to correct the situation. In the views of some analysts, however, these monetary policy shifts were too late and too strong.[11]

In addition to depending excessively on monetary policy to rein in inflation, the Federal Reserve System has been plagued by the variety of monetary policy tools made available to it and the uncertain and variable lags with which these tools begin to act. Moreover, recent confusion about the proper target of these tools has compounded the problem: should the main target be interest rates or money supply growth rates?

In the late 1970s the Federal Reserve System shifted its primary emphasis from interest rates to money supply growth rates. Since this shift, its efforts to stabilize and generally reduce money supply growth have been complicated by extreme fluctuations in the nation's financial markets and by major changes in institutional relationships. NOW Accounts, which are changing savings accounts into the effective equivalent of checking accounts, are just one example.

There is a growing conviction throughout the nation that postwar government spending, fiscal, and monetary policies are important, if not primary, causes of the self-propelled inflation of the late 1960s and 1970s. Table 5.6 illustrates this process in terms of the consumer price index and compares it with fiscal and monetary policy measures over the last three decades. Unfortunately, inflation has now become so virulent and inflationary expectations so widespread that many analysts fear the return to a noninflationary environment can be achieved only gradually over a period of five to ten years. To regain price stability under current economic conditions, a new fiscal and monetary policy thrust must gain dominance. Although energy price increases helped raise inflation, some economists now believe that regulatory impositions on business, the Federal Reserve System's rapid expansion of the money supply, and the federal budget explosion financed by deficit spending were more

important causes of the inflation of the 1970s.[12] The recent use of monetary constraints to cut inflation suggests that reliance on monetary policy alone will not
suffice. Moreover, this approach unfairly burdens the housing, automobile, and consumer durables industries. A balanced combination of fiscal (tax, government spending, and deficit control) and monetary (money supply and interest rate control)
policies will be required to restore economic growth and control inflation. The
orientation of these policies must shift from concern about stimulating demand to
concern about stimulating supply. This new orientation—supply-side economics—
places primary attention on investment, productivity, labor supply, technological
advance, resource availability, and government regulation.

This book's short-term analysis concludes that appropriate fiscal and monetary
policies and government spending targets can be established to lead the nation during
the 1980s to any of the five equilibrium growth paths developed by the midterm
modeling efforts. Achieving the preferred or high-growth paths will be possible only
with major policy changes, however. A need to restrict government spending to a
growth rate somewhat slower or, at worst, no more rapid than the growth of GNP,
when measured on a current-dollar basis and including transfer payments, is indicated. This shift would be a marked departure from the past 30 years during which
government expenditures rose at annual rates averaging 9.6 percent while GNP
growth averaged 7.5 percent. A need for significant boosts in government purchases
of capital goods accompanies an increased emphasis on private capital goods, so it
will be necessary to concentrate on restricting the growth of government expenditures on consumption goods and services and on transfer payments.

The short-term analysis indicates that, although federal budget balance can be
achieved during the 1980s, continuing, but gradually decreasing, deficits may be
necessary during the early part of the decade to permit prompt tax reductions without
major spending pattern disruptions. A fiscal policy focused on tax reductions and
targeted toward encouraging work, saving, and investment is crucial for improving
productivity and economic growth, although socially and politically it is inadvisable
to cut current spending levels drastically. A better procedure would restrict sharply
the growth of spending wherever possible, while improving efficiency and eliminating

TABLE 5.6
Fiscal and Monetary Policies and Inflation, 1949 — 79

Period	Net Federal Deficits as a Percent of GNP	Money Supply (M1B): Average Annual Growth Rates (Percent)	Consumer Price Index: Average Annual Rates of Increase (Percent)
1949–59	0.3	2.5	2.0
1959–69	0.8	3.6	2.3
1969–79	1.9	6.6	7.1

Source: Compiled by the authors.

waste. Drastic changes in government spending might induce similarly drastic economic effects through a combination of psychological and financial shock waves. In contrast, a firm, gradual but sustained change in government spending and fiscal policies can achieve the same results and with less near-term risk.

The influence of monetary policy on fiscal policy is as important for supply-side economics as it is for a Keynesian approach. This study foresees a gradually diminishing money supply growth rate over the next decade, providing just enough additional money and credit to support moderate economic growth while still putting downward pressure on inflationary forces. The authors recommend annual growth rates for M1B (currency, demand, and other checkable deposits of less than $100,000), for example, should decline from the 9 percent range of the 1977–80 period to about 4.5 percent over the last half of the 1980s.

Recommendations

Restraining the growth of government spending to limit government's negative effects on the noninflationary growth of the real economy should not prevent it from fulfilling its basic responsibilities.

To prepare a program that restrains the growth of government spending, it is necessary first to review all current government activities. Two questions should guide this review: can government clearly accomplish the activity more efficiently than a private-sector institution, and is it a legitimate responsibility of government? The legitimate responsibilities of government should include national defense; protecting citizens from the illegal acts of other citizens; setting rules for arbitrating contractual disputes; providing temporary, minimum subsistence livelihood for citizens unable to provide for their own needs; and administering long-established government programs (such as Social Security) that cannot be turned over practically to private sector management. Efforts to restrain government spending should be concentrated initially on activities that fail or only marginally meet these criteria.

The United States should accept moderate, but generally decreasing, deficits in the federal budget through the mid-1980s, while taking the steps necessary to guarantee balanced budgets over business cycles thereafter. The preferred scenario's economic targets can be achieved despite such deficits. In fact, deficits for the next few years may be unavoidable unless a variety of economic factors all evolve in a particular, favorable sequence. More important for the economy's long-range future than an immediate budget balance is the need to provide incentives (and remove disincentives) for private-sector saving and investment in productive facilities, while simultaneously maintaining satisfactory defense expenditures and gradually reducing the dependence of various segments of the society on government.

The nation must establish state and federal government spending targets for the 1980s, expressed as a percentage of a relevant measure of economic output, such as regional personal income or GNP. These targets should aim at gradually slowing the growth of both federal and state spending so that, by mid-decade, growth rates advance no faster than those of the chosen economic output measure. At that time spending should be reexamined to reduce gradually the target percentages for the second half of the 1980s. Under such a program it should be feasible to reduce spending to meet or improve upon the quantitative targets listed in Table 5.2.

Government spending at local, state, and federal levels should be redirected toward long-term investment in capital facilities. Over the years government spending has been concerned increasingly with income maintenance and short-term consumption. To be consistent with government policies directed at shifting the private economy toward more investment and less consumption, government spending will have to move in this same direction. Government expenditures on domestic nondefense programs at local, state, and national levels must be redirected toward renewal and improvement of public capital facilities. At the same time growth of expenditures on short-term consumption must be constrained. The percentage of total nondefense spending allocated to capital facilities should be increased from its current level of 12 percent to 20 percent of spending for goods and services by 1990.

Wherever possible, user charges should be structured so that public capital facilities are more nearly self-supporting than in the past. Emphasis on user charges that tie the charge closely to the service provided is an important means of demonstrating that government spending, like that of the private sector, divides naturally into two categories: spending for investment, and spending for current consumption. Similarly, in both sectors there may be a valid distinction between going into debt to finance capital spending and going into debt to finance current consumption. Such a distinction would argue that government's consumption activities generally should be supported on a balanced-budget, pay-as-you-go basis, while debt financing at times may be appropriate for developing infrastructure that users and taxpayers will be willing to pay for in the future.

Government at all levels must extend its horizons to examine society's longer-term needs for public capital infrastructure. This examination must include an evaluation of replacement needs as well as new facilities to accommodate growth. Several economic growth scenarios similar to those developed in this book should be prepared at local, state, and federal levels. Once long-range programs to provide the necessary facilities have been developed and their financing feasibility established, government must assure the continuity of these programs, as well as their periodic review and updating, despite the continuing changes in administration that occur in our representative democracy.

The primary objective of monetary policy must be to restrain increases in nominal money supply so that within the next five to eight years growth rates of measures such as M1B and M2 are lowered to be compatible with noninflationary growth of GNP. Interest rates should be allowed to fluctuate within rather wide ranges if that is necessary to achieve the primary objective. The government spending recommendations listed in this section will help to reduce the economy's inflationary tendencies. The fiscal policy changes proposed in the investment section, and those dealing with regulatory matters considered later in this chapter, also will reduce inflationary pressures. They will not be successful, however, unless they are accompanied by a suitably restrained monetary policy. This policy should aim at gradual reductions in the growth of the nominal money supply, using all the available tools of the Federal Reserve System.

Government Regulation: Business

The Problem

Densely populated, industrialized societies need more regulations than sparsely populated agrarian societies. Understandably, the United States in 1981 has more regulations than it did in 1781. However, it defies all understanding that the *Federal Register*, the fount of federal rules and regulations, has more than tripled in length in the last decade. A sociologist looking at the post-World War II United States from a Malthusian perspective might postulate the thesis that, as society's complexity grows arithmetically, government regulations increase geometrically.

Excessive, inefficient business regulations add to the cost of producing goods and services, reduce investment and, consequently, productivity growth, increase uncertainties that inhibit individual and business decisions, cause job losses, stifle competition, discourage innovation, and overload the nation's legal and administrative systems. They also lead to the conditions of which *The Federalist Papers* warned so eloquently in the early days of the Republic when they said: "It will be of little avail to the people that laws are made by men of their own choosing, if the laws are so voluminous that they cannot be read, or so incoherent that they cannot be understood, or undergo such change that no man who knows what the law is today can guess what it will be tomorrow."[13] To highlight how widespread U.S. regulatory activity is today, the authors have separated their discussions of regulation into three portfolio papers: this one on regulation of business, and two others later in the chapter, one treating environmental and energy regulation, and the other dealing with electricity pricing; all three issues have significant economic consequences for the nation.

Background

The regulation explosion is not without precedent. After the Civil War, monopolies and trusts flourished ostensibly for the purpose of raising prices. Irate citizens, resentful about paying higher prices, clamored for the federal government and several state governments to pass laws designed either to forbid or regulate monopolies. Natural monopolies such as railroads and utilities were regulated by public agencies and, in other cases, competition was enforced. The Sherman Antitrust Act of 1890 forbade monopolies and sought to prohibit combinations that restrained interstate or foreign trade. The Pure Food and Drug Act of 1906 marked a distinct step in the government's commitment to protect public welfare, as did the Meat Inspection Act passed soon after. The Clayton Antitrust Act of 1914 gave the Federal Trade Commission authority to promote business competition.

With U.S. involvement in World War I, government supervision and direction of production and distribution became essential to effective participation. Government control, to an extent never before exercised in the United States, was effected through federal boards, commissions, and corporations, endowed in some instances with very wide powers and sometimes aided by subordinate state or local bodies.

The Great Depression brought a plethora of regulatory activities. Congress created the Reconstruction Finance Corporation (RFC), which saved banks, railroads, and insurance companies from collapse. With the election of Franklin D. Roosevelt in 1933, two regulatory objectives were institutionalized: recovery and reform. A rapid expansion of the federal bureaucracy occurred, which inevitably meant extended government supervision, control, and activity. During this period more regulatory agencies were established than in any previous decade: the Federal Home Loan Bank Board, the Federal Power Commission, the Civil Aeronautics Board, the Federal Maritime Commission, the Federal Communications Commission, the Food and Drug Commission, the Animal and Plant Health Inspection Service, and the National Labor Relations Board.

Government regulation of business continued to expand rapidly during World War II, but partially reversed itself at the end of the war, and then resumed until the present time. In recent years, however, pressures for expanding regulation have been more social than economic. The interest groups motivating legislation, numbering among them environmental organizations, civil rights groups, and consumer organizations, focus on social rather than economic approaches to public policy, although their combined actions have had major economic impacts.

It was not until around the time of World War II that the entire country adopted compensation laws. Over the next two decades the concern of the unions and the general public for safe working conditions was reinforced by the development of environmentalism and by widespread media interest that publicized controversial industrial health and safety issues to an unprecedented degree. The resulting Occupational Safety and Health Act of 1970, which gave the federal government carte blanche to regulate health and safety matters, probably best typifies these well-intentioned but poorly implemented laws of the 1970s whose mandates have been so debilitating to productivity growth.

Recommendations

The U.S. government should review its business regulations with an eye to improving their economic efficiency and to eliminating unnecessary ones. Existing regulations should be reviewed for their cost-effectiveness, with careful attention given to those that most severely inhibit productivity. Judgments about the productivity and growth-inhibiting effects of specific regulations should be derived by consultation with business and labor. Unless benefits can be shown to outweigh costs by large margins, or unless the regulations definitely prevent serious dangers to human health, they should be abandoned.

Economic impact statements should be prepared periodically for all existing regulations, and for all new regulations before they are adopted. Often significant are the economic costs of plant shutdowns and employment losses, the costs of delays due to uncertainties about future regulations, and the costs of delays due to likely litigation.

The opportunity for both proponents and opponents of newly proposed regulations to prolong litigation unnecessarily should be eliminated. Prompt and limited hearings and appeals processes should be instituted. The full costs of delay due to litigation should be imposed on the person or organization bringing the suit, if litigation shows the suit to have been brought on frivolous grounds. The costs of delay due to extended litigation through several levels of the court system can be so massive in an inflationary environment that many worthy development projects are abandoned — or never initiated because of uncertainties stemming from changing regulatory conditions.

General prohibitions should be established against the retroactive imposition of regulations, except in the case of clear and present dangers to human life. The possibility of retroactive changes in regulations imposes major uncertainties on investment and economic growth. Although particularly prevalent in nuclear plant construction, retroactive regulation applies as well to other activities with long planning or construction horizons. In those few cases where changes are found to be necessary, the cost should be borne by local, state, or national government.

Energy Security

The greatest source of uncertainty in the energy future of the United States results from U.S. dependency on foreign oil, the price and availability of which currently remain beyond this nation's control. When the United States shifted from an economy fueled largely by domestic energy to one heavily reliant upon imports, it left to chance those availability and price issues that it formerly controlled. The gamble proved to be a costly one, as lessons like the 1973 Arab oil embargo illustrated, and its effects have been more far-reaching than observers originally supposed.

Relying on foreign oil might not have proven so disadvantageous had the United States insured itself with the right kind of policy portfolio—that is, had it continued to pursue a sufficient number of other energy options with which to replace conventional liquid fuels given particular combinations of contingencies. However, a series of events—some economic and some political and social—systematically reduced the ease with which options could be substituted for one another. Nuclear power, once the energy hope of the future, at least temporarily has succumbed to public concern about its safety—especially following the Three Mile Island incident—and to regulatory quicksand. A rapid transition from liquids to coal has met with further regulatory restriction, this time inspired by environmental concerns. Decreasing capital availability has delayed research and development in renewables, such as solar; moreover, the failure of the United States to prepare adequate short-term solutions has had predictably adverse effects on the speed with which long-term options can be implemented. The consequence: a self-perpetuating problem.

Some aspects of this problem are easier to tackle than others. Deregulation, for example, removes artificial signals that have confused U.S. consumers about the seriousness of energy price and availability issues. Oil and gas deregulation accomplishes one significant goal for energy pricing: it internalizes energy's high cost. With energy priced properly, consumers and policy makers are, in a sense, freer to evaluate which costs they are willing to assume, some being economic and others, social and political.

This book advocates making decisions—choosing between alternatives and pursuing particular courses of action designed to realize specific goals. Some national goals conflict with others, however, and the task of making these goals complement one another is a formidable one. For example, in order to improve standards of living, the United States has pursued vigorous economic growth. Historically, U.S. economic growth was facilitated by large and cheap energy supplies and the energy input to the economy rose as GNP rose. Supply disruptions and radical price hikes have schooled Americans to seek greater energy self-sufficiency by making the economy less energy intensive. Tremendous headway has been made, in part through a conservation-inspired reevaluation of the KLEM equation, toward shifting emphasis from energy to other inputs. Equally important now is the development of resources that can substitute for expensive and politically vulnerable liquids, particularly oil. Oil prices rising at 4 percent each year, as they do in this study's scenarios with the worst luck on world oil price, provide a certain and consistent amount of pressure to rethink the possibilities inherent in the KLEM equation. Without the impetus of extremely high and continuously escalating oil prices, the likelihood of resolving political and social barriers—environmental and safety-oriented—to other resource options shrinks. But the factors involved in this rethinking of our energy future are more complex than most observers realize or than state-of-the-art models can capture.

Much of the extremely high price that liquid fuels, like Arab light, command, is purely "rent." Production costs are sufficiently low so that, were there no guaranteed demand for the product sustaining current price levels, the cartel could lower posted prices with comparatively little disadvantage to itself to promote energy use and economic growth in other countries. Assuming that such price manipulations occurred, the United States would be forced to reevaluate the goal of reducing import dependency; such a reevaluation would be prompted by the simple economic reality that it would be cheaper to continue using imported oil—priced realistically—than it would be to revamp, rebuild, or construct new plants and equipment to employ other resources. High interest rates can have an effect similar to the price manipulations by simultaneously strengthening the dollar abroad and discouraging investment at home. It pays to note, however, that if the United States does not purchase large quantities of foreign oil, other nations will. Who imports this hypothetically lower-priced oil is important to the United States for security reasons, among others.

The energy assumptions and results, presented in Chapters 3 and 4, respectively, reflect the primary importance of energy pricing. However, many other factors related to supply or extraction technology, for example, influence the viability of a resource's potential contribution to the nation's energy mix. Clearly, the energy issues discussed in the policy sections that follow have greater or lesser degrees of significance depending on the time periods under examination. This book's three time periods—the short, mid-, and long terms—provide a means by which to organize U.S. energy policy options. In the short term the United States must address the liquid fuels question, balancing the goals of energy security and national security. How the United States chooses to implement conservation and to treat oil and gas in its energy mix, in turn, will determine the complexion of the mid- and long terms. The United States must begin—without delay—to answer environmental and safety questions associ-

---

TABLE 5.7
Energy Security Policy Objectives

---

1. The preferred scenario's economic growth calls for primary energy consumption to grow by at least 1.9 percent per year to the year 2000. To achieve this growth rate will require:

   a. maintaining domestic oil and gas production at or close to the current 39-quad production level;

   b. increasing coal and nuclear's current contribution of 17 quads to about 63.5 quads by the year 2000;

   c. increasing hydroelectric, geothermal, biomass, and solar energy's share of primary energy from its current 4 percent to over 7 percent by 2000; and

   d. increasing shale- and coal-based synthetic fuel production so that it accounts for about 5 quads or the equivalent of 2.5 million barrels of oil per day by the year 2000.

2. In the preferred scenario electricity generation grows at approximately 4.3 percent per year. Meeting this growth rate will require a generating capacity growth rate of at least 3.8 percent per year to the year 2000.

3. By the year 2000 sufficient investment must be made for productive conservation to displace 10 quads of primary energy use.

4. Oil imports should be reduced from the 1978 level of 9 million barrels per day (MMBD) to about 3.2 MMBD in 2000. In the interim, the nation's oil import vulnerability must be blunted by increasing the Strategic Petroleum Reserve to offset at least a six-month interruption. Responses to major import disruptions should be coordinated internationally.

5. Decontrolling oil and gas prices should provide sufficient incentive for the transitions from oil and gas to more abundant alternatives; but every effort must be made to price these fuels to reflect the rapid rate at which they are being depleted. The preferred scenario calls for world oil prices to rise 4 percent per year in real terms from 1978 to 2000 and for natural gas to reach parity with oil no later than 1985.

Source: Compiled by the authors.

ated with coal and nuclear power, the energy sources best-suited to providing the nation's midterm energy needs, while research and development, designed to harness the potential inherent in renewable energy sources, focuses on long-term options.

Achieving energy security is a long-range goal designed to preserve national security. The preferred scenario's energy policy objectives all have their roots in the expected rise in the world price of oil and in the growth rates for overall energy and electricity. Table 5.7 summarizes the energy objectives. The corollary recommendations accompany this portfolio's individual energy policy studies: oil, gas, coal, synthetic fuels, nuclear power, solar power, conservation, and environmental and energy regulation. Recommendations concerning oil and gas, and those pertaining to coal and synthetics, are grouped together following those pairs of policy studies because of their interrelationships. These recommendations and the background material presented in each policy study focus on issues of supply and technology, since pricing is discussed in Chapter 3 as a justification for scenario assumptions.

Oil

The Problem

During the 1970s the United States fell into heavy dependence on imported oil, the total of which swelled from 3.5 million barrels a day in 1970 to 8.3 million in 1979. Together with ballooning prices, this rapid increase boosted the U.S. oil import bill from $2.74 billion in 1970 to $56.5 billion by the decade's end.

The hazards of this situation are well-known: a deteriorating balance of payments for the United States, rising domestic inflation, and a sense of helplessness in dealing with the energy-economic dislocation that such dependency creates. Clearly, it is unhealthy for the United States to depend on oil for about half of its energy needs when half of that oil—or nearly one-quarter of all U.S. energy supplies—must be imported. The basic problem of increasing demand for oil has been aggravated by a decline in supply from domestic production.

Background

To see why the oil production decline has occurred and what can be done to reverse it, several factors that affect the oil industry's ability to produce must be considered: the size of the nation's petroleum reserves, oil prices, advances in recovery technology, federal leasing policy, and other regulatory/environmental policies that help create the general climate in which production must operate.

Because uncertainty characterizes each of these factors, a whole range of outcomes is possible. By emphasizing policies in those areas where choice exists, the strategy behind this portfolio is to see that the nation lands on its feet, no matter what bad breaks may occur in those areas beyond U.S. control.

Oil Resources

First, an important distinction must be drawn between the oil that we have and the oil that we actually can get and use. Our oil resources include deposits known or believed to exist in a potentially recoverable form. Reserves, on the other hand, include only that portion that can be extracted economically with current technology and at prevailing prices.

The price part is critical. Rising prices make it economically feasible for producers to recover resources that may have been uneconomic to tap at lower price levels. The result is that these resources move into the category of usable reserves. Other factors that can convert resources into reserves include improved recovery technology and policy changes that may open up new lands for drilling or relieve environmental constraints on development.

According to a recent update of U.S. Geological Survey (USGS) Circular 725 (1975) "median" resource estimates, we now have about 27 billion barrels of proved oil reserves (those that have been confirmed by drilling). In addition, the adjusted estimates envision about 21 billion barrels of inferred and indicated reserves, and about 80 billion barrels of potentially recoverable oil resources still awaiting discovery in the United States, both onshore and offshore.

A reserves-to-production ratio in the range of 8:1 to 12:1 generally is considered necessary to support sustained oil production. Our current ratio hovers around 10:1, but it was considerably better a decade ago. During the eight-year period between 1971 and 1978, the nation used up its proved reserves almost twice as fast as new ones were being found. During the 1970s, proved oil reserves dropped a total of 11.9 billion barrels. As a result, production fell from the 1970 peak of 11.3 million barrels a day to about 10 million a day by the end of the decade.

Depletion of reserves has been particularly severe in the traditional onshore producing areas of the lower 48 states. In 1970 these traditional areas accounted for about 85 percent of domestic oil production and fed about 32 percent of our energy needs. By 1980 these areas were producing only 70 percent of our domestic oil and satisfying only about 18 percent of our appetite for energy. The only major new finds in the lower 48 states, in fact, are the recent discoveries in the Overthrust Belt of the Rockies.

The implication is that producers must look elsewhere for new reserves, and this is exactly what they are doing. A major focus is on offshore possibilities from the Outer Continental Shelf (OCS) of North America. The USGS has estimated that the Continental Shelf out to a depth of 200 meters may contain as much as 31 percent of the undiscovered oil still remaining in the United States. Estimates of the potential reserves—still awaiting discovery there—range from 12.5 billion to 38 billion barrels —a significant amount, no matter which end of the range one chooses.

Alaska also is expected to yield new reserves as drilling increases. Of course, the finding rate (barrels of oil found per foot drilled) is always a matter of uncertainty; but finds in rich and largely untapped Alaskan fields promise to help compensate for a decline in older, increasingly exhausted areas of the lower 48 states. In fact, 1979 may have marked a change in the progressive decline that has characterized U.S. oil finds during the 1970s. Proved reserves still declined in 1979, but the rate of decline slowed down. This promising trend was also evident in 1980. Alaskan reserves, both onshore and offshore, will play a large part in any actual turnaround.

Overall, then, the geologic outlook for boosting U.S. oil production is gloomy in some areas and hopeful in others. Conventional recovery techniques seem to have gleaned about all they can out of many traditional oil-producing areas, but offshore areas in the lower 48 states as well as both land-based and offshore operations in Alaska hold substantial promise for increased production.

Prices

Price levels also will be important in determining whether the potential of these new areas actually can be tapped. Most new discoveries are now being made in remote and inaccessible locations, where exploration is far more expensive than it was when the older oil fields in the interior of the United States were opened early in this century. Higher oil prices can provide the necessary incentive to move into these areas, even though the cost of drilling has risen rapidly.

World oil prices are expected to continue rising between now and the year 2000, and domestic oil prices are expected to follow. The rate of increase is uncertain and will be highly significant. In this book, that rate for world oil is assumed to range between 2 and 4 percent annually, with the higher percentage increase acting as a greater stimulus to production.

Virtually all domestic oil production is currently subject to a Windfall Profits Tax collected at the wellhead. This, in effect, reduces wellhead prices that the producer is able to get for all oil. Although the tax rate (about 30 percent) is lower for newly discovered oil than for most other categories, it is still a disincentive. It will subtract about $5 from the price that the producer receives on every barrel of newly discovered oil. This tax is expected to remain in place through the end of 1988, when it should begin a 33-month phaseout if target revenues have been achieved.

Long-standing tax breaks that help spur oil development include the oil depletion allowance and the allowance for intangible drilling costs. By allowing such drilling costs to be written off as an expense item, the government allows accelerated cash flow to oil producers, making economical certain oil production prospects that otherwise might not be. This volume's analysis assumes the continuation of these financial incentives to oil production, but since their continuation is not guaranteed, they must be counted among the contingencies that could affect domestic oil production in the future.

Technology

The next link in the chain of contingencies that will affect domestic oil production is the status of recovery technology. Enhanced recovery techniques are those that can wring oil out of situations in which, from the standpoint of conventional techniques, a deposit would be considered either too depleted to bother with anymore or too expensive to tap in the first place. Some such techniques already exist, and more are on the way.

The problem is that such techniques are more expensive than conventional drilling. So the expected price that the producer can get on any oil so recovered is once again critical in determining where and how often such techniques will be used. Furthermore, there are sometimes environmental complications, and policy in this area also will affect enhanced oil recovery.

Conventional recovery methods have extracted only about one-third of the oil known to exist in the United States. In addition to the waterflooding technique developed some 40 years ago to boost recovery rates, there are new methods that rely on heat, chemicals, and various other fluids to thin out the oil in rock formations and allow it to flow toward producing wells. Steam injection and the injection of gases such as carbon monoxide are leading techniques. Like newly discovered oil, production made possible by enhanced recovery techniques is taxed at a lower rate under the Windfall Profits Act.

Given favorable conditions regarding technological advancement, prices, and government policies, it is estimated that enhanced recovery actually could double the nation's current proved oil reserves. The Department of Energy reports that these methods added some 270,000 barrels a day to domestic production in 1978 and that the enhanced recovery bonus could grow to over 1 million barrels a day by 1990.[14]

Government Land Policies

The federal government owns one-third of all the land in the United States and all of the OCS beyond state jurisdiction. Until recently, the federal government owned 98.5 percent of Alaska. After completing pending land transfers to the state of Alaska and Alaskan natives, federal agencies still will control about 62 percent of the state's area. The federal government also owns more than 48 percent of Wyoming, 47 percent of California, 37 percent of Colorado, and 33 percent of New Mexico.

The point is that federal ownership, especially in Alaska and the resource-rich Western states, means federal control of access to these resources—and access has not been easy. Only about 13 percent of federally owned onshore lands have been leased to private developers for exploration; and only about 4 percent of submerged OCS lands have been leased. The importance of such access becomes clear when how much domestic oil is currently lying out of reach is considered. The USGS estimates that 37 percent of the nation's undiscovered oil and natural gas liquids lie in the areas under federal control, both onshore and offshore.

Federal land and leasing policy is, therefore, a critical factor in determining the level of domestic oil production. One favorable development in this area is the recent announcement of a bold leasing schedule by the Bureau of Land Management (BLM). This schedule calls for 36 lease sales over the next five years, with 11 for areas in the Gulf of Mexico. This increased access is expected to yield new supplies that will help offset production declines in older Gulf Coast areas.

The BLM leasing schedule will include other offshore areas as well, including areas submerged beneath Atlantic and Alaskan waters. Given the USGS estimates that the total OCS may contain as much as 31 percent of the nation's undiscovered oil, this is a very significant step toward freeing access to these as-yet-untapped domestic oil deposits.

The other main focus of federal land policy is in Alaska and the Rocky Mountain states. It appears likely that the Naval Petroleum Reserve A and the Beaufort Sea in

Alaska will be made available for full resource development. In the Rocky Mountain area, the Overthrust Belt will be important for conventional oil production. Even more important may be gaining access to Western federal lands where some 80 percent of the nation's shale oil reserves are concentrated, especially in Colorado.

Environmental Policy

Inseparable from the issue of federal leasing policy are questions of environmental impact. In fact, the Environmental Protection Agency has considerable influence over the way in which federal lands are used, and it is the charge of this agency to make sure that they are used in ways that protect environmental quality. Some perceive a conflict of priorities between energy and environmental needs, but others insist that a great deal of oil can be extracted from federally controlled deposits without serious damage to the environment.

In addition, environmental regulations affect producers even on private lands. Air quality can be affected by dust and gas releases during the drilling and recovery processes. Water supplies can be affected if drilling and blasting release soluble substances into local groundwater. Noise regulations can prevent drilling near settled areas. Regulations designed simply to preserve the visual appeal of certain areas can ban the presence of unsightly oil rigs.

There is no way to drill for oil in a quiet and inconspicuous manner. Disturbing the peace and beauty of heretofore undeveloped areas is a serious issue to the environmentally concerned both in and out of government, and one that energy developers must face in both public and private sectors. A growing awareness of the urgency of U.S. energy needs could help promote a greater spirit of compromise in this area, but protecting the environment is still an issue—or rather a cluster of issues—that vitally can affect the nation's prospects for increasing domestic oil production.

What, then, do all these contingencies—contingencies of geology, price, technology, and policy—affecting domestic oil production mean for the United States? A glance at this book's scenario results shows considerable variation in outcomes: compared with present domestic output of 19–20 quads per year, production in the year 2000 could range from a low of 15.9 quads in the low-growth scenario to 22 quads in the independence case. This means that U.S. oil production could shrink as much as 19 percent or grow as much as 12 percent, depending very largely on choices made at the federal level.

Natural Gas

The Problem

Natural gas is among the most desirable of fuels. Like its hydrocarbon twin—oil —gas is an energy mainstay of the U.S. economy. It currently fills about one-quarter of all the nation's energy needs. Gas can be substituted for oil in many applications: as a home heating fuel, for example, or as a fuel for utility and industrial boilers. Most of the gas U.S. citizens use is produced domestically, a plus from the standpoint of national security. There are also environmental benefits from substituting gas for oil, since gas burns more cleanly than oil, releasing fewer sulfurous air pollutants. If the United States can secure more gas, it could mean reducing the demand for imported oil. The gas problem, then, is essentially one of supply: how can we maximize gas supplies in the United States over the next 20 years?

Background

There are two ways to get the gas we need: produce it domestically or import it. The primary focus should be on ways to augment domestic production, without ruling out the possibility of increasing gas imports under circumstances that would be compatible with overall energy goals.

Natural gas production in the United States, currently running about 20 trillion cubic feet (tcf) per year, faces a number of contingencies in the years ahead. Major among them are the extent of our recoverable gas resources, wellhead prices for natural gas, government regulatory and environmental policy, the rate of development of unconventional and synthetic gas sources, and the existence of an adequate transportation network to get the gas from increasingly remote production sites to the consuming public.

Resources and Reserves

The first logical question about natural gas is how much the United States has. Here the distinction between resources and reserves—between what is there and what is recoverable—once again applies. To the extent that favorable developments occur with regard to price incentives, extraction technology, and environmental policy, a greater portion of the nation's natural gas endowment can be turned into usable supplies.

Recent updating of USGS Circular 725 (1975) median assessment for natural gas takes account of new gas finds in the Overthrust Belt of the Rocky Mountains, as well as decreased potential in the Permian Basin and Atlantic OCS area. The total comes out to 195 tcf of proved reserves, plus about 200 tcf of inferred reserves and about 500 tcf of undiscovered recoverable gas resources (all conventional).

Our reserves-to-production ratio for natural gas has been falling for some time. While gas production peaked in 1973 and had fallen some 12 percent by 1978, the level of proved reserves peaked in 1967 and by 1978 had fallen nearly 25 percent. New discoveries of natural gas simply have failed to replace what has been consumed. Experts do not know exactly how much remains or what the rate of recovery will be, but they do know that natural gas as a resource is dwindling. The United States probably has no more than 40 years' worth left at current consumption rates (about 20 tcf per year), and many analysts believe that we have considerably less.

Wellhead Prices

Besides the sheer extent of our geologic endowment, another factor that can influence domestic gas output is price. The history of natural gas pricing is one of almost unremitting conflict. For decades, gas producers and gas consumers have been locked in combat around a central issue: should the price of gas be based on its cost of production, or on its value in the marketplace?

Prior to the Natural Gas Policy Act (NGPA) of 1978, only interstate gas—produced in one state and consumed in another—was subject to federal price controls. Since then, gas produced and consumed all in the same state has fallen under similar controls. The controls have been a patchwork of prices for different categories of gas, based on federal calculations as to how much it should cost industry to produce gas in each category. Predictably, the controls have been unpopular with gas producers, who charge that they have choked off potential gas supplies with red tape, encouraging consumption but offering little incentive to build up domestic gas production.

With price decontrol of most categories now in sight—either in 1985 or delayed until late 1987, according to NGPA phased decontrol provisions—gas producers can look forward to market incentives to boost production potential. The delay could occur because skyrocketing world oil prices since the passage of the 1978 act have driven a large wedge between controlled gas prices and the freer-moving price of oil. Assuming that the wellhead price of gas follows the world oil price, the prospect of a catch-up leap in gas prices immediately following decontrol might prompt federal authorities to extend gas controls to the maximum late 1987 deadline allowed by the Natural Gas Act. On the other hand government advocates of free-market pricing have been urging earlier decontrol.

Supply Allocation

In addition to pricing policy, other government policies also affect the gas picture. One has to do with the allocation of gas supplies. The Powerplant and Industrial Fuel Use Act (PIFUA) specifically places natural gas use off limits to certain users under certain conditions. Provisions ban building new oil- or gas-fired power plants, ban fuel-burning industrial plants from using boilers designed to take oil or gas as their primary energy source, and prohibit existing power plants from using natural gas after January 1, 1990, unless a "systems compliance plan" for full gas phaseout by 1995 or 2000 is developed and approved by the Department of Energy (DOE). Exemptions may be granted if the relative cost of alternative fuels (mainly coal) is as much as 30 percent higher than the cost of using oil or gas, or if the installation is unable to meet environmental standards with fuels other than oil and gas.

PIFUA has two broad objectives. One is to reduce dependence on foreign oil by promoting a switch to coal for utilities and other major industrial concerns. The other is to limit industrial use of natural gas, thereby reserving it for residential customers. In this respect, PIFUA reconfirms the Phillips decision of 1954, which established priorities among natural gas users: residential customers, industries using gas as a feedstock, industries burning gas in boilers, and electric utilities.

The so-called gas bubble of recent years has confused the picture somewhat by prompting federal officials to turn around and promote industrial gas use, at least for the present. The gas surplus is expected to be temporary, however, so the long-term trend is still the same: industry, including the electric utility industry, will be last in line if gas supplies tighten again.

Federal Gas Leases

Leasing of federal lands for exploration and development, especially offshore, will affect vitally the pace of domestic natural gas production. Some 30 percent of our domestic gas output already comes from federal leases both on- and offshore. Government studies show that about 43 percent of the natural gas still waiting to be discovered also lies under federal control. The OCS area is considered particularly rich in untapped gas potential. The USGS has estimated that about 21 percent of the undiscovered natural gas remaining in the nation lies under its waters.

As long as OCS development remains a two-stage process, requiring both exploration permits and then federal and state production permits if any recoverable gas is found, the permit process will be a drag on production. On the other hand, leasing federal offshore areas at an accelerated pace and streamlining the permit system could give a substantial boost to domestic gas production prospects. Streamlining the system of environmental regulations that requires lengthy environmental impact statements before drilling can begin also would expedite production.

A hopeful sign is the recent leasing schedule announced by the Bureau of Land Management that will open up 1 million acres of the Gulf of Mexico every year through 1990. Once gas resources in this area have been developed more fully, current estimates suggest that the next logical focus will be accelerated drilling for gas in the waters off Alaska if more federal leases can be secured.

New Domestic Sources

Prospects for synthetic natural gas (SNG) from coal also rest heavily on federal policy. Passage of the Energy Security Act in June 1980 has opened the way for development of a coal gasification industry, but many questions remain as to water supply and other environmental considerations. In addition, capital requirements will be enormous, and the posture of the Federal Energy Regulatory Commission (FERC) on the rates required to keep pioneer projects afloat will be important in determining whether the potential for gas from coal becomes a reality soon enough to help relieve the oil import problem during this century.

Another largely untapped supply of domestic gas would come from so-called unconventional sources: natural gas from Western tight sands, Appalachian shales, coal seams, and the geopressured thermal brines of the Gulf Coast. The main deterrents here are price and technology. Most of these deposits simply are not economic to tap at current prices with existing recovery methods. Given price increases and modest technological advances, such sources may be able to offer a few quads of energy by the century's end, but most experts see no major role for unconventional gas resources in relieving the oil import bind.

The Import Option

The remaining possibility for swelling the U.S. gas supply is simply to import it —an apparently bizarre suggestion in light of the drive against oil imports. The two situations are different, however, in one critical area: reliability. Whereas most of the U.S. imported oil comes from Middle Eastern nations that have shown their willingness to cut off supplies when it suits them, the natural gas now imported by the United States comes almost exclusively from neighboring Canada. Prospects for increased imports hinge on agreements with Canada and Mexico, also a neighbor. Both of these nations have economies that are heavily interdependent with that of the United States, which provides some assurance that they would not be likely to cut off gas supplies for light or transient reasons.

How much gas could Canada and/or Mexico provide? In terms of its reserves-to-production ratio, Canada is in a favorable position. Current Canadian production of 2.5 tcf annually represents only 3.2 percent of proved reserves in contrast with the 9.7 annual percentage rate at which the United States is using up its reserves. Furthermore, while Canada's proved reserves now total roughly 86 tcf, that nation estimates an additional 277 tcf of probable and potential reserves remaining. This all adds up to a 125-year supply of natural gas at current consumption rates, including the 1 tcf (or about 40 percent of total production) that Canada currently exports to the United States.

Mexico's endowment of natural gas is probably even richer, and it is being tapped even more slowly. The potential is high: Mexico has an estimated 300-year supply of natural gas at current production rates. Proved reserves of about 67 tcf are being tapped at a rate of only 2 percent a year (roughly 1.3 tcf), and an estimated 340 tcf of probable and potential reserves remain. So far almost all of it is consumed domestically, and it is uncertain whether Mexico will slip comfortably into a role similar to Canada's as an exporting neighbor.

Price has been a bone of contention with both Canada and Mexico. Canada's recent price increase from $3.45 to $4.47 per million Btus shows its intention to price its gas exports at least equivalent to the cost of its oil imports—a chance factor on the world market—and Mexico is likely to demand parity with Canadian prices. In addition, Mexico's announced energy plan calls for domestic use of natural gas resources in order to free Mexican oil for export. Since Mexican oil export revenues already have overheated that nation's economy, this further reduces whatever incentive may exist to export gas as well. So Canada well may prove a more reliable source of natural gas imports in the immediate future, although negotiations with Mexico can be expected to continue.

Gas Transport

The final major contingency affecting prospects for natural gas use in the United States is transportation. Adequate means of transporting the gas are essential to support any increased traffic between producer and consumer, whether the producers are domestic companies or foreign exporters.

Domestically, the Alaskan Natural Gas Transportation System (ANGTS) scheduled for operation in the mid-1980s will be essential to bring Alaskan gas to customers in the lower 48 states, where gas production from conventional sources is expected to decline. The ANGTS design capacity is 4.5 billion cubic feet (bcf) per day, with increments possible through installation of compression equipment if additional fields in the Prudhoe Bay area prove productive. Imports also depend to some extent on the successful completion of ANGTS. About half of the Canadian gas committed to the U.S. market during the 1980s will come from the Pan-Alberta project, which is tied to ANGTS for delivery.

LNG (liquefied natural gas) from overseas presents another transport issue. The most economical means of moving large amounts of gas over very long distances, particularly across oceans, is to liquefy it by cryogenic techniques and transport it in special tankers. A small amount of LNG, about 0.5 quad, now comes from Algeria by this method, and more is possible from other nations in the Middle East, Africa, Southeast Asia, and Latin America.

Two drawbacks exist. The first is the safety risk involved in handling and storing this highly volatile and flammable fluid, a risk that has meant siting problems for potential LNG terminal and regasification facilities in the United States. The other is U.S. reluctance to depend any further on possibly unreliable foreign suppliers— faraway gas exporters that might behave in the future as the oil-exporting nations have behaved in the past.

This book's estimates of future domestic gas production, like those for petroleum, vary considerably across scenarios. Starting from a 1978 baseline of 19.2 quads, the best that now can be expected in the year 2000 is the continuation scenario figure of 17.5 quads for U.S. output, while production could fall as low as the 11.5 quads per year of the low-growth case. In the high-growth and continuation cases, both of which assume new discoveries and modest real price increases, total gas supplies actually rise over the rest of this century—but only if the United States counts on increased natural gas imports from neighboring Canada and Mexico as well as some contributions from unconventional sources.

Recommendations for Oil and Natural Gas

For domestic oil and gas the preferred scenario policy objective is to maintain production of domestic oil and gas at the 1978 level of 39 quads per year through the year 2000. Several actions will be required to support this objective.

Prices of domestic oil and natural gas must be decontrolled completely. Under price controls, investment returns are not high enough to encourage producers to spend the money and take the risks necessary to turn domestic oil and gas potential into usable supplies. Allowing domestic oil prices to follow world oil prices through phased price decontrol is essential to assure domestic supplies and to promote conservation over the long term. In addition, giving newly discovered oil extracted by enhanced recovery techniques a special tax break would be beneficial. Removal of the Windfall Profits Tax on these categories and eventually on all oil sources would be best. Continuation of other special tax breaks such as expense writeoffs of intangible drilling costs to improve producers' cash flow also would be beneficial.

Accelerated leasing of federal lands on- and offshore is essential to achieving energy independence. The United States possesses vast amounts of oil and natural gas in lands under government control. Accelerated leasing can be achieved while at the same time giving reasonable consideration to environmental concerns. No matter what the financial incentives and the available technology, producers cannot recover oil and gas from lands that they cannot touch. Too much of the nation's resource base lies under government control to exempt these areas from development, either intentionally or as an unintended consequence of a ponderous bureaucratic process.

The nation should encourage expanded domestic oil and natural gas production. Domestic oil and gas supplies can ease the transition to coal, nuclear, and alternative and renewable energy sources. During this transition, enhanced recovery techniques and the use of heavy oil can make a real contribution, and one that should be supported with continuing R&D and favorable price/tax treatment. To capitalize on the nation's domestic energy resources and assure their efficient use will require additional research and development in the areas of secondary recovery techniques, use of heavy oil, offshore production, tight sand sources, and geopressured methane.

The United States must develop increased transport capability for domestic oil and gas. Major domestic energy resources are located in areas remote from major population and industrial centers. In particular, ANGTS must be in place by 1985 to bring gas from Canada and Alaska to the lower 48 states.

During phase-out of reliance on imported oil and gas, the United States should shift to more reliable sources in Canada and Mexico and accelerate the buildup of the Strategic Petroleum Reserve. Weaning the nation away from imported oil of necessity will take time. Substituting natural gas for oil and shifting in both cases to sources in close proximity would enhance near-term national security. By accelerating the build-up of the Strategic Petroleum Reserve to a targeted six-month supply, the nation will cushion substantially the shock of any future cutoff of imported oil supplies.

The United States should allow the continued use of natural gas by electric utilities in existing gas- and oil-fired boilers to reduce the use of oil. In California, for example, state air quality regulations prohibit burning oil with a sulfur content of more than 0.5 percent, and very little such oil is available to utilities domestically. Meeting arbitrary deadlines to reduce substantially gas use in existing boilers by the end of the decade will present many electric utility companies with an even more formidable financing task than the one they already face and will serve to delay completion of new coal and nuclear capacity.

The United States should augment conventional natural gas supplies with production from new gas sources. The stimulus can take the form of price and tax incentives for unconventional natural sources and—probably more important—direct federal assistance for coal gasification projects, which could yield about 1.5 quads of gas annually by the early 1990s.

Coal

The Problem

Coal is the nation's most abundant conventional energy resource. With a proven reserve base of some 437 billion tons, U.S. coal can last some 300 years at current rates of recovery and consumption. Unlike our domestic oil and gas reserves, our coal reserves are in no serious danger of running out.

The main problem with coal, then, is not a problem of supply. It is rather a problem of demand—of finding ways to increase our use of a fuel that we already possess in abundance. Substituting coal for oil and gas is a national energy goal, and one that considerations of both availability and fuel cost tend to support. Simply producing more coal for the marketplace is not enough, however. Some of the most critical challenges lie at the point of use: to use coal safely, without major adverse impacts on health and the environment and to maintain simultaneously its competitiveness with other fuels. The coal policy paper considers direct coal combustion and the synthetic fuels policy paper, which follows, considers its potential as a direct substitute for liquid and gaseous fuels.

Background

For many years, coal was the nation's primary fuel. Then inexpensive petroleum and natural gas became available. Now those fuels are no longer abundant, nor are they inexpensive. They will grow more costly as phased decontrol of oil and gas prices allows them to follow world oil prices upward.

The nation's ability to substitute for oil and gas through the direct combustion of coal depends on a number of factors. Among the most important are the type of coal available, access to low-cost deposits on federal lands, growth in coal-using industries, productivity in the coal fields, adequate transportation for increased coal output, and—probably most important—the search for cost-effective ways to deal with the health and environmental impacts of burning coal.

Resource Variability

The United States possesses two quite different types of coal resources, classified broadly by geographic location. Eastern coal, long the staple of coal-burning industries, forms the nation's oldest and deepest deposits, up to 100 feet thick. These deposits yield coal with a higher energy content than Western coal, a plus from the standpoint of heating efficiency. What is undesirable is that Eastern coals, because they were formed under salt water, also have a considerably higher sulfur content, meaning that they release more sulfurous air pollutants when burned. They also are relatively more costly to recover, since underground mining usually is required.

The Western coals that now are beginning to receive attention tend to run in shallower, thinner veins, closer to the earth's surface. They are typically softer and less efficient as a heat source than Eastern coal, but their lower sulfur content has made them look attractive as a means of minimizing air problems. They are also easier and cheaper to recover, since surface strip-mining can be used. The Office of Technology Assessment (OTA) figures coal in underground mines is only about 57 percent recoverable with currently used technologies, whereas surface mining techniques can recover about 80 percent of coal in shallow Western deposits.

Federal Lands

The extent to which U.S. coal production will shift to the West, which in 1976 accounted for only about 16 percent of the nation's output, will depend partly on federal leasing policy. Like the nation's oil and gas deposits, much Western coal—at least 60 percent of reserves—lies beneath federal lands. A moratorium on leasing prevailed during the 1970s. Whether these lands now will be opened for strip-mining and whether Western water supplies will be adequate to support a burgeoning coal industry are major questions affecting the coal outlook.

Even more basic in the short term, though, is the question of who would buy the output of new Western coal fields. The mining industry estimates that current U.S. coal production capacity is already 15–20 percent greater than output. That is, we can already produce substantially more coal than we can use.

The Market for Coal

The coal market is limited by the fact that direct combustion makes sense today only in very large facilities: in utility power plants and in large industrial boilers. This fact is due partly to difficulties in handling this bulky fuel, and partly to the difficulty of controlling its environmental impact. Only very large enterprises can afford the kind of environmental control equipment that now is required by law for burning solid coal.

The electric utility industry is the coal industry's main customer. In 1980, utilities consumed over three-quarters (81 percent) of all the coal used in the United States. The iron and steel industry used about 9.5 percent, and 8.6 percent went into the boilers of all other industries combined. Commercial and residential coal use as fuel was virtually negligible, totaling less than 7 million short tons, or about 0.9 percent.

What this means is that coal demand is heavily dependent on growth of a very few domestic industries—mostly the electric utilities, with a lesser role for the steel industry—and exports. Growth in the electric utility industry has become highly uncertain in recent years, progressing at a substantially slower rate than historic growth patterns would predict. After humming along for years at an average growth rate of about 7 percent, average growth sagged to 3.0 percent in 1979. It has picked up some since then, and is expected to pick up further during the 1980s, but the exact rate is highly uncertain. This book's scenarios show generation growth rates ranging from 1.7 percent to 5.1 percent over the period 1978 to 2000. Slower growth in the steel industry also has depressed the coal market, especially the market for coking coals, and steel's recovery rate from the 1980 recession is similarly uncertain.

The slower growth in consuming industries, plus the hurdles that attend the conversion of oil- and gas-fired powerplants to coal, are the main reasons why the anticipated coal boom has not materialized on the scale that many anticipated over the short term. In 1977, when annual coal use was about 14 quads (18.4 percent of total energy use), the National Energy Plan called for nearly doubling coal use by 1985. This increase now appears highly unlikely, although by the year 2000 coal use probably will triple. This latter prospect depends on the successful development of coal-based synthetic fuels, as well as on firmer markets for direct coal use.

Labor and Productivity

Coal costs will help determine the level of market demand; productivity in the coal fields will help determine those costs. The history of labor-management relations in the coal industry is one fraught with conflict, as the massive coal strike of 1977–78—a confrontation generally acknowledged to have no winner—has illustrated only recently. Strikes and work slowdowns have played havoc with productivity, although substantial wage and benefit increases of recent years should modify this tendency in the future.

Compounding this problem in the short run is the recent exodus of skilled, experienced miners due to disability or retirement, and the associated influx of young, relatively inexperienced workers in the mines. Some 50,000 experienced miners were replaced by new workers during the late 1960s and early 1970s, a change that seems directly linked to the decline in worker productivity and one that occurred in many other industries as well over the same period. Moreover, management has had its own shortages of highly trained and qualified personnel to keep the mines running smoothly.

The net effect has been an unstable working situation in the coal-mining industry, in which costs have risen as output per worker has declined. Progress has been achieved in this area in the late 1970s but more will be necessary if coal is to provide the bulk of midterm energy supplies.

Transportation

Transportation, too, is a problem. About three-quarters of mined coal moves by rail. Eastern rail lines that could transport greatly increased coal output do exist, but they are not in top condition. Railroads would have to build many new lines to carry coal to market from the developing Western coal fields. Either way, for new construction or simply for upgrading and repairs, the railroads must lay out a substantial investment—and they are understandably reluctant to do this until they are sure that in fact there will be greater coal output to transport.

It takes time to build railroads, and if coal demand surged tomorrow, the railroads would not be ready. On the other hand, they cannot get ready until they are sure that there is something for which to ready themselves. So the question revolves again to the market demand that will trigger coal production and the uncertainties that attend this demand.

An alternative to rail transport for solid coal is the coal slurry pipeline, which carries pulverized coal mixed with water. The most economical way to move the black fuel over long distances, about 5 million tons per year already move by pipeline between Arizona and southwestern Nevada. There are questions, however, as to whether there is enough water available in the West to expand this method, and in any case the railroads have refused to allow slurry pipelines—their competitors—to cross railroad property, which would be essential on most long-distance routes.

Regulatory bodies have allowed sharp increases in railroad rates without using federal power (for example, the right of eminent domain) to open up the slurry pipeline alternative. At the same time, coal movement has been restricted and higher transportation costs have been incurred due to inadequate waterway and port facilities in the East, where some coal moves via canal. So the combination of coal market uncertainty, inadequacy of rail and water transport facilities, lack of action on the slurry pipeline option, and simultaneously rising rail rates could make transportation a real bottleneck in increasing coal use.

Health and Environmental Concerns

Of all the problems retarding coal's ascendancy, the most serious seem to be those that center on health and the environment. There are two critical questions: whether it is possible to control potential hazards in a cost-effective manner and, if so, how to do so without severely restricting coal use.

Like all fossil fuels, when coal is burned to produce heat, it releases a variety of by-products: sulfur oxides, nitrogen oxides, particulates, and carbon dioxide, to name the most important. Sulfur oxides unquestionably contribute to the murky quality and poor visibility associated with air pollution episodes. They also are suspected of making the rain more acidic than it normally would be, and of contributing to human respiratory disorders. Researchers now are trying to determine exactly how great a threat sulfur oxides really pose to human health and the environment so that control standards can be set in a way that assures protection without placing unnecessary costs or constraints on coal use.

The story with nitrogen oxides is essentially the same. When nitrogen combines with oxygen during fossil fuel combustion, one result is nitrogen dioxide, the gas that gives smog its characteristic yellowish brown color. Nitrogen oxides can be converted to weak nitric acid in the atmosphere, so the concern about acid rain applies to them, too. They also have been implicated in studies of chronic respiratory disorders, as well as kidney and heart disease. As in the case of sulfur emissions, investigators are trying to determine whether there is a safe threshold—a level below which the impacts on health and the environment are insignificant—and how close today's air quality standards come to matching that natural threshold, if one exists.

Particulates are tiny particles of solid or liquid airborne material, ranging in diameter from about 0.0005 microns for aerosols (particles that remain suspended in the air) to about 500 microns for flakes of soot. These particles can create, in effect, a smokescreen that limits visibility in areas where burning takes place. They can also work their way into the human lung, where they may cause or aggravate a variety of respiratory conditions. There is even some possibility that they could alter our climate by acting as a filter, blocking out the sun's rays and creating a colder Earth.

An opposite climatic impact has been suggested for carbon dioxide emissions, the source of the much-discussed "greenhouse effect" that now may be occurring in the earth's atmosphere. The atmosphere gains very little of its heat directly from sunlight. Instead, solar radiation is absorbed by the earth, converted to heat, and reradiated from the earth's surface. A blanket of water vapor and carbon dioxide in the atmosphere can trap this heat and hold it close to earth, creating a net heating effect. The consequences of such a climate change could be virtually irreversible and quite drastic, although the onset of such a change could be hundreds to thousands of years away.

The main emissions can be controlled, either through direct use of emissions controls on plant stacks or indirectly, through development of new coal-burning technologies with built-in environmental safeguards. The primary form of direct emissions control is the stack-gas scrubber, which is generally quite effective (80–90 percent) in cleaning sulfur dioxide and all but the smallest particulates out of the gases released by burning coal. Furthermore, injecting small amounts of ammonia into combustion gases can clean out most of the nitrogen oxides. The tradeoff here is that these emission control methods are expensive: by 1978 the utility industry already had spent $4 billion on scrubbers alone.

The other approach is to find new ways to burn coal more cleanly. One example of the new clean-coal technologies is fluidized-bed combustion (FBC). As the pulverized coal burns in a turbulent "bed" of hot air, limestone captures sulfur oxides by reacting with them chemically to produce a harmless, disposable solid. This method also allows coal combustion at lower temperatures than those used commonly (1,500–1,600 degrees F rather than 3,000 degrees F), which simultaneously retards the formation of nitrogen oxides. The R&D pricetag for such new technologies is substantial, however, so this approach to making coal use environmentally acceptable is not a cheap alternative to direct emission control.

Air quality standards have become tougher than ever since the May 1979 passage of updated ceilings on the major controllable emissions from coal-burning. In the case of sulfur oxides, a new twist has been added. Potential emissions—those that would occur if uncontrolled completely—must be reduced by a certain percentage, even if the actual emissions already are controlled to a level that would pass muster.

Specifically, sulfur dioxide emissions already were limited by law to 1.2 pounds per million Btus of fuel consumed. The new standard retains this limit, but it also imposes a percentage reduction requirement of 70–90 percent, depending on the sulfur content of the coal used. Nitrogen oxide emissions are limited to no more than 0.5–0.8 pounds per million Btus, depending on coal type. The ceiling for particulate emissions has been lowered from 0.1 pounds per million Btus to only 0.03 pounds, a very substantial reduction.

A major upshot is that using low-sulfur coal no longer will be sufficient to meet existing air quality standards. With the new percentage reduction requirement, all regulated coal-burning facilities will have to install scrubbers to put the proper distance between potential emissions and actual ones. The implications of this change are several. One is that the cost of using coal will rise if all coal-burning facilities have to bear the additional costs of installing scrubbers. Another is the implicit warning to utilities and other potential investors in coal-fired facilities that the rules for using coal can change, making an economic proposition uneconomic under new and tighter regulations. A third is that the market for low-sulfur coal could fail to grow as expected, throwing the development of Western low-sulfur coal fields even further into doubt. Other air quality rules aimed at the "prevention of significant deterioration" in areas that still have relatively clean air—mostly sparsely populated areas—also could limit the possibilities for mining and burning coal in the Western states.

The whole coal-fuel cycle, then, from mining to use to subsequent cleanup, poses significant health and environmental challenges. Miners directly involved in the cycle and the public at large may suffer respiratory disorders if exposed to sufficiently high levels of emissions. As for the environment, the potential toll runs from the scars of strip-mining to the carbon dioxide buildup in the earth's atmosphere. None of these problems is an easy one to solve and in combination they could limit coal's competitiveness with oil and gas, at least at current price levels. Yet the benefits of increased coal consumption—of using what we have in abundance—are too great for the nation to forego greater utilization in any commonsense approach to today's energy dilemma.

In this book, all five modeled scenarios see coal use increasing between now and 2000. Fossil-fueled powerplants, in particular, will have to rely increasingly on coal. Coal use could more than triple if the nation pursues a vigorous path of energy security by shifting its needs toward consumption of coal-based electricity. Coal as a feedstock for synthetic fuel processes also could face a bright future if a sufficiently strong national commitment to synthetic fuels development prevails.

Synthetic Fuels

The Problem

There is more oil in U.S. shale deposits than in the petroleum reserves of all the OPEC nations combined. A similar amount of oil is present in tar sands, most in northern Alberta, Canada, but some in the U.S. northern Midwest as well. Add to these sources the fact that we now can make oil and gas from coal, a resource that the United States possesses in even greater abundance than shale, and the promise of synthetic fuels in relieving the import squeeze becomes very clear. The problem is how to turn this promise into a reality—using methods that are economically and environmentally sound.

The term "synfuels" (synthetic fuels) actually can apply to a broad spectrum of possibilities: all those fuels that human beings can create from the same chemical building blocks—mostly hydrogen and carbon—that nature has used in the creation of petroleum and natural gas. The Energy Security Act of June 1980 defines a synfuel as one that can be used as a substitute for petroleum or natural gas and that is produced by chemical or physical transformation of domestic resources. Such resources include shale, coal, tar sands, and even water, which can yield combustible hydrogen through electrolysis. Several of these possibilities have been around for a long time, but it was not worthwhile to pursue them as long as petroleum and natural gas were cheap.

During the late 1970s federal legislation established a national production goal for synfuels from domestic resources, a goal likely to change several times in the 1980s. The target was 500,000 barrels a day of crude oil equivalent by 1987 and 2 million barrels by 1992. To this end, the government would provide an initial $20 billion in various forms of assistance to the private sector, as well as create an independent government corporation to oversee the process. The present volume's recommendations for synfuels development focus on shale oil and on synthetic fluids from coal, since these options appear the most likely to provide a significant boost to domestic fuel supplies between now and the century's end.

Background

Technologies

Fortunately, proven technologies already exist for making hydrocarbon fluids from solid shale and coal. Shale oil comes from a waxy substance known as kerogen that is found in sedimentary rock formations, most notably in the rich Green River Formation that encompasses parts of Colorado, Utah, and Wyoming. This area contains an estimated 1,800 billion barrels of shale oil. Kerogen is a natural hydrocarbon, and the oil that comes from it is synthetic only in the sense that it is not "the real thing" that we are all accustomed to—oil from petroleum.

Kerogen is harder to tap than petroleum, since it is locked in solid rock. Heating that rock to very high temperatures (at least 900 degrees F) is the only way to extract the fuel. When heated, the kerogen in the rock breaks down into shale oil, combustible hydrocarbon gases, and a black carbon residue. Any rock that bears kerogen qualifies as oil shale, but only those oil shale deposits that will yield more than 20 gallons of oil per ton of rock by Fisher Assay generally are considered worth development.

The process for heating the rock and extracting the usable hydrocarbons is known as retorting. Traditionally, the rock has been mined, brought to the surface, crushed into fragments from 0.25 to 3 inches in diameter, and heated in a free-standing chimney-like vessel called a retort. More recently, some developers have been trying a riskier method called in situ retorting. The in situ method makes the earth itself a retort, by blasting out a columnar receptacle underground and heating the shale rubble where it lies. The aim of underground retorting is to allow use of lower grades of shale, as well as to sidestep some of the environmental problems associated with surface operations.

In the case of coal, there are a number of technologies for converting the black solid into liquid and gaseous fuels. The point of doing so is dual: to provide fuel for processes that otherwise would have to rely on oil or natural gas, and to avoid the air quality complications that attend the burning of solid coal.

Liquefaction involves transforming coal from solid to liquid form, with impurities being removed in the process. First, the coal is crushed, dried, and pulverized. A solvent is added to the coal, and the resulting slurry is heated and pressurized in the presence of hydrogen to dissolve the coal. What remains is a low-sulfur liquid fuel that can be burned in existing oil-fired industrial boilers, including utility boilers, without major modification. In addition, there is a possibility that coal liquids eventually can substitute for petroleum-based diesel fuel in transportation and other areas. Leading candidates for commercialization currently include the H-Coal and Exxon Donor Solvent liquefaction processes.

Coal gasification is not a new technology.[15] Some U.S. cities depended on coal gas until cheap natural gas began to flow through the long-distance pipelines built to carry petroleum for the war effort. By the mid-1950s, both the domestic and European industries virtually had disappeared.

None of the current gasification technologies can produce coal gas with a heating value equivalent to that of natural gas, which is almost all methane. To gasify coal, processors subject it to partial combustion under carefully controlled conditions. If ordinary air is used in the gasifier, the result is low-Btu gas that is not economical to transport but can still be used for on-site industrial boilers and power generation. If more costly pure oxygen is used in the gasifier, then we get medium-Btu gas that can travel and substitute for natural gas in most industrial applications. If we want high-Btu coal gas—an extra step—most likely expensive methanation would be required. So far only low- and medium-Btu processes have reached the threshold of commercial development.

Contingencies

There are basically two snags in a smooth transition to synthetic fuels: cost and environmental issues. Currently, shale oil, coal liquids, and coal gas are all more costly to produce than traditional oil and gas. All of the synfuels pose environmental problems, some fully known and others still in the process of being delineated.

Costs

The economics of shale oil development always have been tricky. Back when crude oil was less than $2 a barrel, shale oil was considered possible at $3; but domestic inflation and rising production costs, particularly for environmental controls, have pushed up the potential price tag for shale oil nearly as fast as OPEC has boosted the price of imported petroleum. The capital costs of shale oil development are substantial: a shale oil plant that could reach a commercial production level—generally acknowledged to be about 50,000 barrels a day—now is estimated to cost between $1.2 and $1.5 billion (1980 dollars) to build.

Cost projections for coal-based synthetic fuels are even more speculative, and disagreement abounds as to the probable unit costs for production under the many different processes being considered. Resources for the Future reports estimates ranging from $2.80 to $3.80 (1977 dollars) per million Btus for coal liquids, and an even greater range of $1.80 to $5.10 (1977 dollars) for low- or medium-Btu gas.[16] Besides working out technological snags and coping with rising environmental costs, developers of coal-based synfuels must confront uncertainty surrounding the future cost of the feed coal itself. The present volume assumes that real coal price increases could range from a low of 0.5 percent a year in the high-growth scenario to a high of 2.0 percent per year under the least favorable conditions of luck and policy.

For an overall cost comparison, the American Petroleum Institute pegs the per-barrel price ($1980) of shale oil at $30–$50 with current technology. The comparable price of liquid fuel from coal would be roughly the same, with gas from coal coming in at about $30–$36 for equivalent heating value.[17] With world crude oil prices still hovering in the $35–$45 a barrel range, this means that synthetic fuels are on the verge of being able to compete with natural petroleum in a purely economic comparison. The bottom line is that synthetic fuels are expensive, however, and substantial government assistance will be required to bring about the kind of domestic synfuels capability that energy planners have foreseen.

Environmental and Health Issues

Environmental and related health hazards are a big hurdle for synfuel developers. Some of these problems are amenable to known solutions—though at a substantial cost—but others pose thornier issues of resource availability. Questions of access to scarce water resources, for example, especially in the West, go beyond a simple cost calculation. In the arid Western areas, where much of the infant synfuels industry is trying to establish a foothold, water is a precious resource, and any major new use is viewed as competitive with existing agriculture and light industry. Still more problematic is the question of as-yet-unknown environmental and health impacts from coal conversion processes.

For shale oil, the possibility of in situ retorting is seen partly as a solution to these environmental concerns about land, air, and water. Spent shale disposal, for instance, is a major task facing surface developers. Once shale is mined and crushed into tiny fragments for surface retorting, the increased volume will not fit neatly back into the same shaft; in fact, shale can expand almost half again during processing. Assuming a shale grade of 35 gallons per ton, a 50,000 barrels-a-day surface retorting operation must mine at least 60,000 tons of rock daily and be left with some 51,000 tons of spent shale on its hands, day after day.

Revegetating these heaps of spent shale on the earth's surface can be expensive and time-consuming. More serious, there is considerable fear that soluble salts can leach from them into local groundwater. With in situ retorting, some 60–75 percent of the rock never leaves the ground, and high underground retorting temperatures are hoped to bind the salts to the host rock. So the underground technique may help prevent leaching and consequent water supply contamination.

Air quality is also a problem with surface operations: mining, crushing, retorting, and disposal of the hot, dusty shale all release vast numbers of tiny airborne particles. The in situ technology, with its minimal mining and surface activity, also promises to minimize these particulate releases.

Finally, in situ processing would require less water consumption. It is expected to take only one barrel of water to produce a barrel of oil, whereas surface methods are estimated to use from two to four barrels of water for every barrel of oil produced. Much of this difference between surface and in situ water requirements is due to the 40–50 percent consumed in surface operations for wetting down, transporting, revegetating, and otherwise disposing of the spent shale.

It is important to remember, though, that the promise of in situ retorting is so far only a promise. There is not yet any solid proof that underground operations, with their potential for unseen snags, can be expanded to commercial scale at all. So it may or may not be possible to circumvent the environmental blocks to oil shale development by a move underground. Occidental Petroleum and a number of other producers are pressing forward with the in situ technology, but only time will tell whether it is the wave of the future in oil shale development.

Coal-based synfuel production faces many of the same problems environmentally. Mining is again a factor, with its implications for land use and particulate loadings in the air. In addition, coal conversion processes, like shale processing, require substantial amounts of water. These facts alone pose major obstacles to the launching of a full-scale coal conversion industry.

Moreover, the coal conversion processes themselves are suspected of releasing potentially toxic substances into the surrounding air and water. Research is proceeding on how to identify and control such substances, but the cost ramifications are sobering. Controlling all the potentially hazardous by-products of coal-based synfuel production could multiply the costs of liquid or gaseous fuels produced from coal. The fuels themselves are clean, but the processes for producing them tend to be very dirty.

Transportation

A final contingency that affects the future of domestic synfuels is transportation. In the lower 48 states, a network that could transport the products of synfuel plants is already in place, since synfuels could use existing oil and gas pipelines. In the case of coal-based fuels, though, a prior question exists: can we transport the coal feedstock itself on the scale necessary to support commercial operations? Coal generally is transported by rail, and the nation's railroads have deteriorated drastically over the past several decades. A vigorous boost in the railroads' coal-carrying capacity will be essential to feed a growing synfuels industry.

Recommendations for Coal and Synthetic Fuels

Production of about 44.5 quads (about 2 billion tons) of coal for domestic consumption—in addition to that produced for export—will facilitate preferred scenario coal and synfuel policy objectives. This figure includes sufficient coal production to yield 5 quads of synfuels in the year 2000.

The nation should end the leasing moratorium on Western federal coal lands to allow mining of easily recoverable deposits in logical mining units. Gaining access to the coal deposits that are least costly to develop can hold down the average costs of production. In a market economy, expanding the demand for coal is something that cannot be done simply by fiat. It has to be done indirectly—by making it more attractive than competing fuels, including imported oil. If ways can be found to use more of the coal we have available under safe conditions that are still economically competitive, then the market for coal will expand by itself.

Increased efforts should be focused on occupational health and safety problems. Many of the labor problems in the coal fields are linked closely to health and safety issues. Resolving these issues should contribute significantly to higher productivity and lower costs.

Environmental regulations that prevent increased coal use need to be examined from a cost/benefit perspective. It has been suggested that specified reclamation objectives following strip-mining can be accomplished at one-third the cost using the best available procedures rather than those prescribed by regulation. Ongoing revisions of the Clean Air Act and similar environmental legislation offer the nation an opportunity to achieve a better balance between environmental and energy concerns.

The United States must devote greater attention to environmental research. Insufficient information exists about the effects of burning coal and other fossil fuels on the environment; for a better understanding of appropriate cost-benefit criteria, research on problems such as acid rain and the greenhouse effect should receive top priority. This sort of research will provide a firmer scientific basis for setting environmental standards, which, in turn, will provide coal-related industries with a firmer basis for their own long-term planning.

The use of coal must be made financially attractive for utilities and other major customers. Despite government commitments to increasing coal use, public utility commissions in many cases have impeded the switch to coal by allowing utilities to pass through to customers the costs of using expensive oil while hindering a passthrough of capital costs for conversion of plants to coal use. Since the latter easily could prove cheaper in the long run, favorable tax and depreciation treatment for coal-using industries would speed the increased use of coal.

The nation needs to develop transport capability for domestic coal use. Transporting increased volumes of coal could be accomplished more easily and cheaply by coal slurry pipelines. The railroads have opposed this alternative, but the federal government could assist the effort by use of its power of eminent domain. Coal slurry pipelines could provide the competitive alternative to increased railroad tariffs under the Staggers Act freedoms, which will generate sufficient revenues for the railroads to develop increased transportation capability.

The United States should pursue the accelerated development of synfuel technology. Development of the nation's synfuels capability is vital to an overall program for alternative fuels. The preferred scenario target of 5 quads of synthetic fuel by the year 2000 is equivalent to about 2.5 million barrels a day of imported oil. Achieving this goal will require continued private and federal support of the R&D that will help bring down the dollar costs and minimize the environmental/health hazards of an emerging synfuels industry. As a logical extension of this R&D effort, the federal government should also take an active role in supporting pilot/ demonstration facilities that will be a stepping stone to full commercial development. The costs will be undeniably high. But such a move should yield an even higher payoff given the nation's need for an energy buffer against the unpredictable actions of foreign suppliers. What's more, a few quads of synthetic fuels by the year 2000 may be only the beginning. Americans' appetite for oil and gas will not disappear overnight even with the best efforts at conservation, so the prospect of a new and secure source of supply for the future is a welcome one indeed. This goal would require continued private and federal R&D support to help bring down the dollar costs and minimize the environmental and health hazards of an emerging synfuels industry.

Nuclear Power

The Problem

The 1973 Arab oil embargo made it immediately apparent that the nation's future energy security required concerted efforts to reduce import dependence, particularly on oil. More ominously, it was also apparent that the global potential for oil production could no longer be relied upon to rise indefinitely and meet apparently endless increases in world demand. It would be necessary to turn to abundant and reliable oil alternatives, including coal, nuclear energy, and renewable sources, to provide the new energy necessary for economic stability and growth. The first of a series of programs designed to facilitate this transformation of the nation's energy base was called "Project Independence."

The civilian use of nuclear energy is uniquely a concern of the electric utilities, since the only practical use for Btus released in nuclear fission is boiler heat to make steam. In this role, however, nuclear heat can substitute directly for large amounts of residual fuel oil; a single 1,000 mw unit in an import-dependent region of the U.S. can save 30,000 barrels of oil a day, or 11 million barrels a year.

Background

In the early 1970s, all signals looked green for nuclear. Indeed, annual reactor orders peaked at 20 new units in 1973, and by the end of 1975, U.S. nuclear manufacturers could boast a total of 236 commitments for domestic nuclear plants. There were heady projections that installed nuclear capacity might reach or exceed 1,000 gw by the year 2000.

Since the early 1970s, however, the bottom has dropped out of all of these early projections. After 1976, nuclear plant orders slowed to a trickle, and they dried up entirely after 1978. In the meantime, a wave of cancellations wiped out substantial amounts of already ordered capacity. As of September 1980, only 176 units remained in operation, under construction, or in the formal planning stage, 60 fewer than five years earlier, according to the Department of Energy. Projections of future nuclear capacity have been lowered sharply; in 1981 the Energy Information Administration (EIA) projected 125 gw of installed capacity by 1990, equivalent to 3.5 million barrels of oil per day.[18] This figure more than doubles the 53 gw of installed nuclear capacity provided by the 74 nuclear units licensed for operation as of 1980.

The sharply negative turn of events does not reflect any fundamental reappraisal of nuclear energy's potential to displace substantial amounts of oil and gas in electricity generation nor any erosion in the favorable long-term economics of nuclear relative to coal. As the decade of the 1980s opened, utilities were meeting 7.2 quads of their annual primary energy demand—about 30 percent of the total—in the form of oil and gas. Most of this use is for base and intermediate load generation rather than peaking loads. Assuming a world oil price of $35 per barrel (the approximate price of imports by the end of 1980), DOE found it would be economic by 1990 to shift two-thirds of this oil- and gas-fired load, equivalent to 2 million barrels of oil per day, to alternate fuels.[19]

Unfortunately, what makes supreme national economic and strategic sense in the long run has collided head-on with an array of circumstances and short-run factors that are pushing utilities in precisely the opposite direction—toward greater rather than lesser resort to oil and gas for generation. The dilemmas arising from this clash between rational long-term energy goals and short-term realities pose one of the most complex problems facing the United States in the years ahead.

By far the most visible and familiar obstacles to the expansion of nuclear genera-tion arise from public concern about its impact on the environment and the risks it poses to public health and safety. The government responded to these concerns during the 1970s by tightening and extending its regulatory grip on all phases of nuclear generation, from site selection and plant design to plant operation and ultimate storage of spent fuel and radioactive waste disposal. The more exhaustive regulatory effort was accompanied by strenuous efforts of antinuclear interest groups to compel even more stringent and far-reaching regulation of nuclear than that contemplated by the federal government. Often these attempts were successful, as in the Calvert Cliffs decision of the U.S. Court of Appeals for the District of Columbia, which required a thorough environmental impact statement for every individual nuclear facility seek-ing a construction or operating permit. Assembling these mountains of paper for nuclear units was a vast undertaking, resulting in a 17-month hiatus in the issuance of construction permits and a 14-month gap for operating permits.

Small but well-organized antinuclear groups have sought to block construction of new plants by sit-ins and other disruptive tactics, as in the case of the Seabrook, New Hampshire, facility now under construction. It has become routine to find half a dozen antinuclear referendums on state ballots in every national election. While the more extreme proposals, such as the shut-down of existing nuclear plants or the prohibition of new plant construction usually are rejected by the voters, referendums recently have been approved that prohibit uranium mining or the burial of nuclear wastes in a particular state. Antinuclear groups pressing these ballot proposals play heavily on public fear of the negligible levels of radiation associated with routine nuclear operations as well as the exceedingly remote possibility of a major accident involving core rupture and large-scale release of highly radioactive and toxic materials. The weapons proliferation issue also has been exploited to build congressional opposition to reprocessing of spent fuel and other measures necessary to realize the full potential of nuclear energy. Often there is a perceptible undercurrent of opposition to nuclear power simply because of its large-scale and centralized control and because of a conviction, more widely shared in the 1970s than today, that small is somehow better.

Two significant developments in the late 1970s further complicated the nuclear outlook. First, unlike all its predecessors, the Carter administration never committed itself firmly to continued nuclear power expansion. While reluctant to forego the nuclear option entirely, President Carter publicly described it as a "technology of last resort" and indicated a clear preference for renewable energy sources. The second development was the loss-of-coolant accident at the Three Mile Island 2 unit of General Public Utilities near Harrisburg, Pennsylvania, in March 1979. Although the reactor core was damaged severely, putting the unit out of commission, the integrity of its containment was not impaired, there was no possibility of a meltdown or core rupture once the coolant flow was restored, and only negligible amounts of radiation were released to the plant vicinity, exposing the public to no more than what would be considered normal background radiation in Denver, Albuquerque, or other high-altitude cities. Nevertheless, the incident and particularly its exploitation as an "impending catastrophe" by the news media set in motion a wave of reviews of nuclear safety and licensing by the Congress, the Nuclear Regulatory Commission (NRC), and the presidentially appointed Kemeny Commission. Although the meaning of Three Mile Island was immediately apparent to the electric utility industry, which moved swiftly to assure more thorough training for operating personnel, and to nuclear suppliers, who recognized the necessity for deeper consideration of human factors in the design of instrumentation and controls, the government's analysis of the accident consumed considerable time. The net result was another long licensing delay; not until August 1980 did the NRC break this logjam with the issuance of its first post-Three Mile Island license, an operating permit for Virginia Electric and Power Company's North Anna 2 unit.

A major consequence of increased regulatory intensity at the federal, state, and local level has been a relentless increase in the lead time required to bring nuclear capacity from the drawing board to full operation. The time between a decision to proceed with a nuclear unit and its licensing for operation averaged only about six years in the early 1960s. By 1978 the time required to plan, obtain permits for, and build nuclear capacity had increased to 10–12 years, including 6.5–8 years for actual construction.

While regulatory delay and confusion, costly and time-consuming retrofits of plants under construction or already completed, and protracted litigation have tended to make the nuclear option increasingly formidable for utility managements to undertake, two other negative factors must be considered: persistent inflation at levels unprecedented in U.S. history, and the significant slowdown in U.S. electricity growth since 1973. As difficult as regulatory problems have become, direct economic factors are even more fundamental in utility calculations, and it is apparent that they are primarily responsible for the decisions to cancel or delay scores of nuclear units.

The cost of inflation and associated high interest rates are especially acute for capital-intensive industries like electricity generation. No form of generation is more capital-intensive than nuclear, which may cost $900 to $1,100 (in 1980 dollars) per kilowatt of capacity when financing charges are added to the basic cost of building and equipping the plant. Because of the extreme lead times required to bring nuclear capacity into operation and the fact that interest charges must be paid on large amounts of borrowed capital, utilities are finding that the interest load over the period that capital is tied up in construction can run as much as 25 to 40 percent of the actual cost of brick and mortar and equipment. All of these financing charges must be sustained by the utility itself during the construction phase. Not until the plant is licensed for full operation does it become a part of the utility's rate base. Only then may the utility begin to recover the great cost it has incurred for the nuclear unit. In the case of a relatively small investor-owned utility, it is not unusual for the cost of a single nuclear unit to exceed the company's total common stock equity.

The task of financing nuclear facilities is complicated further by regulatory lag in a highly inflationary climate. Public utility commissions are reluctant to impose higher charges for service at a pace equal to the rising costs utilities must pay to maintain the service. Although utilities generally are thought to be assured a reasonable return on common equity investment, actual return has remained mired between 10.6 and 11.7 percent for over a decade while interest rates on long-term debt have soared. Because of intense inflation as well as the faltering return on equity investment, investors are exacting stiffer premiums for utility securities. Long-term utility bond yields have risen along with inflation from 5.5 percent in 1966 to 13 percent in 1980, while returns on equity have dropped from 12.5 percent or more to about 11 percent, with the result that utilities find themselves paying far more for debt than they are earning on their sunk investment.

At the beginning of 1981 a common share of the 100 largest private electric utility companies sold on average for about 72 percent of book value, despite the stock market's overall recovery.[20] High interest rates pushed the cost of money obtained from the issuing of utility bonds far above historic levels.

As daunting as these economic factors may seem, it is nonetheless the case that large-scale nuclear generation offers important long-range benefits to society relative to other increments of capacity, which burn fossil fuels. For one thing the cost of enriched uranium fuel is almost negligible over a nuclear plant's operating life. In contrast, fuel and operating charges constitute the largest cost elements over the life of fossil fuel plants and, as recent experience has shown, there is literally no limit on the price utilities may have to pay for fossil fuels in future years. No similar uncertainty confronts a nuclear system once it goes into operation. Thus, even in today's economic environment, one reasonably might expect utilities to cling tenaciously to planned nuclear capacity and to continue placing orders for additional capacity. However, a second major economic factor must be considered—the slowdown in the growth of demand for electricity since 1973 as a result of price-induced conservation of all energy forms.

Far from ordering additional nuclear capacity, utilities are much more likely to announce additional deferments or cancellations of announced nuclear construction not yet significantly under way. This seems particularly likely for those nuclear expansion plans announced before it became apparent that the slowdown in electricity demand growth was more than a temporary aberration. Of the 169 gw of capacity built, under construction, or still in the planning stage as of late 1980, about 38 gw falls in the "soft" category—that in which work has not commenced actively or is less than 10 percent complete.[21]

Taken in the aggregate, these negative factors raise the question of whether it is realistic to continue pressing the nuclear option. What would be the consequences of its abandonment? One could be heavy financial losses for electric utilities deeply committed to the construction of new projects, which would have to be abandoned or adapted to the use of another fuel. The nation as a whole would lose an important alternative energy source capable of substituting for substantial amounts of fluid hydrocarbons. Future energy security would be diminished, and continued heavy outflows of U.S. dollars for foreign oil would become inescapable. The sole remaining alternative to oil for base load generation would be coal, but in the absence of competition from nuclear and with consequently stronger demand for coal, its price could be expected to move upward more rapidly toward a level approximating that of residual fuel oil. From an environmental standpoint, a demonstrably clean, low-risk, secure energy form would be relinquished, leaving coal with its major transportation, emission, and waste disposal problems as the sole fallback energy source for the United States, not only for electricity generation but also as a feedstock for synthetic fuels.

If the diverse long-term penalties for abandoning the nuclear option are greater than the short-term relief such a step would afford, what reasonably may be expected in the near term? By 1990 the maximum realistic expectation must be that little more than the plant capacity already deeply committed to construction can be brought into operation. If most of the capacity far along in the construction pipeline can be completed, U.S. nuclear capacity in 1990 should exceed 100 gw, twice the present level. If all of the construction work in this category can be completed, it is even possible that EIA's estimate of 125 gw may be realized.

While maintaining nuclear construction schedules now under way would add an average of 7 gw annually to U.S. nuclear capacity during the 1980s, it is evident that there will be a pause of several years after the last of these major units goes on line. This hiatus, of course, reflects the fact that there have been no new nuclear commitments since 1978 and that none are likely as long as the uncertain regulatory climate continues, high inflation persists, reserve margins are ample, and electricity demand grows at only about half its historical rate. Whether this pause commencing in the 1990s is temporary, protracted, or permanent depends upon national perceptions today of the likely demands in the next decade and beyond and on the nature of the policy actions to be adopted as a result of these perceptions.

Aside from the tenfold increase in the world oil price during the 1970s, perhaps the most surprising energy development of the past decade has been the very considerable reduction of U.S. energy demand as a result of conservation efforts. It is obvious that these efforts can be pursued more vigorously, but that incremental energy-efficiency gains will become increasingly costly because the easiest conservation opportunities are invariably the first to be exhausted. While the energy intensity of GNP will continue to decline for years to come, in response to upward price pressure for energy, at some point a crossover will be encountered when it will become more economic to forego conservation measures and to continue specific energy uses.

Most projections of the nation's energy future anticipate a major shift in the energy mix toward electricity. This shift simply reflects the fact that electric utilities are positioned ideally to take maximum advantage of coal and nuclear energy, the two abundant alternatives to fluid hydrocarbons. Moreover, this shift to greater electricity use is most pronounced in scenarios that allow for continued moderate economic growth. While the overall energy intensity of GNP has been declining since the first round of oil price jumps in 1973, the trend of Btus devoted to electricity generation has tracked closely per capita GNP. As economist Fremont Felix has observed, "whereas non-electric energy provides an essential base for the support of the economy, it is, principally, electricity, as it powers the two most GNP-productive sectors of the economy—industry and services—which propels economic growth."[22]

This close linkage between electricity demand and economic growth is also apparent in this book's scenarios, all of which project an increase of primary energy devoted to electricity generation from the present 30 percent to more than 40 percent by the end of the century. In all but the low-growth case, electricity generation and consumption grow one-third faster than GNP and twice as fast as overall energy consumption. EIA projects a somewhat similar trend in its "mid-oil price" case for the period 1978–95: average annual growth of 3.1 percent in electricity generation, about 30 percent faster than annual GNP growth of 2.4 percent.[23]

The world inevitably will begin to experience a long-term decline in fluid hydrocarbon production in a matter of only a few decades. This grim prospect for resource depletion stems from the fact that, even at present near-punitive price levels, global consumption of known reserves is proceeding at a rate approximately a million times faster than the natural processes that form those resources. Therefore, despite the bleak outlook that prevails for nuclear energy in the early 1980s, long-term considerations of national energy security, as well as economic and environmental well-being, require the pursuit of three different goals: continuing the present nuclear contribution to the nation's energy base; completing nuclear capacity now well along in construction with minimum further delay; and establishing an economic, investment, and regulatory climate conducive to the earliest possible resumption of large-scale expansion of nuclear energy in the U.S. energy mix.

Obviously, realizing these goals will require a broad spectrum of policy initiatives. Some are modest and narrowly focused; for the most part, these can be realized promptly through regulatory and administrative action within the executive branch of the government. Other initiatives are more ambitious and will require legislation for their enactment, while still others could involve radical changes in federal energy administration as well as in the rate-making approach employed by public utility commissions.

Recommendations

The preferred scenario calls for 300 gigawatts of installed nuclear generating capacity by the year 2000. Such an objective is in keeping with the mid- and long-term preferred scenario objectives of planning for moderate growth from now to 2000 and continued slower growth in the economy and in energy use beyond the year 2000.

The United States must make a definite national commitment to nuclear energy. The historical origins of nuclear power and its evolution have left considerable misunderstanding and confusion on the part of the public. It will take a strong public commitment and a sustained effort to educate the public about the risks and benefits of nuclear energy. A goal of 300 gigawatts of nuclear energy installed by the year 2000 is possible to achieve. Such a clear and forthright statement of support for nuclear energy by the federal government would be a powerful factor in regaining public acceptance of the nuclear option and assuring its role in the nation's future energy base.

The regulation of nuclear materials transportation, reprocessing, and waste disposal should be placed under exclusive federal control. The federal government should undertake an immediate rulemaking on the transportation of nuclear materials, preempting local jurisdiction and nullifying outright state and local bans on nuclear shipments.

Until the nuclear fuel cycle includes appropriate programs to reprocess and recycle uranium from spent fuel elements, which should be the subject of increased R&D efforts, it will be necessary to store such materials. Spent fuel presently is stored on-site, but additional off-site storage urgently is needed. Immediate establishment of federal storage facilities is essential to prevent premature shutdown of some existing nuclear units. Since spent fuel used in light-water reactors contains as much as one-third of its original content of fissile uranium, U-235, and a much greater fraction of its original energy content, this material represents a national energy treasure whose careful preservation is essential.

Another top priority is the earliest possible enactment of a comprehensive statute providing for safe, permanent disposal of both low- and high-level radioactive nuclear wastes. Government failure to address the long-term problem has given rise to exaggerated fears that waste disposal is laden with unknown risks and dangers and that it represents a major technological obstacle to further expansion of nuclear power. It is, in fact, a relatively straightforward engineering and geologic task to devise means for the permanent burial of such wastes. A federal law controlling waste disposal will immediately terminate the ill-advised antinuclear referendums that have been voted into law in several states.

Streamline the licensing process for nuclear plants. The characteristic lead time for nuclear plants today is 10–12 years, much of which is consumed by review and licensing activity. This period must be reduced to facilitate a new round of nuclear orders. Promising measures include streamlined licensing procedures, replication of standardized units, "stacking" of multiple units at an existing site, and a revival of canceled units for which construction permits already have been issued. NRC development of licensing procedures for standardized plants was suspended following the Three Mile Island incident and should be reinstated immediately because of its great potential for reducing licensing delays. The NRC and DOE should institute studies of the potential for emergency uprating of the authorized power levels of nuclear reactors for limited periods to minimize the effects of a disruption of oil supply. Existing reactors can produce 3–7 percent more thermal power than their licensed levels; realization of this "stretch" capacity could save up to 170,000 barrels of oil per day by 1985, and 240,000 barrels per day by 1990 during oil emergencies, according to DOE. Although the licensing of maximum dependable reactor capacity is based on safety criteria, recent loss-of-coolant studies at the LOFT facility in Idaho suggest that present safety criteria are excessively stringent and may be relaxed temporarily with no increase in risk.

The NRC should resume immediately the issuance of construction and operating permits. Following Three Mile Island, the commission suspended issuing both operating and construction permits. In August 1980 it resumed issuing operating permits on a case-by-case basis, but more aggressive action is needed to assure that completed facilities can reach full power as soon as possible. NRC has not issued a construction permit for more than two years, although several applications are pending. The NRC should issue operating permits to Diablo Canyon 1 and 2 and to Three Mile Island 1 to commence and/or resume full power operation. All three units are located in regions primarily dependent upon oil for generation; activation of the physically completed Diablo units would displace approximately 60,000 barrels of oil per day, while reactivation of the remaining healthy unit at Three Mile Island would relieve another 25,000 barrels of daily oil demand.

Congress also should consider legislation to arrest the tendency of courts to order administrative hearings for minor regulatory decisions. The U.S. Court of Appeals (DC) ruled in November 1980 that a public hearing must precede implementation of any action that has the effect of amending a license, even where no significant hazard is involved. The ruling arose from NRC's authorization to vent krypton at Three Mile Island in 1980, and, unless overturned by the Supreme Court or by legislation, could further congeal the nuclear regulatory process.

The U.S. government should consider additional financial incentive for nuclear development. Utilities building nuclear plants in today's hostile inflationary and regulatory environment are required to devote excessive management attention to nuclear projects and tend to cancel or defer these in preference to restructuring their generating mix. If further erosion and slippage is to be avoided in nuclear construction schedules, congressional action may be necessary to strengthen the financial ability of utilities to maintain extended construction periods for nuclear plants. Deferment of income tax on reinvested utility dividends has been proposed but more vigorous measures may be necessary. Similarly, appropriate assistance should be considered for utilities required to undertake expensive retrofits to comply with policy-motivated regulatory changes.

Proceeding with the development of breeder reactor technology is an important long-term goal. To enhance the credibility of the nuclear commitment of the United States and to encourage further nuclear energy expansion over the long term (beyond 2000), it will be necessary to resume the reprocessing and recycling of spent fuel elements, to reactivate the Clinch River Breeder Reactor Program, and to initiate studies defining a prototype commercial-scale breeder. Although U.S. reserves of recoverable uranium and enrichment capacity can support significant expansion of nuclear capacity based on the present light-water reactor technology, far greater fuel efficiencies will be mandatory if nuclear energy is to realize its full long-term national potential. Fuel reprocessing and advanced converter reactors and breeders will increase the volume of plutonium circulating within the nuclear fuel system and, hence, the risk of weapons proliferation; other nations already are far advanced in the development and use of these technologies. Further U.S. restraint will not alter foreign commitments to proceed with these new fuel cycles, but it can foreclose a vital national energy option, and it will prevent us from exerting any influence over international plans to prevent proliferation.

Solar Power

The Problem

If all the sun's energy falling on the earth could be captured and used, the energy obtained in only one hour could meet the world's current needs for almost half a year. The world's yearly solar energy income at ground level equals 586,666 billion barrels of oil—roughly 1,000 times the energy of all known free-world petroleum reserves.[24] Given such figures, it is no wonder that concern over dwindling oil and gas reserves has led to growing interest in the potential of solar power.

The main problem is that solar is a highly diffuse energy source. To be useful for large-scale needs, it must be collected, concentrated, and often converted into other energy forms; and all this can require costly equipment. The fuel (sunlight) is free, but the equipment necessary to capture and use it prices solar power out of competition with more conventional energy sources.

The immediate challenge, then, is to minimize cost obstacles to the greater use of solar power, either by bringing down actual equipment costs or simply by subsidizing them. Over the longer term, the challenge is to be ready with advanced solar options by the time that continually rising oil and gas prices at last make them cost-competitive—or that the depletion of conventional resources makes their use imperative, whatever the cost.

Background

Solar power is no new phenomenon: a simple solar system heated the ancient Roman baths at Pompeii. Today's renewed emphasis on solar energy covers a broad range of options, which the Department of Energy (DOE) divides into three general categories. Solar thermal applications, making direct use of the sun's heat, can heat air and water in homes and other buildings; biomass applications can use the solar energy stored in organic matter as fuel; and solar electric applications can employ a variety of devices, from the traditional windmill to the futuristic power tower, to convert solar energy into electricity. Examining each of these categories in turn can outline the potential for a variety of solar options, as well as the contingencies that will affect the realization of that potential.

Solar Thermal Applications

Solar thermal technologies, which capture the heat emitted by photons when they strike a surface, offer the most pragmatic means for immediately and substantially increasing the nation's use of solar power. In fact, interest in solar heating systems has been booming for several years: between 1975 and 1977 the solar energy industry leaped from a $25 million to a $260 million one. Passive and/or active solar heating systems can be introduced into new residential and commercial structures, as well as into one-third of the 55 million existing residences.

Passive solar heating works by adapting the design of a building to its environment in order to allow maximum exposure to the sun's heat and to minimize the subsequent loss of that heat. Winter sun is captured through large double-glass windows and retained in the walls at night. With careful design and siting, passive solar heating probably can reduce energy use per square foot to one-half its present value—and, in the future, perhaps to one-third or less. A Texan's U-shaped, energy-conserving home design reduced heating and cooling bills from $850 to $260 per year, while a New England commercial building of 8,000 square feet saved about $400 a month by incorporating passive solar techniques. Of course, such techniques go hand in hand with conservation measures like weatherstripping and insulating.

In active solar heating, panels on the roof catch and concentrate sunlight that heats water, air, or some other medium that flows in pipes through the panels. Pumps or fans circulate the medium through a heat exchanger in a water-filled storage tank. The resulting hot water is used either directly or through a radiator network to heat the house.

Although such systems can mean big energy savings, the capital costs are considerable. The price per square foot of collector ranges from $40 to $84, and the overall price of a combined active space and hot-water heating system can range from $5,000 to $13,000 for a single family dwelling. The savings accrue only gradually, as other fuel prices continue to rise and solar equipment costs are amortized.

Besides this high initial capital investment in equipment, the other main obstacle to greater use of solar thermal applications is outdated building codes. A person who installs solar heating collectors on his or her roof must be assured that the roof will have continued access to the sun, and no current laws forbid the construction of a high-rise building next door that might block the sun. Of the over 1,000 municipal building codes in the United States, only a few provide for solar energy; some of those that do so impose strict aesthetic requirements that wind up adding to the already high cost of solar heating systems.

Biomass

"Biomass" refers to organic plant or waste material that can be burned directly or after being converted to a combustible fuel. Through photosynthesis, plants store more than ten times more energy annually than is consumed by all mankind, yet today biomass meets less than two percent of U.S. energy needs. Its use is confined largely to wood-burning—especially in residential structures and in paper mills where scrap wood is burned to provide heat for the production process.

The role of biomass in the nation's fuel mix could be enlarged greatly if organic wastes were used more efficiently. Because most local governments already collect municipal waste and dump it in a landfill, it has the advantage of accessibility. Although the steam generated by the direct incineration of such material is of inadequate temperature and pressure to generate electricity, the National Research Council reports that methane can be produced from it at a net cost of $2.09 per million Btus.[25] Agricultural wastes likewise can be converted to synthetic liquid or gaseous fuels by pyrolysis or chemical reduction. Currently, Biogas of Colorado uses the manure from 40,000 cattle to fuel a 50 mw power plant by converting the waste into methane gas. However, the collection and transportation of agricultural wastes most often render their use economically impractical, except on site as fertilizer or fuel that can be burned to dry crops. Other means of producing biomass fuel from organic wastes also involve logistical problems. Solid fuel pellets produced from municipal and agricultural waste after glass and metal have been separated mechanically can be fed into boilers, but the cost of collecting and transporting the waste to the fuel-making site, the cost of the fuel-making facility, and the cost of transporting the fuel to the point of use prohibit the large-scale use of the technology.

Growing energy-rich crops on farms specifically devoted to such endeavors is another possible way to develop more biomass energy. Energy farmers would raise rapid-growth, high-energy crops that could be converted to synthetic fuels or fed directly into steam boilers. Biomass farming presents its own set of problems, however. One involves a policy decision on the allocation of scarce resources— particularly land and water—between the production of energy crops and other crops. Furthermore, at today's prices, food and fiber crops are more valuable as such than as energy supplies. Marine energy farms bypass the allocation problem, but present other environment problems. Their impact on the surrounding marine life is not fully known.

Solar Electric

Future increases in the demand for electricity may necessitate the practical application of solar technologies now only in experimental phases—like the proposed power tower, photovoltaic conversion, advanced wind power conversion, and ocean thermal energy conversion — but those applications are contingent mostly upon cost. A short look at some solar options suggests the broad range of possibilities.

The proposed U.S. power tower is a concrete tower topped by a steam boiler, which captures sunlight beamed from heliostats positioned around it. The resulting steam would be piped down the tower to a turbine-generator combination at the base. A plant of similar design is already in operation in France, pumping one megawatt of solar-generated electricity into the conventional energy system. Because such a system can be incorporated easily into the existing utility grid, it offsets any of the potential conflict between industry and on-site solar systems, thus making for a smooth assimilation of solar power.

Unfortunately, the cost of power-tower generated electricity still far exceeds the cost of energy from more traditional sources. The heliostats, which concentrate the diffuse sunlight, comprise about two-thirds of the overall plant cost, and experts doubt that their price could be reduced much below $140 per square meter. The resulting cost to consumers would be approximately $2,000 per peak kilowatt, or three times the average of conventionally generated electricity. By adding the cost of land (one megawatt requires about six acres) and the cost of adjusting and cleaning the huge collector system, the price of any solar tower's electricity soars out of possible range for any near-term implementation. Yet, because fossil fuel costs will continue to rise as the fuels continue to deplete, and because solar innovations should lower expenses, a wise energy policy keeps all reasonable energy options open—even those not directly applicable in the foreseeable future.

Another solar prospect with great potential is photovoltaic conversion. Photovoltaic cells use a semiconductor, such as silicon, that absorbs photons and discharges electrons to generate electricity. Chemical treatment of the cell's front surface produces an imbalance of charge between front and back, creating negative and positive terminals. When a conductor joins them, the result is an electric flow. Because solar cells do not require concentrated sunlight, their use is not limited geographically. Furthermore, because they are small and work as efficiently in isolation as in groups, their use is not limited by scale. They are feasible sources of electricity in applications too small or localized for many other generating systems.

Again, cost is the limiting factor. The only practical application of photovoltaic conversion to date has been in the National Aeronautics and Space Administration program, and the electricity generated for those specialized operations costs about $1 million per peak kilowatt. Technological innovation (perhaps employing thinner cells and an amorphous semiconductor) well may bring prices down to a competitive level, however. The differences in photovoltaic prices, in fact, already have declined drastically with increases in demand and technical expertise. Today a new installation would cost about $3,000 per peak kilowatt, as opposed to $15,000 in 1977. This sort of evidence suggests that the future may be less remote than it seems. During the summer of 1980, Westinghouse Electric, Pacific Gas and Electric, and Southern California Edison announced an agreement to develop a low-cost manufacturing process for photovoltaic cells in hopes of making affordable solar electricity for Sunbelt consumers by the end of the decade.

Windmills juxtaposed with photovoltaics might appear anachronistic, yet wind-powered electrical generation is emerging again as a possible alternative to fossil fuel consumption. During World War II, a fuel-short Denmark used wind-powered turbines to generate 18 million kilowatt-hours of electricity over seven years, and the current energy crisis has renewed interest in wind potential. The major drawback is the inevitable moment-by-moment fluctuations in wind velocity that make it difficult to generate electricity of a standard and consistent current. Because of the highly variable output, a great deal of back-up capacity is required to ensure reliability of service. These limitations render the large-scale adoption of wind power unlikely. Furthermore, the ultimate potential contribution that windmills can be expected to make is quite small. For example, in 1979 the electricity generated every 25 seconds from all sources in the United States equalled the total seven year output from the Danish windmills referred to earlier. Wind power's greatest potential lies in supplementing conventional systems or in particular localized applications.

Harnessing sea power to produce electricity also holds promise for the future. Ocean thermal energy conversion (OTEC) uses the temperature difference between the sun-warmed ocean surface and the cold depths below to produce energy. A typical OTEC station liquefies a low-boiling-point gas by pumping it through a cylinder to the cool depths. As this liquid is pumped back to the surface, the heat of the surface water causes it to gasify. After passing through a turbine-generator the gas is recycled to the bottom of the cylinder and the process is repeated. Although there is no online OTEC generating capacity at present, the technology was tested in 1979 near Hawaii in a plant cosponsored by the state of Hawaii, Lockheed Missiles and Space Company, Dillingham Corporation and Alfa-Laval.[26] The demonstration plant generated 10 kw from a gross output of 50 kw. Still, many technical refinements must be made before OTEC stations become economically competitive. Uncertainty surrounding their environmental impacts and issues of international sea rights further complicate the task of estimating OTEC's potential contribution. However, because of its potential as a source of baseload generation—in contrast to most other forms of solar energy— its development is being actively pursued both in and out of government.

If local utilities are to provide the electricity to back up solar systems, substantial operating problems can arise. It is inefficient and costly to have generating units sitting idle on sunny days, yet they must be maintained to meet the surge in demand that a week of cloudy weather may create. The costs of this inefficient demand pattern eventually must be passed on to the consumer, which simply adds to the cost of using individual solar systems in homes and offices. Improved methods of energy storage for dispersed, on-site solar systems also could make such systems more self-sufficient and therefore less needful of utility backup.

Finally, the full spectrum of solar options sometimes is drawn to include hydro-power, the power of falling water. This energy commonly is converted to electricity and, in fact, supplies about 16 percent of the electricity the United States uses today. As such, it is the only solar-derived option that already occupies a place in the conventional power lineup. The reason this option is not considered at length here is because siting limitations have placed serious constraints on the future growth of large hydropower stations and the total potential is small from the large number of low-head sites available. In this book, the volume growth of hydropower does not vary at all across scenarios: no matter what conditions prevail, hydropower (plus a small contribution from geothermal sources) is expected to increase only modestly between now and the year 2000, from 3.1 quads to 3.4 quads of energy.

In contrast, the future contribution of the "new," unconventional solar options discussed here may vary enormously. In the continuation scenario, solar energy contributes only 1 quad to U.S. supplies in 2000. In the preferred scenario, as well as two others, it contributes five times that amount. (This 5 quads does not even include the contribution of passive solar construction, which is classified in this book as a form of conservation.) The point is that the development and use of solar options, like synfuels, is highly contingent on what happens between now and the century's end, both on policy decisions and on chance outcomes, such as the path of world oil prices.

Recommendations

The preferred scenario calls for 5 quads of solar energy in the year 2000. Maximizing the solar contribution seems to depend on a combination of two strategies, one short-term and the other long-term. Over the next decade or so, the most pragmatic approach is to concentrate on increasing the use of solar thermal systems in residential and other buildings. Supplementing this short-term emphasis would be continuing R&D on the more advanced solar options. Experimentation with today's active solar thermal systems can yield technological improvements that will cut costs to users. Similarly important in holding down user costs will be short-term government incentives—in effect, subsidies—such as tax credits for the purchase of solar equipment and low interest financing.

The nation must make the development of energy storage technology a greater priority. Improved energy storage methods could make home and business solar thermal systems more self-sufficient, thus relieving the strain of widely fluctuating backup demand on local utilities and cutting the consequent high cost of backup power. Furthermore, utilities themselves could make use of improved storage techniques to provide around-the-clock power from the sun, even at night and on cloudy days.

The use of biomass as an alternative energy source should be pursued more intensively. The nation has a potential source of substantial alternative energy supplies in the form of biomass, all of which is formed originally by sunlight. The biomass option could make a significant contribution, especially through the recycling of solid waste that must be collected and disposed of anyway.

A broad public education campaign to make people aware of the costs and benefits of solar power is needed in the United States. Such public education is required to overcome initial resistance to the capital investment required for collectors and other equipment. The education of architects and designers also should include a more sophisticated knowledge of what can be done with both active and passive solar systems.

Revision of building codes and removal of other such institutional barriers will allow greater use of the solar options currently available. More widespread use of existing solar thermal technologies for applications such as home heating could help save oil and gas today, and thus is the logical place to begin. Yet to make solar power a truly versatile energy source, capable of running vacuum cleaners and computers as well as providing heat, affordable ways must be found to convert solar energy into electricity, an essential step in bringing about any truly solar economy in the future and one that both private industry and government must support actively.

One national goal should be to increase research and development in all forms of alternative energy resources. Oil from petroleum is a transitional fuel in our economy. Movement toward alternative power sources must be pursued as rapidly as possible. The promises of virtually unlimited energy from the sun, from nuclear fusion, and from other possibilities on the frontier of energy research are considerably far away. Continuing R&D on advanced options, particularly the possibilities for solar electricity, offers the best prospect for large-scale use of solar energy in the long run. Cutting the very high cost of photovoltaic chips to a competitive level, for example, could expand vastly the applications for solar power.

The government must streamline the approval and regulatory process for all types of alternative energy facilities. "Fast-track" procedures for the review and approval of alternative energy facilities are called for, given the urgent need for expanded domestic energy production. This need warrants the acceptance of at least some short-term environmental costs.

Conservation

The Problem

Like fuels, conservation can be regarded as an energy resource, one with particularly significant effects on the nation's midterm energy future. Productive conservation is the cost-effective substitution of capital, labor, and materials—KLEM equation factors—for fuel that has grown increasingly expensive. While fuel input cannot be reduced to zero, substituting other production factors for lavish fuel use can provide the same goods and services at a lower total cost. Moreover, unlike fuels, productive conservation is an energy resource that cannot run out. It becomes more and more plentiful with advances in education and technology.

Productive conservation stands in sharp contrast to the traditional idea of conservation as sacrifice. The emphasis is not on doing without, but on doing more with less energy input. Productive conservation goes hand in hand with the trend toward neoindustrialization—toward a renewed emphasis on maintaining and raising our living standards through a less wasteful, more efficient technological utilization of the resources at our command.

The problem is that productive conservation requires a rational awareness of alternatives and of the real costs attached to each one. Furthermore, in an ideal conservation system, this awareness would be virtually universal: it would do little good for homeowners to scrimp on electricity if utilities still were generating most of their power from expensive oil and gas rather than substituting less costly coal and nuclear fuels. Likewise, it would do little good for utilities to keep exploring ways to generate more efficiently from cheaper fuels if homeowners and other consumers were unaware of the need to insulate their buildings. To actually plug leaks in our system of energy use rather than simply redistribute them, energy producers and energy consumers both need conservation awareness.

Yet consumers frequently are confused as to what their options really are and which ones are cheapest in the long run. Government conservation measures indeed can help save energy, and they already have; but the ultimate decisions, such as the decision whether or not to obey the government's 55 miles-per-hour speed limit, often fall back into the hands of millions of individuals who are unaware of the energy implications of what they do. When consumers are uninformed, or when real energy costs are camouflaged by market distortions, conservation regulations alone cannot achieve optimal energy savings.

Background

When energy prices rise, people find ways to substitute capital, labor, and materials for energy, thus achieving the same result more economically. If energy always were priced correctly—that is, in a way that would reflect its cost to society and its value to the consumer—then there would be no motivation for consuming too much of it. People would realize that they were paying more than necessary, giving up other benefits (more disposable income, greater national security, cleaner air, and so on) that outweighed the satisfaction they might get from excess energy consumption.

Pricing Issues

While it is unrealistic to imagine that a perfect pricing mechanism can be achieved, several strategies have been suggested for restructuring prices in a way that reflects energy's true costs more accurately and so sends clearer signals to the consumer. The first is removing energy price controls. Artificially low prices for these energy sources not only discourage production but also encourage consumption; in effect, they subsidize excessive energy use. Letting oil and natural gas prices, for example, rise to their more appropriate market levels is one of the surest ways of seeing that people consume less of these dwindling resources.

Besides price decontrol, a second strategy is the internalization of costs. This approach focuses on the overall social costs that are not reflected directly in the price of energy but that, by this reckoning, should be. For example, the price of coal can reflect more accurately the true social costs of using it if that price, paid by coal consumers, is sufficient to cover the full costs of mining accidents, land reclamation, air quality control, and the other health and environmental drawbacks attendant on coal use. Similarly, oil consumers might have to pay—by means of some tax on imported oil—for oil storage to compensate for the very high socioeconomic costs that accompany an import supply cutoff. Or consumers of refined oil products, such as gasoline, would have to pay higher prices to cover the costs of air cleanup in congested urban traffic areas. While it is not always easy to specify such cause and effect relationships between energy use and its consequences, cost internalization should be attempted wherever it is possible to recognize a reasonable relationship between damages and remedies.[27]

The point of cost internalization is to shift unpaid energy costs from society as a whole to energy consumers. The belief is that such measures would not add to energy costs, but merely would convert existing costs into part of the price paid by those actually using the energy. So once again, those using the energy would be motivated by price to use less of it.

The third strategy of pricing reform would apply mostly to gas and electric utilities. Their prices, particularly to small consumers, usually depend on the average accounting cost of all the energy they produce and deliver, rather than the actual economic cost of each kilowatt-hour or therm. In fact, however, the cost of producing a kilowatt-hour of electricity from coal or nuclear energy is substantially less than producing it from oil or gas. Likewise, a kilowatt-hour produced from an older unit typically will cost less than one produced from a newer unit that has much higher financing and construction costs.

One approach, typically referred to as "time-of-day pricing," prices electricity to reflect these cost differences over time. Those who use electricity during periods of peak demand, when peaking turbines that run on oil or gas must be brought into service, pay higher prices than those who consume off-peak electricity produced more cheaply by the baseload units run on coal or nuclear fuel. Of course, it requires expensive metering and record-keeping devices to keep track of each customer's use over time, and pricing under this scheme is not straightforward; extensive cost/benefit analyses by user class must be conducted to determine the best balance between electricity use and metering. Another approach, usually called incremental or marginal cost pricing, prices electricity to reflect the current cost of replacing existing capacity rather than its being averaged in a way that blurs the cost-price relationship.

The success of any such pricing approach in promoting conservation depends on an educated consumer who can respond rationally to price differences. Furthermore, in the real world, market mechanisms rarely function with perfect ease and efficiency. In each sector of the economy—transportation, residential/commercial, and industrial—the interplay of price and other factors will work out somewhat differently.

How each sector of the economy can contribute to energy savings depends on the conservation contingencies at work in each. Industries and homeowners, for example, often have different kinds of calculations and decisions to make, even though they are both part of the same energy system. The transportation sector will be examined first, since it provides a good opportunity to observe the interaction of three variables that turn up repeatedly in conservation scenarios: the effects of technological innovation, of government regulation, and of individual consumer choices in response to price and other considerations.

Transportation

The American automobile accounts for one-ninth of all the oil consumed in the world every day. Clearly, given such a figure, a U.S. driving population educated in the need for energy conservation could have made changes in national driving habits voluntarily and, consequently, in U.S. energy consumption. Likewise, an automobile industry sensitive to marketing needs, if necessary, would have produced a fuel-efficient automobile long ago, similar to those built in Europe or Japan. However, in both cases, unrealistically low oil prices kept gas-guzzlers on the roads, affordable for the customer and profitable for the manufacturer. A substantial part of the reduction of oil consumption between 1978 and 1980 in this sector—12 percent in two years—has resulted from an effective balance of rising gasoline prices, government regulation, consumer education, and the availability of fuel-efficient small foreign cars. Some of the drop may ultimately prove to have been a consequence of the 1980 recession, but almost certainly conservation has also played a role.

The Energy Policy and Conservation Act of 1975 set fuel efficiency standards that, with the reduced speed limit, have cut oil consumption drastically. Even partial compliance with the 55 miles-per-hour limit has saved about 100,000 barrels of oil per day. These standards set an average minimum of 18 miles per gallon for 1978 models with an average minimum of 27.5 mandated for 1985. In fact, 1978 models already reached an average 19.6 miles per gallon—a figure that marks a 44 percent increase over 1973's average 13.6 miles per gallon. Since the average car is on the road for more than ten years, however, the impact of new mileage standards on national gasoline consumption is felt only gradually. For example, despite the large numbers of new small cars now in use, average mileage in 1979 was only 14.3 miles per gallon, up somewhat from the 1973 low, but still only slightly better than 1967's figure of 13.9.[28]

One attractive feature of the fuel efficiency standards for both consumers and producers is that the average applies to fleet production. This approach allows manufacturers to produce a larger, heavier, and less energy-efficient model as well as the compact, light, energy-efficient model, as long as the fleet average miles per gallon meets the minimum standard. This method of regulating consumption has proved far more effective than the alternatives originally discussed (a tax on the gas-guzzler or a 50-cent increase in gasoline prices by 1985), while allowing the producer a degree of freedom in design and size responsive to market demands.

Another possibility that is still just a dream among conservation planners is the advent of the electric car for widespread consumer use. The electric car substitutes a more plentiful fuel for a less plentiful one: that is, electricity made from abundant, inexpensive coal for gasoline made from increasingly scarce, expensive petroleum.

Electric cars could save the nation large quantities of oil—about 290 million barrels yearly, assuming 12 million such cars—if problems with battery recharging, limited ranges (40–50 miles on a charge), and overall servicing requirements were overcome sufficiently to gain consumer acceptance. The federal government, the U.S. Postal Service, and selected utilities across the country have been experimenting with electric vehicles for fleet use, paving the way for what is hoped will be consumer interest in the electric vehicle as an energy-efficient alternative for local commuting, shopping, and other short-distance driving needs. If auto manufacturers are allowed to include the energy-efficient electric vehicles in calculating their compliance with federal fleet standards, they will have a substantial incentive to produce electric cars for the consumer market.

The situation in the Middle East and the attendant surge in gasoline prices probably have done most to educate Americans about the need to conserve oil, but the need for conservation education in this sector still exists. Most people are aware that car pools and mass transit mean energy savings, even if they do not choose to cash in on such savings. However, fewer individuals are aware that a careful eye toward proper automobile maintenance can result in cash savings. Tire pressure, for example, makes a difference in use efficiency, with higher pressures yielding greater gasoline mileage. One of the keys to productive conservation in the transportation sector is an educated awareness of the potential for huge price increases in the future.

Housing

The National Energy Plan II reports that the 75 million U.S. residences, using on an average 130 million Btus per year apiece, coupled with approximately 30 billion square feet of commercial floor space, account for about 38 percent of U.S. energy consumption. The number of variables associated with building design and production has limited attempts toward productive conservation in this sector, and the overall improvement in recent years is below that of the other sectors.

Yet, increased concern and education have sparked conservation measures. An American Gas Association spokesman, citing an informal survey of 40 gas utilities, predicted a 1.5 percent improvement in building energy efficiency over each of the next ten years. The American Architects Institute Research Corporation says design efficiency for new residential and commercial structures, already offering a 20 percent improvement, can mean a 50 percent improvement in the near future.[29] In California, the State Energy Commission has established standards designed to boost energy efficiency in new commercial construction some 20 percent by 1985. However, the nation's commercial and residential housing stock has an average lifetime of 30 to 50 years or more, so the low turnover rate limits the pace at which energy-efficient design changes can be incorporated—unless they are amenable to retrofitting existing structures.

The 1976 Energy Conservation and Production Act provided funds for weatherization for the elderly and the handicapped, and the 1978 National Energy Act, offered a 15 percent credit for residential conservation measures, with a limit of $300. Although the $300 limit is inadequate as a measure of the energy conservation potential of retrofitting homes, it can be useful as an incentive. The problem is again one of bringing consumer awareness beyond the bygone era of decreasing real energy prices. Often an individual will avoid seemingly expensive residential improvements because current energy prices mask actual savings based on future real energy costs. Over the lifetime of a building, such savings could grow greater every year as energy costs rise.

The Natural Gas Policy Act of 1978 (part of the National Energy Act) established a system that puts all of the higher costs of new natural gas first on industrial consumers, up to the point at which the cost of gas forces industrial users to change to alternative fuels. When all industrial facilities served by a pipeline reach the Btu equivalency of the cost of an alternative fuel, the higher rates will be shared by other customer classes as well. This provision hides marginal costs of natural gas from many customers and encourages them to continue making unwise investments in gas-consuming equipment—investments that might cost, not save, in the long run.[30] Similarly, government regulation concerned merely with counting the number of Btus per square foot per year as a gauge for energy efficient buildings (for example, like the Building Energy Performance Standard) fails to account for the depletion costs of some energy sources or to define the quality of the energy consumed. Such measures effect only a short-term masking of a long-range issue and suggest an unorganized and underdeveloped government policy toward residential/commercial conservation.

Government measures that are aimed at education, like the Energy Extension Service, now are operating on an experimental basis in ten states. Similar to the Agricultural Extension Service, the Energy Extension Service could be a major center for models, methods, and other information on energy conservation tailored to local needs. It is hoped that these education efforts will be a major force in improving the so far unimpressive track record for conservation in the residential/commercial sector.

Industry

Between 1973 and 1978 output in goods and services rose 12 percent, while energy consumption stayed essentially unchanged. This represents a significant improvement in industrial energy efficiency. Industry cut its share of energy consumption from 40 to 36 percent and its costs by $15 billion. Though such figures appear to ignore a historically low growth rate, they do indicate (given recession conditions and higher prices) that industry has made important conservation advances, largely through improved management, waste recovery, and innovative technology. Industry's response to the need for energy efficiency reveals an awareness of conservation's role as a crucial economic factor.

The 1978 National Energy Act provided an additional 10 percent tax credit for conservation investment, bringing the total to 20 percent. Voluntary measures by industry, including many that require no capital outlay, have accounted for improved efficiency across the board. Better management alone can reduce energy cost as much as 10 to 30 percent in some instances, while R&D already has meant billions in savings. A new system of paint-curing, for example, saves 80 percent of the natural gas necessary to the task, and a new crude-oil distillation process nets 40 percent savings. Significant fuel savings also can be garnered from the recovery of waste, such as waste heat in industrial production or the reclamation of waste products. Recycling aluminum, for example, requires only 7 percent as much energy as producing aluminum from ore.

Cogeneration, the combined production of electricity and steam (the latter for either space-heating or process purposes) is a key area for waste recovery. Almost one-half of industrial energy consumption goes to produce steam. If the production of electricity is integrated with the production of steam, the process can save up to half the fuel necessary to produce the two separately.

In theory, the process itself is relatively simple and the economic gains are clear, but, in practice, many factors complicate its application. Small cogenerating units located at manufacturing sites often can only burn oil because of environmental restrictions. For larger units on utility sites where coal burning might be practical, the economics of moving steam require the manufacturer using the steam to be in the immediate vicinity of the generating station. Current cheap electricity rates based on average cost sometimes discourage cogeneration, just as they did when U.S. manufacturers gradually abandoned the process earlier in the century. Utilities, likewise, do not always want and cannot always use efficiently the electricity produced by cogeneration, which, in order for the cogeneration to be economic, may be priced higher than other energy sources. The cogenerator also runs the risk of selling electricity and finding himself labeled a utility, and subject to utility regulation. Finally, many manufacturers are reluctant to divert scarce and expensive capital funds from their primary business in order to build power-producing facilities with unfamiliar operating problems and pay-off periods that may reach 30 years or more. This matrix of problems suggests the need for increased cooperation and dialogue among government, industry, and utilities, all of which (with the consumer) stand to profit from any additional energy savings as rates and demand increase.

California is one of the leaders in the effort to develop cogeneration. The state has implemented interim policy to comply with the provisions of the Public Utilities Regulatory Policies Act of 1978, with purchase price guidelines and incentive standby power rates now in effect. The governor has established a task force to help implement cogeneration and set a statewide goal of 6,000 megawatts by 1995.

Electric utilities, being energy producers as well as energy consumers, can help promote conservation in a variety of ways. The greater agility of oil- and gas-fired generators in meeting demand surges makes them the fuels of choice for peaking generators. Therefore, the utility industry goal to conserve expensive oil and gas by substituting coal and uranium as fuel inputs in electricity generation is not always easy to effect.

Consequently, the industry has devised several strategies for reducing dependence on and use of peaking generation. Among them are direct load control and time-of-use rate structures, both designed to smooth out the peaks and valleys of customer demand so as to increase the proportion of total output which can be met with baseload coal and nuclear plants. Another option is energy storage, now largely limited to pumped-storage hydro facilities, which use power generated by baseload plants during periods of low demand to pump water into a storage reservoir. When demand rises, the utility then can provide inexpensive hydropower from its storage reserves rather than having to run its expensive-to-run oil- and gas-fired peaking generators. Research is proceeding on other bulk-power storage methods, such as batteries, but presently pumped storage is the only practical method for storing large quantities of energy.

Besides substituting plentiful fuels for less plentiful ones, utilities continually are working on technological innovations that will help cut energy losses as fuels are converted to electricity and then transported to the consumer. R&D efforts, such as the superconducting generator and the ultrahigh voltage transmission line, exemplify this ongoing technological thrust.

As energy producers, utilities are also in a good position to see the total system of electric energy use and help plug leaks at the consumer end of the system. Education in conservation awareness is perhaps the major help that utilities can offer, through modestly priced energy audits, information enclosed in monthly bills, and other consumer services. Some utilities offer low-cost financing for customer home insulation, as well as help in selecting a competent company to do the job. Several California utilities have been asked by the Public Utilities Commission to develop zero-interest financing to help homeowners purchase energy conservation items. In addition, projects are being formulated that are designed to reduce the first-cost burden and shorten payback periods for residential use of solar water-heating hardware.

Industry, including the electric utility industry, has developed a high degree of conservation awareness in response to rising prices. Increased tax credits for investments in energy-saving equipment and a greater government commitment to mutually funded R&D would reward and augment such conservation measures in the industrial sector.

Productive Conservation

Productive conservation focuses on the least-cost way to achieve a certain outcome—for example, adequate heating of a building. From this point of view, it does not matter whether this goal is accomplished by substituting coal for oil at the power plant, by using improved technology to cut generation and transmission energy losses, by insulating the building itself, or by a combination of all three approaches. What counts is achieving the goal at the lowest total cost. In an era of rapidly rising energy prices, this goal generally will mean the substitution of capital, labor, and materials for energy, or simply the substitution of cheaper energy inputs for those that are more expensive.

This book views the potential for productive conservation as substantial. The 30 quad difference in energy consumption between the high and the preferred scenarios (147 versus 117 quads) in the year 2000 can be attributed partly to a nonproductive lag in economic growth, but 10 quads are expected to come from the preferred's economic substitution in response to a more rapid escalation of world oil and other energy prices. In the preferred case, productive conservation as an energy resource meets some 10 percent of our total energy needs by the century's end.

Recommendations

The preferred scenario policy objectives call for conservation to substitute for 10 to 12 quads of energy in the year 2000. To reach this objective the energy intensity of the economy must decrease 1.1 percent per year.

The action of completely decontrolling oil and gas prices will spur conservation more than any other action. This book supports a national program emphasizing voluntary action and avoiding unnecessary regulation.

The concept of productive conservation recognizes energy as an economic variable—one that it makes sense to save as energy prices rise. *Every effort should be made to eliminate those pricing distortions that mask energy's true cost.* Oil prices held artificially low by federal controls, for instance, encouraged the lavish use of a dwindling resource. Measures designed to reveal the true cost of energy use all set the stage for more rational and more conservation-minded energy decisions.

The nation should adopt the concept of productive conservation as an approach to the efficient and economic use of energy. Without sacrificing our quality of life, U.S. citizens will be using substantially less energy input per unit of output in the year 2000 than we are using today. The same amount of energy, used most effectively, certainly can accomplish more than it does now. This is a goal that will take education and cooperation, but not deprivation, to achieve.

Productive conservation encompasses both energy producers and energy consumers. Piecemeal approaches that benefit one at the expense of the other are ultimately self-defeating. Utilities, for example, are working both to hold down generating costs and to help consumers reduce energy losses at the other end. Likewise, the government functioning as partner, rather than regulator, could help fund demonstrations of promising new energy-saving technologies for use at both ends of the energy system. Federal and state governments should remove restrictions that prevent utilities from entering into wholesale conservation activities.

The nation should encourage and, in a few cases, require the public to adopt efficient energy consumption and conservation measures. Energy consumers—each one a decision maker—must be given adequate information for making energy use choices. Energy costs of appliances, industrial equipment, and building features must be presented in a way that easily can be added to the initial purchase cost for overall purposes of comparison. Educated consumers with sufficient information to calculate the comparative cost of various energy alternatives are the cornerstone of any sound conservation effort. Two areas where mandatory conservation requirements are justified are automobile mileage standards and building codes. In general, however, mandatory conservation measures should be limited to those situations where the resulting savings are certain to be major and a market imperfection precludes the effectiveness of price-induced conservation.

The government should set reasonable performance standards for energy end-use devices. Government standards and incentives can be helpful stimuli to conservation. Auto, appliance, and insulation standards, speed limits, tax credits, and similar incentives and educational measures can all be beneficial. However, such regulations should be used selectively and sparingly, supporting, but not substituting for, the educated consumer's response to rising real energy prices.

Government Regulation: Energy and Environment

The Problem

For years various segments of the energy industry have been subjected to economic regulations more intensive and extensive than those governing the average private business in the United States. The price and conditions of sale for electric energy have been regulated for nearly a century on the basis that electric utilities are natural monopolies. Natural gas sold in interstate markets has been price regulated at the wellhead and again at the point of use by customer class for nearly 25 years, while crude oil has been under price and allocation controls since shortly after the Arab oil embargo of 1973.

An analogous situation has prevailed with regard to environmental regulations: those applying to the energy industry have been more numerous and intrusive than those imposed on other industries. Generally, this has been due to the very nature of energy industries, which are deeply involved in extracting large quantities of raw materials, or which require large facilities to refine, convert, or transport the energy. Pollution control has become a major public policy issue and a source of conflict and controversy in government and industry.

The regulatory approach to environmental problems often does not structure incentives in a way that promotes the best solution at the lowest cost. It lacks the flexibility to deal with a diverse and changing economy. A Brookings Institution study, for example, suggests that existing water effluent limits requiring the best available technology discourage improving that technology, since costly innovations then would be imposed automatically on the industry. Arbitrary EPA deadlines often can force the adoption of makeshift technology because time is inadequate for fundamental engineering and retooling. The Brookings study concludes that the regulatory approach is "cumbersome, corruptible, and arbitrary and capricious in its impact."[31] Although EPA was created to achieve a coordinated administration of environmental laws, inconsistent approaches are still being taken, and Congress is still legislating in piecemeal fashion. The National Environmental Policy Act merely sets forth that federal agencies are to take environmental considerations into account when undertaking major federal actions. Although the courts have held that it is a procedural law not conferring substantive rights, many of them have upheld challenges to the adequacy of environmental impact statements and the result has been tremendous delays in energy and other development in the United States.

Background

As environmental regulation burgeoned throughout the nation in the 1960s and 1970s, the energy industry increasingly became a target. Using price controls as the warp and environmental restraints as the woof, the government gradually wove a constricting net around the industry, delaying or frustrating its attempts to respond to changing supply and demand conditions. The industry's slow or incomplete responses then sometimes induced further regulations. This tendency to pile regulation on top of regulation became particularly apparent after the Arab oil embargo of 1973. To a significant degree the nation's indifferent success in reacting to the post-1973 supply interruptions and price increases has been due to ill-advised and maladministered regulations.

Of course, price and environmental controls were hardly the only two causes of the energy "crisis." Far from it. A foreign policy for the Middle East that was, by turns, cynical, unbalanced, and vacillating was a primary cause. A widely held view in the 1960s — as typified by studies such as *The Oil Import Question* — that we could safely import as much oil as we wished so long as it was cheaper than domestic supplies, was another important contributing factor.[32] Finally, a failure on the part of both government and industry to recognize the pace at which cheap domestic energy reserves were being depleted was the most crucial factor of all. Other parts of this book touch upon some of these factors. Here the focus is on some of the ways in which regulation accelerated the onset of the "crisis" in the years before 1973 and then aggravated it in the years that followed.

Electric utility price regulation, which began nearly a century ago, for example, was essentially the regulation of a production and distribution process: there was no attempt to constrain prices of the basic raw materials from which electricity was produced. It was only with the advent of natural gas wellhead price controls that the federal government began regulating the prices of depletable natural resources.

This fateful step was taken in compliance with a 1954 Supreme Court decision that extended the coverage of the Natural Gas Act of 1938 to prices charged by gas producers to interstate pipelines as well as to prices charged by the pipelines to local distributors. Sales within a given state were not affected. The Court directed that prices be set at levels that were "just and reasonable" but gave the responsible agency, then called the Federal Power Commission (FPC), no specific criteria to define those terms. Lacking other guidance, the FPC set prices based on the regulators' assessment of the cost of producing the gas. In contrast, the intrastate prices continued to be set by supply and demand factors, that is, by a joint buyer-seller determination of the gas's value.

For about a decade after 1954 the regulation was ineffective but harmless: inter- and intrastate prices moved in lockstep. By the mid-1960s, however, the supply-demand balances were changing and the value-based intrastate price began to move steadily higher than the FPC's cost-based interstate price. In 1966 the former was only 18 percent higher than the latter (based on new contract prices in each market). By 1975· the intrastate price was nearly 150 percent higher. Regulation had become increasingly effective and seriously harmful: effective in that it retarded the price increases of interstate gas, and harmful since it discouraged producers from exploration and bled increasing fractions of gas into the intrastate market while encouraging even higher consumption of gas by interstate consumers who recognized a bargain and took advantage of it.

The ultimate consequences of these short-sighted cost-based price controls of a depletable resource were seen in the winter of 1976—77 in the form of cold houses, closed schools, and layoffs. The damage from gas curtailments would have been even greater and occurred even sooner except that long-term contracts with the pipelines arranged years earlier had committed about two-thirds of total U.S. gas production to the interstate markets. By the early 1970s, however, that same fraction of the newly discovered reserves was being dedicated to the intrastate market.

At the same time, a variety of newly erected environmental roadblocks was wreaking similar havoc on the domestic oil markets. During the 1967 Arab-Israeli War, the U.S. oil industry still enjoyed some excess producing capacity that could be brought into use to offset most, if not all, of any likely foreign oil cutoff. As a result, there was no cutoff.

Between 1967 and 1973 conditions changed, however. Environmental protection rules limiting sulfur dioxide emissions from electric generating stations caused massive substitution of low-sulfur oil for coal; as a result, the demand for oil in 1973 was 1 million barrels per day greater than if coal had kept its 1967 market share of utility fuels. Increasingly tough auto emission standards during this same period reduced combustion efficiencies and boosted oil demand by another 0.5 to 1 million barrels per day.

The North Shore oil discoveries in Alaska also were being developed and pipelines planned—one across Alaska to Valdez and another eastward from the Pacific Coast across the Southwestern United States. Deliveries to Valdez, through a pipeline estimated to cost $900 million dollars, and then by tanker to the West Coast, were scheduled to begin in the summer of 1973. A variety of environmental restrictions delayed completion of the Trans-Alaska pipeline four years and contributed to escalating its final cost to seven or eight times the original estimate. The line across the Southwest eventually was canceled outright.

In sum, by 1973 environmental rules had raised oil consumption by 1.5 to 2.0 million barrels per day and reduced domestic production capacities by yet another million barrels or so per day. In the autumn of 1973, OPEC could see that the U.S. excess production capacity had disappeared and that it now had the upper hand.

Domestic oil production capabilities both before and after 1973 were held down in other ways as well. Off-shore California drilling was stymied. Lease sales in Alaska and the Gulf of Mexico were slowed. Areas adjacent to the North Slope finds, including the Naval Petroleum Reserve, were declared off-limits. Exploration off the Atlantic Coast was discouraged, although initial seismic work in that area paralleled early North Sea exploration—and North Sea production now exceeds 2 million barrels per day.

Meanwhile, efforts to build coal and nuclear generating stations often were frustrated as well. The Kaiparowitz coal plant cancellation in Utah is one example. After completing literally hundreds of applications that fruitlessly consumed more than a decade, the prospective owners abandoned the entire effort a few years ago. The record with regard to nuclear plants is similar. If accelerated construction had been ordered early in 1974 at the end of the Arab oil embargo, all plants then on order could now be in operation.

Instead, while one arm of public policy has tried to keep current electric rates as low as possible and, in the process, weakened the financial ability of utilities to raise construction funds critical to keeping future rates as low as possible, the other arm, in effect, has maximized the cost and time required to complete nuclear plants. Together, the two policy arms have caused serious delays for some plants, outright cancellations for others, and a de facto moratorium on new orders.

Public policy has been equally perverse with regard to oil price controls. Instead of recognizing the damaging results of natural gas price controls and acting promptly to remove them when new supplies of domestic energy so clearly were called for in 1974, the federal government slapped price controls on domestic crude oil and later extended the natural gas controls to include intrastate sales. The price controls on domestic crude had an effect similar to that of the gas price controls: they discouraged the search for new domestic crude and encouraged consumers to turn to the only available supplement — imported oil.

Finally the light has dawned, however. The last of the oil price controls were removed in early 1981 and natural gas price controls are scheduled to be removed gradually over the next five or six years. Many other energy policy initiatives proposed by the Reagan administration also seem headed in a sensible direction — at last.

Recommendations

The primary criteria for judging the desirability of energy regulations should be whether they reduce oil imports significantly from insecure sources; whether they contribute to additional and diversified domestic energy supplies at reasonable free-market price levels; and whether they encourage productive conservation. The preferred scenario policy objectives should seek to reduce our dependence on imported oil, increase domestic supplies of all energy sources, and assure their proper pricing. Any regulations that frustrate or complicate these objectives must have absolutely overriding advantages before they can be imposed.

New fuel supply prices should be decontrolled promptly, and serious consideration should be given to the accelerated price deregulation of those old sources of fuel still under controls. Energy price controls are aimed primarily at helping consumers. Only if prices reflect true costs of providing energy will consumers receive the proper incentives to conserve and producers receive the proper incentives to produce.

The impact of energy prices on the low income households of the nation must be recognized and offset through welfare measures targeted to those in need. The government can respond to the increasing prices of necessities such as energy through adjustments in direct transfer payments such as Social Security, unemployment compensation, welfare, and energy stamps. Tax rebates or tax credits also can be used, but such methods often benefit all income classes and thus serve to insulate all consumers from the market's discipline.

In performing economic impact studies of existing and newly proposed environmental regulations, particular attention should be paid to the effects on the supply, demand, and price of various energy forms. The U.S. energy situation for the next decade or two will be so critical and its effect on economic output and productivity so important that serious consideration should be given temporarily to boosting energy supplies even at the expense of a certain measure of continued environmental pollution. Even with the most vigorous and well-directed conservation efforts, the long-term productivity consequences of energy price increases will be seriously negative. Costs will be higher and output per man-hour will be lower than if the energy price increase had not occurred. This is true because existing production processes, designed to operate most efficiently with a specific mix of capital, labor, and energy, are being distorted to reduce the use of energy. Adding to these costs is the expense of retiring economically obsolete equipment.

Research and development efforts aimed at measuring pollutants and evaluating their environmental effects should be expanded. Tax incentives should be structured to encourage additional efforts in this area by the private sector. Since the mid-1960s, some environmental regulations have been imposed on the basis of fragmentary data from less than fully adequate experiments. While regulators' natural tendency to err on the side of safety is not without value, it most often involves higher economic and social costs than if more adequate data were available.

Except for national parks, wilderness areas, and other restrictive regions of rare and unique value or with unusually sensitive ecological conditions, efforts should cease to keep pollution levels below the standard judged to be nationally adequate. The primary objective of environmental protection regulations should be the optimization of the total human environment: physical, social, and economic. Although protecting rare flora and fauna and preserving sections of the United States in a completely unspoiled condition are laudable objectives, the focus should be on the human inhabitants of the United States and the rest of the world, and on their progeny in future generations. Providing a safe, healthy, and economically vigorous society for 230 million Americans should be the government's primary concern.

The nation should strive to achieve a better balance between conflicting national and local needs and desires relative to protection of the environment. We continually should encourage local and state management of their own affairs wherever possible. When major national policy imperatives are at risk, as in the promotion of additional domestic energy supplies, the national interest should be able to override local objections promptly. Lacking major national policies at risk, however, local or state jurisdictions should be favored as the source of regulations.

Government Regulation: Pricing Electricity

The Problem

As natural monopolies, electric utilities have been regulated for nearly a century primarily on a statewide basis, although the Federal Energy Regulatory Commission controls interstate and wholesale sales. State and federal regulatory bodies establish electricity prices or "rates" that are "just and reasonable" to both the producer and the consumer of electricity. The typical regulatory process requires setting aggregate rates to provide adequate revenues to the producer and developing a rate structure to apportion costs fairly among various customer classes. Both tasks have been complicated over the 1970s by rapid inflation and the aftereffects of the 1973 energy crisis. Because electricity bills now constitute such a significant part of the average individual's and business's budget there is growing concern about how bills are determined. Furthermore, because electric rate structures can affect levels of consumption, the federal government, a strong proponent of conservation, has entered the regulatory process more forcefully in recent years. Ultimately this federal intervention may submerge state-to-state and company-to-company differences in favor of national average rate-setting standards.

Background

Government regulation of public utilities derives from English common law as modified by a series of landmark U.S. judicial decisions handed down from 1877 through 1943. These decisions gradually defined a public utility as a business whose activities are essential to the public welfare and that operates at lowest average cost in supplying a particular market when it is free from competition from others selling the same service. This second criterion defines a natural monopoly.

A combination of local, state, and federal regulatory bodies has been established throughout the United States to regulate electric utilities under the authority described in the foregoing paragraph. Investor-owned utilities are regulated primarily at the state level. Virtually all states have public utility commissions charged with regulating the production and intrastate retail sale of electricity of these investor-owned companies. The Federal Energy Regulatory Commission (formerly the Federal Power Commission) is charged with regulatory responsibility for all interstate transactions and wholesale sales.

Rate-making procedures and guidelines have been developed over the years by legislative actions and judicial decisions aimed at assuring that rates are just and reasonable to both the customer and the utility company. To qualify as just and reasonable, rates must: permit producers to be adequately compensated for expenses incurred and services rendered; allocate costs fully and fairly among classes of customers within limits of reasonable practicality; compensate fairly the owners of all capital funds employed in the business so that adequate supplies of new capital funds can be attracted to finance needed expansion of facilities; promote efficient utilization of the fixed plant facilities of the utility company; to the extent possible, provide stable trends in revenues over time to facilitate planning for the future by both customers and company; and be simple enough to be administered efficiently by the utility company and understood by the customers. Setting rates that perform these functions efficiently involves two distinct steps: setting an adequate level of rates in the aggregate and developing an appropriate structure of rates. The level of rates determines the degree to which total revenues cover operating expenses, provide a reasonable return on invested capital, and attract the new capital required. The rate structure determines the way by which total costs are apportioned among customers.

Each of these rate-setting steps requires judgment and compromise. The task of determining a fair rate of return on the common equity investment of the utility is the most difficult part of setting aggregate rate levels. Past court decisions have established that the equity owner's return should be commensurate with returns on other investments having comparable risks and that the return should be sufficient to assure the financial integrity of the utility and permit it to attract new capital funds when needed. Neither of these criteria are quantitatively sufficient; both require interpretation and judgment.

Inflation further complicates the rate-making process when, as in recent years, it is so severe that the costs under which the utility company operates change appreciably during the very regulatory process through which utilities appeal to commissions for rate relief. Under these circumstances, regulatory lag—the time between a company's appeal and the commission decision—makes it effectively impossible for a utility company to realize the rate of return approved by the regulatory authorities. Regulatory lag can result in realized rates of return that are 2 to 4 percentage points lower than allowed rates of return on common equity. (Typical rates under current circumstances are 14 to 16 percent allowed and 10 to 12 percent realized.) A failure to find some solution to regulatory lag will mean inadequate rates of return on common equity, which, in turn, will impose financial penalties on companies seeking new capital funds to finance construction. The penalty is particularly severe when the construction plan involves capital-intensive forms of electric generation, such as nuclear or coal plants. One solution to the regulatory-lag problem is to set rates based on "prospective" or "future" test years, using forecast data, rather than on historic information. Another, at least partial, solution is to accelerate the regulatory process. Most state commissions are trying to incorporate one or both of these solutions—or variants of them—into their rate-making procedures.

The step in the regulatory process that requires establishment of rate structures is perhaps even more complex. It requires, first of all, a decision about whether rates should reflect the cost incurred by the utility in providing the service or the value of service to the customer. This question normally is resolved in favor of a cost-of-service determination because value-of-service is a highly subjective measure not readily determinable and likely to vary greatly among individual customers. In addition, to the degree electric service has become a necessity, its value in many instances would be judged to be far above its cost, so that value-of-service regulation would yield total revenues well in excess of those required to meet the comparable risk and financial integrity criteria set by the court decisions.

Several factors related to the technical characteristics of electricity production and use make even cost-of-service determinations very difficult. First, a substantial portion of a utility's generation, transmission, and distribution facilities is used to supply electric service to all or large numbers of customers. Thus, only part of the total costs of service can be identified as relating only to a given customer or a group of customers. The sizable, joint-cost remainder must be allocated using methods that necessarily involve assumptions and judgments.

A difficult, but related problem of setting rate structures on a cost-of-service basis has to do with the relationship between customer costs, energy costs, and demand costs. Demand costs refer to those that derive primarily from the operation of the utility's capital equipment. In general, these may be thought of as fixed costs and the source of most of the joint-cost allocation problem. In addition there are energy costs that may be thought of as variable costs and that are primarily fuel costs. Finally, there are customer costs, such as meter reading, billing, and some distribution costs, that are incurred by the utility merely to get ready to serve a customer. These three cost categories vary from customer to customer and, in some cases, from minute to minute for each customer. Thus, accurate cost-of-service regulations would require separate measurement of at least some of the cost components for each customer each minute. Major compromises with this theoretically perfect cost-of-service regulation are necessary, of course.

Over the past century of electric pricing many of these compromises have been developed and used. The degree of compromise has been influenced strongly by the cost of electricity, by the technology of the metering, recording, accounting, and billing functions, and by a host of other subsidiary factors. In recent years the combination of rapidly rising costs and improvements in technology has accelerated a move toward more complex rate structures. The trend is toward recording the time as well as the intensity (kilowatts of demand) and quantity (kilowatt-hours) of use for more and more customers and billing them accordingly. These more complex procedures provide customers with more accurate measures of the true cost of the electricity they consume and give them better information with which to judge the costs and benefits of services. At the same time, these more complex procedures impose an increased cost burden on the utility—and thus on the customer—so continually changing compromises between billing complexity and costs are required.

Among the most important, yet controversial, developments in electricity pricing techniques in recent years has been the strong advocacy of marginal (or incremental) pricing principles. These principles require that the price of all units of a product or service be set equal to the total cost of production of the marginal (or last) unit produced. As generally interpreted, the marginal unit is assumed to be produced by the plant facility most recently brought into operation or by the facility next scheduled to be brought into operation. Such a pricing technique is in sharp contrast to the currently dominant pricing theory in the United States that assumes all units of electricity to be produced by an average of all plant facilities used by the utility and included in its "rate base." Marginal cost pricing advocacy generally is based on an assertion that economic theory requires such pricing in order to assure a socially optimum resource allocation—a situation in which each resource is put to its best use and consumer satisfaction is at its maximum. This is a particularly appealing advantage in the current era of generally high energy prices and limited availability for some energy forms.

Unfortunately, marginal cost pricing is much more complex and controversial in reality than in theory. Therefore, it has not yet been put into general practice in the United States, although a few utilities have incorporated approximations of such pricing principles to some customer groups. As with all such new developments, it is important to balance the costs and benefits involved. The literature describing marginal cost pricing techniques and attempting to measure their costs and benefits has grown exponentially over the last five years and is now immense.[33] The most vexing problems currently inhibiting the widespread application of marginal cost pricing are measurement limitations, the distinction between short and long run, the difference between revenues collected and allowed, the need for accurate price elasticity estimates, and the difference between the actual current U.S. economic environment and the theoretical economic environment on which the theory of marginal cost pricing is based.

In the true economic sense the short- and long-run distinction relates not to time periods but rather to the variability of the physical plant. Over the short run, it is assumed that the physical plant is unchangeable and that only the degree to which that plant is employed can change. Over the long run, it is assumed that the physical plant is completely changeable. Thus, those who advocate short-run marginal costs are concerned primarily with energy cost changes as the demand for electricity changes, while those who contemplate long-run marginal cost must estimate the marginal cost of the last (or next) increment of physical plant to be added to the utility's system.

From the short-run perspective, the marginal energy cost might be nuclear at one moment and coal or oil at another, with changes occurring continually through each 24-hour period and each week as the output of the utility system responds to customer demand. From the long-run perspective, the marginal capital cost might be that of the unit actually scheduled to come into production on the utility system, or, more appropriately, it might be a minute increment of the ideal system that the utility theoretically would be able to construct under current cost conditions as a replacement for its entire existing system. A number of other possible variations of short- and long-run marginal costs are also conceivable.

The difference between revenues collected and revenues allowed arises from the fact that electric rates based on marginal cost pricing principles, in general, will yield total revenues that are different than those that regulatory commissions will allow under a doctrine by which revenues must cover all reasonable costs incurred, including capital costs, but no more. When a company operates under increasing cost conditions, in which marginal costs are higher than average costs, the use of marginal principles results in excess profits (that is, profits larger than necessary to recover all expenses and earn a satisfactory return on investment). In contrast, operation under decreasing cost conditions would force the utility to endure continuing deficits. Decreasing cost conditions are those that prevail when average costs decline as output increases and the company expands in response to the increased demand.

Since normal regulatory processes—and conventional financial considerations—in the United States require that total revenues be based on average (that is, "imbedded") costs, the use of marginal costs would require that rate levels be adjusted from the marginal levels to the average levels by either a subsidy or a tax. In the United States, neither of these avenues has proven practical, because the regulatory agencies charged with setting prices do not have the authority either to tax or to subsidize.

Marginal cost pricing proponents maintain that economic theory provides a suitable guideline—within the purview of the regulatory agencies—that can guide deviations from basic marginal pricing concepts. The proponents argue that use of this guideline, along with marginal pricing, prevents the utility company from collecting more or less than its revenue requirement while still preserving a great measure of the resource allocation potential of the marginal pricing concept. The guideline would set rates below or above the true marginal costs by a sufficient amount to achieve the proper revenues, but would concentrate the reductions or increases in those markets where demand is inelastic—where a price change would affect consumption by relatively small amounts.

These cost concepts are problematic for several reasons. First, any significant deviations from true costs on the basis of demand elasticities could be defined as inconsistent with regulatory requirements that rates be nondiscriminatory, that is, just and reasonable for all customers. Second, and closely related, the price elasticity of each customer class must be known. The currently available methods for estimating price elasticities are approximate at best, so that all that can be expected is an informed judgment about relative elasticities among customer classes.

Perhaps the most serious shortcoming of marginal cost pricing, one that has attracted very little attention of late, is the great difference between the theoretical economic foundations on which marginal cost pricing is based and the actual real-life economic environment that prevails in the market for electricity, other energy forms, and products and services of all sorts. Economic theory proposes that if producers in a competitive market set their output at such a level that price equals marginal costs, then profits will be maximized and resources will be used efficiently. However, this is only true if the producer is operating in a competitive market; if all other producers of goods, services, capital, and labor also are operating in competitive markets; if all producers are seeking to maximize profits; and if the existing income distribution in the society is optimum. None of these conditions prevail in the electricity market and none prevail in the markets for other energy forms or for other goods and services in the United States.

It is interesting to summarize the conditions that would be necessary for the existence of such a competitive market: many firms producing a homogeneous product; each firm so small that it has no perceptible influence on the prices of things it buys or sells and has no pricing policy except to meet the market or go out of business; markets absolutely free of institutional restraints, so there are no restrictions—regulatory or otherwise—on prices; factors of production—land, labor, and capital—that are completely mobile and can be reapplied essentially without delay or loss from one productive effort to any other; all economic units, whether they be producers, laborers, suppliers of capital, or consumers, possess complete knowledge about the present and complete certainty about the future; price is constant for all levels of output of a given product; and real costs are increasing.

Clearly, none of these conditions exist in any market for any good or service anywhere. Consequently marginal cost pricing may well provide an incorrect price signal and certainly cannot assure optimum resource use.

Closely related to marginal cost pricing is the concept of economic rent. Although the concept was developed to describe "excess profits" said to be accruing to owners of particularly fertile land in eighteenth-century England, the concept has a direct analogy in the twentieth-century energy industry. For example, imposition of marginal cost pricing principles in the energy industry would result in economic rent accruals to owners of older, low-cost oil and gas wells and electric generating stations. It is not surprising that the issue of equitable distribution of "excess profits" has become an issue in the energy industry or that people are proposing that government recapture the energy industry's economic rent and distribute it to society in what they consider "an equitable manner."

What is surprising, however, is that some of the same consumer activist groups that have opposed the institution of marginal cost pricing in the oil and gas industries have been the most vigorous advocates of marginal cost pricing for electric utilities. In view of the nation's urgent need to reduce consumption of scarce oil and gas, especially imported oil, by encouraging the use of abundant resources such as coal and nuclear energy, including the breeder, it is hard to devise a more perverse combination of policies than these groups advocate.

It is important to distinguish among the several consequences of the payment of economic rent to the energy industry, namely: reduce demand for scarce resources, encourage development of new sources of production, and provide "unwarranted" profits to members of a privileged or lucky group. Nearly everyone would agree that the first consequence is a desirable one and a majority would applaud the second consequence, while very few would care to advocate the third.

There are major differences across the energy industry between the two desirable consequences. In the case of a truly scarce, nearly depleted resource, such as domestic oil is now thought to be, the demand reduction consequence must dominate because only limited amounts of new production can be developed. In other words, a true scarcity exists that capital investment, such as would be available from economic rent payments, would not solve. In the case of electricity, however, the problem is not so much a depleting resource as it is a shortage of readily available capital. Here modest economic rent payments would fulfill both of the two desirable consequences. In fact, the more important objective is the second, since a sensible national energy policy will encourage rather than reduce the use of electricity whenever it could be used as a substitute for oil.

Recommendations

State and federal regulatory commissions must provide adequate and timely rate relief to allow companies to pursue long-term energy supply strategies that minimize costs to the customer, permit the utility to attract new capital funds on favorable terms, and contribute to the nation's energy policy objective of shifting consumption away from oil. Achieving the preferred scenario's energy policy objective — shifting from oil to coal, nuclear, and other fuels in greater domestic supply — requires full participation by the electric utility industry. Adequate rate relief and a financially healthy industry can reduce both prices to ultimate consumers and dependence on imports. For most of the last decade the deteriorating financial condition of the industry has restricted the ability of companies to shift to coal and nuclear power as their primary base and intermediate load generation sources. This condition has forced delays and extensions of construction plans, which, in the end, have resulted in substantially higher cost electricity than if construction had proceeded promptly.

Methods for offsetting the adverse effects of regulatory lag in an inflationary economy should be adopted by all utility commissions to accomplish the objective of providing adequate rate relief. A variety of such methods exist, such as the use of forecast data, construction-work-in-progress expenditures in the rate base, automatic adjustment clauses, and temporary rate increases to take effect before regulatory hearings, with provision for possible refunding after hearings. Each commission should be allowed to choose those provisions best suited to local conditions without federal impositions that attempt to force nationwide consistency.

Regulatory authorities should be allowed similar latitude in determining rate structures. Federal mandates implementing marginal cost or time-of-day pricing should be avoided. However, commissions should be encouraged to investigate the practical application of such pricing methods because of the potential that such methods theoretically have for sending appropriate price signals to consumers.

Marginal cost pricing should be considered whenever it can help achieve substitution away from imports by providing access to additional capital for new construction, but not as a device solely for reducing electricity consumption. Modified application of marginal cost pricing should be implemented only after sufficient information is gained to determine the effects on various classes of customers and to avoid price discrimination.

Notes

1. Harry Max Markowitz, *Portfolio Selection, Efficient Diversification of Investments* (New Haven, Conn.: Yale University Press, 1976), p. 3.

2. See Hans H. Landsberg et al., *Energy: The Next Twenty Years* (Cambridge, Mass.: Ballinger, 1979); Sam H. Schurr et al., *Energy in America's Future: The Choices Before Us* (Baltimore: Johns Hopkins University Press, 1979); National Research Council Committee on Nuclear and Alternative Energy Systems (CONAES), *Energy in Transition: 1985–2010* (San Francisco: Freeman, 1980).

3. Thomas G. Cowing, ed., *Productivity Measurement in Regulated Industries* (New York: Academic

Press, 1981); Edward F. Denison, *Accounting for Slower Economic Growth: The United States in the 1970s* (Washington, D.C.: Brookings Institution, 1979); Gregory Christiansen, Frank Gallop, and Robert Haveman, *Environmental and Health/Safety Regulations, Productivity Growth, and Economic Performance: An Assessment,* a report prepared for the Joint Economic Committee and the Senate Committee on Commerce, Science, and Transportation of the U.S. Congress (Washington, D.C.: U.S. Government Printing Office, 1980); Ali Dogramaci and N. R. Adams, eds., *Aggregate and Industry Level Productivity Analyses* (Boston: Martinus Nijhoff, 1981); Ali Dogramaci, ed., *Productivity Analysis: A Range of Perspectives* (Boston: Martinus Nijhoff, 1981); Soloman Fabricant, *The Economic Growth of the United States: Perspective and Prospect* (Washington, D.C.: National Planning Association, 1979); Martin Feldstein, ed., *The Economy in Transition* (Chicago: The University of Chicago Press, 1980); Jerome M. Roscow, ed., *Productivity Prospects for Growth* (New York: Nostrand Reinhold, 1981); George M. von Furstenberg, ed., *Capital Efficiency and Growth* (Cambridge, Mass.: Ballinger, 1980).

4. See Dale W. Jorgenson, "Energy Prices and Productivity Growth," a report prepared for Edison Electric Institute, 1980, available from EEI upon request; Dale W. Jorgenson and Barbara M. Fraumeni, "Substitution and Technical Change in Production," in *The Economics of Substitution in Production,* ed. Ernest R. Berndt and Barry Fields (Cambridge, Mass.: Ballinger, forthcoming).

5. Based on wage rate and employment data from Wharton Econometric Forecasting Associates, Inc., *Wharton Annual Model Post-Meeting Control Forecast, November 1980* (Philadelphia: WEFA, 1980) and factory sales figures for cars and light trucks from U.S. Department of Commerce, *Survey of Current Business* (Washington, D.C.: U.S. Government Printing Office, October 1980).

6. For a description of the success of such committees in various communities, see National Center for Productivity and Quality of Working Life, *Establishing a Community-Wide Labor-Management Committee* (Washington, D.C.: U.S. Government Printing Office, 1978).

7. See Figure 3.3.

8. U.S. Congress, Joint Economic Committee, *The 1980 Report* (Washington, D.C.: U.S. Government Printing Office, 1980).

9. Quoted in *Business Week,* June 30, 1980, p. 61.

10. Quoted in "Why Supply-Side Economics is Suddenly Popular," in *Business Week,* September 17, 1979, p. 116.

11. See, for example, Allen H. Meltzer et al., "Policy Statement," in *Business News and Trends* (Pittsburgh National Bank), February 1980 and Edward R. Tufte, "Political Control of the Economy," in *Business Week,* May 22, 1978, pp. 108–9.

12. See, for example, Paul W. McCracken, "Our Unmysterious Inflation," *Wall Street Journal,* April 23, 1979; Tilford Gaines, "A Primer on Inflation," *Economic Report,* September 1979; Lawrence A. Kudlow, statement to the House Budget Committee, Task Force on Inflation, U.S. House of Representatives, June 19, 1979; W. Philip Gramm, "Inflation: Its Causes and Cures," a paper presented to (and distributed by) Federal Reserve Bank of St. Louis, February 7, 1975.

13. From *The Federalist,* No. 62 (no date indicated) in *The Complete Madison: His Basic Writings,* ed. Saul K. Padover (1953; reprinted ed., Germany: Kraus Reprint Co., 1973), p. 244.

14. U.S. Department of Energy, Energy Information Administration (EIA), 1980 *Annual Report to Congress* (Washington, D.C.: U.S. Government Printing Office, 1981), Vol. III, Table 3.21, p. 85.

15. For a fuller treatment of coal gasification see CONAES, *Energy in Transition,* p. 173, to which this discussion is greatly indebted.

16. Schurr et al., *Energy in America's Future,* p. 263.

17. American Petroleum Institute, *Two Energy Futures: A National Choice for the 80s* (Washington, D.C.: API, August 1980), p. 105.

18. EIA, 1980 *Annual Report,* Vol. III, Table 3.15, p. 70.

19. Ibid, Figure 3.10, p. 67.

20. Salomon Brothers, *Electric Utility Common Stock Market Data,* March 2, 1981.

21. EIA, *1980 Annual Report,* Vol. III, Table 3.17, p. 74.

22. Fremont Felix, "Our Top Priority: Expanded Electrification Will Substantially Reduce Oil Use, While Propelling Economic Recovery," paper delivered to the Economy, Energy, and Electricity Confer-

ence, sponsored by the Atomic Industrial Forum, Toronto, October 14–15, 1980, mimeographed, p. 6.

23. EIA, *1980 Annual Report,* Vol. III, pp. 66, 102.

24. Data derived from solar radiation and worldwide energy consumption data in *McGraw-Hill Encyclopedia of Energy,* 2d. ed. (New York, 1981), p. 616.

25. CONAES, *Energy in Transition,* p. 374.

26. U.S. Library of Congress, Congressional Research Services, *Pursuing Energy Supply Options: Cost Effective R&D Strategies,* a report prepared for the Joint Economic Committee of the U.S. Congress (Washington, D.C.: U.S. Government Printing Office, 1981), p. 312.

27. For a discussion of cost internalization, see Schurr et al., *Energy in America's Future,* pp. 444–45.

28. U.S. Department of Energy, Energy Information Administration, *Monthly Energy Review,* June 1981, p. 15.

29. Roger W. Sant, *The Least-Cost Energy Strategy: Minimizing Consumer Costs Through Competition* (Pittsburgh: Carnegie-Mellon University Press, 1979), p. 23.

30. Landsberg, *Energy: The Next Twenty Years,* p. 149.

31. Allen V. Kneese and Charles L. Schultz, *Pollution, Prices, and Public Policy* (Washington, D.C.: Brookings Institution, 1975), p. 91.

32. U.S. Cabinet Task Force on Oil Import Control, *The Oil Import Question,* a report to the President on the relationship of oil imports to national security (Washington, D.C.: U.S. Government Printing Office, 1970).

33. The Electric Power Research Institute's report to the National Association of Regulatory Utility Commissioners provides a useful overview: EPRI, *Rate Design and Load Control* (EURDS-61) (Palo Alto: EPRI, November 1977).

EPILOGUE

We have presented some perspectives on the past and some visions of the future in the hope not only of informing readers but also of inspiring them to use this information productively in their various roles as policy makers, teachers, students, and consumers.

Our country is at one of the most decisive points in its history. As the 1980s begin, major uncertainties at home and abroad plague policy makers to an unprecedented degree. Business sector efforts to expand economic output are blunted by low investment, stultifying regulations, and stagnant productivity. Government sector programs to promote the general welfare are judged by many taxpaying citizens to be overly expensive and often only marginally effective, and by others to be insufficient. The resource sector, particularly with respect to critical fuels, is plagued with problems of increasing real costs, adverse environmental impacts, and questions about continued availability. International relations are complicated by economic and political barriers to the increased cooperation and interdependence that modern world conditions demand. Superimposed on these societal problems are the complexities of achieving a consensus in a democracy whose people increasingly stress individuality and pursue a multitude of diverse, and at times contradictory, goals. In such an environment the nation either can succumb to the passivity of spirit that infected national decision making in the 1970s, hoping that chance events turn out favorably in coming years, or it can engender a renewed boldness of spirit through a series of positive policy choices that have the strongest likelihood of insuring better years ahead for all our citizens.

National decision making in the face of current uncertainties must recognize that the future will depend on a combination of conscious choices and uncontrollable chances. Policy choices that promote growth in the quality of life, that incorporate flexibility in our economic system, and that create a state of preparedness to ward off the worst consequences of adverse chance developments can lead us to a future much like the preferred scenario.

Any preferred future most probably will be achieved by a coordinated set of policies — a policy portfolio — aimed at enhancing economic vitality and increasing energy security. Economic vitality can be enhanced by returning to greater reliance on a free market system and its incentives, by significantly boosting private domestic investment, by streamlining the regulatory process so that it complements productivity improvements, by controlling government spending in order to promote the growth of total national output, and by reorienting more of that spending toward improving the nation's human resources and public capital facilities. Energy security, vital to productivity growth, can be increased by eliminating price controls of all raw energy sources, by encouraging cost-justified conservation by all energy users, by supporting new technological developments aimed at greater utilization of domestic energy supplies and less consumption of imported supplies from insecure sources, by boosting domestic availability of all conventional raw energy supplies, by encouraging the economic use of unconventional and renewable energy forms, by facilitating efforts to eliminate adverse environmental impacts of energy use, and by removing regulatory restraints that needlessly hamper the use of some energy supplies.

As this book goes to press in late 1981, the mood of the country, the leadership initiatives of the President, and the initial responses of the U.S. Congress signal a major shift in national direction—a shift away from the passivity of the 1970s toward a renewed boldness of spirit—such as occurs no more than once in a generation. Several of the policy portfolio recommendations in Chapter 5 have been embodied in recent legislation and others are being advocated vigorously by members of both major political parties. This book provides a strong foundation for understanding and justifying these and other related policy initiatives. It should encourage at least a moderate amount of forbearance from those segments of society that expect, initially at least, to be affected adversely by the policy shifts. This forbearance will be necessary if the new policies are to prevail until they can reverse existing trends and move the country once again toward healthy, noninflationary growth. As the short-term analysis clearly demonstrates, turning a $3 trillion economy around cannot be accomplished overnight—or even in a year's time. Something close to four or five years probably will be needed. As the mid- and long-term analyses show with equal clarity, however, near-term patience will be rewarded as the economic vitality and energy security benefits increase in years to come.

All contributors to this book will be rewarded properly if it plays a part in moving the nation toward choices that will lead to a better future for all U.S. citizens. We are confident that it will.

SELECTED BIBLIOGRAPHY

American Petroleum Institute. *Two Energy Futures: A National Choice for the 80s.* Washington, D.C.: API, 1980.

"An Economic Dream in Peril." *Newsweek,* September 8, 1980, pp. 50–69.

Bénard, André. "World Oil and Cold Reality." *Harvard Business Review* 58 (November–December 1980):91–101.

Choate, Pat. *As Time Goes By: The Costs and Consequences of Delay.* Columbus, Ohio: Academy for Contemporary Problems, 1980.

Christiansen, Gregory, Frank Gallop, and Robert Haveman. *Environmental and Health /Safety Regulations, Productivity Growth, and Economic Performance: An Assessment.* Prepared for the Joint Economic Committee and the Senate Committee on Commerce, Science, and Transportation of the U.S. Congress. Washington, D.C.: U.S. Government Printing Office, 1980.

Cooper, Ronald L. "The Energy-Economy Connection: 1974–1979 and Beyond." *Business Economics,* September 1980, pp. 5–11.

Cowing, Thomas G., ed. *Productivity Measurement in Regulated Industries.* New York: Academic Press, 1981.

Crew, Michael A., ed. *Problems in Public Utility Economics and Regulation.* Lexington, Mass.: Lexington Books, 1979.

Denison, Edward F. *Accounting for Slower Economic Growth: The United States in the 1970s.* Washington, D.C.: Brookings Institution, 1979.

Dogramaci, Ali, ed. *Productivity Analysis: A Range of Perspectives.* Boston: Martinus Nijhoff, 1981.

Dogramaci, Ali, and N. R. Adams, eds. *Aggregate and Industry Level Productivity Analyses.* Boston: Martinus Nijhoff, 1981.

Easterlin, Richard Ainley. *Birth and Fortune: The Impact of Numbers on Personal Welfare.* New York: Basic Books, 1980.

Edison Electric Institute. *Economic Growth in the Future: The Growth Debate in National and Global Perspective.* New York: McGraw-Hill, 1976.

Energy Laboratory of MIT. *Independent Assessment of Energy Policy Models.* Final report (EA1071) to the Electric Power Research Institute. Palo Alto: EPRI, 1979.

Energy Project. *Energy Future.* Edited by Robert Stobaugh and Daniel Yergin. New York: Random House, 1979.

Etzioni, Amitai. "Choose We Must." In *The Individual and the Future of Organizations.* Franklin Foundation Lecture Series, Vol. 9, edited by Carl A. Bramlette, Jr. and Michael H. Mescon, pp. 25– 39. Atlanta: Business Publishing Division, College of Business Administration, Georgia State University, 1980.

Fabricant, Soloman. *The Economic Growth of the United States: Perspective and Prospect.* Washington, D.C.: National Planning Association, 1979.

Feldstein, Martin, ed. *The Economy in Transition.* Chicago: The University of Chicago Press, 1980.

Ginzberg, Eli, and George J. Vojta. "The Service Sector of the U.S. Economy." *Scientific American,* March 1981, pp. 48– 55.

Hogan, William W. et al. *Energy and the Economy.* 2 vols. Report (EA620) prepared by the Energy Modeling Forum of the Institute for Energy Studies at Stanford University for the Electric Power Research Institute. Palo Alto: EPRI, 1978.

Hudson, Edward A., and Dale W. Jorgenson. "Energy Prices and the U.S. Economy." *Natural Resources Journal* 18 (October 1978):877– 97.

————. "U.S. Energy Policy and Economic Growth, 1975– 2000." *Bell Journal of Economics and Management* 5 (Autumn 1974):461– 514.

Hyman, Edward J. *Attitudes Toward Economic Growth and the Environment.* Berkeley: Center for Social Research, 1980.

Kendrick, John W. *Understanding Productivity: An Introduction to the Dynamics of Productivity Change.* Policy Studies in Employment and Welfare, no. 31. Baltimore: Johns Hopkins University Press, 1977.

Kneese, Allen V., and Charles L. Schultz. *Pollution, Prices, and Public Policy.* Washington, D.C.: Brookings Institution, 1975.

Landsberg, Hans H. et al. *Energy: The Next Twenty Years.* Cambridge, Mass.: Ballinger, 1979.

National Research Council, Committee on Nuclear and Alternative Energy Systems. *Energy in Transition: 1985– 2010.* San Francisco: Freeman, 1980.

"Revitalizing the U.S. Economy." *Business Week,* June 30, 1980, pp. 56– 142.

Sant, Roger W. *The Least-Cost Energy Strategy: Minimizing Consumer Costs Through Competition.* Pittsburgh: Carnegie-Mellon University Press, 1979.

Schurr, Sam H. et al. *Energy in America's Future: The Choices Before Us.* Baltimore: Johns Hopkins University Press, 1979.

Sommers, Albert T. "Inflation: The Crucial Challenge in the 1980's." In *The Economy and the President: 1980 and Beyond,* edited by W. E. Hoadley, pp. 34– 73. Englewood Cliffs, N.J.: Prentice-Hall, 1980.

Taber, George M. "Capitalism: Is It Working . . . ?" *Time,* April 21, 1980, pp. 40– 55.

U.S., Congress, Joint Economic Committee. *The Joint Economic Report.* Annual reports to Congress on the annual *Economic Report of the President* for 1979– 81. Washington, D.C.: U.S. Government Printing Office, 1979– 1981.

————. "The U.S. Economy in the 1980s." In *Midyear Review of the Economy: The Outlook for 1979.* Washington, D.C.: U.S. Government Printing Office, 1979.

U.S., Council of Economic Advisors. "The Annual Report." In the *Economic Report of the President.* Annual reports to the President for 1979– 81. Washington, D.C.: U.S. Government Printing Office, 1979– 81.

U.S., Department of Energy. *An Assessment of National Consequences of Increased Coal Utilization,* Executive Summary. 2 vols. Report prepared by Argonne, Brookhaven, Lawrence, Berkeley, Los Alamos, Oak Ridge, and Pacific Northwest laboratories for the Department of Energy. Washington, D.C.: U.S. Government Printing Office, 1979.

U.S., Department of Energy, Assistant Secretary for Policy and Evaluation. *Reducing U.S. Oil Vulnerability: Energy Policies for the 1980's.* Report to the Secretary of Energy. Washington, D.C.: Government Printing Office, 1980.

U.S., Department of Energy, Energy Information Administration. *1980 Annual Report to Congress.* 3 vols. Washington, D.C.: U.S. Government Printing Office, 1981.

————. *Survey of Research into Energy-Economy Interactions.* 2 vols. Washington, D.C.: U.S. Government Printing Office, 1979.

U.S., Executive Office of the President, Office of Energy Policy and Planning. *The National Energy Plan* (NEP-I) NEP-II (1979) and NEP-III (1981) prepared by the Department of Energy. Biennial reports to Congress. Washington, D.C.: U.S. Government Printing Office, 1977.

U.S., Library of Congress, Congressional Research Services. *Pursuing Energy Supply Options: Cost Effective R. & D. Strategies.* Prepared for the Joint Economic Committee of the U.S. Congress. Washington, D.C.: U.S. Government Printing Office, 1981.

U.S., President's Commission for a National Agenda for the Eighties, Panel on American Economy: Employment, Productivity, and Inflation. *The American Economy: Employment, Productivity, and Inflation in the Eighties.* Washington, D.C.: U.S. Government Printing Office, 1980.

von Furstenberg, George M., ed. *Capital Efficiency and Growth.* Cambridge, Mass.: Ballinger, 1980.

Wilson, Kenneth D., ed. *Prospects for Growth: Changing Expectations for the Future.* New York: Praeger, 1977.

INDEX

ABOUT THE AUTHORS

WILLIAM F. THOMPSON is Economist for the Philadelphia Electric Company. He holds bachelors, masters, and doctor of philosophy degrees in mechanical engineering, business administration, and economics from Lehigh, Drexel, and the University of Pittsburgh, respectively. Dr. Thompson's career has ranged from engineering and engineering management activities with Westinghouse Electric Company in the fields of aviation gas turbines and nuclear reactors, to responsibilities as corporate economist for the Atlantic Richfield Company, and the Philadelphia Electric Company. He previously directed a major economic growth study published as *Economic Growth in the Future: The Growth Debate in National and Global Perspective* (1976) and served as executive director of this project.

JEROME J. KARAGANIS is currently Director of Energy Modeling for the Edison Electric Institute. He earned his undergraduate and masters degrees from the University of Buffalo and Western Michigan University, respectively, and is ABD in mathematics from American University. He came to EEI from the Electric Power Research Institute where he spent four years managing a wide variety of energy-economic related studies. Mr. Karaganis has been associated with the Federal Energy Administration, the Office of Energy Data and Analysis, and the U.S. Geological Survey.

KENNETH D. WILSON is Executive Assistant for Corporate Planning and Policy Analysis at Southern California Edison Company. He received his Doctor of Public Administration degree from the University of Southern California School of Public Administration, where he teaches a core seminar in Public Administration. He also teaches at the Center for Public Policy and Administration, California State University, Long Beach, and for the UCLA Extension Department. Dr. Wilson served as co-staff member on a large-scale study of the growth issue, *Economic Growth in the Future: The Growth Debate in National and Global Perspective* (1976), and also as editor of *Prospects for Growth: Changing Expectations for the Future* (1977).